Acta Regia: Or, An Historical Account, In Order Of Time, Not Only Of Those Records In Rymer's Foedera, On Which Mons. Rapin Has Grounded His History Of England - Primary Source Edition

Paul de Rapin-Thoyras, Thomas Rymer, Stephen Whatley, Jean Le Clerc, Michael Van der Gucht

ACTA REGIA:

OR, AN

Historical Account,

In Order of Time,

Not only of those RECORDS in *RYMER's* FOEDERA, on which Monf. *RAPIN* has grounded his History of *England*;

But of feveral Grants from the Crown, Summons's to Parliament and Convocation, Royal Mandates to the Clergy and Laity for General Maffes, Subfidies, *&c.* Proclamations and Memorials of divers Kinds, *Congé d'Elires*, Difpenfations for Marriages, and numerous other publick Acts relating to particular Families, and our own Domeftick Affairs:

From the Reign of King HENRY the Firft, to that of King CHARLES the Firft.

Which never yet appear'd elfewhere in the *Englifh* Tongue:

And which are abfolutely neceffary to be known by all that read *Rapin's*, or any other Hiftory of *England*.

Tranflated from the *French* of M. *RAPIN*.

With the HEADS of the KINGS and QUEENS, curioufly engrav'd by Mr. *Vandergucht*.

To which is prefix'd, The LIFE of the AUTHOR.

IN FOUR VOLUMES.

VOL. I.

Beginning with the Reign of HENRY I. and Continued to the Acceffion of RICHARD II.

LONDON:

Printed for J. and J. KNAPTON, D. MIDWINTER and A. WARD, A. BETTESWORTH and C. HITCH, F. FAYRAM and T. HATCHETT, J. OSBORN and T. LONGMAN, J. PEMBERTON, C. RIVINGTON, F. CLAY, J. BATLEY, and R. HETT. M.DCC.XXXI.

William the *Conqueror*.

TO

William Benſon Eſq;

SIR,

ACCORDING to your Commands I have begun the Tranſlation of that Work which you judged ſo neceſſary to be rendered into *Engliſh*.

THE Public Voice, *Sir*, juſtifies your Surprize that an Account of that noble *Collection of Records* publiſhed in our *Metropolis*, has been printed no where but abroad; and that ſo judicious and uſeful an Abridgment of them as that given by Mr. *Rapin*, who ſeems to have been Maſter of the Aim and Motive of every ſingle Act in the *FOEDERA*, ſhould lie ſo long dormant in a Foreign Language.

AT the ſame time that I attend you, *Sir*, with this *Firſt Volume*, I acknowledge the Honour you did me in laying the pleaſing Task on me. I am ſure you will be ſo candid as to excuſe any ſmall Errors in the Performance; and I hope you will forgive the Importunity with which I courted the favour of your Patronage, there being nothing that can give me greater Satisfaction than this public Opportunity of thanking you for the many Acts of Friendſhip with which you have honoured,

SIR,

Your moſt obliged and moſt

devoted humble Servant,

STEPHEN WHATLEY.

INTRODUCTION.

THERE *never was yet seen so noble a Collection of publick Acts and Monuments of History as that compiled by the late Historiographer Mr.* Thomas Rymer, *under the Title of* FOEDERA, CONVENTIONES, LITERÆ, *&c. consisting of the LEAGUES, CONVENTIONS, LETTERS, and all the other PUBLIC ACTS between the Kings of* England *and all other Emperors, Kings, Popes, Princes or Communities, beginning with the Reign of King* Henry *the First, and ending with that of King* Charles *the First.*

THIS was an Undertaking worthy of the Generosity of the late Great Queen, and of those able Councils that were about her when it was directed and set on foot: For it is universally allow'd to be a Repository of the best Materials that can be had for embellishing and illustrating the British *History, and that of all Countries in general with which our Crown has negotiated ever ſince the beginning of the twelfth Century. By this we diſcover a great many Faults, which have eſcaped the moſt exact Hiſtorians who have wrote of our Affairs ſince that time, both in Facts and Dates. We find ſeveral conſiderable Chaſms in our Hiſtory fill'd up by the help of many ſecret* Acts *which were never publiſh'd before, or never came into the hands of Hiſtoriographers, either before or ſince. We are thereby enabled to diſcover the Anceſtors of many illuſtrious Families of* Europe, *how they conducted themſelves in all Revolutions and Parties in the State; and in fine, we have the Satisfaction to ſee every Fact eſtabliſh'd upon the authentic* Acts *of the ſeveral Reigns, and on ſuch Originals as are indiſputable.*

AFTER this, it cannot be doubted but the Public is infinitely obliged both to her Britannic *Majeſty, and to her Miniſtry, who, in the midſt of ſo expenſive a War, generouſly contributed to promote this Undertaking. I own, it was a great Pleaſure to me to ſee ſuch a Regard had to Poſterity, as to put it in a Condition to be better inform'd of paſt Tranſactions than even the preſent Age was till now: This was a Thought we were not to expect but in great Souls, too ſublime*

lime to be affected by the vicissitude of the Times. In many Places, Dust and Vermin prey upon the few antient Records they have left, till perhaps they are quite destroy'd by Fire, or some other Accident; while no body laments the Loss, because it falls on the Indolent, *who despise the Knowledge of what is past or to come, provided they enjoy the time present. But the Philosophers tell us, That the Curiosity of knowing things past, the Attention which a Man gives to it in order to form Rules for his present and future Conduct, and the Regard he shews to Posterity, are some of the chief Characters which distinguish Man from the Beasts of the Field. One of the *Antients, no less fam'd for his Knowledge than for his Eloquence, says, "That the Difference betwixt Men and "Brutes lies chiefly here: A Beast is only "mov'd by the Senses, and looks no far-"ther than the Time present, having "little or no Perception of what is past, "or to come; on the contrary, Man being "endow'd with Reason, sees both the "Causes and Consequences of Things, "knows their Beginning and Progress, "compares like with like, and even joins "Futurity with the Time present."*

* Inter hominem & belluam hoc maxime interest, *&c.* *Cic. Offic. Lib.* 1. *cap.* 4.

IT was therefore a singular Pleasure to see Persons of the first Rank in Britain *correcting the Vice of their Age, and setting an illustrious Example, which, 'tis to be hoped, will some time or other be follow'd by its Neighbours.*

OF all the Histories that were consulted by Mr. de Rapin Thoyras, *'tis granted by the Editors of his eight Volumes in* Quarto, *that this valuable Collection was of the greatest help to him in compiling that large Work; for it enabled him to rectify the Dates in an infinite number of places, to discover a world of Mistakes in the best Writers of all Nations that have treated of our History, to pass a true Judgment on those Articles wherein they happen to contradict one another, and to bring to light a great many Events which other Historians have not so much as mention'd, or but slightly touch'd.*

'TIS now above twenty Years since the FOEDERA *first began to be publish'd. In the Year* 1708, *it made six Volumes, which are since increas'd to seventeen large Folios, and have been sold for a hundred Guineas; there being, I may venture to affirm, not one important Act omitted in it, that the Records of* England

land *can shew in any of the Reigns it mentions.*

WHAT is now propos'd is an Abridgment of this voluminous expensive Collection, translated from that made by Rapin *himself in* Holland, *and publish'd in the* French *Bibliotheques of the famous M.* le Clerc, *who being furnish'd with the* Fœdera *by the late Lord* Hallifax, *one of the principal Promoters of it, lent the several Volumes to Mr.* Rapin *for that very purpose.*

THO' it is an Abridgment, it is so judiciously and accurately done, that it has pass'd the Approbation of all the Curious who have seen it; for we have not only the Titles and Pages of the several Acts recorded by Mr. Rymer, *but a well connected Series of the Events to which they relate; together with many useful Remarks, for which we are obliged to the learned Publisher above-mention'd, as well as to his deceased Friend* Rapin.

THE Disposition as well as Leisure of the present Generation to read modern History, *especially since the Study of it has been recommended so particularly from the* British *Throne, seem very much to encourage the publishing of this Work in the* English *Language, which is intended to come*

come out monthly, and to be finish'd in about a Year. And to make it still further useful, the Translator has added some Notes from the best Authorities, which are not to be met with either in the Fœdera, *or the* French *Abridgment of it; and he has mark'd the Pages in the Margin, referring to the Originals at large in the* Fœdera.

MARIE

MARIE R.

WHEREAS We have directed our Trusty and Well-beloved *Thomas Rymer*, Esq; our Historiographer Royal, to transcribe and publish all the Leagues, Treaties, Alliances, Capitulations and Confederacies, which have at any time been made between the Crown of *England*, and any other Kingdoms, Princes and States, as a Work highly conducing to our Service, and the Honour of this our Realm: For the better enabling him, therefore, to carry on the said Work, Our Will and Pleasure is, That the said *Thomas Rymer* have free Liberty and Access, from time to time, to search into the Records in our Tower of *London*, in the Rolls, in the Augmentation-Office, our Exchequer, the Journals of both Houses of Parliament, or any other Places where Records are kept, for such Records as we have or shall direct, and the same to transcribe. And that he also have access from time to time to our Library at *St. James's*, and our Paper-Office, upon such Matters as We have or shall appoint for Our Service, without paying any Fees; whereof the respective Officers, and all other Persons whom it may concern, are to take notice, and to yield due Obedience to our Pleasure herein declar'd.

Given at Our Court at *Whitehall*, the 26th Day of *August*, 1693, in the fifth Year of our Reign.

By Her Majesty's Command,

J. TRENCHARD.

At the COURT at *WHITE-HALL*, the 12th of *April*, 1694.

PRESENT,

The KING's most Excellent Majesty in COUNCIL.

WHEREAS his Majesty hath appointed *Thomas Rymer* Esq; Historiographer Royal, to transcribe and publish all the Leagues, Treaties, Alliances, Capitulations and Confederacies, which have at any time been made between the Crown of *England* and foreign Princes and States: His Majesty in Council is pleas'd to order, That the Right Honourable the Lord Keeper of the Great Seal of *England* do cause a Writ to be seal'd, and directed to the Right Honourable the Lords Commissioners of his Majesty's Treasury, and to the Chamberlains of the Exchequer, authorizing and requiring them to deliver, or cause to be deliver'd, to the said *Thomas Rymer*, from time to time, all such Leagues, Treaties, Alliances, Capitulations and Confederacies, with all other Records relating thereunto, remaining in the several Treasuries of the Exchequer, which he shall have occasion of and desire; to be deliver'd back by him into the said Treasuries.

Wm. BRIDGEMAN.

ANNE R.

WHEREAS we have directed our trusty and well-beloved *Thomas Rymer* Esq; our Historiographer Royal, to transcribe and publish all the Leagues, Treaties, Alliances, Capitulations and Confederacies, which have at any time been made between the Crown of *England* and any other Kingdoms, Princes and States, as a Work highly conducing to our Service and the Honour of our Crown; wherein he has already made such Progress, that several Volumes thereof have been published: For the better enabling him to carry on the same, Our Will and Pleasure is, That the said *Thomas Rymer*, and *Robert Sanderson*, who has hitherto been employ'd by him as his Assistant, have free Liberty and Access, from time to time, to search the Records in our Tower of *London*, in the Rolls, the Augmentation Office, our Exchequer, the Journals of both Houses of Parliament, or any other Place where Records are kept, for such Records as we have directed, or shall direct, and the same to transcribe: And that they also have Access from time to time to our Library at *St. James's* and our Paper Office, upon such Matters as we have appointed or shall appoint for our Service, without paying any Fees: Whereof the respective Officers, and all other Persons whom it may concern, are to take notice, and to yield due Obedience to our Pleasure herein declared.

Given at our Court at *Kensington* the 3d Day of *May* 1707, in the Sixth Year of our Reign.

By her Majesty's Command,

SUNDERLAND.

Bp *Nicholson's* Character of the *Fœdera*, *p*. 182. of his *English Hist. Libr*.

THIS *great Work we have from* T. Rymer, *Historiographer Royal, commanded and supported by her Majesty; and it may justly be reckoned one of the many Glories of her Reign. We have here not only finished Treaties, but Letters of great Princes, and their chief Ministers of State; Instructions to Ambassadors, and other Ministers residing in foreign Courts; Papal Bulls of all Kinds,* Conge d'Elires, *and Writs of Restitution of Temporalities, Royal Mandates to the Clergy for Commemorative Masses, Fasts and Thanksgivings,* &c. *Sculptures of Hands and Seals, and multitudes of other curious Pieces of Antiquity.*

BOOKS

ACTA REGIA.

VOL. I.

Henry I.

Convention between K. Henry I. *and* Robert *Earl of* Flanders.

THE firſt Volume begins with a Convention at *Dover*, dated *May* 17, 1101, between King *Henry* I. of *England*, ſurnamed *Beauclerc*, and *Robert* * Earl of *Flanders*; by which the King obliged himſelf to pay him 400 Marks Sterling *per Annum*, in Fee, on condition of *Robert*'s Engagement, in caſe of need, to ſend 500 Horſe into *England* to ſerve the King. And there was another Convention afterwards, the ſame Year, by which the ſaid Earl obliged himſelf to furniſh 1000 Horſe upon the ſame Terms. *P.* 4.

* THIS Earl was called *Robert* of *Jeruſalem*, becauſe of his being at the taking of that City from the *Saracens*, by *Godfrey* of *Bouillon*. In his time, *Flanders* was ſo afflicted with Plague, Famine, Inundations, and continual Rains, from *October* 1108, to *April* 1109, that many of the Inhabitants were forced to retire into *England*, where they were planted in a Colony in the Eaſt part of the Country, by King *Henry* I. He was the firſt of the Earls of *Flanders* choſe by the Emperors to be Protector of *Cambray*.

AFTER his Return from the Holy-Land, he took part with the *French* King, who was called *Lewis the Groſs*, againſt the *Engliſh*, and beſieged the City of *Mante*, on the *Seine*, then in their hands; but was trampled under Horſes Feet in one of their Salleys, and died of his Wounds at *Arras*, in 1111.

THESE

Henry I. THESE being not the most inconsiderable Pieces in the Collection, Mr. *Rymer* has made Remarks upon them in his Preface, that deserve to be taken notice of; to which we shall join others, when we come to the mention of some particular Passages in these two Acts.

AFTER having mentioned the Witnesses on the part of the King and Earl, the first Act goes on thus:

'ROBERTUS comes Flandriæ, fide & sacramento assecuravit regi Henrico, vitam suam, & membra quæ corpori suo pertinent, & captionem corporis sui, ne rex eam habeat ad dampnum suum, & quod juvabit eum, ad tenendum & defendendum regnum Angliæ, contra omnes homines, qui vivere & mori possint; salva fidelitate Ludovico regis Francorum. Ita si rex Ludovicus regnum Angliæ invadere voluerit, comes Robertus, si poterit, regem Ludovicum remanere faciet; & quæret quocumque modo poterit, consilio & precibus, per fidem absque malo ingenio, sine datione pecuniæ, ut remaneat. Et si rex Ludovicus in Angliam venerit, & Robertum comitem secum adduxerit, comes Robertus tam parvam fortitudinem hominum secum adducat, quam minorem poterit; ita tamen ne inde feodum suum erga regem Franciæ forisfaciat.' *i. e.*

ROBERT Earl of *Flanders* solemnly swears to subject himself, Life and Member, to King *Henry*, that he shall not come to any damage by him, and that he will assist him to maintain and defend the Kingdom of *England* against all Men living; saving his Allegiance to *Lewis* King of *France*: In such manner, that if King *Lewis* offers to invade the Kingdom of *England*, Earl *Robert*, if he can, shall prevail with King *Lewis* to forbear, and shall for that end use all manner of

Ad-

Advice and Intreaty, without any ſiniſter Intention, or Bribe. And if King *Lewis* ſhall come into *England*, and bring Earl *Robert* with him, the ſaid Earl *Robert* ſhall take as ſmall a Number of Men with him as poſſible: Provided nevertheleſs that he doth not depart from the Fealty which he oweth to the King of *France*. *A.* 1101.

THEN follow certain Conditions, particularly one in theſe Words, *Et ſi quis comes Angliæ, vel alii homines ejuſdem terræ boſiaverint, ita quod rex comitatum, vel valens comitatum amiſerit: i. e.* And if any Earl of *England*, or other Perſons of the ſaid Realm ſhall rebel, ſo as that the King ſhall loſe the County, or the Value thereof, &c. There are likewiſe Guarantees on both ſides for this Treaty, who are termed *Obſides, i. e.* Hoſtages: And in the ſecond Act, theſe Guarantees oblige themſelves to pay 100 Marks for him they are bound for, in caſe he does not obſerve the Treaty. The King of *England* engages on his Part to pay the Earl of *Flanders*, *unoquoque anno* 400 *marcas argenti in feodo*; *i. e.* 400 Marks Sterling every Year, in way of Fealty.

THE Remarks which Mr. *Rymer* makes upon theſe Conventions are, 1. That *Eadmer* the Hiſtorian of that time ſhews that the common People knew nothing at all of the Reaſon why *Robert* came over into *England*; which Reaſon we find in this Inſtrument, and which probably was kept ſecret for fear of offending the King of *France*.

2. THAT the Hiſtorians of *Flanders* miſtook the 400 Marks Sterling for a Tribute, becauſe the King gave it to the Earl of *Flanders*, *in feodo*, as a Fief, by virtue of which the Earl was obliged to do him certain Service, as appears by this original Convention, and by many others; tho' ſome Hiſtorians, both antient and modern,

Henry I. have related the matter quite otherwise, for want of being well informed of the Fact.

3. THAT this Act is a more ancient Proof than any the *French* have yet been able to produce, that the old Earls of *Flanders* were Vassals to their Kings.

4. THAT *Lewis* is here named for his Father *Philip* *, because the latter was then excommunicated, upon account of his carnal Commerce with *Bertrade*, Wife to *Fulk* Earl of *Anjou*, tho' *Lewis* had not begun to take care of the Affairs of the Kingdom: Which is a Confutation of *David Blondel*, who in his Book *de formula regnante Christo*, has asserted that the Title of King was never granted to this *Lewis* in any Act whatsoever, during the Life of his Father.

To these Remarks Mr. *Rapin* adds, 1. That for all this, King *Philip* is named several times in the second Convention, probably because this Instrument was drawn up in the Interval, when the Bishops of the *Low Countries* approved of the King's pretended Marriage with *Bertrade*: For which it may not be amiss to consult the *French* Historians.

2. THAT it is remarkable a Pension is here called *Feodum*, or Fief, a Term seldom given to any thing but Lands; from whence it comes to pass, that a *Fief* is defined in Law to be *ususfructus rei immobilis, sub conditione fidei*; *i. e.* The holding of Land upon condition of Fealty. Mean time, it is specified in both Conventions, that the

* HE put away his Wife on pretence that she was too near a-kin, and married another, for which he was excommunicated; but obtained an Absolution afterwards from the Pope, and a Confirmation of his last Marriage. He wasted himself by his Debaucheries, and died in 1108, not at all lamented by his Subjects, because he was a great Oppressor.

STEPHEN.

400 Marks Sterling ſhall be given to Earl *Robert*, *in feodo*, or in Fee, as if it was ſo much Land. *A.* 1101.

IT muſt be obſerved by the way, That if any one would undertake to inrich M. *du Cange*'s Gloſſary of Vulgar *Latin*, he would here find a great many new Examples of Words which M. *du Cange* has explained; and without doubt many more of which he has ſaid nothing at all. There is a Neceſſity of having either his Book, or *Spelman*'s, for the perfect underſtanding of thoſe Acts. Without ſuch Helps who could imagine that *boſiare* ſignified to rebel; that *exonium* ſtood for Moleſtation, *forisfacere* for rejecting, renouncing, or loſing, which occur in the foregoing Acts; and many more ſuch Words that we meet with afterwards?

Source of the French *Language.*

AS the *French* Language, in its preſent State, is derived immediately from the vulgar *Latin*, it is there we muſt ſeek for the Etymology of moſt Words, as M. *Menage* plainly demonſtrates, in his Origin of the *French* Tongue. For inſtance, they who are only acquainted with the ancient *Latin* would be at a loſs to gueſs from whence comes the Expreſſion *il ſera quitte de cela*; but ſuch as have read the foregoing Acts will know that it then meant *quietus erit de illa*; *i. e.* he ſhall not be moleſted on that head. To inſtance in the Etymology of one Word, which does not derive its Origin from the old *Latin*; the Orthography of the Word *Feodum*, Fief, and the Senſe which it bears in the abovementioned Acts, perſuade me to believe, that they * who derive that Word from the old *Saxon Feo*, which ſignifies Reward, are in the right.

* *See* Stephen Skinner'*s* Etymologicon, *upon the Word* Fee.

II. HERE

K. Steph.

1137. Pope's Bull for the Church at Aldgate. Page 7.

II. HERE we have a Bull of * Pope *Innocent* II. in the Year 1137, whereby he takes *Aldgate* Church at *London* into his Protection, and confirms the Donations which had been given to it. Mr. *Rymer* has caus'd the Beginning and the End of it to be engrav'd, to please the Curiosity of those who never saw such Instruments: There we plainly see the Pope's Sign Manual, his Cypher, or those interwoven Letters which he subjoin'd to his Name; and last of all, his Seal. Its being dated in the Year of our Lord, 1137, shews, according to the Remark of Mr. *Rymer*, that Father *Papebroch*, the Jesuit, was mistaken, when he deny'd that Bulls were dated after that manner before Pope *Eugene* IV. and pretended that those produced to disprove him were fictitious. Father *Mabillon* was in the right to oppose him, and this antient Monument is a Proof of it. The

P. 11. same thing will appear in a like Bull, granted by Pope *Eugene* III. which is a little lower; and

P. 227. in another by Pope *Honorius*, which is produced among the Acts of the Reign of *Henry* III. so that we need go no farther for Proofs of it.

1141. In the Year 1141, the Empress *Maud*, Daughter of King *Henry* I. created *Milon* of *Gloucester*,

P. 8. Earl of *Hereford*; and here we have his Patent, by which we understand that the Earldoms of *England*, at that time, were real Fiefs, and not

Grant to the Earl of Hereford. mere Titles as they are now. That Princess gave to *Milon* the *Moat of Hereford*, and *all the Castle*, with many Prerogatives therein specify'd. 'Tis suppos'd that this is the most antient

* This Pope had an Interview with the King of *England* in *France*, and would have persuaded him to take a Voyage into the *Holy-Land*.

Charter,

Charter, or Patent, for creating an Earl, of any in Being. *A.* 1153.

FINALLY, The last of the Acts that we find here, under the Reign of *Stephen*, is the Convention which he made in the Year 1153, after a long War with *Henry*, Son to the Empress *Maud*, whom he declares for his Successor after his Death, on condition that himself should enjoy the Kingdom during his Life *. The Historians of *England* make mention of this Act which Mr. *Rymer* has given at full length.

Convention between King Stephen and Maud's Son Henry, about the Succession.

III. AFTER this come the Acts of the Reign of King *Henry* II. called *Plantagenet*. The first is a Brief dated in 1154, from Pope † *Adrian* IV. wherein he heartily approves of *Henry*'s Design to conquer *Ireland*, on condition that every House of that Island pay St. *Peter*'s Penny to the Apostolical See, according as the King had offered to the Pope: But this Conquest was not executed till a long time after.

Acts of K. Henry II. 1154. *Page* 15. *Pope gives him encouragement to conquer Ireland.*

IN the Year 1163 there was another Convention at *Dover*, between the King of *England* and his Son on one part, and ** *Thierry* of *Alsace*, Earl of *Flanders*, and his Son, on the other part; by which the Earl of *Flanders* received five hundred Marks of Silver by way of Fealty, as was said before, on condition that he should send a thousand

1163. *Another Convention betwixt our King and the Earl of Flanders.* P. 23.

* *See* Polydore Virgil, *in his Account of King* Stephen.

† This Pope was an *Englishman* called *Nicholas Breakspear*, of a mean Parentage, at *Abbats Langley* in *Hertfordshire*; his Father was a Lay-Brother of the Abbey of *St. Albans*, where he himself received Alms every Day at the Gate, and did much of their Drudgery for it.

** THIS *Thierry* made four Voyages to the *Holy-Land* against the Infidels, and had to his first Wife the Dowager of *Charles*, called the Pious, King of *France*; and to his second, a Daughter of *Fulk* of *Anjou*, King of *Jerusalem*.

Hen. II. thousand Horse to the King of *England*, when he had need of them. There is moreover another Convention much like the preceding one,

P. 27. whereby certain *Flemish* Lords, Vassals to the Earl of *Flanders*, make the like Promises to the King of *England*, according to the *Fief*, or Money which they were to receive from him every Year.

1169. K. Henry's *Letter to the Pope, against* Thomas Becket. P. 28.

IN the Year 1169, there is a very warm Letter from King *Henry* to Pope *Alexander* III. against *Thomas Becket*, Archbishop of *Canterbury*; in which the King demands of the Pope, That he absolve certain Bishops and Abbats, which the said Archbishop had excommunicated. It is surprizing that there are no more Acts mention'd relating to the Dispute betwixt the King and *Becket*; but perhaps they were suppressed by the Authority of the Popes, who had a mind that *Becket* should pass for a Saint, because he had defended the *Liberties of the Church*, as they called it, against his King.

SEVERAL Acts follow relating to the Affairs

P. 35. of that time, such as the Disputes which *Henry* had with his Sons, and with a King of *Ireland*;

P. 41. those betwixt the Kings of *Castile* and *Navarre*,

P. 43, &c. of which they acknowledge the King of *England* Arbitrator; the Pope's Concessions in favour of

P. 54, &c. the Knights Templars of *Jerusalem*, &c.

King Richard I.

IV. RICHARD I. for his exceeding Valour called *Cœur de Lion*, Son to King *Henry* II. having resolved to go into the Holy-Land,

P. 63, &c. with *Philip* King of *France*, passed several Acts with him, some of which follow.

P. 65. THERE are some very severe Regulations which he made at *Chinon* in *France*, 1189, for keeping the Soldiers and Sailors in awe, whom he embarked for that Country. If any one kill'd another

another on board, he was to be tied to the dead Man and cast into the Sea; if he kill'd him ashore, he was to be bury'd with him. If a Person drew his Knife against another, and wounded him, he was to have his Hand cut off. He that struck another with his Hand, was to be duck'd over Head and Ears three times in the Sea. If any one call'd another hard Names, he was to give him the same number of Ounces of Silver. Thieves were to have their Heads shav'd, to have boiling Pitch dropp'd upon their Crowns; and after having Cushion-Feathers stuck upon the Pitch, they were to be set ashore in that figure, at the first place they came to. These Punishments indeed kept the common Soldiers from quarrelling; but the greatest Mischief of all proceeded from the Division of the Princes, which render'd most of the Voyages beyond sea fruitless.

A. 1189. *P. 65.* *His Orders for regulating the Soldiers and Sailors when he went to the* Holy-Land.

HERE we have several Treaties of King *Richard*, with *Tancred* King of *Sicily*, and *Philip* King of *France*, when he arriv'd at that Island, in his way to the *Holy-Land*. There is no Piece that informs us what *Richard* did in *Judea*; but we know by History, that as he came back, he was arrested in 1192, by the * Archduke of *Austria*, and deliver'd up to the Emperor, who wou'd not release him for less than a hundred thousand Marks *Sterling*, which was then a very great Sum.

His Treaties. *P. 63, &c. 66, to 69.*

Imprisonment.

HERE you have Facts to illustrate and support all the Particulars of this History. 1. In a Letter from the Emperor *Henry* VI. where he tells how *Richard* fell into the hands of *Leopold*, Archduke of *Austria*, who arrested him, to be reveng'd

The History of it. *P. 70, &c.*

* THE *German* Historians say, That *Richard* I. took down the *Austrian* Banner at *Joppa*, and threw it into a House of Office; that the *English* were oblig'd to sell their Church-Plate to pay his Ransom; and that not only *Vienna* was fortified and enlarged, but the Towns of *Ens*, *Heimburg*, and *Newstat* were wall'd therewith.

Rich. I. for an Affront he receiv'd from him at *Ptolemais*,
or *St. John d'Acre*, in the *Holy-Land*. 2. In a
remarkable Letter from *Vetus de Monte* to the
Duke of *Austria*, wherein he declares that it was
he, and not *Richard*, who had caus'd the Marquis
de Montferrat to be assassinated at *Tyre*, because
he had put one of his Subjects to death, in order
to be Master of his Money: and he protests, that
they only caus'd those to be assassinated who had
P. 72. done them any mischief. 3. In three Letters
74. from King *Richard*'s Mother, Queen *Eleanor* to
76. Pope *Cælestin**, desiring him to interpose his Authority, in order to oblige the Emperor to re-
P. 80. lease the King her Son. 4. In some Letters from
83. the said Prince to the Queen his Mother, to the
84. Archbishop of *Canterbury*, and to the Nobility
of *England*, wherein he tells them the Conditions
on which it was agreed he shou'd be ransom'd.
P. 84. After this also there comes *Richard*'s Contract
with the Emperor, promising him a hundred thousand Marks *Sterling*.

P. 85, 91. ALTHO' there were several Treaties of Peace
between *France* and *England* before *Richard* was
in the *Holy-Land*, and that there have been several since, of which here are the Copies at length,
yet the two Kingdoms were soon after this
His Treaty embroil'd. This was the reason why *Richard*
with an in 1197, made a League offensive and defensive
Earl of against *France*, with *Baldwin* Earl of *Flanders*,
Flanders which was to be perpetual. The latter in this
against Treaty talks no longer in the humble Phrase
France. of a Vassal of the King of *France*, as he did
P. 94. formerly, of which the *French* Historians who
have wrote about this Treaty give a Reason.
Not long after, *Richard* enter'd into a War

* This Pope took part with King *Richard* against his Barons, and engag'd him in the Croisadoes for the recovery of the *Holy-Land*.

with

with *France*, and gain'd ſome advantages over that Nation near *Giſors*, a little Town of *Normandy*, of which the King himſelf ſent word to the Biſhop of *Durham* on the 30th of *September* in the ſame Year. *A.* 1197. P. 96.

POPE *Innocent* III. labour'd to bring the two Kings to an Accommodation; and here we have the Letters which he wrote with that view in 1198. In the end, a Truce was concluded, on which there are ſome Acts mention'd which we need not inſiſt on. P. 98, 100. P. 109, &c.

V. THE Acts paſs'd in the Reign of King *John*, begin with ſome Privileges granted to the Inhabitants of the Iſle of *Oleron* in 1199. There follow a great many particular Acts, which may ſerve for particular Purpoſes, or to prove the Certainty of Facts or Dates, when required, but of no neceſſity to be mention'd here. P. 111.

THERE is a very particular Writing of *Sancho* King of *Navarre*, by which he makes a perpetual Alliance with *John* and his Succeſſors, and promiſes to relieve them againſt all, the King of *Morocco* only excepted. This Writing is dated in 1201. Sancho K. *of* Navarre, *his Treaty with King* John. P. 126.

HERE are alſo ſeveral Letters from King *John* to the Abbats of the *Ciſtertian* Order, and to his Clergy, wherein he calls upon them for aſſiſtance, as well againſt the King of *France*, as to ſupport the Emperor *Otho*. For as the beſt part of his Kingdom was given away to Monks and Churches, ſcarce any but the Clergy were able to furniſh the ready Penny. It came at length to that paſs, that Kings were forced to beg Alms, as it were, of thoſe very Perſons who had enrich'd themſelves by no other means than the Alms of Kings and People. 'Becauſe 'tis but reaſonable, ſays King *John*, in 'a Letter to the aforeſaid Abbats, dated in '1202, that all the Members in general ſhould 'ſup- P. 129, 132. K. John's *Letter to the Clergy for a Supply.* P. 132.

K. *John.* ‘ ſupport and defend the Head, we have thought ‘ fit to deſire your Society, ſince you were founded and enrich'd by the Goods and Liberality ‘ of our Predeceſſors, to give us free and effectual ‘ Aſſiſtance to repel the Violence of ſo great an ‘ Enemy. We ſhall be much oblig'd to you for ‘ it, and ſhall make the utmoſt diſpatch in what ‘ your Devotion ſhall think fit to ask of us. Know ‘ alſo that we will not draw the Supply you ſhall ‘ give us into a Precedent.’ *Quia ad defenſionem capitis æquum eſt univerſalem membrorum ſubventionem accurrere, univerſitatem veſtram rogandam diximus quatenus vos qui de bonis & largitionibus Prædeceſſorum noſtrorum fundati eſtis & ditati, ad tanti hoſtis propulſandam violentiam, gratuitum nobis & efficax conferatis auxilium; ita quod vobis inde debeatis grates condignas impendere, & in his, quæ a nobis duxeritis expetenda, devotionem veſtram benignius expedire.*

His Character. HISTORY tells us that King *John* thereby embroil'd himſelf with his Clergy; but he treated the Laity every whit as bad, for he was a covetous ambitious Prince, who aim'd only to enrich himſelf with the Spoils of his Subjects, and obſerv'd no Laws.

Takes the K. of Man *into his Protection. P.* 137. THERE's an Act in 1205, where he takes into his Protection the King of *Man*, which is a little Iſland between *England* and *Ireland*. There is another like it not long after in *p.* 234. See moreover *p.* 339.

K. John's *Quarrel with the Pope.* 'TIS known that King *John* quarrell'd with Pope *Innocent* III. becauſe he had, without his Conſent, procur'd the Election of a Man for Archbiſhop of *Canterbury*, whom the King did not like, and therefore refus'd to own, inſomuch that the Pope excommunicated him. *P.* 143. There is a Letter upon it from the Pope, wherein he complains againſt him for his Diſobedience. It was written in the Year 1207. *P.* 147. There's another Letter alſo from the ſaid Pope written

written in the following Year, upon the same subject, to the Barons of *England*. In the Year after, the said Pope wrote him a very menacing Letter, to oblige him to restore the Estate of *Berengaria* to the Queen Dowager of *England*. There are many other Pieces on this Subject among the Acts of this Reign.

A. 1213. P. 152. P. 142, 194, 208, 210, 213.

THE King being under Excommunication, was necessitated to reconcile himself to the Pope, who in the Year 1213, prescrib'd the Terms to him, upon which he was willing to receive him, for the Peace of the Church. Mr. *Rymer* has inserted a Copy of them, together with the Instructions of *Pandulph* the Pope's Legat, and other Pieces concerning this Affair. The most remarkable and scandalous thing of all was, the Resignation he made of the Kingdoms of *England* and *Ireland* to the Pope, which Mr. *Rymer* has taken from a Manuscript of the *Cotton* Library. This King, who was as cowardly in Adversity, as he was insolent in Prosperity, there says, 'That without Force or Fear, but of 'his own Free-Will, and by the common 'Consent of his Barons, he offers and freely 'gives to God, to the Holy Apostles, St. *Peter* and St. *Paul*, to the Holy *Roman* Church 'his Mother, to his Lord Pope *Innocent* III. 'and to all his Catholic Successors, the whole 'Kingdom of *England*, and all the Kingdom of '*Ireland*, with all their Rights and Appurtenances, for the Remission of all his Sins, and 'those of his Family, whether living or dead. 'That from thenceforth he receives and holds 'his Kingdoms from God, and from the *Roman* Church as its Feudatary.——That he had 'publickly perform'd Homage for them to the 'Church——And that he had oblig'd his Successors to do the like——That for a proof 'of such Concession, he wou'd have a thousand

His Reconciliation and Submission to the Pope. P. 166, 167.

His Resignation of England *and* Ireland *to his Legat.* P. 176.

 'Marks

K. *John.* 'Marks *Sterling* paid to the Pope out of his Revenues arising from his two Kingdoms, besides 'St. *Peter*'s Penny *——And if any of his Successors fail'd herein, he should forfeit his Right 'to the Kingdom.'

Pope's Civility to him. *P.* 177. AFTER this there follows a kind of Oath of Fidelity, which he took to the Pope as his Vassal. There is no cause to wonder if the Pope was extraordinary civil to him afterward, and took his part against the Barons of the Kingdom, who wou'd oblige him to govern according to the Laws, and to whom he was forced to grant what they call *Magna Charta.* Mr. *Rymer* has inserted a great many Briefs from *Innocent* III. in his favour, which are only owing to that King's mean-spirited Behaviour. Among other things, the Pope granted him as an extraordinary Favour, by a Letter dated in the Year 1214. that he cou'd not be excommunicated but by express Order from his Holiness.

P. 177, *to* 181. *P.* 183.

P. 201. Magna Charta. HERE we have a remarkable Act touching the Execution of *Magna Charta*, made in 1215. the very Year in which the Charter was granted. By this Act the King gives a Lease of the City of *London* to the Earls and Barons of his Kingdom, till the Day of the Assumption of the Virgin *Mary*, in the 17th Year of his Reign. He also resigns the Tower of *London* to the Archbishop of *Canterbury*, to keep it till the Term aforesaid; and neither the City nor Tower was oblig'd to receive any of the King's Forces. Mean time, the whole Kingdom was to take an Oath to the Barrons, to be obedient and assisting to the 25 Barons chose out of their Body, on purpose to take care of the Observation of the

* SEE *Henry Spelman*'s Glossary upon *Romescot*, where it appears that this Tribute consisted of 300 Marks *Sterling*, and that it was much more antient than this Reign.

Peace

Peace and Privileges granted them by the King, and confirm'd by his Charter. And all that the King and the Barons thought fit, was to be restor'd. If Restitution was made in this Term, or if the King did not oppose it, the City and Tower were to be deliver'd up to him without delay. But if it was not perform'd in the time prefix'd, the Barons were to keep the City, and the Archbishop the Tower of *London*, till it was done; and in the mean time, every one was to recover the Castles and Lands which he held before the War betwixt the King and the Barons. *A.* 1215.

HOWEVER, the King wou'd not perform his Promise, and got himself absolv'd by the Pope, from the Oath he had taken to restore the antient Laws, and to observe *Magna Charta.* The Pope did not care how much the King tyranniz'd over his Subjects, provided he was but submissive to the Church, which had consequently the greatest share in that Arbitrary Power which the King pretended to claim.

HERE therefore we have, 1. A Letter of the same Year 1215, wherein the Pope entirely disapproves of the Agreement which had been made between the King and the Barons. 2. Another, in which he exhorts the Barons to renounce that Agreement. 3. A Letter from the King to the Pope, wherein he complains, that the Barons were not so submissive to him since he was become the Pope's Feudatary, and that they blam'd him for it in an especial manner; wherefore he intreats the Pope to take care of a Kingdom which was his. 4. A general Excommunication against the Barons of *England*, because they disturb'd a Kingdom which belong'd to the Church of *Rome*. 5. Another more particular than the former.

P. 203, &c. *Letters betwixt the Pope and the King.* P. 205. P. 207. P. 208. P. 211.

K. *John.* In this manner did the Court of *Rome* favour the Tyranny of a very wicked King, when the Laity only were to be the Sufferers by it; but she oppos'd some Attempts which he had made, as she pretended, against the Rights of the Church, with that Violence, as to excommunicate him. If we compare these Acts with *Polydore Virgil*, and other Writers of the History of *England*, it will evidently appear, That the same may be of great Service to correct and supply many Errors and Defects, which 'tis not so material to mention here.

K. Henry III. VI. THE rest of the Acts of this Volume relate to the Reign of *Henry* III. which lasted 56 Years, taking in the time that *Simon de Montfort* ruled in his Name, while he kept him Prisoner.

P. 215. THE first Act is a Letter dated *Anno* 1216, in which *Henry* acquaints his Chief Justice of *Ireland* of the death of his Father, and his Accession to the Crown. There is a great number of Acts here relating to both public and private Affairs, which are of vast Service to those who are to write a History of that Reign.

Pope's Bull in favour of Scotland. P. 227. ANNO 1218, Pope * *Honorius* III. sent a Bull to *Scotland*, in which he grants divers Privileges to that Kingdom, *viz.* That no Person could put it under an Interdict, except the Pope and his Legats; that none but a Native of *Scotland* should act there as a Legat, unless he was one chose by the Apostolical See; that if Quarrels happen'd in the Kingdom about the Right to the Crown, no Foreigner shou'd judge thereof, without Appeal to the Pope; and, that the Im-

* THIS Pope excommunicated the Emperor F[illegible]eric II. and order'd Kneeling at the Elevation of the Host.

munities

munities and Privileges granted by the preceding Popes, should always subsist. 'Tis evident that in the main, the Pope, according to the Custom of that Age, took more for himself than he gave to the *Scots*, and that at the same time he would have it all esteem'd as special Favour. This is one of those Bulls, of which, as we said before, Mr. *Rymer* has caus'd the Beginning and End to be engrav'd, to shew the Form thereof to those who never saw them. *A.* 1218.

HE observes also in his Preface, that *George Buchanan* in the seventh Book of his History of *Scotland*, was in the wrong to charge *Henry* III. King of *England*, with Breach of his Promise to match the two Sisters of *Alexander* King of *Scotland*, his Brother-in-Law, within a certain time, because it appears by two Acts in this Collection, that they were actually marry'd. There is first of all a Declaration of King *Henry*, dated *June* 15, 1220. by which he promises to give his eldest Sister *Joan*, when she came into his Hands (for she was then with the Earl of *March* in *France*) to *Alexander* King of *Scotland*, by *Michaelmas* Day following; or if he could not get her over, that then he would match his youngest Sister *Isabel* to the said King *Alexander* in the space of a Fortnight after; and that he wou'd match the two Sisters of the said Prince, who were *Margaret* and *Isabel*, in *England*, within a Year, reckoning from St. *Dennis*'s Day 1220. If *Henry* broke his Word, it was only in point of Time; because it appears by an Act of *May* 12. 1225. that the said *Isabel* was then marry'd to the Son of the Count *le Bigod*; and by another, dated *November* 13. 1232. that the other Sister *Margaret*, was marry'd to *Hubert du Burgo*.

A Mistake of Buchanan's *in the History of this King, rectify'd.* P. 278, 327. P. 240. P. 278. P. 327.

IT appears likewise by the Acts of the Year 1221, that the Earl of *March*, who marry'd the Mo- P. 252, 253.

Hen. III. Mother of *Henry* King of *England*, after the death of his Father, sent him his Sister *Joan*, and that she was marry'd to the King of *Scotland*. This seems to have been the Motive of King *Henry*'s restoring to his Mother the Lands that were assign'd to her in *England* for her

P. 253. Dowry, as appears by two Acts of the Year 1222. Nevertheless they had Disputes afterwards, in which the Pope intermeddled, as may be seen by other Acts.

A Prince of Wales *disturbs King* Henry, *and is excommunicated by the Pope.*

THE Kings of *England* were frequently embroil'd with the Princes of *Wales*; and in this Volume we have a great number of Acts relating to *Lewelyn*, a Prince of that Country, who was often at variance with King *Henry*, tho' he had marry'd that King's Sister. As the Popes were always for weaving themselves as far as possible into the Concerns of temporal Princes, Pope *Honorius* excommunicated *Lewelyn*

P. 261. in 1223, in case he did not satisfy the King of *England*. He also took this King's part very often against others, probably because of the Submission which he paid to the See of *Rome*: Of this there are a great many Instances in the Acts of his Reign.

Marriage of the King's Sister to the Emperor. P. 353.

THERE we have likewise the Marriage Contract between the Emperor *Frederic* II. and *Isabel*, Sister to King *Henry*, made in 1236, and divers other Pieces relating to the same Affair. It appears by the Acts, that the Person sent over hither

P. 362. on this Errand, was one *Peter de Vinea* *, alias *des Vignes*.

* THE Emperor's Chancellor and most familiar Counsellor, who afterwards, with others of the Emperor's Servants, was suborn'd to murder him, and had accordingly provided a Physician and a Dose; but the matter being discover'd, the Doctor was hang'd, and *Peter* had his Eyes put out, and was carry'd up and down, by the Empe-

Vignes. King *Henry* promised his Sister 30,000 Marks *Sterling* in Marriage, and wrote to Pope *Gregory* IX. to intreat him to engage for him to the Emperor for that Sum, submitting himself to the Ecclesiastical Censures if he did not pay it within the Terms stipulated; and it appears by the Sequel, that he actually paid the whole Sum. By this Marriage the Emperor had a Son nam'd *Henry*, to whom he gave the Island of *Sicily*, as appears by an Act of the Year 1237. Mr. *Rymer* complains in his Preface, of some Historians who have not vouchsafed to make mention of this Marriage of *Frederic*, or of his Son *Henry*; tho' he was a Youth of the most promising Genius and Person, according to *Matth. Paris*, and three *Italian* Writers, the only Historians, according to *Rymer*, who have taken notice of him.

A. 1236. P. 362. *The Pope K. Henry's Bondsman for her Dowry.* P. 373. *Her Issue.* P. 374.

HERE is a Brief or Letter from Pope *Gregory*, dated *July* 7. in the same Year, *viz.* 1237, in which he demands of *Henry* the *Yearly Quit-Rent of the thousand Marks Sterling* of the preceding Year, which had not been paid. There is a like Compliment from *Innocent* IV. his Successor, in the Year 1247.

Pope's Demands upon K. Henry. P. 374. P. 444.

THE Pope in requital, took part in all the Quarrels of the King of *England*; and here we have a Declaration of the above Year, *viz.* 1237. for putting an end to all the Disputes which the King of *England* had with the King of *Scotland*. This Reconciliation was made in pre-

P. 374, &c.

Emperor's Command, thro' most of the Cities of *Italy*, to make known the Design, till he came to *Pisa*, where, in Despair he dash'd out his own Brains. See *Lib.* 8. *cap.* 14. of *Albert Krantz*, Doctor of Laws and Divinity, and Dean of the Church of *Hamburg*, who liv'd in the fifteenth and sixteenth Centuries, was a Man of great Piety as well as Learning, and writ several Books.

Hen. III. fence of the Pope's Legat, and was sign'd, according to Custom, by many Bishops and Barons of *England*. What is surprizing here, is, that the very next Piece is a Letter from the King P. 377. of *Scotland* to the Pope, whom he calls *Innocent*, tho' the then Pope's Name was *Gregory*, and *Innocent* was his Successor.

Emperor Frederic's *Quarrel with the Pope.* P. 382, &c.

THE Emperor and the Pope quarrel'd not long after; and here we have very bitter Complaints of * *Frederic* against the Pope, and against the *English* too, who suffer'd the Pope's Excommunication denounc'd against him, to be publish'd in their Kingdom. 'Tis pity that there were not more Facts in the Emperor's Writings, and less of the Rhetoric of that time, which is by no means pleasant to read. It appears by the Emperor's Complaint, that his Brother-in-Law, the King of *England*, was very much inclin'd to favour the Pope, who perhaps, to reward him, wrote over into *England* the next Year, which was 1239, to order that no Persons disagreeable to the King, should be elected to the Sees P. 387, 388. of *Winchester* and *Durham*; for at that time of day the King did not dare to nominate to Bishopricks. There are other Letters from the same Emperor, wherein he acquaints *Henry* of P. 393. his Success in the War which he carry'd on in *Italy*, and afterwards of the Death of his Sister P. 399. *Isabel*, whose Marriage we have already mention'd.

* DR. *Nicholson* says, That this Emperor was Master of the *Greek*, *Latin*, *German*, *Italian*, and the *Turkish* Languages; and understood most Arts and Sciences; that he was equally wise and brave, and stood out no less than five of the Pope's Excommunications. The Story of this noble Emperor, and of his Controversy with the Pope, whom he describ'd to be the *Antichrist*, is at large in the first Volume of the *Book of Martyrs*.

NOT

NOT to insist upon the Acts relating to France, with which Nation *England* always had some Quarrel or other, nor on those relating to the Principality of *Wales*, which was not yet fallen into the Hands of the Kings of *England*, there's a great number of Acts relating to both, which consider'd indeed distinctly, are of no great Importance, but are of vast Use to such as write the History of that Reign, were it only to fix the Dates, and to range the Events in order of Time. *A.* 1250.

IN 1250, Pope *Innocent* IV. publish'd a Bull for a Croisado, which is in this Collection, together with other Briefs relating thereunto; and the History of that time informs us, that they were not without effect. There is another Bull to the same purpose, which was issu'd *Anno* 1252, and other Acts concerning the same thing. The Popes were very glad to send the Western Princes into *Asia*, because in their Absence they had more Authority in their Dominions, and because these Princes commonly returning Beggars from beyond Sea, they were more submissive to the See of *Rome*, than if they had been in a better Condition.

P. 452 *to* 457, &c.

Popes political Reason for their Croisadoes.

P. 468, &c.

BESIDES the thousand Marks *Sterling*, which *England* paid every Year to the Pope, the Clergy of this Kingdom complain'd in 1252, that the Court of *Rome* drew away fifty thousand Marks more for the Grant of Benefices. * *Innocent*

English Clergy's Complaints against the Pope's Exactions, P. 471.

* THIS Pope was a violent Persecutor of the learned and pious *Grosthed*, Bishop of *Lincoln*, for calling him Antichrist: and *Matth. Paris*, *Cestrensis*, and other Historians of that time, say, That he was frighten'd by the Bishop's Apparition after his Death, summoning him to Judgment; and that he thereupon sicken'd and languish'd for a short time, till he died. He first instituted Cardinals red Hats.

wrote

Hen. III. wrote a Letter upon it to pacify the Complaints of the *English*; but in his Writings there's more Flattery than Sincerity, according to the Custom of the Church of *Rome*. There are also several of this Pope's Letters relating to the Dissolution of the Marriage betwixt the King of *England* and the Daughter of the Count *de Ponthieu*, on pretence that she was his Cousin in the fourth Degree; and likewise to the Confirmation of his Marriage with *Eleanor*, Daughter of the Earl of *Provence*.

After some Disputes with the King of *Castile*, the King of *England* made a perpetual Alliance with him in 1254, *contra omnes homines de mundo, salva fide Ecclesiæ Romanæ*; *i. e.* against all Men in the World, saving his Allegiance to the Church of *Rome*. There are several Pieces upon this Article, very proper to illustrate the History of that Time. P. 503, 504, to 510.

Conrad King of *Naples*, and Son to *Frederic* II. having put to death his Brother *Henry* King of *Sicily*, the King of *England*'s Nephew, he gave advice of it to his Uncle in 1254, by a Letter, wherein he pretended to be very much griev'd for his unhappy End. P. 514. Pope *Innocent* gave the Kingdom of *Sicily* to *Edmond*, Son to our King of *England*, who was as yet a Child; and he left no Stone unturn'd to engage his Father to put himself in possession of it, as may be seen in many Acts of that Reign; and even order'd the Clergy of *England* to borrow Money for this Prince upon their Church-Livings; all which Money was squander'd away by the said Pope, who died about the latter end of the Year, and so the whole Project was disconcerted. P. 511, to 518.

K. *of* Castile's *Resignation of* Gascoigne *to our Prince* Edward.

Edward, eldest Son to the King of *England*, having marry'd *Eleanor*, Sister to *Alphonsus* King of *Castile*, the latter yielded up to *Edward*

ward all his Pretensions to *Gascoigne* by certain Letters Patent, of which Mr. *Rymer* has caus'd a part to be engrav'd. There's a Gold Seal of the Weight of about a Mark *Sterling*, fix'd to this Patent, of which *Matth. Paris* makes special mention: there are likewise other very particular Ornaments. Mr. *Rymer* was of opinion, that this is an Act not unlike those Privileges which are call'd in *Spanish*, *Privilleios Rodados*, from the Mark of a Wheel in the Royal Signature. A. 1255. P. 53

ALEXANDER IV. who succeeded *Innocent* IV. wrote several Bulls and Briefs in the beginning of his Pontificate, which he sent into *England*. He could not rest till he had depriv'd *Mainfroi* or *Manfred*, natural Son to *Frederic* II. of *Sicily* and the Kingdom of *Naples*, which he had made himself Master of by putting *Conrad* to death; and therefore he chang'd the Vow which the Kings of *England*, *Norway*, &c. had made to go to the *Holy-Land*, into a Vow to conquer *Sicily* and the Kingdom of *Naples*, in favour of the Church. P. 536, &c. P. 548, &c.

THERE follow a great many Acts proper to illustrate and confirm the Circumstances of this Undertaking, particularly a Letter from the King in 1256, to certain Cardinals, wherein he says, That the Barons of this Kingdom thought the Conditions upon which the Pope had engag'd him to go and take possession of the Kingdom of *Sicily* very hard; namely, that he shou'd go thither in Person before the Feast of St. *Michael* next ensuing, or send a Captain to command the Army with 135,541 Marks *Sterling*, or else the Treaty shou'd be of no effect, the King should be excommunicated, and the Kingdom put under an Interdict. At the end of the *Acts omitted*, there's the very Bull of P. 587. *Barons of* England *complain of the Pope's Exactions.* P. 893.

 Pope

Pope *Alexander* IV. in which theſe Conditions are expreſs'd more at large. Nevertheleſs the King enter'd into a Treaty upon theſe Conditions; and while Affairs ſtood thus, there happen'd a Diſaſter to the Pope's Army, which put the *Engliſh* ſo much out of conceit with it, that they diſſuaded the King from going thither; but he declares in this Letter, that he was reſolv'd to puſh on the Enterprize, tho' he could not execute it ſo ſpeedily as the Treaty requir'd, by reaſon of the Impoſſibility of raiſing ſo great a Sum of Money. However, there the Affair ſtopp'd, and the King of *England* was not willing to engage in ſo deſperate an Undertaking; but he could not help furniſhing great Sums of Money for it, to the Court of *Rome*, as may be ſeen by a great many Acts; inſomuch, that *Simon de Montfort*, in the King's Name, renounc'd his Pretenſions to the Kingdom of *Sicily*, as we ſhall ſee hereafter.

Pope's Army betray'd to Manfroi *the Uſurper of* Sicily.

King *Henry* declares, That the Treachery of the Marquiſs *de Herebroke* was the Cauſe of the Misfortune in the Army above-mention'd. Mr. *Rymer* has given the whole Hiſtory of it in his Preface, as he had it from *Matthew Paris*, a very ſincere Hiſtorian, who liv'd in that Reign, and was highly eſteem'd in *England*. To be ſhort in the Narrative, *Manfroi* lay at the Town of *Nocera*, in *Campania*, with an Army of *Saracens*, which was ſaid to amount to 60,000 Men, whom *Frederic* II. had ſent for into *Italy*, to make head againſt the Pope's Followers. *Alexander* IV. having ſent a conſiderable Army againſt the Town, commanded by the Marquis *de Herebroke*, under the Cardinal *Octavian*, the ſaid Army ſtopp'd to block up *Nocera*; but committed no Hoſtility againſt the Town, nor did *Manfroi* make any Motion within it. As they

they were not like to come to an Engagement, the Marquis persuaded the Cardinal to disband the greatest part of his Army, in order to save Charges, so that there remain'd but 10, or 12,000 Men; after which, he went and acquainted *Mainfroi* himself with what he had done to serve him, who thereupon made a Salley, and cut the Pope's Army in pieces; but *Octavian* having timely notice from a Friend, made his Escape. This was the Event that disgusted the King of *England* against the Descent upon *Sicily*; to which, however, as I said before, he could not avoid paying a great deal of Money to support the Pope's Interest. *A.* 1255.

In *June* 1256, *Alexander* wrote a Letter to King *Henry*, and sent a Man to him to receive the Money promis'd without delay. At the same time, he impos'd a Tenth upon the Clergy of *England*, *de Maneriis propriis*, to be rais'd out of their own Manors, or from the Lands belonging to every Bishop in the Abbey. There were likewise some Merchants at *Rome*, who having advanc'd Money to the Pope upon what was due to him in *England*, came hither for Payment, and brought with them a *Bull* directed to the King, which the Pope granted them by way of Recommendation. And afterwards he employ'd some *Florence* Merchants, whose Credit he vigorously supported by thundering Excommunications, against those who did not pay them.

Pope's Message to K. Henry for Money. P. 593, &c.

His Tax upon the Clergy. P. 595.

P. 595, &c.

By other *Bulls* in that Year, the Pope granted to the King, 1. The Revenue of the vacant Benefices in *England* which were in the Pope's Collection, that he might fulfil the Vow he had made to go to the *Holy-Land*. 2. The Revenue of those Non-Residents who absented without Leave or Dispensation. 3. One Year's

Pope's Grants to the King. P. 597, to 601.

Hen. III. Revenue out of all the Benefices that should happen to be vacant within five Years. 4. The Tenth of all Ecclesiastical Revenues, according to their just Valuation. 5. The Houshold Goods of those who died intestate. After this manner the Popes were always liberal of other Mens Goods, if it is proper to call a Concession Liberality, which came back again to themselves by another Canal; for what they granted to the Kings for Journeys to the *Holy-Land*, they employ'd against the *Gibelines*, by permitting them to commute their Travelling Vow for a Fighting one, in favour of the Church.

Pope's Tax on the Scotish *Prelates* P. 608, &c. P. 611.

HERE we have certain *Bulls* that impose Taxes on the Prelates of *Scotland*, in order to pay the Debts contracted by the Pope for the Expedition to *Sicily*. There are *others* which grant the King of *England* a longer Term to repair thither himself, or to send a Captain with Money into *Apulia*, but the Prince did neither.

King's Brother elected King of the Romans. P. 622.

THERE was another Affair at that time, which gave *England* employment, and put the Nation to Expence without any manner of Profit; which was the Nomination of *Richard* Earl of *Cornwal*, Brother to *Henry*, to be King of the *Romans*. Here we have a Letter from the said *Richard* to *Edward* his Nephew, the King of *England*'s eldest Son, advising him of his Coronation at *Aix la Chapelle*: The Letter is dated *May* 18, 1257. But *Richard* was never own'd by all the Princes and States of *Germany* *.

AT

* MR. *Daniel*'s History of his Reign tells us, That Earl *Richard* carry'd this Election against no less a Competitor than *Alphonsus* King of *Spain*, after having first sent over the Earl of *Glocester* and Sir *John Mansell* to try the Princes Affections; and that the King of *Spain* pretended he

AT this time, the King of *England*, being weary of laying out so much Money for the Business of *Sicily*, and no good like to come of it, order'd Mr. *Rostand*, the Pope's Chaplain and Nuncio in *England*, to deposite all the Money which he had rais'd in this Kingdom upon that score, in the new *Temple* at *London*, and hinder'd him from paying it to the Pope's Bankers. The Pope was horridly vex'd at it, and order'd his Nuncio, in spite of the King's Prohibition, to employ all the Sums he had out of the Tenths, the Redemption of Vows, and all the other Methods that he had used to draw Money from the *English*, towards paying the Debts of the Holy-See. It appears that this Affair was afterwards accommodated, tho' the King of *England* declar'd from that time, that he was ready to renounce the Kingdom of *Sicily*. *A.* 1257. *The King lays an Embargo upon the Money levy'd by the Pope's Nuncio for the Business of Sicily.* P. 624, &c.

IT appears by some *Acts*, that the Jews then in *England* endeavour'd, according to Custom, to make an Interest at Court. For certain Services which two Jew Brothers *Cresse* and *Hagen* had perform'd to *Richard* his Brother, the King discharg'd them in 1257 from all Taxes, &c. for five Years, on paying down a Mark and a half of Gold, of which the said *Cresse*, who was Son to Mr. *Moses* a Jew at *London*, was to pay the Mark, and *Hagen* the half. By a *Patent* of this Year, the King deposed a Jew nam'd *Elias*, P. 623, 636. P. 636.

he was first elected, but he being a Philosopher, and studious of the Mathematics, which he reviv'd in *Europe*, was drawing Lines when he should have drawn his Purse, and so lost his Hopes, and *Richard* stept in before him.

DR. *Howel* says he paid a large Sum of Money for the Honour, and that he was reputed at this time to possess as much ready Coin, as would every Day, for ten Years, afford him a hundred Marks upon the main Stock; besides his Rents and Revenues in *Germany*, and the *English* Dominions.

Hen. III. whom he calls a Bishop and Sacrificer of the Jews, which is as much as to say a Rabbi, for a Fault he had committed against his Majesty, and against *Richard* King of the *Romans*. The two Jews above-mention'd gave the King three Marks of Gold, to obtain Leave for the Society of *Jews* in *England* to chuse whom they pleas'd for Rabbi.

English *Nobility's Letter to the Pope, about the Affair of* Sicily. P. 660, &c.

In the Year 1258, there's a remarkable Letter sign'd by eleven *English* Noblemen, and sent to the Pope in the name of all the rest of the Nobility, complaining of the King's having accepted the Kingdom of *Sicily* for his Son, contrary to their Opinion and Consent; because *England* was in no manner of Condition to support such a Charge. They add, however, that in respect to the Apostolical See, if he would please to redress the Disorders in this Kingdom, and obtain *Sicily* for them upon better Terms, they wou'd support him in the Undertaking, tho' he engag'd in it without their Consent. They tell him that the King, and his eldest Son Prince *Edward*, consented to the Choice of 24 Persons, of whom the King was to name one half, and the Barons the other; and that they both engag'd themselves by Oath to follow what the whole Body or the Majority should agree to. Nevertheless, according to this Letter from the *English* Lords, the King's * Brothers, who were come from *France*, had hinder'd the King from performing his Promise. *Ademare* was as great an Obstacle as any, who, being elected Bishop of *Winchester*, tho' he had not yet taken Orders, fed the King with those Notions, promised him whatever Money he shou'd

* The Children of the Earl of *March* and of the Queen, Mother to *Henry* III. born in *France*.

want

want in the Controversy, tho' it should exhaust his Bishopric; and in short, he made Confusion every where, and shook the Kingdom. The Barons did all they could to get the Laws re-establish'd according to the Agreement; but the King's Brothers aim'd at breaking all their Measures, and caused very great Disorders in the Kingdom; so that, say the Barons, *neither their Inferiors, now their Equals, nor their Superiors, could live or converse with them.* They were therefore summon'd before a Court of Justice, to give an account of their Conduct, so that two of them were permitted to retire to *France*, on condition that two should stay in *England* to appear at the Bar of Justice; but they all withdrew to *France* with a *Passport* from the King, which comes after this Act. A. 1258. P. 662.

THE Barons, after having told their Story to the Pope, desire he would so order it, that the King's Brothers might stay in *France*, and especially *Ademare*, who being elected to the See of *Winchester*, and the chief Cause of all the Mischiefs, they even desir'd the Pope to deprive him altogether of his Bishopric, the very People of *England* hating the Thoughts of his coming back again; which was the more easy for the Pope to do, because he had only the Administration of the Bishopric, and had never yet been consecrated.

Peace between K. Henry *and* Lewis IX. *of* France.

BY reason of these Broils, *Henry* clapp'd up a disadvantageous Peace with *France*, as we are inform'd by the Historians of both *France* and *England*. We have the Articles both in *Latin* and *French*, dated *May* 20, 1259. and several other Acts relating to it, particularly *one* in *October* following, in *French* and *Latin*, on which we cannot insist. P. 675, &c. P. 688.

Hen. III. The Pope's Bull to absolve those who had taken an Oath to observe the Laws. P. 722.

The Pope answers afterwards by two Bulls, where, instead of exhorting the King to the Observance of the old Laws of the Kingdom, he sent an *Order* to certain Prelates, to absolve all those who had engag'd themselves by Oath to execute what the Majority of the 24 Barons had resolv'd on, and to excommunicate those who wou'd not break their Engagements. This Reign was embroil'd every day more and more, and besides the Quarrels which the King had with the Kingdom in general, he had one in particular with *Simon de Montfort*, Earl of *Leicester*, who had marry'd his Sister *Eleanor*; and putting himself at the Head of the King's Enemies, did him a great deal of Mischief, as will appear hereafter. There are *Letters* dated in 1261, in which *Henry* signify'd his desire to refer his Dispute with the Earl *de Montfort*, to the Arbitration of his Sister-in-law *Margaret*, Queen of *France*; but it came to nothing, and the People of *England* were still the more incens'd.

King's Quarrel with the Earl of Leicester

Henry *offers to refer it to the Arbitration of* Margaret *Queen of* France. P. 724.

Obtains the Pope's Absolution of his Oath to the Barons. P. 736.

In 1262, the King, by a Letter dated the first Day of *January*, demanded of Pope *Urban* IV. *Alexander*'s Successor, to be absolv'd from the Oath he had taken to the Barons; which Absolution, the Pope, without much Deliberation, sent him on the 25th of *February* following, together with Orders to the Archbishop of *Canterbury* to dissolve and annul all the Engagements which he had enter'd into with the Barons. In this manner the Popes made a Jest of the Oaths of Kings and People, as if neither the one nor the other had any right to take them without their Leave.

Sicily, *given away by the Pope.*

In 1263, *Urban* wrote word to the King and Prince *Edmund*, that he was resolv'd to give the Kingdom of *Sicily* to another, because they were not able to perform the Conditions upon which

which it had been granted to Prince *Edmund*; *A.* 1263.
and afterwards he invested in it *Charles* of *Anjou*, Brother to St. *Louis* King of *France*. Thus after the See of *Rome* had squeez'd great Sums of Money out of *England* upon this very score, they depriv'd her of all hopes of the Island. The worst on't was, that either the King of *England* wou'd have been oblig'd to refuse that Crown, or at least to have renounc'd it soon after. For to give a Kingdom in which the Donor has no Right in reality, on condition that the Person to whom it is granted, shall go and conquer it at his own Hazard and Expence, is making a Present as unjust as it is mischievous, and as injurious to him who accepts it, as dishonourable to him who gives it.

King of France *chose Umpire of* Henry's *Quarrel with the Barons.* *P.* 776, &c.

IN the Year 1264, the King of *England* on the one part, and the Barons on the other, chose the King of *France* Arbitrator of their Quarrel, as we see by their Letters of the same Year; and *Lewis* accordingly pronounc'd his Verdict at *Amiens*.

The French *King's Sentence in favour of K.* Henry. *Confirm'd by the Pope.* *P.* 781, *to* 785.

AFTER the Example of the Pope, with whose Authority he had cloth'd himself, he annull'd all that the Barons had obtain'd of the King, and decided perfectly in his Favour, tho' he left things in the same state they were in before the Treaty, which the Barons had made with the King. Pope *Urban* confirm'd the Sentence of the King of *France*, and enjoin'd Excommunication against those who refus'd Submission to it, as we see by his Bulls to the Archbishop of *Canterbury*, and the Abbat of *St. Dennis* in *France*.

Folly of the Barons.

THE Barons were not to be commended for referring the Laws and Privileges of their Country to the Arbitration and Award of a Prince, who was not only their King's Brother-in-law, but

Hen. III. but moreover a King himſelf; a Title which thoſe beyond Sea generally hold to be incompatible with the Liberties and Privileges of the People. Beſides, *Lewis* was a blind Bigot in Religious Affairs; and the Pope's declaring for *Henry*, was Warrant enough for him to be of the ſame ſide of the Queſtion. Nor was it good Policy in a King, who had a great many powerful Vaſſals of his own, to give Judgment in favour of Vaſſals againſt their Sovereigns, for fear, leſt that in a like Caſe, the Vaſſals of the Kings of *France* ſhou'd, one time or other, try the ſame Expedient.

Of the Fr. *King.*

Barons Contempt of the French *King's Award.*

HOWEVER, the Barons of *England* refus'd to ſtand to *Lewis*'s Award: They took no more notice of it, than the King did of the Oath in 1258, from which the Pope abſolv'd him, as has been already ſaid. At length the Sword was drawn, and a * Battle was fought between both Parties in *April*, in which the Barons were worſted, but maintain'd their Courage; and on the 14th of *May*, gave † Battle again to the Royal Army, which they defeated, and took the King Priſoner, together with his Brother *Richard*, who came to his Aſſiſtance. His own Son, Prince *Edward*, and *Henry*, Son to *Richard*, ſurrender'd themſelves into the Barons hands as Hoſtages. From that time to *May* 28, 1265, *Simon de Montfort*, Earl of *Leiceſter*, govern'd the Kingdom in the King's Name, who, though he ſeem'd to be under no Reſtraint, was narrowly watch'd. He made him ſign what Orders he

They defeat and take their King Priſoner.

Simon de Montfort's *Government.*

* THIS happen'd at *Northampton*.

† IT was fought near *Lewes* in *Suſſex*. This diſcovers the Miſtake of ſome Hiſtorians, who date this Battle on *May* 19.

pleas'd,

pleas'd, and summon'd a * Parliament to meet at *London* in the Month of *June*, by whose Advice the King was to be conducted. Mr. *Rymer* has taken care to distinguish the Acts made during the King's Captivity, so as to be easily known from the others; for which see the Pages from 790, to 815. *A.* 1265.

THE Pope hearing what had happen'd in *England*, sent over *Guy* Bishop of *Sabine*, who was afterwards Pope, by the Title of *Clement* IV. but the Barons refus'd to admit him into *England*; upon which he excommunicated them, and enjoin'd 'em to release the Prisoners, by a Letter which we have here.

His Party excommunicated, because they wou'd not admit the Pope's Legat. P. 798.

MEAN time *Edward* found means to escape from his Keepers on the 18th of *May*, 1265, and with all possible speed assembled a Body of Troops to rescue his Father. Upon this *Simon de Montfort* made his Father sign several Orders against him; particularly one to the King's Vassals to assemble and oppose him, another to apprehend him, and a third to excommunicate him. Among the Acts of that time, there is a Power likewise which the King gave to *Simon de Montfort*, to *Peter* of *Savoy*, and *John Mansell*, Treasurer of *York*, to renounce the Kingdom

Prince Edward's *Escape.*

P. 810. 811. 812.

K. Henry's *Renunciation of* Sicily. P. 815.

* DR. BRADY thinks this was the first Convention wherein the Sheriffs were order'd to return two Knights for each County, and the Cities and Burghs two Citizens and Burgesses respectively, and that *Simon de Montfort* summon'd this Convention, and alter'd the antient Usage, because of the Danger, that he and his Friends apprehended from the Concourse of the Nobility and their great Retinues, and the Example of his and the Barons Practices at *Oxford*. *Dr.* Brady's *Introduct.* p. 143. But *Spelman*, *Bede*, *Selden*, Dr. *Hody*, and other authentic Historians, have prov'd that there was the same sort of Conventions, even so early as the *Saxon* Times, tho' under different Denominations.

Hen. III. dom of *Sicily* in the Names of Himself, and his Son *Edmund*. The Earl of *Leicester* did not fail to make this Renunciation in favour of *Charles* of *Anjou*.

PRINCE *Edward* made light of all Proclamations, &c. against him in the Name of the King, and assembled a sufficient number of Troops to give battel to those of *Simon de Montfort*, whom he attack'd on the 4th * of *August*, when *Montfort* was kill'd; and all the Heads of the Party being either kill'd or taken, the King was set at liberty, and revok'd all that the Earl of *Leicester* had done in his Name. On the other hand, the Bishop of *Sabine* being chose Pope as aforesaid, made use of spiritual Weapons, and sent a great number of unnecessary Bulls into *England*, before he knew what had pass'd there.

Pope's Bulls against Simon *E. of* Leicester, *&c.* *P.* 817, *to* 829.

IT seems that *Edward* had much ado for some Years past, to excuse himself from travelling to the *Holy-Land*; but now he prepares for a Journey thither, along with *St. Louis* King of *France*: and we have two Acts in *French* this Year, by which the King of *England*, and his Son, borrow 70000 *Livres Tournois*, to fit out *Edward* for the Voyage, who left the Guardianship of his Children, during his absence, to his Uncle *Richard*, King of the *Romans*, as a *French* Act in the Year 1270 makes appear. There are also Passports from *Charles* of *Anjou*, King of *Sicily*, for *Edward*, who actually went to the *Holy-Land*; tho' his Father finding himself sick, and fearing he should die in his Son's absence, recall'd him by a Letter dated *February* 6, 1271. He recover'd however of that Illness, and made a Vow to go himself with the Cross to the *Holy-Land*, as he declares

P. 862. Edward *makes a Voyage to the* Holy-Land. *P.* 866, *to* 869. *P.* 869. K. Henry *makes a Vow to do the like.* *P.* 871.

* THIS Battle was fought near *Evesham* in *Worcestershire*.

declares in a *French* Act of the 16th of *April* in the same Year; for he thought he could not give the Lord a greater Proof of his Thankfulness for having just restor'd him to his Health. *A.* 1271.

Gregory X. being advanc'd to the Pontifical Throne, notify'd it to *Henry* by a Bull dated the 26th of *March*, 1272, and in two days after he publish'd a Croisado, requiring all the Members of it to repair to the *Holy-Land*, within the space of two Years, reckoning from the first of *May*, 1274. *Pope* Gregory's *Creation.* P. 879. *His Croisado.* P. 881.

Here we have Prince *Edward*'s Last Will and Testament made at *Acre*, some time after his arrival in the *Holy-Land*. It is in the *French* Language, and he there appoints his Executors and Guardians for his Children, in case the King his Father shou'd happen to die, before the eldest was of Age to govern by himself. This shews to what hazards Princes expose their Dominions and Families by going to the *Holy-Land*; and the Popes took care to send them thither as often as they cou'd, because the absence of the Princes gave the Clergy at home the more room to increase their Power and Wealth. *Edward*, as History tells us, had like to have been murder'd by an Assassin, who gave him several Stabs with a Dagger; but recovering of his Wounds, and hearing that *Lewis*, King of *France*, whom he expected, was dead in *Africa*, he set out on his return home; and we have a Letter here, dated *December* 23, 1272, whereby the Grandees of the Kingdom gave him advice of his Father's Death. *Prince* Edward's *last Will.* P. 885. *An Attempt to murder him.* P. 888.

Mr. Rapin, when he concludes his Account of the first Volume, makes this very pertinent Remark; that Mr. *Rymer* has not inserted any of the Acts relating to the Re-establishment of the Laws, and in particular of *Magna Charta*;

which,

Hen. III. which, according to our Hiſtorians, *Henry* made in the fifty-firſt Year of his Reign. This is confeſs'd to be at leaſt as material an Omiſſion as any that cou'd have happen'd of the Acts in his Time; becauſe the Non-obſervance of thoſe Laws was one of the principal Cauſes of the Civil War therein mention'd. Perhaps, ſays *Rapin*, in ſome Reigns, when the bare mention of Privileges and Laws was Treaſon, and where Arbitrary Power happen'd to be the only View of the Princes, there was a deſign to remove thoſe Acts out of ſight, which ought to have been preſerv'd in the Records, preferable to all others. On the other hand, it is not to be doubted, but that Length of Time, and the Negligence of thoſe who had the Care of the Records, may have innocently robb'd us of the ſight of a great many conſiderable Pieces, which the State Hiſtoriographer might have ſearched for to Eternity.

Edw. I. THE SECOND VOLUME of Mr. RYMER'S *Fœdera*, begins with the public Acts paſs'd before King *Edward* was return'd from the *Holy-Land*, and takes in all the Acts of that King's Reign from 1273, to 1307, which was the 35th Year of his Reign, and the laſt of his Life; for he died the 7th of *July*, that very Year, as appears by a particular Account thereof at the end of this Volume. (P. 1059.)

To make an Abridgment of all the Acts of this Volume, and at the ſame time to take in all the Events to which thoſe Acts have a Reference, wou'd be a Work of great Labour and length of Time. What I propoſe therefore, is only to give you an Idea of the principal Occurrences, that you may be able to point your Readers to the Acts which they refer to, and to draw

draw ſuch Inferences from them, as may be to the ſatisfaction of thoſe who have a Curioſity for ſuch Inquiries. I confeſs that ſome perhaps might look into this Collection with another View than I have done; and for example, might be induc'd to take particular notice of the Forms of the Acts, and of the *Latin* or *French* Terms which are therein uſed: And others perhaps, according as their different Studies lead them, might have a particular Inclination to take notice of ſome important Facts, with reſpect to certain Affairs, which I have paſs'd over in ſilence. But 'tis not poſſible to ſatisfy the Curioſity of all ſorts of Readers, unleſs one was to write a Hiſtory, as I have already ſaid, of all the Events to which the numerous Acts have a Reference, which would ſwell the Work in hand beyond meaſure. Therefore I have confin'd myſelf to what I thought moſt curious; and to do it with Accuracy, inſtead of following the Order of Time in which thoſe Acts are rang'd, I ſhall conſider them according to the different Subjects of 'em, reſerving to myſelf the liberty of giving an Account of ſome things afterwards, which have no dependance one upon another. A. 1273.

THE principal Matters treated of in this Volume are,

I. THE War in *Wales*, which ended in the Conqueſt of that Country by *Edward* I.

II. THE Differences between the two Families of *Arragon* and *Anjou*, of which *Edward* I. was choſe Mediator.

III. THE War in *Scotland*, with the Origin and Cauſes of that War, which was attended with ſuch fatal Conſequences.

IV.

Edw. I.

IV. The Disputes which *Edward* had with *France*.

V. The Affairs which concern *England* in particular.

VI. The Ecclesiastical Affairs, or rather the Controversies which *Edward* had with the Popes.

VII. Some Acts relating to *Edward* in particular.

VIII. And lastly, some distinct Acts which contain divers things Important and Curious.

I. *The Affairs of* Wales.

King Edward's *Archbishops excommunicate the Prince of* Wales. P. 79.

In this Volume we find several Acts relating to *Wales*, and the War which *Edward* carry'd into that Country; but there are few of them very important. It wou'd appear very strange at this time of day, if a Prince shou'd take it into his head, to put the Chief of his Clergy upon excommunicating the Princes with whom he happens to be at War. Nevertheless at that time such a Proceeding cou'd not be for nothing; for we find here that the Archbishop of *Canterbury*, after having excommunicated *Leolyn* Prince of *Wales*, requires the Archbishop of *York* to do the like.

English *Nobility pass Judgment against him.* P. 68.

This War in *Wales* was not began till after a solemn Judgment pass'd against *Leolyn*, by the great Men of *England*, in the Year 1276. They condemn'd him for refusing to come and do Homage to *Edward*, and the Excuses he alledg'd for not coming were not admitted. They are only mention'd here in general, tho' the Exactness required

quired in History made, it absolutely necessary to give the particulars*. *A.* 1276.

AT length this War was determin'd by the Death of *Leolyn*, who was kill'd in Battle in 1282†. There's a Letter from the Archbishop of *Canterbury* to King *Edward*, dated in this Year, which Mr. *Rymer* copy'd from the Records at *Lambeth*; wherein he tells the King, that some Letters were found in Cypher in *Leolyn*'s Pocket, by which it appear'd that he held a Correspondence in *England*. *His Death.* P. 224.

AFTER the Death of this Prince, his Brother *David* was taken and sent to *Edward*, who caus'd him to be try'd by the Parliament of *Shrewsbury*, where he was condemn'd, and suffer'd death as a Traytor, which never used to be inflicted before upon Persons of Distinction ‖. It cannot be deny'd but there was a vast deal of Barbarity in King *Edward*'s Treatment of this Prince, the last of the Race of the antient *British* or *Welsh* Princes. Thus you have all that *Death of his Brother David.*

* THEY are mention'd in *Powel's* Chronicle of *Wales*, and if true, seem very substantial; but *Edward* having resolv'd on the Conquest of that Country, only wanted a Pretence for it.—— Dr. *Kennet*, in his Note upon Mr. *Daniel*'s Account of this Affair, taxes him with not speaking so much in favour of the *Welsh* as he might have done; and the Doctor quotes the aforesaid Chronicle, to shew that they had other more substantial Reasons for the War, that *Leolyn* and his Brother gave the Archbishop of *Canterbury* above a dozen Articles of Grievances, most of them very weighty, which provok'd them to take Arms; and that King *Edward* refus'd to treat with them.

† THIS rectifies another Mistake in our Historians, who place his Death in *December* 1283.

‖ MR. DANIEL says, he was first drawn at a Horse's Tail about *Shrewsbury*, and then beheaded, his Body quarter'd, and his Heart and Bowels burnt; his Head was sent to be set on the Tower with his Brother's, and his four Quarters to these four Cities, *viz.* *Bristol Northampton*, *York*, and *Winchester*.

Edw. I. is of any importance in the Acts relating to this Affair.

II. *Acts relating to the Differences between the Kings of* Arragon *and* Sicily.

Conradin's *Execution.* THERE's a great number of these Acts in this Volume, which relate to these Differences, and to *Edward's* Negotiation for accommodating those two Families; but to be enabled to understand these Acts at the first view, one must look back to the History of the Quarrel on which they were founded; which is in substance this. When *Conradin*, whom *Charles* of *Anjou* had order'd to be beheaded, was mounted on the Scaffold, the young Prince threw his Glove into the Square, desiring the Person that took it up, to carry it to a Relation of his, as a Mark of the Investiture which he gave him of the Inheritance of the Family of *Swabia*, of which he was the last Heir Male. They say that this Glove was carry'd to *Peter* King of *Arragon*, who marry'd *Constantia*, Daughter of *Mainfroi*, the last King of *Sicily*, and who was natural Son to the Emperor *Frederick* II. *Peter* was not in haste to improve what Pretensions he might have to *Sicily* in Right of his Wife, till a Resolution was form'd by *John de Procida*, a discontented *Sicilian* Nobleman, in concert with Pope *Nicholas* III. who was also incens'd against *Charles* of *Anjou*, to stir up the *Sicilians* to a Rebellion. Sicilian *Conspiracy*, After they had consulted the necessary Measures, *John de Procida* went and communicated the Conspiracy to the King of *Arragon*, and told him of his Design to deliver *Sicily* from its Tyrant. *Peter* was at first afraid of entring into a War, because he did not foresee how he cou'd get out of it with honour; but *Procida* remov'd remov'd all his Difficulties. 1. By furnishing him with the Money he had receiv'd from the Emperor of *Constantinople*, who, in order to divert *Charles* from a Design to make War upon him, had deposited great Sums of Money in *Procida*'s Hands to carry on the Conspiracy. 2. By secretly giving him the Investiture of *Sicily* in the Name of Pope *Nicholas* III. And, thirdly and lastly, by giving him to understand, that there was no manner of necessity for his engaging in this Undertaking, till the *Sicilian* Conspiracy had taken effect. For this end it was agreed between them, that the King of *Arragon* should equip a considerable Fleet, on pretence of making War against the *Saracens*, and that he shou'd lie upon the *African* Shore ready to sail for *Sicily*, if the Conspiracy took effect; and that if it miscarry'd, he might then, without seeming to have had any manner of Concern in it, go on to make War against the *Saracens*. These Measures being concerted, *Peter* carry'd his Fleet to *Africa*, and there besieg'd a Town, which the Historians of *Sicily* call *Andacalle*. Mean time *Procida*'s Plot succeeded, and the *Sicilians* cut the Throats of all the *Frenchmen* upon the Island, which was what they call to this day, the *Sicilian Vespers* *. *Charles* of *Anjou*, who had a Fleet ready equipp'd to fall upon the Emperor of *Greece*, sail'd immediately towards *Sicily*, and besieg'd *Messina*; the Inhabitants whereof offer'd to surrender to him on this only Condition, that he wou'd spare their Lives; but he was so enrag'd beyond measure, that he refus'd 'em that Condition, which made them resolve to defend

A. 1282.

Sicilian Vespers.

* It had that Name, because the Bell which rung to Evening Prayers was their Signal. The Massacre was upon *Easter-Eve*.

Edw. I. themselves to the last Extremity. During this Siege, *Procida* went over to the King of *Arragon*, then in *Africa*, and inform'd him how much the Inhabitants of *Messina* were press'd for want of

P. 208. his Assistance. Before *Peter* quitted the Coasts of *Africa*, he wrote a Letter to King *Edward*, dated in the Year 1282, from *Altoyl*, (I know not whether it may not be the same Place with *Andacalle*;) in which he tells the King, that while he was employ'd in the War against the *Saracens*, the *Sicilians* had sent Deputies to him, to desire him to go and take possession of *Sicily*; which he was resolv'd to do, since that Kingdom belong'd to his Wife *Constantia*. He sail'd therefore for *Sicily*, and arriving at *Palermo*, was receiv'd and crown'd there as King. From thence he sent a Note to *Charles*, wherein he acquainted him of his Arrival on the Island of *Sicily*, which was adjudg'd to him by Authority of the Church, Pope, and Cardinals; and he commanded him to quit the Island immediately after the receipt of his Letter, on pain of being compell'd to it by Force. *Charles* answer'd this by another Letter of the same Strain, wherein he calls him a Miscreant and Traitor to God, and the Holy *Roman* Church*. Mean time *Charles*, who, while he besieg'd *Messina*, did not expect the Town cou'd have any Relief, was afraid of being block'd up and starv'd by the King of *Arragon*'s Fleet, and therefore he abandon'd the Siege, and retir'd to *Calabria*; from whence he went to *Rome*, to complain to the Pope against his Enemy, whom he call'd perfidious Traitor, and dar'd him to single Combat. While *Charles*

Challenges between the K. of Arragon *and* Sicily.

* Both these Letters are in *Italian*, but in a Style not much above the Advertisements of our Heroes at *Fig's Amphitheatre*, the one challenging, the other defying.

lost

loſt Time in complaining, *Peter* made good uſe of it in *Sicily*, by cauſing himſelf to be acknowledg'd in *Meſſina*, and all over the Iſland; after which he ſent his Ambaſſadors to *Rome*, where there was a new Pope that ſucceeded *Nicholas* III. viz. *Martin* IV. a Creature of *Charles* of *Anjou*, by whoſe Intrigues, or rather by a Force put upon the Cardinals, he was elected. *Peter*'s Ambaſſadors made the beſt Anſwer they cou'd for their Maſter, and according to their Inſtructions, accepted for him the Duel propos'd by *Charles* of *Anjou*. This procur'd a Truce, during which the two Kings agreed to chuſe twelve Perſons each, in order to regulate the Time, Place, and Conditions of the Combat. Theſe twenty-four met accordingly, and drew up ſome Articles, which the two Kings ratify'd. It was therein agreed, that they ſhou'd fight at *Bourdeaux* upon the firſt of *June*, 1283, each accompany'd by an hundred Horſe. The very *Articles* are to be ſeen in this Volume. Their being never made publick before, has led ſome of the beſt Hiſtorians into Miſtakes, and has been very prejudicial to the Reputation of the King of *Arragon*. The chief of thoſe Articles were in ſubſtance as follow.

A. 1282.

Articles of the Duel. P. 226, &c.

1. THAT the Duel ſhall be at *Bourdeaux*, in ſuch Place as the King of *England* ſhall judge beſt, which ſhall be rail'd in.

2. THAT the two Kings ſhall make their perſonal Appearance before the King of *England*, in order to fight this Duel on the firſt of *June*, 1283.

3. THAT if the King of *England* cannot be at *Bourdeaux* in Perſon, the two Kings ſhall then appear before ſome Perſon whom that King ſhall depute, to record their Appearance in his room.

Edw. I. 4. THAT if the King of *England* be not there, either in Perſon, or Proxy, the two Kings ſhall then be oblig'd to appear before the Perſon who commands at *Bourdeaux* for him.

5. IT was alſo agreed *, *that the ſaid Duel ſhall not be fought before any Perſons whatſoever in the King of* England'*s Service, unleſs the ſaid King is actually preſent in Perſon.* Saving to the two Kings the Liberty of agreeing between themſelves, by mutual Conſent, to fight the ſaid Duel in that manner; that is to ſay, in the abſence of *Edward*.

6. THAT if the King of *England* is not perſonally preſent at the Place and Time appointed, the two Kings ſhall be oblig'd to ſtay for him thirty Days.

7. AND in order to procure the King of *England*'s Preſence by all means, the two Kings promiſe and ſwear to do their utmoſt, *bona fide*, and without Fraud, to obtain of the ſaid King, that he wou'd appear at the Time and Place aforeſaid, and to take due care that their Letters be actually put into his Hand.

AFTER ſome other Articles relating to the Truce, and the Securities which the two Kings give reciprocally; it is farther agreed,

8. THAT which ſoever of the two Kings fails to appear at the Time and Place aforeſaid, he ſhall be deem'd a vanquiſh'd, perjur'd, falſe, faithleſs Traitor; that he ſhall never aſſume to himſelf either the Name or Honours of a King; that he remain for ever depriv'd and ſtripp'd of the Royal Title and Honours, and be incapable of any manner of Office and Dignity, as a Perſon vanquiſh'd, perjur'd, falſe, faithleſs, traitorous, and eternally infamous.

* THIS is a remarkable Article.

ALL

ALL the *French*, *Spanish*, and *Italian* Historians have unanimously affirm'd, that *Edward* actually settled and took care of the Place of Combat; perhaps they were led into this Error by the Appearance of *Charles* of *Anjou* at *Bourdeaux* with his hundred Horse, for they cou'd not imagine that this Prince wou'd come with his Troop in a posture to fight, and that he wou'd stay at *Bourdeaux* from Sun-rise to Sun-set, if he had not thought of fighting: but we have a *Letter* here from King *Edward* to that same Prince, whereby he acquaints him, *That were he to gain both the Kingdoms of* Arragon *and* Sicily, *he wou'd not appoint the Field of Battle, nor suffer the two Kings to fight a Duel in any place of his Dominions, or in any other whatsoever, if it were in his Power to hinder it.* In the *Letter* which he wrote to the Prince of *Salerno*, he tells him, that instead of having granted his Father's Demand touching this Duel, he had deny'd him *tout-outre* (or point blank,) that's the Term he makes use of; for both Letters are in *French*. There is no reason therefore to suppose, that *Edward* gave any Sanction to this intended Duel, either by his Presence, or by sending any one to represent him, or by giving the two Kings any Letters of safe Conduct, or, finally, by causing the Place to be prepar'd: and yet the Historians suppose it as a thing certain, when they say that *Charles* came to *Bourdeaux*, and that he made his Appearance on the Field of Battle, and stay'd there from Sun-rise to Sun-set, without seeing his Enemy. The Truth of the Fact is, that *Charles* of *Anjou* actually came to *Bourdeaux* on the Day fix'd, that he stay'd there till towards the Evening; and that hearing the King of *Arragon* was yet a great way off, he retir'd that same Day. But he was

A. 1282.

Another great Mistake of Historians rectify'd.

P. 239.

P. 240.

Edw. I. ſcarce gone, when *Peter*, who was all the while in the Town diſguis'd under the Name of one of the Noblemen of his Court, went before the Seneſchal of *Guyenne*, took a Record of his Appearance, and left his Arms as a Teſtimony; after which he made the beſt of his way out of Town, and poſted towards his own Dominions. This Conduct of his gave a handle to the *French* Hiſtorians to accuſe him of Cowardice, and want of Courage to meaſure Swords with his Enemy. But if we conſider the Tenor of the Articles agreed on between the two Kings, 'tis manifeſt that the Appearance of theſe two Princes before the Seneſchal of *Guyenne*, was only to comply with the fourth Article, and with no manner of deſign to fight; becauſe it appears by the fifth, that there was to be no Duel there, if the King of *England* was not preſent; and by King *Edward*'s Letters above-mention'd, that nothing was farther from that Prince's Intention, than to be preſent at ſuch Duel. Therefore let them accuſe the King of *Arragon* of Faint-heartedneſs as much as they will, I admit that he was afraid; but then his was not a Fear to engage in a Duel with his Enemy, becauſe by their Conventions he was not oblig'd to it: And yet this is the Ground of their Charge againſt him, this the Reaſon of all the Jokes that have been put upon his Conduct. What was he then afraid of? The *French* Hiſtorians, who were very glad of an opportunity to vilify this Prince, who was an Enemy to the Royal Family of *France*, have been far from explaining to us the Ground of his Fear; but the *Sicilians* and *Neapolitans* have done him that Juſtice, by telling us, that he had Intelligence not only that *Charles* had brought his hundred Horſe

Horſe with him into *Bourdeaux*, but that he had, *A.* 1283.
as ſome ſay, three thouſand, and according to others, five thouſand Horſe but a Day's Journey from the Town; and ſome add moreover, that the King of *France*'s Nephew was at the head of 'em: which is a Circumſtance that *Mezeray* left room to conjecture, when he ſaid, *That* Peter *retir'd, pretending that he was afraid of ſome Surprize on the part of* France. Now if the King of *France* had not had Troops near *Bourdeaux*, how cou'd *Peter*, when he was in the Dominions of the King of *England*, pretend the Fear of any Surprize from the King of *France?* There are two things therefore to be conſider'd for the Juſtification of the King of *Arragon*; firſt, whether he perform'd the Terms of Agreement, and of this there can be no doubt with any one that has read the abovemention'd Articles; and, ſecondly, whether he had any reaſon to be jealous of *Charles*, and of the King of *France*. As to the former of theſe Princes, the Hiſtorians of *Naples* and *Sicily* ſay, that he publickly boaſted that he wou'd be the Death of the King of *Arragon*; which was ſufficient to give the latter juſt Reaſon to be afraid of him, when he found himſelf in a Country remote from his own Dominions, not far from thoſe of the King of *France*, and without any ſafe Conduct from the King of *England*, or any other Security than the bare Word of an Enemy, upon whoſe Sincerity he cou'd by no means depend, after he had openly threaten'd he wou'd have his Life. As for the King of *France*, the *Italians* ſay that he had a Body of 5000, or at leaſt of 3000 Horſe, no more than a Day's Journey from the Spot. *Mezeray*, and the other *French* Hiſtorians, who cou'd not be ignorant of what the *Italians* ſaid, do not deny it, and

Edw. I. are content to say nothing of it; so that there is at least as much Probability of the thing's being true, as there is of its being false. But after all, supposing that *Peter* had been struck with a groundless Panic, for fear of some Surprize on the part of the King of *France*, I don't see what great harm it cou'd have done to his Reputation. *Garibay*, a *Spanish* Historian, who, no doubt, was not ignorant of the Conventions between the two Kings, has taken the freedom to say, that the King of *Arragon* came to *Bourdeaux*, but went away again because *Charles* was not there. *Des puez que el Rey D. Pedro se apoderò del Reyno de Sicilia, viviò cinco anos y dando orden en las cosas del nuevo Reyno, tornò à Espana y tuvò rieptos y desafios con el Rey Carlos, y disfracado passò por la Provincia de Guipuscoa, para la ciudad de Burdeos. que por ser en este tiempo de Ingleses era el lugar de la batalha a la qual por no acudir el Rey Carlos, tornò el Rey D. Pedro en Arragon y Cataluna: i. e.* after *Peter*, King of *Arragon*, had taken possession of the Kingdom of *Sicily*, and manag'd the Affairs of his new Government about five Years, he return'd to *Spain*, where he accepted a Challenge from King *Charles* to fight him at single Combat, and went disguis'd thro' the Province of *Guipuscoa* to the City of *Bourdeaux*; which being then in the hands of the *English*, was to be the Place of Battle: but King *Charles* not coming thither, King *Peter* return'd to *Arragon* and *Catalonia*.

I have been the longer upon this Subject, because it seems to me that the Acts in this Collection, relating to it, give us such an Idea of this Affair as is perfectly new.

Pope's Bull of Excommunication against the King of Arragon. P. 252.

THE other important Acts here, relating to the Quarrels between those two Families, of which King *Edward* was Mediator, are a *Bull* of of Pope *Martin* IV. which excommunicates the King of *Arragon*, and gives his Kingdom to *Charles* of *Valois*, Son to *Philip* III. King of *France*. A. 1283.

HERE we likewise see what pains our King took to procure the Liberty of *Charles* the Prince of *Salerno*, who being taken Prisoner in a Sea-Fight by *Roger Lauria*, Admiral of *Arragon*, would certainly have suffer'd the same Death as *Conradin*, by way of Reprisal, had it not been for Queen *Constantia*, *Peter* of *Arragon*'s Wife, who commanding at that time in *Sicily*, took him by force out of the hands of Revenge, and sent him into *Arragon* to the King her Husband. The Liberty of this Prince was the present Subject of King *Edward*'s Negotiations, and of a great number of Acts and Letters in this Volume. The chief are the Articles which *Edward* agreed to with the King of *Arragon*, at *Oleron* in *Bearn*. A *Bull* of Pope *Nicholas* IV. which disapproves those Articles. The Confirmation of those Articles made at *Campo Franco* in *Arragon*. The Bond, into which *Edward* himself enter'd for the Security of the King of *Arragon*, by virtue whereof the Prince of *Salerno* was set at liberty, on condition of returning to his Prison if he did not perform the Treaty. A *Certificate* of the said Prince, call'd afterwards *Charles* King of *Sicily*, of his coming to a certain Place to surrender himself to Imprisonment; and two Letters from the King of *Arragon* to our King *Edward*, complaining of the Prince of *Salerno*'s Insincerity, and Non-performance of the Treaty; which being altogether foreign to the History of *England*, I thought it sufficient to take notice of only the principal Acts relating to this Affair.

Happy Deliverance of the Prin. of Salerno.

P. 346. P. 358. P. 371. P. 375. P. 435. P. 450. P. 456.

Edw. I.

III. *The Affairs of* Scotland.

Settlement of the Succession of the Crown of Scotland.

For the better underſtanding of the Acts of this Volume, which relate to *Scotland*, it muſt be noted, That it was ſtipulated by the Marriage-Contract between *Margaret*, the Daughter of *Alexander* II. King of *Scotland*, and *Erick*, King of *Norway*, that if *Alexander* ſhould happen to die without Male Iſſue, his Daughter *Margaret* and her Deſcendants ſhould ſucceed to the Crown of *Scotland*. This Contract is to be ſeen amongſt the *Acta Omiſſa*, and is dated on St. *James*'s Day 1281. It happen'd that the two Sons of *Alexander* died in their Father's Life-time, and that their Siſter *Margaret*, Queen of *Norway*, died alſo, leaving a Princeſs of the ſame Name behind her, who was juſt born. Now as *Alexander* II. died in the ſame Year, *viz.* 1282, young *Margaret* of *Norway* ought to have been recogniz'd, as Heireſs of the Kingdom of *Scotland*, immediately after the Death of her Grandfather; but the Nobility of *Scotland* did not oblige themſelves to own her for their Queen till 1284, which was about two Years after, as appears by the *Act* itſelf. In the mean time, *Margaret* continu'd in *Norway*, undoubtedly becauſe of her Minority; and *Scotland* was govern'd by Regents till the Year 1289, that her Father *Erick* ſent Ambaſſadors to *Edward*, to treat with him about certain Affairs relating to his Daughter, who was the ſaid *Edward*'s Grand-Niece. *Edward* being return'd home from *France* that ſame Year, the Regents of *Scotland* ſent Ambaſſadors to *England* to treat in the King's Preſence with the Ambaſſadors of *Norway*. Theſe Ambaſſadors met at *Salisbury*, and drew up certain Articles, wherein it was ſtipulated, that *Mar-*

P. 1079.

P. 266.

P. 416.

P. 431.

garet ſhould be ſent to *Edward*, free from any Engagement of Marriage, and that this Prince ſhould deliver her in the ſame Condition to the *Scots*, provided the latter would engage on their part not to match her without the Conſent of the King of *Norway* her Father, and of the King of *England* her great Uncle. Theſe Conventions are recorded here both in *Latin* and *French*. Mean time, King *Edward* having a mind to marry his Son of his own Name to *Margaret*, ſollicited and obtain'd a *Diſpenſation* from *Rome* for the Marriage, which he afterwards propos'd to the Regents of *Scotland*, by whom it was approv'd. Then *Articles* were drawn up to be inſerted in the Contract; by which it appears, that the *Scots* took all the Precaution poſſible that the Liberty of *Scotland* might receive no manner of Prejudice by means of this Marriage, which was to unite the two Kingdoms under the Dominion of young *Edward*. They ſtipulated, that the Kingdom of *Scotland* ſhould always remain entirely ſeparate from and independent upon *England*, to which *Edward* made no oppoſition. But all theſe Projects vaniſh'd into Smoke by the Death of young *Margaret*, who died before ſhe left *Norway*; or rather, as ſome ſay, on a little Iſland where ſhe was oblig'd to put in for Refreſhment. Amongſt the *Acts omitted*, there's a Letter to *Edward* from the Biſhop of *St. Andrews*, wherein he lets him know the Report of the young Queen's Death, and expreſſes his Apprehenſion of the Troubles which the Loſs of her was like to occaſion in *Scotland*.

A. 1289.

P. 446. P. 448. P. 450. P. 471, &c. P. 482.

Scots *take care to ſecure their Independency on the Crown of* England.

UPON the Death of *Margaret*, the main thing in diſpute was to ſettle the Succeſſion; to which ſome great Men, who were deſcended from the Royal Family by the Mother's ſide, laid

Diſputes about the Succeſſion betwixt Baliol *and* Bruce.

Edw. I. laid claim. The two most considerable Competitors were *John Baliol* and *Robert Bruce*, both very powerful and highly esteem'd in *Scotland*, so that in a short time the whole Nation was divided into two Parties, which render'd the Determination of this Contest exceeding difficult; and had they been able to have ascertain'd which of the two Claimants had the best Right, it would have been very difficult to execute the Sentence without involving the Kingdom in a Civil War. The *Scots* Historians say, that their Country-men pray'd *Edward* to be the Arbitrator of the Difference, while the *English* affirm on the other hand, that *Edward* was the natural Judge or proper Umpire of it, by virtue of the direct Right of Lordship which he had over *Scotland*. 'Tis difficult to know whether *Edward* made use of this Pretension at first, or whether he declared it before he accepted of the *Scots* Proposition; and there is nothing in this Collection which seems to justify what *Buchanan* says upon this Subject: on the contrary, we find that *Edward* neglected nothing for establishing his Sovereignty over *Scotland*; but all the while this is no Proof that he discover'd his Pretensions before he was acknowledg'd as Arbitrator of the Difference. Be this as it was, he summon'd the States of *Scotland* to *Norham*, a Town upon the *Tweed*; which, whether he did as an Act of mere Authority, or at the Desire of the *Scots*, is a Point which I think cannot easily be settled; but this however is certain, that King *Edward* look'd upon this as a very favourable Opportunity to establish his Authority over *Scotland*, so as not to be disputed for the future.

King Edward *convenes the States of* Scotland *at a Town on the* English *Borders.*

The States of *Scotland* being conven'd at *Norham*, *Edward* went thither attended by a great

great many of the *English* Nobility, and a small number of Troops, as appears by the Summons which he sent to several Lords to repair to *Norbam* by such a Day, with the Arms and Horses with which they were oblig'd to furnish the King. The first Assembly was held on the 10th of *May Anno* 1291, from which Day to the very end of the Session Mr. *Rymer* has given a Journal of what pass'd, of which I shall here give an Abridgment. Mean time, I think my self oblig'd to advertise, that the said Journal ought to be read with Precaution, because it was writ by Mr. *John de Cadam*, Clerk to King *Edward*, and probably by order of this Prince; who being accus'd by the *Scots* of having nothing in view from first to last but his own Interests, and sacrificing those of *Scotland* to his Ambition, it may be presum'd he took special care that nothing should be inserted in the said Journal to his own Prejudice, or that might discover a Design of which he had been suspected, of making use of this Conjuncture to aggrandise himself, under the specious Pretext of rendring exact and impartial Justice. The Remarks which I shall add at the end of the Journal, which is a sort of verbal Process, will shew that this Caution is not unnecessary.

A. 1291.

P. 525.

P. 542 *to* 589.

Journal of their Proceedings.

I HAVE already said that *Edward*'s Project was to make use of this Opportunity, to extort a Recognition from the *Scots*, that *Scotland* was a Fief of the Crown of *England*; an Acknowledgment which the last King of *Scotland* had absolutely refus'd: and this was the Business which he intended to bring first upon the Stage, postponing the grand Point of all, which was the Affair of the Succession, till this was determin'd. For this end, in the first Assembly at *Norbam*, on *May* 10. 1291, he tells the *Scots*,

Edw. I. by his Spokesman *Roger Brabanzon*, Chief Justice of *England*, that the Consideration of the State of the Realm of *Scotland*, which was then without a King, had engag'd him to require them, by his Letters Patent, to repair to that Place; and that he was come thither to meet them in order, as direct Sovereign Lord of the Kingdom of *Scotland*, to do Justice to the Claimants of the Crown, and to establish a solid Tranquillity in the Realm: That it was not his Intention to retard Justice, nor to usurp the Right of any body, or to infringe the Liberties of the Kingdom of *Scotland*, but to render to every one their Due. And to the end this might be done with the more ease, he requir'd the Assent of the States of *Scotland ex abundanti*, and that they should own him as direct Sovereign of the Kingdom, offering upon that Condition to make use of their Counsels to do what Justice demanded. Upon this Proposal, the States desir'd time to consult their absent Members, and to consider of a proper Answer. *Edward* caused it to be signify'd to them, that tho' he had Reason to be persuaded that they were come ready prepar'd to answer that Article, because they could not be ignorant of his Intention, he would give them time till next Day. The same Proposal being accordingly made to the *Scots* on the Day following, they insisted again upon more time; whereupon *Edward*, by the Advice of his Council, granted three Weeks, reckoning from the 10th of *May*, to prepare what they had to alledge against his Pretension.

King Edward's *Pretension to the Sovereignty of* Scotland. *P.* 544.

On the second of *June* another Assembly was held, which, according to the Time given by King *Edward*, ought to have met the Day before: The Reason of this Remark will appear by by and by. In this Aſſembly the Biſhop of *Bath and Wells*, then Chancellor of *England*, was Spokeſman for the King, and told the States that in the preceding Aſſembly the King had granted them three Weeks to prepare what they had to object againſt his Pretenſion; but that ſince they had not given any abſolute Anſwer, nor ſet forth any thing to invalidate his Right, it was his Majeſty's Intention to act in the Affair in queſtion, by virtue of his acknowledg'd Right of Sovereignty, and to examine and determine the Difference, in quality of direct Sovereign of *Scotland*. Then the Chancellor, addreſſing himſelf to *Robert Bruce*, one of the Claimants of the Crown of *Scotland*, demanded of him whether he was willing to receive Judgment, as to his Pretenſions to that Crown, from the King of *England*, as Sovereign and direct Lord of the Kingdom; to which the latter anſwer'd in clear and expreſs Terms, That he recogniz'd him for ſuch, and that in that Quality he was ready to ſubmit to his Deciſion.

A. 1291.

P. 545.

THE ſame Queſtion was afterwards put to the other Claimants, *viz. Florence* Count of *Holland*, *John Haſtings*, *Patrick Dunbar* Earl of *March*, *William Roſs*, *Walter de Huntercumbe*, *William Veſey*, *Robert de Pynkeny*, and *Nicholas de Soules*, who all return'd the ſame Anſwer as *Robert Bruce*. After this, a Knight ſtood up, who made an Excuſe for the Abſence of *John Baliol*, and deſir'd he might have time granted him for his Appearance till the next Day; and *Baliol* appearing accordingly in the next Aſſembly, the ſame Queſtion was put to him, and he return'd the ſame Anſwer as the others.

Competitors for the Crown of Scotland. P. 546.

P. 548.

IN the fifth Aſſembly the Biſhop of *Bath* and *Wells*, after having recapitulated all that had paſs'd to that time, proteſted on the behalf of

P. 549.

King

Edw. I. King *Edward*, That altho' in the Dispute which was arisen between several Claimants, touching the Succession of the Kingdom of *Scotland*, that Prince acted in quality of Sovereign, in order to render Justice to whomsoever it was due, yet he did not mean thereby to exclude himself from the hereditary Right which he himself might have to that Kingdom, which Right he intended to assert and improve when he should think fit: and the King himself repeated this Protestation with his own Mouth in *French*. This made *John Commin*, Lord of *Badenoch*, desire leave to exhibit his Pretensions to the Crown; which was accordingly granted him, after he had own'd *Edward* for direct Lord and Sovereign of *Scotland*, as the others had done.

P. 555.

Their Recognition of Edward's *Sovereignty over* Scotland.

BEFORE they proceeded further, the Recognition which the Claimants had made of *Edward* for Sovereign of *Scotland* was committed to Writing, and form'd into an authentic Act, which was sign'd by all the Claimants; which Act we find at length in the Journal, in the *French* Tongue. Next Day the Claimants made and sign'd another Act, whereby they consented that King *Edward* should be put in possession of the Kingdom of *Scotland*, in order that he might deliver it up afterwards to the Candidate to whom it should be awarded.

P. 555. P. 529.

THE Sovereignty of *Scotland* being thus establish'd, they came at last to the grand Affair; I mean to the Examination of the Claims of the several Competitors to the Crown; and that the same might be conducted impartially, it was agreed that *John Baliol* and *John Commin* on the one part, for themselves and all the Claimants who should approve of their Nomination, should chuse forty Commissioners of Inquiry; and that *Robert Bruce* on the other part, for

P. 555.

for himself, and the rest of the Claimants, should in like manner chuse forty others; and that King *Edward* should add twenty four on his part, to be as Mediators between the eighty Commissioners, who were all to meet in a Body, and make a Report of their Opinions to the King, that he might judge of the Merits of each respectively. *A.* 1291.

In the Assembly of the 5th of *June* they did nothing but read and register the Names of the Persons chose Commissioners, whom King *Edward* appointed next Day to agree among themselves about the Time and Place of meeting, to hear the several Pretensions; and they pitched upon the Town of *Berwic*, about four Miles from *Norham*, on the other side of the *Tweed*, and in the Kingdom of *Scotland*; for it must be observed, that the *Scots* had obtained of King *Edward* that the Affair might be tried in their own Kingdom, tho' the Letters Patent which he granted them for this end are not dated till the 12th of *June*, which was six days after the Nomination of *Berwic*; but it is not unlikely that he gave them a verbal Promise. The Commissioners not being able to agree about the time, King *Edward* himself fixed it on the second of *August* ensuing. *P.* 556. *P.* 554. *P.* 554.

On the 11th of *June* the Regents resigned their Commissions to the King, who took, but delivered them back again to them to govern in his Name; after which, he made the Bishop of *Caithness* Chancellor of *Scotland*, with whom he joined in Commission one *Walter* of *Hamondesham*, an *Englishman*.

On the 12th the Chancellor took an Oath of Allegiance to *Edward*. *P.* 557.

Scots swear Allegiance to Edward.

On the 13th the Regents and chief Nobility of *Scotland* did the same.

 On *P.* 558.

Edw. I. On the 14th and following Days, all the other Lords, Magiſtrates, Governors of Places, &c. took the ſame Oath.

Pag. 567 to 573. p. 574.

King *Edward* removing afterwards to *Berwic*, together with all the Commiſſioners, made a Proteſtation there; in which he declared, that tho' he had granted that the Affair of the Succeſſion ſhould be tryed in *Scotland*, yet he did not thereby intend to prejudice the Right which he had in the like or any other caſe to exerciſe Juſtice in *England* hereafter, touching Affairs which might relate to *Scotland*.

On the third of *Auguſt*, the Commiſſioners being met at *Berwic*, every one of the Claimants preſented his Petition, ſetting forth his Pretenſions to the Crown of *Scotland*; which, as they were all founded on their Deſcent from ſome Perſon of the Royal Family of *Scotland*, would appear plainer to the Reader in the genealogical Table than in a long Diſſertation. But the Nature of this Work will not admit of Trees of Genealogy; ſo that we can but juſt touch upon the Deſcents by which they claimed.

Claimants Pleas of Deſcent. p. 575 to 580.

Florence, Count of *Holland*, deſcended from *Ada* Siſter to King *William*.

Patrick *Dunbar*, Earl of *March*, deſcended from *Ilda* Daughter of King *William*.

William *de Veſci*, deſcended from *Margaret* Daughter to King *William*.

William *de Roſs*, deſcended from *Iſabel* Daughter to King *William*.

Robert *de Pynkeny*, deſcended from *Margery* Siſter to King *William*, by a Daughter of King *William* named *Alice*.

Nicholas *de Soules*, deſcended from *Margaret* Daughter of *Alexander* II.

Patrick *Galythly*, deſcended from *Henry* the Son of *William*.

Roger

ROGER *de Mandeville*, descended from *Africa*, second Daughter of King *William*.

JOHN *Comyn*, Lord of *Badenoch*, descended from *Donald* formerly King of *Scotland*.

JOHN *Hastings*, descended from the third Daughter of *David* Earl of *Huntingdon*, Brother to King *William*.

JOHN *Baliol*, descended from *Margaret*, eldest Daughter to *David* Earl of *Huntingdon*.

ROBERT *Bruce*, descended from *Isabel*, the second Daughter of *David* Earl of *Huntingdon*.

IN order to form a right Notion of all these Pretensions, 'tis necessary to observe that *Florence* Count of *Holland*, *Robert de Pynkeny*, and *John Comyn* being descended, the two first from the two Sisters of *David* Earl of *Huntingdon*, and the last from *Donald*, younger Brother to *Malcolm* III. 'tis manifest they could not in Law claim Preference before the Descendants from *David*. As to *Nicholas de Soules*, *William Ross*, *Patric Dunbar*, *William Vesci*, *Patric Galythly*, and *Roger de Mandeville*, if their Genealogy was well set forth, 'tis certain that in the Succession of a Fief, which was not Male, they ought to have been preferred before the Descendants of the Earl of *Huntingdon*, because they were descended from *William* King of *Scotland* his elder Brother; but 'tis probable either that they had not well set forth their Genealogy, or that they from whom they derived their Descent were Bastards, and by consequence incapable of transmitting any right to their Descendants. What confirms this Conjecture, is, that in the Petition presented by *Baliol*, wherein he gave a particular Account how the Crown should have devolved from one to another, till it came to him, after having mentioned the death of *Margaret* of *Norway*, he said, That after the death of that

Edw. I. Princess the Crown should have devolved to *Margaret* her great Aunt, Daughter of *Alexander* II. and from the said *Margaret* to one *Magoth* her Daughter; but that this *Magoth* dying without Issue, the Succession came to *Margery* her Sister, who died also, as he says, without Issue: and yet *Nicholas de Soules* called himself the Son of this *Margery*, and consequently by *Baliol*'s own Acknowledgment this same *Nicholas* ought to have been preferred before him, if he had been really *Margery*'s Son, as he had asserted he was. It is not to be supposed that *Baliol* would have been contented with combating the Right of *Nicholas de Soules* with a bare Negative, if it had not been manifest and notorious to the whole World, that this *Margery*, the pretended Mother of *Nicholas de Soules*, died without Issue.

In like manner *Baliol* in his Petition, after having said that *Isabella*, the third Daughter of *Alexander* II. died without Children, asserts that the Crown ought to have returned to the Descendants of *David* Earl of *Huntingdon*; and at once leaps over all the heads of *Henry de Galythly*, *Isabella*, *Ilda*, *Margaret* and *Aufrica*, Daughters of King *William*, from whom *Patrick de Galythly*, *William Ross*, *Patrick Dumbar*, *William Vesci*, and *Roger de Mandeville* claimed their Descent. What gives room to conjecture that the above *Henry* and his three Sisters, admitting they were *William*'s Children, were no more than Bastards, is, that afterwards the Competitors who derived their Origin from them, very readily gave up their Pretensions, even before they came to be examined; a certain Proof that *Baliol* was in the right to pass them over in silence, as what could be no great Prejudice to him.

WHAT

WHAT remained therefore to be done, was only to regulate the Succession between the Descendants of *David* Earl of *Huntingdon*, Brother to King *William*, whose lawful Branch was just extinct by the death of young *Margaret* of *Norway*. This *David* had several Children, four of whom died before him; and he left three Daughters, *Margaret*, who married *Alan* of *Galway*, *Isabella*, Wife of *Robert Bruce*, and *Ada*, who was married to *Henry Hastings* an *Englishman*. From *Margaret*, the eldest of the three, came *Deverguldе* and *Marione*; the latter of whom was married to *John Comyn*, and in all probability died without Children: but be this as it was, neither she nor her Children, if she had any, appeared in this Process. *Deverguldе* her eldest Sister, who was married to *John Baliol*, had by him this *John Baliol*, who demanded the Crown by virtue of his Mother's Right, who was still living. *Isabella* the second Daughter of *David*, Wife of *Robert Bruce*, had a Son named *Robert* after his Father, which Son was one of the Claimants. Lastly, *Ada* had by *Henry Hastings* her Husband, *John Hastings*, who had also formed Pretensions; but foreseeing that the Descendants of his two Aunts, who were his Mother's elder Sisters, would carry it from him, he contented himself with the Plea that *Scotland* was a divisible Fief, and that by consequence it ought to be shared between the three Daughters of *David* Earl of *Huntingdon* his Grandfather. The main Point in dispute lay therefore between *John Baliol* and *Robert Bruce*: The first alledged for himself, that he was Grandson to *Margaret* the eldest Daughter of *David*; and the latter pleaded that he was Grandson to *David* himself, and that by consequence he was nearer by one Degree: and it being objected to him, that *Devergulde*, who was still alive,

Edw. I. alive, was in as near a degree of Consanguinity as he, and that she had the advantage of being the Daughter of *David*'s eldest Daughter; he answered, that where the Degrees of Proximity were equal, the Men ought to be preferred to the Women. That was the Sum and Substance of the Reasons on both Sides, and the subject Matter of the ensuing Inquiry. Let us go back now to what passed in the following Assemblies.

ALL the Petitions of the Claimants being read, *Edward* fixed the second Day of *June* in the following Year 1292, for hearing the Report of the Commissioners of Inquiry, who had by this means nine or ten Months to inform themselves.

P. 580. WHEN the Day appointed was come, the Ambassadors of *Erick* King of *Norway* appeared, and demanded, in the name of their Master, that he might be admitted into the number of Claimants, as the Father and lawful Heir of *Margaret* his Daughter; which was granted him after his Ambassadors had first of all recognized the Sovereignty of the Kings of *England* over *Scotland*.

THIS done, the Commissioners proceeded to the Examination of the Petitions of each of the Parties; but *Edward* thinking that this way of proceeding would spin out the Affair to a great length, he was for examining the Rights of *Baliol* and *Bruce* before all others, without prejudice to those of the other Claimants. This being settled accordingly, he ordered the Commissioners to examine by what Laws they ought to proceed to Judgment; upon which the Opinions were so various, that in order to give them time to agree, or to inform themselves better, he prorogued the Assembly to the 14th of *October*, with a design, as he said, for his

A. 1292.

own part, to consult the Lawyers of foreign Countries.

IN the next Assembly, which was held on the 14th of *October*, *Edward* put two Questions to the Commissioners of Inquiry, and wish'd to have their Opinion. 1. By what Laws and Customs they ought to proceed to Judgment; and supposing there could be no Law or Precedent found in the two Kingdoms, how then? 2. Whether the Kingdom of *Scotland* ought to be taken in the same View as all other Fiefs, and to be awarded in the same manner as Earldoms and Baronies? To the first of these two Questions it was unanimously answer'd by the Commissioners, That the King ought to give Judgment in this Affair conformable to the Customs establish'd in the two Kingdoms, if any certain Laws or Precedents could be found for that purpose; but that if there were none to be had, then the King might, by the Advice of the great Men of his Kingdom, establish a new Law. As to the second, Answer was made, that the Succession of the Kingdom might be awarded in the same manner as that of Baronies and Earldoms. These two Articles being done with, King *Edward* addressed himself to *Baliol* and *Bruce*, demanding to know if they had any thing more to alledge in maintenance of their Right; And each of the two having spoke for himself, and insisted on the Pleas already mentioned, which they always laid down as the Basis of their Right, King *Edward* declared, that on the sixth of *November* he would pronounce Sentence; and when that Day came, *Robert Bruce*'s Pretensions to the Crown of *Scotland* were entirely set aside; whereupon he protested, that he had a Design to prosecute his Right under another Form.

P. 581, &c.

Edw. I.

THEN *John Hastings* stood up, and after asserting that the Kingdom of *Scotland* was a divisible Fief, he demanded that it might be divided between the Descendants of the three Daughters of *David* Earl of *Huntingdon*, whose third Daughter was his Mother. *Robert Bruce* stood up at the same time, and made the same Demand; whereupon King *Edward* ordered the Commissioners to examine whether *Scotland* was a divisible Fief, and gave them time to consider of it till the 17th of that Month.

WHEN that Day came, King *Edward* demanding to know the opinion of the Commissioners of Inquiry, they answered, that the Kingdom of *Scotland* was not divisible; whereupon the King pronounced, that neither *John Hastings* nor *Robert Bruce* had any Claim to the Succession of the Crown. This Sentence was as yet of no advantage to *Baliol*'s Cause, because there were so many other Claimants besides; but these at length spared King *Edward* and the Commissioners the trouble of further Inquiry, by intirely dropping their Pretensions. There being nothing now remaining which could stand in the way of *Baliol*'s Right, King *Edward* pronounc'd Sentence in his favour, and declared him King of *Scotland*; after which he exhorted him to govern his People with Equity, and in such a manner as to give them no reason to complain of him, and to bring their Complaints to the direct Lord and Sovereign of *Scotland*. He then appointed a day for him to take the Oath of Allegiance, and another for him to perform Homage for the Kingdom of *Scotland*: which things were done accordingly; the first at *Norham* upon the 20th of *November*, and the second at *Newcastle* upon St. *Stephen*'s day the 26th of *December*. Here

Crown of Scotland *awarded by* K. Edward *to* Baliol. P. 589.

His Oath and Homage to K. Edward. P. 591, 593.

is

it may not be improper to remark, that King Edward's Chamberlain, demanding perhaps too much of *Baliol* for his Fee, when that Prince performed his Homage, or not knowing what to demand, *Edward* fixed his Fee himself at twenty Pound; which was double to what was paid by an Earl, as appears by the King's Order establishing the said Fee. A. 1292. P. 600.

Mr. Rapin's Remarks on the whole Process, as well as on the Merits of the Cause.

Now, to look no further than this Journal, one would think nothing could be more exact nor more impartial than *Edward*'s Proceeding in the Determination of this famous Process. In the first place he demands of the *Scots*, that they own *ex abundanti* that *Scotland* is a Fief depending on *England*; and the *Scots* Convention making no opposition to his Pretensions, he sets himself up for Judge of this Difference, by virtue of his recognized Sovereignty; and that he may be able to judge of the matter impartially, he causes eighty Commissioners of Inquiry to be chose by the two principal Claimants, and does not pronounce Sentence till he has had the opinion of the said Commissioners. This seems so fair, so exact, that what in the World could have a better Face? Yet for all this, the *Scots* do not fail to complain of him, and affirm that he had regard only to his own Interests. Therefore to have a clear and distinct Idea of this Affair, it is worth while to look into the Complaints of the *Scots*, and to see on what they are founded, tho' this is what Mr. *Rymer*'s Collection takes no notice of.

The *Scots* say therefore, that King *Edward*'s only View was not to make *Scotland* easy, but to improve this Conjuncture, that he might be recognized Sovereign Lord of the Kingdom, and that the Crown might be placed on the head of that Person who was least able to dispute this

Edw. I. this Right with him; that is to say *Baliol*, who had a Genius far inferior to his Rival, and fewer Friends and less Credit in *Scotland*. They charge King *Edward* with obstructing the Freedom of voting; and that while he professed the strictest Impartiality in publick, he acted underhand by Threats and Promises to incline the Commissioners to vote as he would have them. They say, that at first he offer'd the Crown to *Robert Bruce*, if he had been disposed to ingage to do him Homage for it; and that the latter refusing it upon those Terms, the King proposed it to *Baliol* on the same Terms, which he accepted, and was therefore promised the Crown. They observe in excuse for *Robert Bruce*'s recognizing King *Edward* as Sovereign of *Scotland* afterwards, That he did it, because he was very sensible of what Prejudice his Refusal was to him. They add as a Proof, That the Meeting of the States at *Norham* was not a free Assembly; that in the first place King *Edward* brought Troops thither; and secondly, that they made no Answer to the Proposal which King *Edward* made to them, of owning him for Sovereign Lord; but if they had thought this Right was indisputable, why did they desire time to consider of it? And if they thought the contrary, how came it to pass that the Assembly of States could not find so much as one single Reason to dispute the Right pretended to? which it is certain the late Kings of *Scotland* always opposed. The *Scots* add moreover, that for all this it does not appear that the States recognized this Sovereignty, and that it is plain what Recognition was made, only came from the Regents corrupted by King *Edward*, or from the Claimants, whose Interest it was to court his Favour, and who were, for most part, his Vassals or

his

his Subjects; and who, when all is done, had no Power to bind the whole Nation of *Scotland* by their particular Submission. They say also that it was King *Edward*, who by his Intrigues summoned all the Competitors to meet together, exclusive of *Baliol*, *Bruce*, and *Hastings*, on purpose to embarrass the Affair, to shew the two principal Candidates that they had need of his Favour, and that he might have the Majority of Voices among the Candidates to favour his own Ends; which say they manifestly appears from this Circumstance, *viz.* That as soon as ever *Robert* lost his Cause, all the other Competitors (except *Baliol* and *Hastings*) dropped their Pretensions; an evident Proof that what they had done, was but meer Grimace in compliance with the King, by whom they were acted. For how can it be imagined, say they, that the Sentence passed against *Bruce* should be prejudicial to the other Claimants, and oblige them to quit their Pretensions? It appears still more evident, that the Intervention of the King of *Norway* was sollicited, because it is very unlikely that his Ambassadors would have dared to betray the Interest of their Master, if they had not had secret Orders to act according to the Directions of King *Edward*, who had no longer need of him after *Robert Bruce* was set aside. It seems likewise as if there had been something mysterious in the Conduct of *Baliol*, who absented himself from the first Assembly at *Norham*, on purpose to let the others make the first step in acknowledging the King of *England* for Sovereign, as if he was the farthest of any from such an Intention; which, say they, could only proceed from the Assurance he had of obtaining the Crown: but, notwithstanding this Precaution, he could not hinder public Fame from ac- A. 1292.

cusing

Edw. I. cusing him, as the first of the Candidates for the Crown who had engaged himself to King *Edward*. This was also what they still continued to upbraid him with; and though he afterwards lost the said Crown for offering to retract, yet he could never regain the Esteem of his Subjects, who afterwards tack'd about to his Rival's Son.

Here I cannot avoid making a Remark, which, by the way, I only give as my own private Conjecture; namely, That in the second Assembly, which was held at *Norham* on the 2d of *June* 1291, *Edward* granted a delay of three Weeks, reckoning from the 10th of *May*, in order to give time to the *Scots* to prepare what they had to answer to his Pretensions to the Sovereignty of *Scotland*. According to this delay, the Assembly ought to have been held on the first of *June*, and yet we don't find that any was held till the second Day; on which, tho' it does no where appear that the *Scots* had been ask'd what they had to offer by way of Answer, the Chancellor opened the Conference by saying, that since they had not given in any Answer, the King of *England* was resolved to make use of his Prerogative. This gives me cause to conjecture, that probably another Assembly was held the day before, in which the States of *Scotland* produced their Reasons, but did not think fit to insert them in the great Roll of *Scotland*, from whence this Journal was taken; for how could the Chancellor be supposed to open the Assembly, by saying that the *Scots* had not return'd any Answer, before he had summon'd them for that purpose? And if they were summoned, and did return any Answer, it was perhaps either that the Homage demanded was not due, or that they owned *Scotland* to be a Fief of

Eng-

England. In the former case, there was an absolute necessity of inserting at least a part of their Answer in a Journal so exact as this, where the very words are reported and often repeated *verbatim*; and in the latter case, nothing surely could have been of more advantage to the King's Interests than such a Confession. And if, in short, no Answer was returned, though demanded, the Summons given them for that purpose ought at least to have been inserted, with the Addition that they remained mute; for it must be observed, that this is a sort of verbal Process, in which the very Words made use of are set down; and not a Narrative, the Expressions of which depend on the caprice of him that gives it. *A.* 1292.

THIS Conjecture, and what the *Scots* oppose, seems to have a Foundation the more solid, because the Reasons which King *Edward* made use of, to shew that *Scotland* had been always heretofore a Fief dependent on the Crown of *England*, seem not to be conclusive. It is this Act which I am now to examine, having not done it hitherto, tho' it is inserted in the middle of the Journal, because I was not willing to interrupt the Process.

Proofs fetched from Antiquity of the King of England's *Sovereignty over* Scotland. *P.* 559 *to* 573.

IN the Speech which the Chancellor made at the second Assembly at *Norham*, he says, that the King his Master would prove his Right to the Sovereignty of *Scotland* by indisputable Documents; and it was with this design therefore that King *Edward* caused the Proofs of it to be drawn up in Writing. The Act being by much too long to transcribe here, I shall only take notice in a word, that all the Proofs are founded upon Passages extracted from certain Historians, such as *Marianus Scotus*, an *Irishman*, *William* of *Malmsbury*, *Roger* of *Hoveden*, *Henry* of *Hun-*

Vol. I. *tingdon*,

Edw. I. *tingdon*, *Raoul de Dicet*, and other *Englishmen*; that the main Point for which those Historians are quoted, is to shew, that the Kings of *England* have often vanquished the *Scots*; that they have sometimes placed Kings upon the Throne of *Scotland* by force of Arms, and that the Kings of *Scotland* have often rendered them Homage. The *English* Historians, who boast of the Sovereignty of their Kings over *Scotland*, lay mighty stress upon this Memorial or Manifesto of King *Edward*; out of which, by the way, they give us but few Particulars. Tho' this is a dispute, which not many are concerned in at present, yet I persuade myself that there are curious Persons who would be glad to see some Remarks upon the Proofs here produced by King *Edward*.

Mr. Rapin's Remarks on them.

1. The Authors from whom the Passages are extracted are all *English*. To go about to prove by *English* Writers, that *Scotland* is a Fief of *England* seems very extraordinary; and is no less than making the Parties Judges in an Affair which was then the Subject of the Process between the two Nations. It would be a very good Jest if such Passages should be brought only to confirm more authentic Proofs.

2. The Discovery that the Kings of *Scotland* have paid Homage to the Kings of *England*, is far from amounting to a Proof, that *Scotland* was long since a Fief depending on the Crown of *England*, because it ought to be proved beyond Dispute, that they paid that Homage for *Scotland*. For, by example, if the King of *France* should go about to prove that the Kings of *England* ever paid Homage to his Predecessors, he could easily do this by a Cloud of Historians; but if he should offer to conclude from thence, that *England* is a Fief of the

the Crown of *France*, such Consequence would *A.* 1292.
be perfectly ridiculous, because the Homage which the Kings of *England* have formerly paid to the Kings of *France* was not for *England* it self, but for the Provinces which they possessed in the Kingdom of *France*. The same thing may be pleaded with respect to the Kings of *Scotland*, who possessed *Huntingdonshire*, and some Lands upon the Frontiers of both Kingdoms, for which they did Homage to the King of *England*.

3. But if they had not enjoyed a foot of Land in *England*, it would not follow from their having done Homage to the Kings of *England*, that *Scotland* was a Fief of that Crown; because 'tis certain, that Homage was often performed for meer annual Pensions, without expressing the Cause of the Homage; of which there are more Instances than one, in the first Volume of the *Pag.* 1.
Fœdera, with respect to the Earls of *Flanders*, who did Homage to the Kings of *England* for a Pension of 500 Marks. So that there is no Conclusion to be drawn in support of this Claim of Sovereignty, from the Homages performed by the Kings of *Scotland*, unless it had been expressed that they were performed for the Kingdom.

4. Every body knows how punctually those to whom Homage was due, had it paid to them upon every Change, either of Sovereign or Vassal, in presence of many Witnesses; that authentick Acts were drawn up for that end, and that he who had performed it, gave an Instrument of it under his Hand and Seal. How comes it to pass then, that King *Edward* did not produce any of these Homages in due form, but was fain to prove his Right from historical Passages? Was it not plainly confessing that he had no better Proofs?

5. It

Edw. I. 5. It may be objected perhaps, That in King *Edward*'s Memorial, there is a long Account of the Homage which *William* King of *Scotland* paid for *Scotland* it self to King *Henry* II. and his Son, and that moreover this Homage is not contested. But it may be answered, That as this Homage had been extorted from the said King *William*, as one of the Conditions of his Liberty, after he had been taken Prisoner by *Henry* II. so *Richard* the Son and Successor of the said *Henry*, voluntarily departed from it, as is affirmed by the *English* Historians themselves, and as may be proved by an Act in the first Volume of the *Fœdera*, among those of King *Richard*: so that this Article makes no Proof at all. p. 64.

6. It is true indeed that the Kings of *England* have often demanded Homage of the Kings of *Scotland*, for *Scotland* it self: but this is a proof of their Pretensions only, not of their Right; for if such a bare Demand be sufficient to prove their Right, it is as certain that the bare refusal of the Kings of *Scotland* may prove the contrary: and it is notorious beyond all dispute, that the Kings of *Scotland* have sometimes refused to do Homage for their Kingdom. *Alexander* II. having performed Homage to King *Henry* III. his Father-in-Law, for the County of *Huntingdon*, *Henry* demanded the same Homage of him for *Scotland*: but this Prince, tho' very young at that time, excused himself, by saying, that he could not do it without the Consent of the States of his Kingdom: and it is particularly remarkable, that *Edward* in his Memorial quotes that Instance of the Homage paid by *Alexander* to *Henry*, to prove his Right, artfully confounding the Homage which *Alexander* paid for the County of *Huntingdon*, with that which he refused for the Kingdom of *Scotland*. For when *Alexander*

ander

ander came to perform Homage to King *Edward* himself, he protested that it was not for the Kingdom of *Scotland*; and his Homage was received with the said Protestation, and with the following Restriction, as plainly appears by an Act in this Volume: *Et idem Rex Angliæ homagium ejusdem Regis Scotiæ recepit, salvo jure & clamio ejusdem Regis Angliæ, & hæredum suorum, de homagio prædicti Regis Scotiæ, & hæredum suorum, de Regno Scotiæ, cum inde loqui voluerint.* A. 1292. P. 126.

7. When one reads the Passages quoted by King *Edward* from Historians, one cannot help perceiving how weak are the Consequences which he would infer from some general Expressions.

8. In the last place, as to the Passages produced to shew that the Kings of *England* have sometimes placed the Kings of *Scotland* upon the Throne, this does not infer that *Scotland* was dependent on *England*. For example, if *Lewis* XIV. had been so lucky as to restore King *James* II. to the Throne, it would not follow from thence that *England* must have been obliged to recognize the King of *France* and his Successors for its Sovereigns.

I Might add several other Remarks upon the Proofs brought by King *Edward*: but this is sufficient, I believe, to shew how astonishing it is that the States of *Scotland* should make no Answer to K. *Edward*'s Pretensions; which makes me think either that the Journal is not exact, according to my former Conjecture, or that if they did not answer, they were intimidated by King *Edward*, from whom they had every thing to fear, as matters then stood.

I Have been a little the longer upon this Journal, because the Subject of it was the Foundation of all the Wars which afflicted the two

Edw. I. Nations for 300 Years; and as to the Remarks which I have added, my View was to hinder every body from being prejudiced in favour of a Writing which has such an authentic appearance, as if it ought to be the sole foundation of Truth, tho' it was drawn up by Order of one of the Parties concerned *.

The other Acts of greatest importance in this Volume, relating to *Scotland*, are the Demand which *Baliol* made that the Causes of *Scotsmen* should be tried in *Scotland*, together with King *Edward*'s Denial, and *Baliol*'s Declaration whereby he gives up the Concession which King *Edward* granted on the same account to the Regents and Claimants of the Crown, which we find in *Page* 532.

P. 596, 597.

Macduff's *Imprisonment.* P. 604.

Not long after we come to an Act, whereby *Macduff* Earl of *Fife* was condemned to Imprisonment by the Parliament of *Scotland*. This is a remarkable Piece, because that Complaint or Appeal which *Macduff* made to King *Edward*, was one of the principal Reasons of the Quar-

* To justify what has been said by Mr. *Rapin*, a great deal more might be added from several eminent Historians, both *English* and *Scots*: but there being not room here for Quotations, the Curious, who have a mind to be more fully satisfied of the Independency and Sovereignty of the Kingdom of *Scotland*, will not take it amiss to be referred to those Pieces wherein this Subject is treated more at large; particularly Sir *George Mackenzie*'s Observations upon the Laws and Customs of Nations as to Precedency, *Cap.* 3. Sir *Thomas Craig*'s Dispute concerning Homage, entituled, *Scotland*'s *Sovereignty* asserted; Mr. *Tyrrel*'s General History of *England*; Sir *James Dalrymple*'s Collections concerning the *Scottish* History; Mr. *Anderson*'s Essay, shewing that the Kingdom of *Scotland* is Imperial and Independent; and to close all, the late *Treaty* of *Union* concluded betwixt *England* and *Scotland* as two Independent Nations.

rel

rel that happened betwixt him and the King of *Scotland.* The Fact was as follows. *A.* 1293.

WHILE King *Edward* was in possession of *Scotland*, by the Concession of the Regents, and of the Competitors for the Crown, he ordered that *Macduff* Earl of *Fife* should be put in possession of certain Lands, to which he laid claim. The Affair of the Succession being settled, and *Baliol* acknowledged for King, *Macduff* was summoned to Parliament, for having put himself in possession of those Lands which ought to be left to the King of *Scotland*, and he was therefore condemned to suffer Imprisonment. When he was set at Liberty, he went and complained to King *Edward* of the Injustice that had been done him, and upon this Complaint *Edward* summoned the King of *Scotland* to appear before him; which the latter obeying, he was treated like a private Man, says *Buchanan*, and obliged to go and stand at the Bar to plead his Cause; which exasperated him to the last degree. *Pag.* 606. *King Edward's Summons to* Baliol.

BUT this was not the only occasion which *Edward* took to assert his Sovereignty over *Scotland.* Here are no less than eight several Summons sent to *Baliol* upon very trifling occasions, to appear in Person before King *Edward.* *P.* 605 *to* 641. It was this Treatment that made *Baliol* think of ways and means to shake off such a cruel Yoke. The War which then broke out between *France* and *England*, seemed to give him a favourable opportunity. He made an offensive and defensive Alliance with *France*, and married his Son *Edward* to a Daughter of *Charles de Valois*, Brother to *Philip* the Fair; and at last by an Act for the purpose, renounced the Homage he had paid to King *Edward.* *P.* 695. *P.* 697. *P.* 707. *Baliol* imagined that *France* would cut out so much Work for King *Edward*, that he would not have time to think of him:

 but

Edw. I.

but the contrary happen'd; for *Edward* did not so much mind his Affairs in *France*, because he had set his heart upon the punishment of the King of *Scotland*, who was vanquished, and obliged to go to King *Edward* and resign his Kingdom to him: after which Act of Resignation, he was committed to the *Tower*.

Baliol *forced to resign his Crown to* K. Edward. P. 718.

The *Scots* revolted several times, but were always defeated, and at last obliged to own King *Edward* for their Sovereign.

Scots *recognize King* Edward*'s Sovereignty*. P. 950.

Robert Bruce, Son to him who was a Candidate for the Crown, fled from *England* into *Scotland*, where he kill'd *John Comyn* who had betray'd him, and caused himself to be crowned King of *Scotland*. He was defeated, and endeavoured to hide himself, while those of his Party that were taken Prisoners, were ill-treated by King *Edward*. We have no other Acts here that make mention of King *Edward*'s last Expedition to *Scotland*, in which he died.

J. Comyn *murdered by* Robert Bruce. P. 988. Bruce's *Overthrow*. P. 1012.

IV. *The Affairs of* France *in this Reign*.

King Edward's *Treaty with* France. P. 134.

The first Piece we shall mention is a Treaty dated at *Amiens*, *May* 23, 1279. between King *Philip* III. called the Hardy, and King *Edward*, which confirmed that made between *Henry* III. and St. *Louis*, whereby the King of *France* was obliged to quit the District of *Agenois* to the King of *England*.

His Letter to the Bishop of Agen. P. 139.

Here is a Letter from King *Edward*, wherein he desires the Bishop of *Agen*, to whom, according to Custom, he ought to have taken the Oath in Person, that he would please to receive it by his Seneschal of *Guienne*. It is dated at *Abbeville*, *June* 4, 1279.

P. 167.

The next is a Letter from King *Edward* to *Philip*, wherein he intreats him to make no Alterateration in the Customs of the Province of *Gascoigne* without his Consent. 'Tis dated *March* 4, 1281. *Gascoigne* and *Guyenne* were at that time synonymous. A. 1281.

Letter from the Nobility of Gascoigne *to King* Edward. P. 168.

HERE we have a Letter to King *Edward* from the Nobility of *Gascoigne*, desiring him not to subject their Lands to *Arnold de Seuil*. This Letter begins, *Domino præ cunctis mortalibus diligendo, Edwardo*, i. e. To our Sovereign Lord *Edward* beloved above all Mortals: Yet they don't spare to tell him their minds, *Dominationem vestram volumus pro constanti, quod nullatenus nobis placet, ut altam justitiam terrarum nostrarum in Arnaldum Raimundi de Solio, vel aliquem alium, maxime ignobilem, conferatis*; i. e. We would have your Majesty to take it always for granted, that we shall by no means be pleased with your subjecting of our Lands to *Arnold Raymund de Seuil*, or any other Person of mean Rank. And a little lower they say, *Nunquam enim præmissa proponimus sustinere, nisi id faceremus, quod absit, coacti a vobis*; i. e. For we never propose to bear the Premises, unless, which God forbid, we should be compelled by you. It is dated the first of *May*, 1281.

King Edward's *Homage to* Philip *of* France. P. 320.

HERE we have the Restrictions contained in the Homage which King *Edward* paid to King *Philip*, *A.* 1286. the Bishop of *Bath* and *Wells* being his Spokesman: where it must be observed, that under the Reigns of *John* and *Henry* III. King *Edward*'s Grandfather and Father, *France* had taken several Provinces from the Kings of *England*; and that after frequent Wars upon this very score, there were some Treaties of Peace, which King *Edward* complained were not observed. Therefore, after having protested against those Infractions, he only made his Homage in general Terms, for fear of ex-

Edw. I. excluding himself from the Claim which he intended to make to those Provinces, if he only performed Homage for the Lands then in his possession, and mentioned them particularly by name. The Homage therefore was couched in these Terms: *I become your Man for the Lands which I hold of you on this side of the Sea, according to the Form of the Treaty which was made betwixt our Ancestors.* And after this manner was the Homage received.

Treaty between King Edward *and* Philip *the* Fair.

IN this Page we have a Treaty of Peace between *Philip* the Fair, and our King *Edward*, dated in *August*, *A. D.* 1286.

P. 336. *The K. of* France *summons our K. to* Paris.

A PARTICULAR Quarrel between two Seamen, one an *Englishman*, the other a *Norman*, having occasioned a Rupture between *France* and *England*; *Philip* summoned *Edward* to appear in Person at *Paris*, before the Court of Peers.

P. 617.

FOR the better understanding of the Acts that follow, and the Grounds of the Controversy between *Philip* the Fair and *Edward*, the Reader must be acquainted that *Edward* being engaged in the *Scots* War, sent *Edmund* his Brother to *Paris* to appear for him, with Orders to do whatever he could to prevent a War with *France*. The *French* Historians say, that *Philip* being angry with *Edward* for not appearing in his own Person, confiscated *Guyenne*, and sent into this Dutchy his Constable *Raoul de Nelle*, who made himself Master of it. To hear how easily this General took *Guyenne*, is at first surprizing, till one turns to the Page in the Margin, where we find the whole Affair unriddled, together with the Stratagem which *Philip* made use of. He gave *Edmund* to understand that all he had a view to upon this occasion, was his Honour and his Right of Sovereignty; and that provided *Edward* would but make some advances to

Ground of their Quarrel.

P. 620.

satisfy

satisfy him, he would be content with Externals. For this end he demanded that Edward should deliver up to him certain Towns in *Guyenne*, together with some Persons in that Province, of whom he had reason to complain. *Edward*, who was for avoiding a War, did not only give the King of *France* this external Satisfaction, but delivered up all *Guyenne* to him, believing that *Philip*, content with such Submission, would restore it back to him out of hand, according to his Promise. But he was tricked by the King of *France*, who sent the Constable into *Guyenne* to take possession of the Province, which was done without opposition, and *Philip* afterwards refused to part with it. *A. 1286.*

HERE we find King *Edward*'s Order to his Officers of *Guyenne* to pay his Brother *Edmund* the same Obedience as to himself; together with *Edmund*'s Order, in consequence hereof, to deliver up *Guyenne* to the King of *France*. It is scarce to be doubted, but the thing was transacted in the manner as it is related in the above Page by *Edmund*, because divers Acts and Letters of *Edward*, under the Pages in the Margin, do manifestly hint at the Cheat complained of by *Edward*. *Pag. 619.* *P. 642 to 645, 652, 687, 789, 937.*

IN the Year 1294, King *Edward* made a formal Renunciation of the Homage which he had paid to *Philip*. *King Edward's Renunciation of his Homage to the King of* France. *P. 650.*

IN 1296 we find certain Conventions made for a Marriage between *Edward*, Son of King *Edward* I. and *Philippa* Daughter of *Guy* Earl of *Flanders*. But as she was kept at *Paris* by *Philip* the Fair, who was against the Marriage; *Edward* and *Guy* made new Conventions for a Match betwixt young *Edward*, and *Guy*'s youngest Daughter *Isabella*. *P. 741.*

Edw. I. P. 789. THERE is a Letter from King *Edward* to the Gentry of *Gascoigne*, to apologize for suffering himself to be tricked by *Philip*, in the secret Treaty betwixt him and his Brother *Edmund*, without consulting with them.

Kings of England *and* France *refer their Quarrel to the Pope.* P. 108, 812, 817. HERE we have a Compromise between *Philip* and *Edward*, to make *Boniface* VIII. Umpire of their Differences, not in quality of Pope, but as a private Person, under the Name of *Benedict Cajetan*.

P. 818. POPE *Boniface* annuls the Conventions for the Marriage betwixt young *Edward* and *Philippa* of *Flanders*.

P. 819. IN the next Page we have the Pope's Sentence of Arbitration, for putting an end to the Dispute betwixt the two Kings. This is the Sentence which *Mezeray* says so nettled the Court of *France*, that when it was delivered to *Philip* by an Ambassador from *Edward*, *Robert* of *Artois* snatched it from him, and threw it into the Fire. Other means were therefore to be consulted, for putting an end to this Quarrel. For this purpose the Ambassadors of the two Kings met at *Montreuil* upon the Sea-coast, and concluded a Truce, by agreeing to a Marriage between King *Edward* the Father, and *Margaret* Sister to King *Philip*, and to another between *Edward* the Son and *Isabella*, *Philip*'s Daughter *. Several Historians have spoke of this Truce as of a final Treaty of Peace, in which they are mistaken; for it appears by the very Terms of the Treaty, that that which was made in 1299, was no more than a Truce.

Another mistake of Historians rectified. P. 840, &c.

* By consulting the *Fœdera*, it appears that Mr. *Rapin* was mistaken when he calls this *Isabella Philip*'s Sister. We have also rectified some of his Pages which are misprinted from the Original.

The

The Peace was not made till the Year 1303, by the Articles whereof printed in this Volume, it may be observed, that the two Kings entirely abandoned those of their Allies who were most attached to their Interests; *Philip* having left the *Scots* in the lurch, and *Edward* the Earl of *Flanders*, of whom there is not one word said in the Treaty.

A. 1303.

Peace betwixt England *and* France.

P. 923.

Both Kings drop their faithful Allies.

P. 929.

THERE is a remarkable Letter upon this occasion from some *Scotsmen* at the Court of *France* to their Friends in *Scotland*, wherein they tell them, that they ought not to be surprized if they are not included in the Treaty, because *Philip* has promised not to abandon them; and that he would do them more Service in any Interview which he was to have with King *Edward* at *Amiens*, than if he had caused them to be comprized in the Treaty: but what the King of *France* told them, was only to amuse them, for he had no Interview with *Edward*, and did nothing for them. On the other hand, the *Flemish* Historians tax King *Edward* with the blackest of Treachery, for having thus abandoned their Earl, and solely contributed to his Ruin, in despite of the most solemn Oaths which he had taken, never to consent to any Peace with *France* without including him in it.

P. 952.

AMONGST the Acts omitted in this Volume, we find that the King of *France* was offended with the Clause *Regnante Edwardo Rege Angliæ*, in the Charters of *Guyenne*, which he insisted should be *Regnante Philippo Rege Franciæ*. After a great many Debates upon this Clause, it was agreed between *John de Grailly* the Seneschal of *Guyenne*, and the Court of *France*, that it should be altered thus, *Regnante Philippo Rege Franciæ, Edwardo Rege Angliæ tenente Ducatum Aquitaniæ*; i. e. *Philip* being King of *France*, and *Edward*

P. 1083.

King

Edw. I. King of *England*, holding the Dutchy of *Aquitain*. But it does not appear in this place that King *Edward* approved of this Expedient.

V. *The Acts which relate to* England *in particular.*

IT may be observed in the first Acts of this Volume, that by their being passed in *England*, during the absence of King *Edward* who was in *Palestine*, he was owned for King, tho' he had not been crowned, the bare Proclamation of him being thought sufficient to vest him with all the Authority of a King: Consequently all those Acts were past in his Name, and by his Authority, only with this difference; that whereas when the King was present, the words *Teste Rege*, or *Teste me ipso*, i. e. Witness the King or my self, were underwritten; while he was absent, the Subscription was *Teste W. Eborum Episcopo, Ed. Cornubiæ, & Gilb. Glocestriæ Comitibus*, i. e. Witness *W.* Bishop of *York*, *Edward* Earl of *Cornwal*, and *Gilbert* Earl of *Glocester*, who were the three Regents of the Kingdom; or else they put, *Per manum W. Norton Cancellarii nostri*, i. e. by the Hand of *W. Norton* our Chancellor.

Provision for K. Edward's Coronation. P. 21.

AMONG the first Acts, after the King's Return from the *Holy-Land*, we find one that ascertains the necessary Provisions to be made for the King's Coronation, every County being taxed to furnish a certain Quantity therein specify'd. For example, *Gloucestershire* was obliged to furnish 60 Beeves, 60 Hogs, 2 fat Boars, 60 Sheep, all alive; 3000 Capons and Hens, and 40 Gammons of Bacon; and other Counties in proportion, which were all to be brought to *Windsor*, and delivered to the Constable of the Castle, on pain of incurring the King's Displeasure.

HERE

A. 1275. P. 34.

Here we have a Memorandum of the day, when King *Edward* arrived at *Dover*, and of that also on which he was crowned.

P. 49.

There's an Act in 1275, the third Year of this Reign, by which Sir *John Bohun* and his Lady resign to King *Edward* the Serjeantship of his Chapel, and the Office called *Officium Spigornellorum*, of which I know not what to make. *Du Cange* speaks of it, but he does not explain it to my liking; for he only quotes a passage which seems to import that it was an Office belonging to the King's Chapel. Sir *Henry Spelman* mentions also in his Glossary, the word *Spigurnelli*, and quotes a passage or two where it is used, but he does not say what it was *.

Irish *offer a great Sum to K.* Edward *to establish the* English *Laws among 'em.* P. 78.

Anno 1277, King *Edward* writes to his Chief Justice in *Ireland*, that 8000 Marks were offered him to establish the *English* Laws in that Country; and that he consents to it, because, says he, those which the *Irish* make use of, are abominable in the sight of God, and by consequence ought not to be deemed Laws. Mean time he orders him to get in the Money with all the dispatch possible.

P. 124.

In 1278, *Alexander* King of *Scotland* being upon a Journey to *England*, King *Edward* orders all the Bailiffs to take care that Provisions be not sold to him above the common Price. Such a Precaution is often wanted elsewhere, especially in *Holland*.

Duels permitted by the Kings of England. P. 56, 157.

It appears that the Kings of *England* formerly permitted Duels between private Persons.

* This was the Office for sealing the King's Writs, so called from *Galfridus Spigurnel*, who was appointed to the Office by King *Henry* III.

'Tis

Edw. I. 'Tis recorded that *Guildhall*, now the Town-house of *London*, belonged in the Year 1280 to *German* Merchants.

Guildhall *to whom it belonged formerly.* P. 161.

An Order to destroy Wolves. P. 168.

We find that formerly Wolves came down from the Mountains of *Wales*, which infested the neighbouring Counties of *England*; for in the Year 1281, King *Edward* gave a Commission to one *Peter Corbet*, to destroy all the Wolves he could find in the Counties bordering upon *Wales*.

P. 427. Here we have another Memorandum of the day on which King *Edward* landed at *Dover*, when he returned from *France* in 1289, after three Years stay in that Kingdom.

P. 783. In 1297, there is an Act wherein King *Edward* excuses himself to his Subjects, for loading them with heavy Taxes; and tells them the reason why he took away the Offices of Constable and Grand Marshal from *Humphry Bohun*, and *Hugh Bigot*; in order to obviate the Reports which were spread abroad, that he did it because those Lords had made some Remonstrances to the King for the publick Benefit of the Nation.

P. 813. In 1298, we find a Commission from King *Edward*, to enquire into his Subjects Grievances, with a design to redress them.

Pierce Gaveston's *Banishment.* P. 1043.

In 1307, King *Edward* made *Gaveston*, a Favourite of his Son *Edward*, take an Oath never to set foot again in *England*; and compell'd his Son *Edward* to take another Oath never to recall him. This Act may be of some use to refer to in the following Reign.

King Edward's *Death.* This King *Edward* died the 7th of *July*, 1307, of which here is a Memorandum.

P. 1059. *The* Jews *banished.* By a Grant passed in 1281, it appears that the High-Priest, or Head of the *Jews* Synagogue

gogue at *London*, was appointed by the King. *A.* 1284.
In this Reign the *Jews* were all drove out of *England* *.

VI. *Affairs betwixt King* Edward *and the Popes.*

IN this Volume there's a great number of Letters from *Edward* to the Popes, and likewise of Bulls from the Popes to the King. The Subject of most of those Bulls and Letters, was an Expedition which *Edward* pretended he would make into the *Holy-Land*, that he might obtain Leave to raise the Tenths upon the Clergy of his Kingdom, as well as on those of *Scotland* and *Ireland*: He endeavoured to amuse the Popes with this Pretence, during the whole course of his Reign. The Popes, who were afraid of being bubbled, were willing enough to grant an Order for levying the Tenths; but they insisted that the King should first of all take the

* DR. *Kennet*, in his Notes upon Mr. *Daniel*'s History of this Reign, after having observed that their High-Priest was confirmed in his Office by the King, says the *Jews* came in with *William* the Conqueror, and were settled in certain Streets by themselves in *London*, of which *Old Jewry* was the chief; and that, being always hated by the People for their Extortion and Usury, they were rather tolerated than lov'd by our Kings, because they now and then fleeced them: but now they were grown so intolerable by their Witchcraft, Poisoning, clipping of Money, counterfeiting Hands and Seals, crucifying of Children privately, and cruel Usury, that nothing would satisfy the People but the utter extirpating them out of the Kingdom; to which King *Edward* did not very unwillingly consent, because they were allowed to carry nothing away with them, except some small matter to bear their Charges, and so left him a vast Treasure. They went most of them into *Italy* and *Germany*. Dr. *Howel* says, 297 *Jews* were executed at *London* at one time, for defacing this King's Coin.

Cross

Edw. I. Cross upon him for the Holy War, and then they would consent that he should receive a part of the Tenths so raised, on condition that the rest should remain in the hands of their Commissioners, to be disposed of according to their Discretion, and always under the specious Pretext of the Holy War; but this was what King *Edward* would by no means consent to. If the Clergy of *England* were to be ruined, he was resolved that no-body should be the better for it but himself; and this sort of Game was carried on to the very end of his Reign. Sometimes the King and the Pope were good Friends upon this Subject, and at other times as much at variance: However it was, 'tis plain, by the History of this Prince, that after he came back from *Palestine*, he never intended, in good earnest, to go thither again.

Bulls and Letters betwixt K. Edward *and the Popes.*

THE Bulls and Letters betwixt the Popes and King *Edward*, upon this Subject, are to be found in these Pages, 119, 122, 202, 235, 259, 273, 316, 321, 323, 341, 413, 432, 459, 460, 475, 495, 499, 501, 509 to 523, 872, 876, 915, 968, 1006, 1036, 1039.

Pope's Receipts for the Tribute from England. *P.* 107, 267, 280.

IT appears by several Acquittances of the Popes, inserted in this Collection, that King *Edward* punctually paid them that annual Tribute, for which King *John* engaged himself to the See of *Rome* *. Indeed he once made an Attempt to alter the nature of this Tribute, by proposing to the Pope to assign the Revenues of

* HERE Mr. *Rapin* seems to question the Truth of a Quotation from *Cooke*'s Institute, Fol. 15. inserted in the Memorial presented by the *English* Protestants to the Prince and Princess of *Orange*; which asserts, That King *Edward* I. refused this Tribute to Pope *Gregory* X. This Memorial was publish'd in *Holland*, and supposed to be written by Dr. *Burnet*, afterwards Bishop of *Sarum*. Vide *Collection of State Tracts in K.* William's *Reign*, Vol. I.

of certain Abbeys in his Kingdom for the Payment of it; but the latter would not consent to it. *A.* 1274. P. 121.

AMONG others, here is a Bull of Pope *Gregory*, exhorting King *Edward* not to meddle with the Revenues of the Churches vacant in *Gascoigne*, in the Year 1274. P. 36.

AND in 1279, *Edward* on his part intreats Pope *Nicholas* not to usurp the Privileges of *England*. P. 130.

IN 1282, King *Edward* forbids his Subjects to export the Money, raised for the Service of the *Holy-Land*, out of the Kingdom. It is not improbable that the Pope had a Design to lay hands on it. P. 201.

IN 1284, Pope *Martin* IV. issued a Bull for absolving King *Edward* of all Crimes which he had committed, as well during the Barons War in the Reign of his Father, as in the War against *Wales*. P. 272.

IN 1289, Pope *Nicholas* IV. issued a Bull for abrogating the Custom in *Scotland* of refusing to admit Foreigners into their Monasteries; and denying them, if not the Habits, at least the Honours of their Orders. P. 417.

NEXT Year King *Edward* complained to the Pope, of the Abuses committed by the Court of *Rome* in *England*, in Collations to Churches: and there's a Letter of the like nature from the Nobility. P. 493.

THE Pope's Answer, inserted in the next Page, is perfectly shuffling; and several Acts testify that the Popes continued their old Pranks. P. 494.

IN 1296, Pope *Boniface* VIII. issued a Bull, forbidding the Clergy to pay any Tax to their Princes without his Leave *. The Clergy of Eng- P. 706.

* THIS Bull is inserted likewise in *Foxe's Martyrology*, fol. 320. And the same Author tells us, That not long

Edw. I. *England*, thinking this Bull a sufficient Warrant for them to refuse the King the Money which he demanded, were out-lawed: which made them comply.

P. 787. NEXT Year, King *Edward* having caused some private Persons Corn to be seized, forbad the Archbishop of *Canterbury* to excommunicate his Officers that made the Seizure. And as it is probable that Prelate threatned them, notwithstanding the King's Prohibition, we find in the very next Page an Order from his Majesty, to commit to Prison all Persons that should dare to publish the Excommunication.

P. 989. 1002, 1020, 1021. WE find afterwards, that King *Edward* complained against that Archbishop to the Pope, and that at last he caused him to be suspended.

P. 844. IN 1299, Pope *Boniface* issued a very haughty Bull, wherein he sets himself up for Judge of the Controversy betwixt the King of *England* and the *Scots*: and not content with ordering *Edward* to send his Ambassadors to *Rome*, there to see the Determination of the Affair, he begins with a flat Lye; for he says, That it is publickly notorious that *Scotland has at all times been a Fief of the Church*. It is from this Bull

long after, at a Parliament at *St. Edmondsbury*, an Eighth being granted to King *Edward* of all Cities and Boroughs, the Clergy, by reason of this Bull, stood out stoutly, and refused to pay a Farthing; and that insisting still upon the same, in the next Parliament at *London*, the King was so offended, that he declared them *out of his Protection*, and that they should have no Benefit of his Laws: and *justly* too, says our Author; for why should they that will contribute nothing to the support of the Government, expect any Advantage by it? As for *Pecham*, the Archbishop of *Canterbury*, who was the Ringleader of the Nonsolvents, the King caused all his Goods to be seized; which so terrifyed the rest of the Clergy, that they freely contributed a Fifth of their Goods to his Majesty's Use, and so were received into Favour.

that

that I took some of the Arguments which I have brought elsewhere against *Edward*'s Sovereignty over *Scotland*, in which Point it is probable *Boniface* had been instructed by the *Scots*. *A.* 1299.

To this there is a smart Answer from the *English* Nobility *, and the King return'd another every whit as sharp, with a Writing inclos'd, in which he asserted his Sovereignty over *Scotland*, from the Proofs contain'd in the Paper presented to the *Scots*, as abovemention'd: all the difference is, that in this he traces the Sovereignty of *England* over *Scotland* farther back, *viz.* from *Brutus* the first fabulous King of *Britain*; whereas in the former, he goes no higher than *Athelstan*, one of the *Saxon* Kings. He knew very well that the Pope would not trouble himself to examine all those Facts. In 1306, the King sent a Letter to the said Pope, wherein he prays him not to usurp the Rights of the Crown of *England*. P. 873, 883. P. 1026.

VII. *Acts relating immediately to* Edward I.

In the Year 1284, *Philip* Count of *Savoy* granted Letters Patent, by which he conferr'd a Right on King *Edward* to nominate his Successor to the said County. P. 290.

Ganday, in the Life of *Alphonso* II. King of *Arragon*, says, That he might well be call'd the *Chaste*, because he was never marry'd: *Y dignamente se puede cognominar el Casto, porque toda sua vida vivio en castidad, sin casarse jamas.* It is true indeed, that he was never marry'd, or rather, that he did not consummate his Marriage; K. Edward *matches his Children.*

* Dr. *Howel*, in his *Medulla Historiæ Anglicanæ*, has given the Names of all the Subscribers, to the number of a hundred Peers, which he calls *a List of those worthy Patriots who withstood Papal Usurpation.*

G but

Edw. I. but it was not his Fault. We find in this Volume, that his Father *Peter* had agreed to a
P. 14. Match propos'd for him with the Princess *Eleanor*, the eldest Daughter of King *Edward*,
P. 173. *Anno* 1273. And his Agreement was confirm'd
P. 187. in 1281, by a Letter from King *Edward* to
P. 210. his Ambassadors, by the full Powers he gave
P. 349. them the Year following, and by Conventions that were pass'd that same Year betwixt the two Kings. In 1287, King *Edward* promis'd by his Letters Patent to have the Marriage consummated; but some Obstacles retarded the Princess's being sent into *Arragon*, and *Alphonso* died before she arriv'd *.

P. 18. In 1273, we find also King *Edward*'s Agreement to a Treaty of Marriage (during his first Voyage to *Guyenne*) betwixt his eldest Son *Henry*, and *Joan* the sole Daughter and Heiress of *Henry* King of *Navarre*; but the young Prince died before he came of Age to be marry'd.

P. 70. Again in 1276, we find a Marriage concluded between *Hartman* Son of the Emperor *Rodolph*, and *Edward*'s second Daughter *Joan*; but the Consummation of it was prevented by *Hartman*'s death. There's a great number of Pieces relating to this Marriage, in this second Volume of the *Fædera*.

P. 175. Here are also several Acts relating to a Marriage propos'd *A. D.* 1281, between *Alphonso* Son of King *Edward*, and *Margaret* the Daughter of *Florence*, Count of *Holland*; but the young Prince died at the Age of twelve.

* This was *Alphonso* III. who, say the *Spanish* Historians, drove the *Moors* out of *Majorca* and *Minorca*, but was despis'd by his Subjects, because of a scandalous Treaty he made with the Pope and the King of *Naples*: he died of the Plague.

It

IT would be needless to make mention here of all the numerous Acts which relate to the Marriages or Proposals of Marriages of the other Daughters of King *Edward*, or of his own with *Margaret* of *France*, and that of *Edward* his Son with *Isabella* Daughter of *Philip de Valois*, in pursuance of the Treaty of *Monstreuil*. *A.* 1274.

King Edward *challeng'd to a Tournament.*

THE *English* Historians say, that King *Edward* passing into *Burgundy*, in his Return from the *Holy-Land*, was challeng'd by *John de Chalon* * to a Tournament in that Province, that he accepted the Challenge, and that the *Burgundians* having play'd him an ill-natur'd Trick, the Tournament was chang'd into a real Combat, which was call'd the Skirmish of *Chalon*, in which King *Edward* had the Advantage. Here are two Bulls of Pope *Gregory* X. † who was then at *Lyons*, in which he exhorts King *Edward* not to be present at a *Tournament, which was to be in* France; which Bulls seem to have a regard to this Tournament of *Chalon*, only a perplexity arises from the difference of Dates, the Bulls being dated in the middle of the Year 1274; whereas *Edward* in his Return from *Palestine* must have enter'd *Burgundy* in 1273: so that it is very probable the Historians have mistaken the Time. P. 29, 30.

Pope endeavours to dissuade him from accepting it.

* DR. *Kennet* calls him the Count *de Chalons*.

† THIS Pope was chose while he was in *Syria* with K. *Edward*, after the Chair had been vacant almost three Years; wherefore to prevent the Inconveniencies of such tedious Elections for the future, in a Council held at *Lyons* in 1273, they contriv'd and settled the Form of the Conclaves.

VIII. *Acts relating to different Affairs.*

Gaston de Bearn's *Homage to King* Edward. *P.* 3.

It is agreed both by *French* and *English* Historians, that when *Edward* return'd from the *Holy-Land*, he went first to *Guyenne* in order to be recogniz'd by the *Gascons*, and that *Gaston* Viscount *de Bearn* refusing to pay him Homage, he was sent for to *Bourdeaux*, where he was arrested, and at last compelled to pay the Homage demanded. It is surprizing that of such a number of Acts in this Collection relating to *Gaston de Bearn*, there is not one touching this Homage, but only about some Disputes betwixt him and King *Edward*, in which the Vassalage of *Gaston* is evidently suppos'd. For example, in 1273, *Gaston* engages himself not to leave the King of *England*'s Court without his Consent, on pain of losing the Lands which he holds of him. This Dependance is farther suppos'd in one other Act of that Year, and in short in all the rest relating to *Edward*'s Differences with this Nobleman. It is true that in *Page* 16. we find King *Edward* complaining that *Gaston* had not obey'd a Summons that was sent to him; but it does not follow from thence that he disputed the Homage which he ow'd to King *Edward*. Yet this is what *Mezeray* asserts positively, and probably he had his Authorities for it; but however it was, it is strange that in none of the Acts of this Volume relating to this *Gaston*, (specify'd in the Margin) there is no mention of the Homage which it is pretended he refus'd.

P. 13. *P.* 14. *P.* 16. *P.* 25. *P.* 28. *P.* 93, 94. *P.* 106, 107.

P. 17, 143, 144, 145, 156, 178.

In the Year above-mention'd, we have the Process of Pope *Gregory* X. against *Guy de Montfort*, Son to *Simon* the late Earl of *Leicester*, for having

having murder'd in the Church of *Viterbo*, *Henry* *A.* 1273.
Son to *Richard*, King of the *Romans*, and Earl of *Cornwal*. This was done at the Sollicitation of this King *Edward*, Cousin to the said *Henry*, who during his stay at *Rome*, in his retnrn from the *Holy-Land*, obtained the Condemnation of the Murderers. As for the Consequences of this Affair, which is in it self of small Importance, see the Pages in the Margin. P. 185, 188, 189, 192, 193, 197, 1068, 1069, and 1077.

As in the first Volume of the *Fœdera*, we find that the Earls of *Flanders* paid Homage to the Kings of *England* merely for Pensions; so we see the same thing in this with respect to the Counts of *Savoy*, *Burgundy*, and *Kasenellebogen* in *Germany*. All the difference is, that the latter mortgag'd some of their Lands, which they own'd they held in Fief of the King of *England*, on the payment of a Pension agreed on betwixt them. P. 1, &c. Vol. 1. and Numb. 1. *Acta Regia*. P. 12, 41, 56, 162, 663.

THE famous Civilian *Francis Accursius*, Professor at *Bologna*, was in the service of K. *Edward*, who made use of him upon several Occasions, and especially in his Affair with the abovemention'd *Gaston de Bearn*. He likewise sent him to the Court of *France* to support his Interests in the general Assembly of the States of that Kingdom, and gave him an annual Pension. P. 4, 25, 28, 37, 50, 52, 125, 180, 496.

THIS Extract is sufficient to shew of what great Use the Acts contain'd in the second Volume of the *Fœdera*, may be to all that have a mind to write the History of *England*, or of the Countries with which it has had any dispute. Tho' some of the Acts may appear of less importance than the others, nevertheless the Collector was certainly in the Right not to omit them, because it is difficult to foresee all the occasions for

Edw. I. for which any one of the Acts may be wanted *.

* It may not be improper to conclude this Reign with the general Character Mr. *Rymer* has given of it, in the Dedication of this second Volume to the late Queen *Anne*.

' This second Volume, ' *says he*, gives a View of ' what passed worthy of Memory during the Reign of ' your most Noble Progenitor King *Edward* the First, ' a Prince the *most Renown'd* ' *for Arms* in that Age.

' And that was an Age ' of much War and Action, ' and of many famous Captains; among others *Albert* the *Great* Duke of ' *Brunswic*; *William* the ' *Great*, Marquiss of *Montferrat*; *Amadaus* the *Great*, ' Count of *Savoy*; three of ' King *Edward*'s nearest Kindred, and his Familiars: ' each of whom by their signal Conduct and Bravery ' had the Title *Great* added ' for their Surname.' *Thus far* Mr. *Rymer*.

As to the first of these Heroes, he was the second Son and Successor to that *Otho*, who according to Mr. *Disney*'s Genealogy of this Family was created Duke of *Brunswic* and *Lunebourg* in 1235. by the Emperor *Frederic* II. whose Diploma is still in the Archives of *Zell*. This *Albert* married *Adelheid*, Daughter to *Henry* the *Magnanimous*, Duke of *Brabant*, whose Portion was to be paid by *Henry* III. K. of *England*, who advis'd him to the Match; as appears by a Letter at the end of this Volume, *p.* 1063. amongst the *Acts omitted*, from the Dutchess her self to King *Edward*, wherein after congratulating him upon his Success in the *Holy-Land*, and upon his Return from thence, and his Coronation, she puts him in mind of the Portion which his Father had promised her with his Consent; and *A. D.* 1280, after the Death of her Husband the Duke, she wrote to him again, *p.* 1076. desiring he would take her Sons into his Protection. It is observable, that in these Letters she calls her self *Adelbeid*, so that there must be a mistake both in Mr. *Disney*, and the *Atlas Historique*, who make *Adelheid* Daughter to the Marquiss of *Montferrat*, *Albert*'s second Wife, and the Mother of his Sons: And the Author of the History of the House of *Brunswic Lunenburg*, printed at *London* in 1715, must also be mistaken in calling her *Elizabeth*, since the contrary appears by her Letters in the Appendix to his Book; and *p.* 40. of the Book itself, where he calls her *Adelhaida*, and says she was Queen *Leonora*'s Cousin, and married in *England*. It is farther observable, that this *Albert* her Husband must have had *Bremen*, for there is a Let-

Letter of his *p.* 1065. in 1276 to K. *Edward* I. in behalf of the Townsmen whom he calls his Subjects, there being then a Controversy betwixt them and the *Londoners* about Trade. The *Atlas Historique* adds, that *Albert* made War upon *Gerrard* Archbishop of *Mentz*, and *Conrad* Count of *Eberstein*; that he took them both Prisoners, and order'd the latter to be hung up by the Feet. He died afterwards of a Wound he receiv'd in Battle against the Marquiss of *Misnia* in 1279, having had Issue six Sons and a Daughter.

THE same Author gives the following Account of the last of these Heroes, *viz.* *Amadæus* V. He defeated the Count of *Geneva* and Dauphin of *Vienne*, who made War upon him. He join'd with *Albert* of *Austria* against *Adolph*, who disputed the Empire, and went afterward to assist King *Edward* I. against the *Scots*. He was successful against the Marquisses of *Montferrat* and *Saluffes*; Having made Peace betwixt the King of *France* and the Count of *Flanders*, he went with a powerful Fleet to assist the Knights of St. *John* of *Jerusalem*, against the *Turks*, whom he defeated, took their Admiral, kill'd their Commander, sunk most of their Brigantines and Galleys; and by this famous Victory sav'd the Isle of *Rhodes*, when it was just ready to surrender to the *Turks*. He had the Town of *Ast* from the Emperor *Henry* VII. and was his Vicar in *Italy*. Those of *Bern* and *Geneva* submitted to him, and he was successful over the *Dauphin* and several other Princes. When the Emperor *Henry* VIII. died, he was unanimously chose at *Pisa* by the *Italians*, who pray'd him to mount the Imperial Throne; but he would not accept it, and died in 1323, after having made thirty-two Sieges, and very much enlarg'd the Domain of *Savoy*.

WE *come now to give an Account of the* Third Volume *of the* Fœdera, *which Mr.* Rapin, *in order to communicate a more perfect Idea of the general Usefulness of that noble* Collection *of* Records *than he had yet done, introduces after this manner.*

AS every one of the numerous Letters, Treaties, Proclamations, Memorials, Patents, and other Pieces of that kind, relating to the *English* History, which are inserted in the *Fœdera*, bear the Dates not only of the Year, but of the Month and Day, there is no room to doubt but those Dates must be of very great use to illustrate Facts, and explain Passages even the most obscure and perplexing. As we find that the discovery of one single Letter in a Cypher leads us to find out a second, and these two a third; just so the Date of an Act, be it of ever so little importance, helps us very often to range a Fact of more consequence in its due Place and Order. But what renders this Collection still more valuable, is, that it mentions the Dates of Place as well as Time, which is of no little service to the Reader, because he is thereby enabled as it were to trace the Prince from one place to another, from the beginning to the very end of his Reign.

Before I had duly consider'd this Advantage, I thought with myself that Mr. *Rymer* was a little to blame, and wonder'd that he should swell his Collection with a very great number of Pieces which at first view seem'd to be of little consequence, if not altogether unnecessary; but after maturer reflection, I am convinc'd that there is not one Piece in the *Fœdera* but what may be of use, especially to such as would write the History of *England*.

The History of *France* is capable likewise of receiving great Lights from it, by reason of the Connection it has with the History of *England*, on account of the Affairs that have been frequently transacted between these two Kingdoms in particular. For my own part, I have discover'd that the best Historians of *France* may be often improv'd by the help of this Collection.

I SAY the ſame thing of the Hiſtory of *Scotland*, the Hiſtorians of that Country having err'd many times in Dates, and even in certain Facts, as I could eaſily inſtance more than once in *Buchanan*.

THE Affairs which *England* had from time to time with the Princes of the *Netherlands*, occaſion'd the inſerting of ſome Pieces in this Collection, which probably never came from the Archives of thoſe Princes; ſuch as Letters, Treaties, and other things which may be uſeful for the Hiſtory of thoſe Provinces.

WE need only look back to the firſt and ſecond Volumes of this Collection, to be convinc'd how the Hiſtory of *Sicily* may be illuſtrated with a great number of Particulars there mention'd, of which one does not ſee the leaſt trace in the Hiſtorians either of *Sicily* or *Naples*.*

THE Hiſtories of *Caſtile*, *Arragon* and *Portugal*, may alſo be furniſh'd from this Collection with certain Facts that were not known to their beſt Hiſtorians, or elſe were never well explain'd; of this we had an Inſtance in the ſecond Volume, with reſpect to the Duel intended betwixt the Kings of *Arragon* and *Sicily*. †

THOSE who undertake to write the Lives of the Popes, may alſo find in it the Popes Briefs or Bulls, and the Letters to them from the Kings of *England*; which, beſides the particular Facts they contain, may be of vaſt help to them, were it only for the exactneſs of the Dates.

IN ſhort, ſeveral private Perſons may here find Circumſtances they knew nothing of before

* Vide p. 38, 36 *to* 39, 41, 48 *to* 51, *of* Acta Regia, *for* September.

† *See* p. 50. *of* Acta Regia *for* September.

re-

Edw. II. relating to their Families, or the Persons of their Ancestors, which is no little Satisfaction; tho' indeed it is what scarce any will be the better for but the *English* and the *Gascons*: I say the *Gascons*, because *Guyenne* having been for a long time under the Dominion of the Kings of *England*, there is a multitude of Pieces in the *Fœdera* which relate to that Province.

'Tis plain therefore, that this Collection is of vast use to those who affect the Study of History, and particularly that of *England*; for which reason such can never enough extol the Bounty of that august Queen who made them so fine a Present, or the Generosity of those Noblemen who procured it. If all other Nations would follow this Example, one might have a History of the several States of *Europe*, at least as to what relates to the seven last Centuries, as perfect as could be wish'd.——Thus far Mr. *Rapin*.

When Mr. *Rymer* waited on her late Majesty with his third Volume, he addressed her with a Dedication so descriptive of the Reign it refers to, that we cannot help quoting a part of it as a necessary Preface to the Account which follows it.

'In this *Volume* You present the World with 'the *Acts of State* in the Reign of K. *Edward* II. 'in a very nice Juncture, or time of great 'Struggling and Difficulty, of great Trouble 'and Disorder all *Europe* over; your three Kingdoms had each their share, and drank deep of 'the bitter Cup.—— In this the darkest Period 'of Time, from your Royal Archives You 'set up as it were a *Pillar of Fire*, for the direction of Travellers in their way to Truth; and 'with an unparallel'd Bounty give out, and 'make such provision, that in this uncultivated, 'in 'in this so barren Track, in this very *Desart*, 'the Curious want not for their Entertainment, 'not to say their *Quails* and their *Manna*.

'AMONGST the Negotiations in this Book 'publish'd, may be noted, that during the most 'unprosperous and disastrous Administration, 'amidst the greatest Confusion, and dismal 'Jumble of Affairs (so it pleas'd Almighty 'Providence) that with *William the Third*, sur'named *the Good* *, Count of *Holland*, was con'tracted an Alliance, whereby those Measures 'were concerted, which in the next succeeding 'Reign carried the *English* Arms into *France*,

* HE was the second Earl of *Hainault*, that was stil'd Earl of *Holland*, *Zealand* and *Friesland*; which Provinces, according to *Guicciardine*'s History of the *Netherlands*, fell to his Father by Marriage. This was a gallant Prince, and for his Piety, Justice and Mildness, had the Surname of *Good*, as his Brother *John*, who was killed by the *Flemings*, was for his contrary Temper surnamed the *Merciless*. In his Reign *Holland* was afflicted with a Plague and Famine, which destroy'd many of their People. In 1328, *Philip* of *France*, by the assistance of this Earl, obtain'd a great Victory over the *Flemings* at *Mount-Cassel*, where they lost 10000 Men. There is a memorable Story of an Act of Justice done by this good Earl not long before his Death upon the Bailiff of *South-Holland*, who had taken away a poor Man's Cow (he refusing to sell her, because she gave Milk enough to subsist his Family) and sent him another in exchange, that was not to compare with her. The Earl commanded the Bailiff in the first place for the wrong done to the Countryman, to pay him 100 Crowns, and afterwards for the Injury done to himself and his Government, to be beheaded. He reign'd 33 Years, and had by his Wife *Jane* of *Valois*, 3 Sons, *William*, *Lewis*, and *John*, with 4 Daughters, *Margaret* Dutchess of *Bavaria* and Empress, *Jane* Countess of *Juliers*, *Philippa* Queen of *England*, and *Elizabeth*. He advis'd his Son *William* upon his Death-bed to maintain Peace with his Neighbours, and lay no grievous Impositions on his Subjects.——See the *Atlas Historique*.

'to

Edw. II. ' to *Cressy* and to *Poictiers*; and thence brought ' the *French* King from the Field of Battle into ' this your Kingdom Captive.'

It is time now to return to Mr. *Rapin*'s Account of the third Volume of the *Fœdera*, which takes in the first sixteen Years of the Reign of *Edward* II. The Method observed by the Collector in ranging all the Acts according to their Dates, tho' upon different Subjects, is somewhat confounding to such as have not the Events to which those Acts relate, fresh in their Memory. To remedy this Inconvenience in some measure, and to give a more distinct Idea of the most important Articles in the third Volume, I will range the whole under four Heads, which take in the chief Contents of this Volume.

I. The domestic Troubles of *England* upon account of *Gaveston*, and the *Spensers*, who were King *Edward* II's Favourites.

II. The Transactions betwixt this Prince and *Scotland*, which are a continuation of the Account taken from the second Volume.

III. The Disputes with the Court of *Rome*, and other Ecclesiastical Affairs.

IV. The Affair of the Knights Templars, whose Order was abolish'd in this Reign.

Article I. *The Domestic Troubles of* England.

King Edward IId's Character.

EDWARD II. was a weak Prince, of a mean Genius, who engaged readily in Affairs, without considering the Consequences, and without the necessary Abilities to extricate himself out of the Difficulties into which he plung'd. His excessive Attachment to *Gaveston*, a

History of his Favourite Gaveston.

KING EDWARD THE II.ND

a Gentleman of *Gascoigne*, to whom he entirely abandon'd himself, and upon whom he heap'd his Favours without measure, embroil'd him with the most considerable Lords of the Kingdom, who united together to ruin the Favourite. In short, they demanded his Removal, and the King promis'd it, but afterwards did all that was in his power to be excus'd from his Engagement: and when he could not come off any other way, he found means to turn his Favourite's Banishment to his advantage, by making him Governor of *Ireland*; an Expedient with which the Nobility would however have been well satisfy'd, if his extreme Fondness for *Gaveston* had not induc'd him to recall him almost as soon as he had sent him over; and not only so, but to bring him to a Tournament, where that imprudent Favourite eclips'd all the other Lords by the Splendor of his Equipage, and the numerous Train of Gentlemen who attended him, both as his Companions and Guards. The Nobility finding themselves deceived by the King, took new Measures. Being assembled in Parliament, they presented a Petition to him, setting forth in plain Terms that the State and his Houshold were both so ill govern'd, that there was a necessity of a proper Regulation; and therefore they pray'd him to let them chuse a certain number of Persons who might be impower'd to make Rules for better governing the State and the King's Houshold, and to cause the same to be duly observ'd. *Edward* being in no condition to resist them, granted what he did not dare to refuse: whereupon the said Commissioners, of whom *Thomas* Earl of *Lancaster* was Chief, were chose, and went by the Name of *Ordainers*. They made a Regulation, and had the necessary Powers from the King and Parliament A. 1312.

Edw. II. ment, to cause it to be observ'd. There was no mention in it of *Gaveston*; but the *Ordainers* seeing that the King continued to heap his Favours upon him, made a new Regulation containing 41 Articles, by one of which *Gaveston* was condemn'd to perpetual Banishment, and the King was oblig'd to conform to it.

Insurrection of the Barons.

This Prince had scarce given Consent to the Exile of his Favourite, but he repented of it, and re-call'd him without saying any thing to the *Ordainers*; which made the Barons rise. They took Arms *, and march'd with the Earl of *Lancaster* at their head towards *York*, where the King then was, in order to force him to deliver up *Gaveston*. Upon the Report of their coming, *Edward* retir'd to *Newcastle*; but when he heard that the Barons Army was advancing that way, he thought it unsafe to stay there any longer; and being more afraid for his Favourite than for himself, he quitted that Town, and carried him to *Scarborough* Castle, then the strongest Place in all the *North*, where he left him, and went himself for *Warwick*, intending to assemble an Army there to oppose the Barons. The latter arriv'd at *Newcastle* the very Day that the King left it; and after pillaging his Moveables and Baggage, sent a Detachment to besiege *Scarborough*. The Earl of *Pembroke*, who had the Care of this Siege, carried it on with so much Vigour, that *Gaveston* was oblig'd to capitulate †, on condition he might have Leave to

* Dr. *Kennet* in his Notes upon Mr. *Daniel's* History of this Reign says, that the Bishops were such zealous Confederates in this Action, that the Archbishop of *Canterbury* excommunicated *Walter* Bishop of *Coventry*, because out of a loyal Principle he refus'd to join with them.

† Dr. *Brady* affirms, upon a Record in the *Tower* which he

to ſpeak with the King, and be tried according to the Laws and Cuſtoms of the Realm. The Confederate Lords were not very well ſatisfy'd with this Capitulation; but the Earl of *Pembroke* having engaged upon his Honour to carry *Gaveſton* to the King, and afterward to bring him back to the Lords, they at length conſented, notwithſtanding the Oppoſition made by the Earl of *Warwick* and ſome others. As the Earl of *Pembroke* was upon the Road with his Priſoner, the Earl of *Warwick* hearing that *Gaveſton* was in a Caſtle where there was not Accommodation for *Pembroke*, went thither in the Night, forced the Guard, took and carried the Priſoner to his own Caſtle of *Warwick*, and there cut off his Head †. *A.* 1312.

Gaveſton's *Tragical Exit.*

How nettled ſoever *Edward* was, by the Affront which he had receiv'd, he was again obliged to ſue to the Barons for a Peace, by the Mediation of two of the Pope's Legates, who happen'd to be in *England*. By the Agreement which was concluded not long after, the Lords engaged to make the King publick Satisfaction, and to reſtore all the Plunder carried off from *Newcaſtle*, together with the Jewels taken from *Gaveſton*. And the King, on his part, promis'd to grant an ample Amneſty to the Barons and all their Adherents. The Barons executed their Part ſpeedily, and *bonâ fide*; but the King delay'd almoſt a Year before he publiſh'd the promis'd Pardon; which made the Lords ſo diffident of him, that the Troubles would have

Peace betwixt the King and the Barons.

he mentions in his Appendix to his *Comp. Hiſt.* that *Gaveſton* did not ſurrender to the Earl of *Pembroke*, but to the Lord *Piercy*; and this is confirm'd by an Act in the 3d Vol. of the *Fœdera*, p. 334.

† Dr. *Kennet* ſays, this was done on the 19th of *June*, 1312.

broke

Edw. II. broke out afresh, if *Edward*'s Father-in-law, the King of *France*, had not sent his Brother, the Count *d' Evreux*, into *England*, along with *Enguerrand de Marigny*, who obtain'd of the King, that the Amnesty should be publish'd.

So much for the First Part of the Domestick Troubles, which ended in *October* 1313: They were indeed attended with some Consequence in the following Years, to 1318; but it is not worth while to insist upon it.

The History of the Spensers.

In the Year 1314, fresh Troubles arose between the King and his Nobles, upon account of a new Favourite, *viz. Hugh Spenser*, who made the same ill use of his Favour as *Gaveston* had done before: He got his Father *Hugh* to be made Earl of *Winchester*; and they two govern'd the whole Kingdom, *Edward* blindly approving every thing they did. The Earl of *Lancaster*, who, after his Reconciliation with the King, receiv'd a terrible Affront from that Prince, made the great Favour of the *Spensers* a Pretext to renew the Confederacy of the Barons: He rais'd Troops, and caus'd the Lands of the said Favourites to be wasted by *Roger Mortimer*, jun. who committed as much Spoil on them as amounted to 60,000 *l.* Sterling. This done, the Lords publickly demanded the Banishment of the *Spensers*, which the King did not dare to refuse, when he saw that the Commons of *England* took their part. *Spenser* jun. was carried to *Dover*, and there put on board *, the Father being at that time absent from the Realm about the King's Affairs. This Prince now found

* *Adam Murymuth* in his History of this King, in *Magdalen*-College Library, *Oxon*, writes, that the younger *Spenser* turned Pirate, and robb'd all the Merchant-ships he could meet with.

him-

himself in a very miserable Plight, being forced to receive Law from his own Subjects, and not knowing which way to extricate himself from such a State of Slavery; but at last a new Affront which the King received from one of the Confederate Lords, drove his Patience to its Extremity, and made him resolve to shake off a Yoke so disagreeable. A. 1314.

King Edward's Queen grosly affronted. P. 897.

HIS Queen intending a Progress to *Canterbury*, ordered her Officers to provide a Night's Lodging for her upon the Road, at a Place called *Leeds*-Castle, belonging to *Bartholomew Badlesmere*, one of the Confederate Lords; but * the Governor of the Castle denied Entrance to the Queen's Servants, some of whom were killed: Upon which her Majesty complained of it to *Badlesmere*; but he had the Insolence to approve of the Governor's Action, and to say, *That he had done nothing but by his Orders. Edward* could not stomach such a gross Affront as this was; but raised Troops, went and besieged *Leeds*-Castle, and hung up the Governor. And having this Power in his Hands, he laid hold of the Opportunity, and pushed the Confederate Lords, without giving them time to look about; so that after having got most of their Castles in his own Hands, they were glad to submit to his Will and Pleasure; and then he made no Scruple to recall the *Spensers* to Court.

* Thomas Culpeper.

Earl of Lancaster's *Rebellion and Death.*

THE Earl of *Lancaster*, who was afraid to trust the King, raised Troops in his own Defence; but being abandoned by most of his Friends, he was not in a Condition to make head against him, which made him resolve to withdraw to the *North*, and join the *Scots*, who had promised him Assistance. The King pursued him; and as the Earl, to avoid a Battle with him, endeavoured to force the Passage of a

Edw. II. Bridge which was kept by *Harclay* †, he was taken Prisoner and carried to *Pontefract*, where the King took off his Head. This Lord, who was King *Henry* the third's Grandson, was cried up for a Martyr by the Populace, and was afterwards canonized for a Saint in the Reign of *Richard* II.*

THIS is the Sum and Substance of the Acts of this Volume, which relate to the Domestick Troubles of *England*, as far as comes within the first sixteen Years of the Reign of *Edward* II. the four others being referred to the fourth Volume of the *Fœdera*.

AMONG all these Pieces, which are very numerous, I shall but barely point out the chief that have a relation to the Events abovementioned.

Edward's *Gifts to* Gaveston. *P.* 1, and 87, 136, 164.

IN this third Volume of the *Fœdera*, we have the great Gifts which *Edward* made to *Gaveston*, particularly the Earldom of *Cornwall*, the City of *Exeter*, and fifteen other Territories or Castles; which made him in an instant the greatest Lord in the Kingdom.

THE first of those Acts is dated from *Dumfries* in *Scotland*, the 5th of *August* 1307, *viz.* a Month after the death of *Edward* I. who had banished *Gaveston* but a little while before, and

† Sir *Andrew Harclay*, Constable of *Carlisle*.

* The People flocked in Pilgrimage to his Tomb at *Pontefract*; and after the *Spensers* had got the King to order a Guard, to prevent their coming, they did it privately. In the next Reign a Church was built over his Tomb, and Queen *Isabel* wrote to the Pope, to justify the Miracles done there, and to desire his Canonization; which was granted, *A.* 1389. An Honour, which indeed he deserved much more than any of his Countrymen, who had acquired it since the Conquest; for if the Love of his Country may be called Piety, he was truly, and unalterably, a pious Man. *Dr.* Kennet's *Notes on Mr.* Daniel.

made

made his Son take an Oath that he would never recall him. *A.* 1307.

HERE is also a Patent constituting *Gaveston*, *Custos Regni*, that is to say, Viceroy of the Kingdom during the King's absence in *France*, whither he went to consummate his Marriage with *Isabel*, Daughter of *Philip the Fair*. It is signed by the King at *Westminster*, *Dec.* 26. 1307. *He makes him Viceroy of the Kingdom.* P. 47.

I HAVE taken particular notice of this Act, to shew the Error of most Historians *, who affirm that *Gaveston* accompanied the King into *France*; and, in particular, Father *Orleans*, who says, that the first time the King saw *Gaveston* after his Banishment, was at *Boulogne*: Which cannot be, for he was then *Custos*, or Viceroy of the Kingdom; and, in the *Fœdera*, there are several Orders signed by him in that quality during the King's Absence, with this Subscription, *Teste* Gaveston. *A mistake in our English Historians rectified.* P. 57.

IN a Memorandum relating to the Coronation of *Edward* II. we find that *Gaveston* carried St. *Edward*'s Crown at that Solemnity †. P. 63.

IT was not long after, that the Lords demanded that *Gaveston* might be banished; and here are the King's Letters Patent dated at *Westminster*, May 18, 1308, in which he engaged, that he should be out of the Kingdom by the Feast of St. *John the Baptist* next ensuing. P. 80.

ON the 7th of *June* following, *Gaveston* and his Wife, who was the King's Niece ††, received P. 87.

a

* This is an Error which has escaped the Correction of the Learned Annotator upon Mr. *Daniel*'s History of this Reign, as well as of Dr. *Howel*, and other celebrated Historians.

† It was performed *Feb.* 25, 1307-8. Thomas Wike's *Chron.*

†† She was the Daughter of *Joanna* of *Acres*, Sister of *Gilbert* Earl of *Glocester*, who was against the Match, according

Edw. II. a Present from that Prince which was worth 3000 Marks a year, in Castles, Lands, and Tenements: The Grant is dated at *Langelye*.

P. 92. AND on the 16th of the same Month, he made him Governor of *Ireland*, by Letters Patent dated at *Reading*.

P. 136, 164. AFTER *Gaveston*'s return, we find that the King conferred many Grants upon him. *

P. 204. THE King's Order for establishing the Ordainers, is dated at *Westminster*, *March* 16, 1310. †

THE second Regulation they made consisting of 41 Articles, one of which sentenced *Gaveston* to perpetual Banishment, is not to be met with here: but there are some Acts afterwards, which seem to confirm that there was such a Regulation; and probably it was made in the Year 1311.

P. 278. WE find afterwards a Protection for *Gaveston*'s coming to Court, by the King's Order, dated *Oct.* 8, 1311, at *London*.

P. 294. THE Lords complaining of his being recalled, he lurked about *incog.* and the King was forced to grant a Warrant for discovering and apprehending him; it is dated at *Westminster*, *Nov.* 30, 1311.

P. 298. THE King recalled him again, and sent an Order to all the Sheriffs, to make Proclamation

cording to *Kennet* upon *Daniel*; but his Notes upon that History differ from the *Fœdera*, both in her Name, and in the date of her Marriage, *October* being mistaken for *June*, and *Joanna* for *Margaret*.

* One of the Patents for this purpose is dated at *Westminster*, *May* 15, 1309. Another, the 28th of *August* following.

† Mr. *Rapin* has mistaken this Act for the First that was made by the *Ordainers*, which contains six Articles, and is dated at *Northampton* the 2d of *August*.

in

in their respective Counties, that he looked upon Gaveston as a good Subject: It is dated *Jan.* 18, 1312, at *York*. A. 1312.

AFTER this Favourite was beheaded, the King issued an Order for apprehending of those who were guilty of his death: It is dated *July* 31, 1312, at *London*. P. 331.

AN Accommodation being made between the King and the Lords, towards the end of that Year, the Lords restored the Jewels, *&c.* that were taken from *Gaveston*; which, according to the List given of them in above five Pages, and the Weight and Price therewith marked, were very great both in Number and Value, and it appears that many of them belonged to the King or the Crown: The Acquittance, or Royal Receipt for them, is dated *Feb.* 27. 1313, at *Windsor*. Gaveston's *immense Wealth in Jewels.* P. 388, &c.

AFTER this, we meet with two Amnesties, the one for those who had favoured *Gaveston*'s Return, and the other for the Confederate Lords, to the number of 468; each of which had a particular Pardon to himself, word for word the same with the rest: They are dated *Oct.* 16, 1313, at *Westminster*. P. 442, 443

THUS an end was put to the first Troubles of this Reign.

As for the second Period of Troubles, we find certain Orders made by the King, to enquire into, and suppress the Confederacies which were formed at *London* and elsewhere, against the *Spensers*: They are dated at *Westminster*, *Jan.* 14, and 30, 1320. P. 866, 867

On the 20th of *August*, 1321, we have the King's Letters Patent, containing the Resolution of the Parliament at *Westminster* against the *Spensers*. *Parliament's Resolution against the* Spensers. P. 891.

Edw. II. ON the 16th of *October* following, there's the Letter from *Edward*, dated in the *Tower* of *London*, giving an Account of the (abovementioned) Affront put upon his Queen at *Leeds* Castle, and the insolent Answer of *Badlesmere*.

P. 897.

P. 898. THERE'S a Proclamation of the same Date, giving notice that the King did not raise Troops to make War against his Subjects, but only to punish the Governor of *Leeds* Castle.

P. 907. THE Recalls of the *Spensers* are dated *Dec.* 8. at *Westminster*, and *Dec.* 26. at *Cirencester*.

P. 936, &c. THE Trial and Condemnation of the Earl of *Lancaster* at *Pontefract*, is dated *May* 2. 1322, at *York*.

P. 1033. THERE'S a Letter from *Edward* to the Bishop of *London*, ordering him to put a stop to the Devotion which the People paid to the Picture of the Earl of *Lancaster*, which was hung up with many others in St. *Paul*'s Church: 'Tis dated *June* 28, 1323, at *York*.

THESE being the chief Acts which are contained in the Collection under this Head, I leave the rest, and proceed to

ARTICLE II. *Of the Affairs of* Scotland.

THE Death of King *Edward* I. was the Preservation of *Scotland*; for after he had already conquered that Kingdom three times, he returned thither with an absolute intention to put it out of the power of that Nation to revolt a fourth time; but death prevented the execution of his Designs. That was the Affair he had most at heart during his whole Reign, and what he most vigorously recommended to his Successor: But *Edward* II. was otherwise disposed; for about a Month after the death of his Father, he quitted *Scotland*, into which he was advanced as far

far as *Dumfries*, and leaving his Army in the Hands of *Cumin*, a *Scotsman*, he returned into *England*, to consummate his Marriage, and be crown'd. In 1308, *Robert Bruce*, the new King of *Scotland*, being dangerously ill, *Cumin* took that opportunity, and advanced to attack him. *Robert*, sick as he was, stood his ground, beat him, and drove him out of the Kingdom: *Edward Bruce*, his Brother, won another Victory likewise, in the County of *Galway*; which put the Affairs of the *Scots* in a very good Situation. *A.* 1308.

Cumin *defeated by* Bruce.

THE King of *England* returned into *Scotland* next Year with a powerful Army; but for want of having concerted proper Measures to subsist it, he was obliged to return without striking a Blow.

IN the Years 1310 and 1311, *Robert* entered *England* several times, and carried off great Booty.

Bruce *enters* England.

IN 1312, he took *Perth* alias St. *Johnstoun*, *Dumfries*, *Lanerk*, *Roxbourgh*, and at last *Edinburgh*; while *Edward* was so harassed with domestick Broils, that he was not in a Condition to oppose his Progress.

Returns and takes Towns in Scotland.

IN 1313, he caused the strong Town of *Sterling* to be besieged by *Edward* his Brother; the Governor of which, after a brave Defence, capitulated, and promised to surrender the Place if it was not relieved in a Year; that is to say, before the Feast of St. *John Baptist* in the Year following.

IN 1314, *Edward* put himself at the head of an Army of 100000 Men, in order to go and raise the Siege; but was beat by *Robert*, and lost 50000 Men, if we may believe the *Scots* Histo-

Defeats K. Edward *at* Sterling.

Edw. II. Hiſtorians: after which time the *Engliſh* generally acted defenſively *.

His Brother's Succeſs in Ireland.

In 1315, *Robert* ſent his Brother to *Ireland*, to ſupport the Natives, who had rebelled againſt *Edward*; and his Brother made ſuch a Progreſs there, that he was at length crowned: But after having lived in that Iſland almoſt three Years, he was killed there in Battle, at a time when *Robert* was haſtning to his Aſſiſtance.

In 1317, Pope *John* XXII. ſent Legates into *England*, to make a Peace betwixt the two Kings, and by his ſingle Authority cauſed a Truce to be proclaimed for two Years; but *Robert*, who was never once conſulted about it, made a Jeſt of the Pope's Proclamation, and took *Berwick*; for which the Legates excommunicated him.

In 1318, he was obliged to paſs over into *Ireland*, to relieve his Brother, whom he found there dead. The King of *England* took the Opportunity of his Abſence to beſiege *Berwick*; and while he was employed in that Siege, the Earl of *Murray*, General of *Scotland*, entered *England* at another Place, and defeated the

General Murray's *Expedition to* England.

* Dr. *Kennet* in his Remarks upon Mr. *Daniel's* Hiſtory of this Reign, ſays, this was called the Battle of *Bannockburn* (on the Banks of which River it was fought the 25th of *June*, 1314.) and is remarked by our Hiſtorians as a Divine Puniſhment of the Leudneſs and Exceſſes of the *Engliſh* Army, who ſpent the Night before the Battle in Drunkenneſs and Intemperance; but as a reward of the Piety of the *Scots*, who entered upon it with ſolemn Confeſſions, and receiving the Sacrament: wherefore God gave them ſuch a miraculous Victory, as ſo few Hands, without a ſpecial Aſſiſtance of God, could not have effected. ——— Dr. *Howel* ſays alſo, that the *Engliſh* in this Expedition, had adorned themſelves as for a Triumph, with all ſorts of Riches, Gold, Silver, and the like, in a kind of wanton manner, correſponding to the Prince they followed.

Militia

Militia of *Yorkshire*, consisting of 10000 Men, which obliged the King of *England* to raise the Siege of *Berwick*. *A.* 1319.

THE Year 1319 was spent almost intirely in Negotiations, which were followed with a Truce for two Years. *Truces betwixt the two Nations.*

AT the Expiration of the said Truce, in the beginning of the Year 1322, the *Scots* entered *England*, and carried off great Booty.

AT length in *May* 1323, a Truce was concluded betwixt the two Nations for thirteen Years.

THESE Matters are the Subject of the Acts of this third Volume relating to *Scotland*.

THO' there's no express mention in those Acts of the Losses sustained by the *English*, yet there are several which manifestly imply that they were very great; as for Instance, *Orders* repeated every Year *for raising Troops*, and to prepare Armies against *Scotland*: which is a sign that the Affairs of the *English* in that Country were not in the most flourishing state; for it is said in most of those Orders, that it was to *repel* the *Scots*. One of the most express Acts, which supposes the Loss of the Battle at *Sterling*, is a Commission to the Earl of *Pembroke* to take upon him the Command of the Army; which Commission, it must be observed, is dated at *York*, *August* 10, 1314. The King's Words are these, *Ad refrænandam Scotorum inimicorum & rebellium nostrorum obstinatam malitiam, qui flagitiis per ipsos in terra nostra Scotiæ, ac in propinquis finibus Regni nostri Angliæ, diversimode perpetratis, non contenti, ipsum Regnum jam hostiliter, in nostri, ac omniam Fidelium nostrorum dedecus, opprobrium & dispendium, sunt ingressi, ibidem homicidia, deprædationes, incendia, sacrilegia, & mala innumerabilia committendo:* i. e. To restrain the obstinate Malice of our rebellious Enemies the *Scots*, who not

Edward's Commission to E. of Pembroke. P. 491.

Edw. II. not content with the flagrant Acts of various kinds by them committed in our Kingdom of *Scotland*, and on the Borders of our Kingdom of *England*, have now, to the dishonour, reproach and damage of us and our good Subjects, entered this very Kingdom in a hostile manner, committing Murders, Depredations, Burnings, Sacrileges, and other Evils without number. By the Capitulation of *Sterling*, that Place was to be either relieved or surrendered before the 24th of *June* 1314; *Edward* entered *Scotland* with a powerful Army to relieve it: nevertheless we find the *Scots* ravaging the *English* Borders upon the 10th of *August* following; an evident Proof that they had defeated and drove the *English* back.

The Pope's Partiality against Robert Bruce.

I Pass over a great many Acts of less Importance, to come to what is most curious upon this Article, and that is, to shew the Partiality with which Pope *John* XXII. acted against *Robert Bruce*. The Particulars which this Collection contains upon this Subject, are such as perhaps are not easily to be met with elsewhere; and therefore I shall give a short History of it.

King *Edward*, who longed mightily to put an end to the War with *Scotland* by a Truce, or by a Peace, as the Acts of this Collection abundantly manifest, had engaged Pope *John* XXII. in his Interests, who for his sake undertook to compel *Robert* to make a Peace with *England*. For this purpose he sent over two Legates, furnished with several Bulls, the first of which

P. 594.

being dated at *Avignon* in *Jan.* 1317. ordered a Truce of two Years between both Nations, *by virtue of the Authority* conferred on the Prince of the Apostles and his Successors, as Vicegerents of the King of Peace, to procure a Peace throughout the Catholick Church, and to cause it to be punctually observed. The second Bull dated the 16th of *April*, impowered the two Car-

Cardinals *Gaucelin* and *Luke*, who had the Titles *A.*1317.
of St. *Marcellin* and St. *Mary*, to make a Peace
between *Edward* King of *England*, and *Robert* P. 613.
Bruce, who assumed the Title of King of *Scotland*. This Commission was as ample as it could well be, for it not only gave them a Power to regulate the Conditions of the Peace as they thought fit, but it also authorized them to force the two Parties into it with their Subjects and Adherents, whether Clergy or Laity of what Quality soever, by Suspensions, Excommunications, Deprivation of their Privileges, and of the Right of making Wills, or of succeeding to Estates; even though *Edward* or *Robert* had obtained of the Holy See the Privilege of being exempted from all Excommunication.

The Pope knew very well that *Edward* would make no scruple to submit to an Authority so extraordinary, and that he would be glad of a Peace or a Truce upon any Terms whatsoever; therefore by a third Bull of the same P. 614.
Date with the second, he gave a Power to the Legates to excommunicate *Robert Bruce*.

In a few days after he dispatch'd three other P. 619.
Bulls, the first of which excommunicated all
the Enemies of the King of *England*; the se- P. 620.
cond being directed to the Archbishops of *Dublin* and *Cassels*, permitted them to excommuni- P. 630.
cate *Robert* and *Edward Bruce*, who had invaded *Ireland*; and the third was against the Friars Mendicant of *Ireland*, who by their Intrigues and Preachments favoured the Invasion of *Edward Bruce*.

These were the Sentiments with which the Pope endeavoured to procure a Peace between *England* and *Scotland*, not in quality of Mediator, for *Robert* had never owned him for such, but *by the Fulness of his Apostolical Power*; as if

Edw. II. he had been born the Judge and Sovereign Magistrate of Christian Princes.

The other Acts relating to this Affair, shew that *Robert* refused to submit to the Authority of the Legates, that he denied them admission into his Dominions, and that he would not so much as return an Answer to the Pope's Letters, on pretence that the Pope did not own his Title of King; and that, in short, he laughed at the pretended Truce which the Legates had proclaimed in *England*, by making no scruple to besiege and take *Berwick* that very Year. *Robert's* Disobedience provoked the Pope to order his Legates to make use of the Authority they had received from him to excommunicate the said Prince, of whom he speaks in these words, in his Bull dated *July* 4, 1318, from *Avignon*: *Ipse vero intelligere nolens ut bene ageret, sed aures suas, more aspidis surdæ, ne audiret vocem Patris sapienter exhortantis, obturans; quasi de impensa à nobis super hiis benignitate, superbiæ concepisse videatur audaciam, iniquitatem, de exhibita sibi per Apostolicam sedem mansuetudine, non absque ingratitudinis vitio parturivit, contemnens ipsas nostras recipere Literas, per Nuncios ipsos eidem oblatas.* ——*Ne non fore posset ambiguum, quicquid malignitatis in hac parte conceperit, licet Treugæ prædictæ per vos, vel alium, seu alios de Mandato nostro per Angliam solemniter publicatæ fuissent, ita quod verisimiliter potuerat ad ejus notitiam hujusmodi publicatio pervenisset, ne lateret eum cominùs positum quod aliis eminùs constitutis non credebatur occultum: Ipse tamen Treugas istas, non absque multa insolentiæ temeritate & plectibili nostro & sedis prædictæ contemptu, spretâque sententiâ antedictâ observare contempsit, villam Berewici nequiter invadens.* i. e. But he refusing good Instruction, like the deaf Adder, stopt his ears, that he might not hear the Voice of his Father wisely exhorting him; and as if our Good-

Will

Pope's Excommunication of Robert Bruce.
P. 707.
P. 711.

Will towards him had made him proud and insolent, he wickedly and ungratefully abused the Favour offered him from the Apostolical See, disdaining to receive our Letters when brought to him by the Nuncios themselves. And as a plain Indication of his malign Disposition, altho' the aforesaid Truces were by our Command published in a solemn manner by you and others throughout *England*, so that the Publication thereof could hardly fail of coming to his Ears, unless it could be imagined that he who was nigh at hand was ignorant of what could not be supposed to be a Secret to those afar off, nevertheless the said *Robert* with daring Insolence, in contempt of us and the See aforesaid, and also of the Sentence aforesaid, hath scorned to observe the said Truces, and wickedly invaded the Town of *Berwick*, &c. *A.* 1319.

MEAN time the Pope seeing that *Robert* despised all his Thunder-bolts, was not willing to expose his Authority to any further Contempt, and therefore recalled his Legates.

IT appears from several passages, that during the two years Truce, which was at length agreed to about the end of the Year 1319, *Robert* sollicited his Absolution, of which the Pope gave advice to *Edward*, by a Letter dated in *September* 1320 from *Avignon*, to this effect. 'That he had appointed a certain time for '*Robert* to appear before him in Person, or by 'Proxy; and that not having done either, the 'Pope had renew'd the Sentence of Excommu'nication against him, and put *Scotland* under 'an Interdict; but that at the Prayer of the '*Scots* Ambassadors, he had suspended the ef'fects thereof.' P. 848.

'TIS very probable, as *Buchanan* positively asserts, that *Robert* had obtained the Pope's promise,

Edw. II. mise, that the Excommunication and Interdict should both be taken off; for we find by the rest of these Acts, that the Pope, instead of acting authoritatively and imperiously as before, P. 846. offered to be a Mediator between the two Kings, P. 860. and that he exhorted the King of *England* to the Peace.

Truce of 13 Years with Scotland. THE last Act we find in this Volume relating to *Scotland*, is the Truce of thirteen Years, which was made the 30th of *May*, 1323, at P. 1022. *Thorp* near *York*. In this Treaty the Title of P. 1030. King is not given to *Robert*; but that Prince's Ratification of it, dated the 7th of *June* following at *Berwick* upon *Tweed*, begins with these words, *Robert Bruce*, &c. and ends with these, *We* Robert *King of* Scotland *aforesaid*.

IT is plain from divers passages, that *Elizabeth*, *Robert Bruce*'s Wife, was detained Prisoner in *England*, from the beginning of *Edward*'s Reign, till *July* 1314 at least, as appears from several Orders made for removing her from one Prison to another, till at last in *July* 1314, *Edward* caused her to be brought before him at P. 489. *York*. This was done in all likelihood to restore her to her Husband, for there is no mention of her afterwards. It seems that *Edward* allowed her but twenty Shillings a Week for her Maintenance, as appears by his Warrant di- P. 385. rected to the Sheriff of *Somerset* and *Dorset*, and dated at *Windsor* in *February* 1313, when she was a Prisoner at *Shaftsbury*.

THE Countess *Isabella*, Wife to *John* Earl of *Boghan*, whom *Edward* I. had confined in a Cage for assisting at the Coronation of *Robert Bruce*, was delivered out of it by *Edward* II. and committed to the Custody of *Henry de Beaumont*, by virtue of the King's Warrant, dated *April* 28,

28, 1313. at *Westminster*, and directed to the Constable of *Berwick Castle*. A. 1313. P. 401.

Article III. *Affairs Ecclesiastical.*

KING *Edward* II. had not those notable Disputes with the Court of *Rome*, which were the occasion of so much Disturbance in *England*, during the Reigns of King *Henry* II. and King *John*; but there was the same Cause for a Quarrel with that Court in this Reign, as in theirs. Tho' the two Kings I have now mentioned were brought under subjection to the Popes, one may venture to say that the Kingdom of *England* was not, but always preserved its Prerogatives without ever abandoning them; and the several Accommodations that were made between the Popes of *Rome* and the Kings of *England*, were never approved by the Kingdom, and by consequence the *English* always kept up their Pretensions: which will not seem strange to those who know the Constitution of the *English* Government. It is certain that the Parliament never failed to defend the Rights both of the Laity and Clergy, upon all occasions that offered; and if they did not act always with the same Vigor, it was because the *English*, when they lost their King, *John*, had the misfortune to fall into a weak and impotent Reign, under a King who was a Minor at first in Age, and always in Understanding, and who ran headlong, as one may say, into the Pope's Clutches, instead of making any Efforts to stop what the *English* looked upon as Usurpations of the Court of *Rome*. The King I mean was *Henry* III. His Successor *Edward* I. having been both an Eye-Witness, and an Agent in the Troubles which had disturbed the Reign of his Father, was

Edw. II. was afraid of renewing them, by giving a handle to the Popes to meddle with the Affairs of his Kingdom, and to ſupport the Malecontents. It may be ſaid therefore that the Controverſies between the *Engliſh* and the Court of *Rome*, were rather huſhed than determined by that ſcandalous Accommodation which King *John* made with Pope *Innocent*; and that neither the Lords nor Commons did in the leaſt imagine that their Rights were forfeited by the ſuperior Force which obliged *John* to take that ſtep, or by the Complaiſance of *Henry* III. for the Pope, or by the Moderation of *Edward* I. Nor did they fail upon proper occaſions to make the Court of *Rome* ſenſible that they were not in a humour to ſuffer themſelves to be robbed of their Privileges, tho' in good truth the Oppoſition which they made to the Enterprizes of that Court from time to time ſeemed to be rather a precaution to avoid Preſcription, than a formal Reſiſtance: which made the Popes always gain ground.

Incroachments of the Court of Rome.

THIS was the ſtate of Affairs when *Edward* II. came to the Crown. The Popes undertook from time to time to confer Benefices, and even Biſhopricks, contrary to the Right of Patrons and Chapters, and very ſeldom troubled themſelves to ask the Conſent of the King, who inſiſted nevertheleſs that his Approbation was neceſſary, before a Biſhop could be put in poſſeſſion of the Temporalities. The Popes cited Clergymen to their Court, in ſpite of the King's Prohibition, and would not ſuffer them to be tried by the Laity, notwithſtanding all the Proteſtations that both the King and Parliament could make upon that Head. They frequently ſent over Nuncios and Legates veſted with ſuch a prodigious ſhare of Power, as ſwallowed up all the Authority of the two Archbiſhops. This is not

not a place to examine which of the two had Right on their side, whether the Pope or the *English*; it being sufficient to observe here, that it was a perpetual subject of Disputes and Quarrels between *England* and the Court of *Rome*. But the Court of *Rome* had a great advantage over the other, in that it acted always uniformly and consistently; whereas *England* being governed by Rulers whose Interests were sometimes different from those of the State, was always a Loser by the Cowardice, by the Complaisance, and sometimes by the private Interests of its King. This is a general View of the Subject of the Acts of this Volume, which relate to the Affairs of the Church, out of which I shall only select three Articles, upon which this Volume furnishes some Particulars. 1. The Disposal of Benefices. 2. Ecclesiastical Jurisdiction. 3. Personal Citations to the Court of *Rome*, or before the Pope's Delegates. *A.* 1313.

As to the Disposal of Benefices, this Collection abounds with Complaints made by the Kings of *England* upon this Article, setting forth that the Popes very often injured the Rights, not only of private Patrons, but of the King himself. The Popes on their part were no less persuaded that they had an extraordinary Right to the disposal of Benefices, when the good of the Church required it, of which they pretended to be the sole Judges. And as if this had not been a reason sufficient, they did not fail to back their Pretension with other Pleas, which seemed rather to hurt their Cause than strengthen it.

Popes Presentations to Benefices, in violation of the Rights of Patronage, &c.

FOR Example, They had made a Decree, that when a Bishop happened to die at their Court, it was their Prerogative to dispose of the vacant See. And it was upon this Foundation

Edw. II. dation that *Clement* V. disposed of the Archbishoprick of *Armagh* in *Ireland*. In like manner

P. 13. when a Bishop resigned his Bishoprick to the Pope, the latter never failed to fill the See vacant by such Resignation, as that very Pope

P. 273. did in the case of the Archbishoprick of *Dublin*. Sometimes the Pope reserved to himself beforehand, the disposal of a Bishoprick when it should come to be vacant. Thus *Clement* disposed of the Archbishoprick of *Canterbury* in favour of *Walter Raynold* Bishop of *Worcester*, tho' the Prior and Chapter had canonically elected *Thomas Cobbam*, a Prebendary of *York*, whose Elec-

P. 439. tion was therefore made void. *Non personæ dicti Thomæ vitio*, said the Pope, *sed utpote post Reformationem, & Decretum prædicta attemptatam*, i. e. Not for any personal Fault in the said *Thomas*, but because it was undertaken after the Reform and Decree aforesaid.

As to inferior Benefices, the Popes never wanted a Pretext to confer them, and often produced no other reason for it, but their own Will and Pleasure; which raised a great Clamour among the Patrons who had the Right of Presentation. Besides the Pretences just now mentioned, that of the Vacancy of the See on which the vacant Benefices depended, was one of the chief; and forasmuch as the See was looked upon to be vacant till the Pope had confirmed the Person elected, there was often a great Interval of Time between the Death of a Bishop, and the Confirmation of his Successor, which gave the Pope an opportunity to confer the Benefices that happened to become vacant in such Bishoprick, on whom he thought fit.

BUT

BUT what most of all provoked the *English* was, to see that very often the Pope gratified Foreigners * with those Benefices, sometimes Cardinals, or others who sucked the Revenues thereof

A. 1313. *Benefices given by the Popes to Aliens.*

* BY an Inquisition taken of this matter in 1253, it appeared that the Ecclesiastical Revenues in *England* enjoyed by Aliens, of whom many were Boys, and more Dunces, amounted to no less than 70000 Marks a Year, which was then reckoned a greater Revenue than that of the King; which occasioned the sharp Letter of *Robert Grosthead* to the Pope, and the Pope's disdainful Reception of it, related at large by *Matt. Paris.*

AT a Parliament held *Anno* 1379. (*Rot. Parl. Ang.* 3 *Rich.* II.) great Complaint was made of Foreigners holding Ecclesiastical Benefices; many Cardinals at *Rome* having the best Promotions, and Livings conferred on them, or granted to hold in *Commendam*, of which there are Catalogues yet extant. (Acts and Monum. *Tom.* 1. *f.* 389.) And from hence many Mischiefs arose; as little or no Divine Service, or Instruction of the People: No Hospitality kept for relief of the Poor: Decay of Houses, and Increase of Barbarism; so that between the *Italian* Hospitality, which none could ever see, and a little *Latin* Service, which few, or none could understand, the poor *English* were ill fed, but worse taught: And lastly, the exhausting the Wealth of the Land, to the impoverishing of the People, and weakning of the King and Kingdom, in case of Invasion or any Attempts against them.

IT is memorable also, that in the Reigns of *Henry* VII. and VIII. the Bishoprick of *Worcester* had four *Italians* successively that never lived there, whose Names we find in *Godwin de Præsulibus Angliæ.* And such prevalence had the Popes and Cardinals in this matter, that once K. *Edward* I. having promised the Cardinal Bishop of *Sabine*, at his Instance, to present one *Nivianus* an *Italian*, his Chamberlain, to a Benefice in *Lincolnshire*, then in his Gift by the Death of another *Italian*, the Pope's Chaplain, and forgetting his Promise, presented his own Clerk to it; but being reminded of his Promise, he revoked his first Presentation in favour of *Nivianus*, as appears by his Patent for that Purpose, still preserved among our Records (Pat. 25. E. I. m. 16. *De Præsentatione pro M. Antonio de Niviano.*) Matt. Paris *An.* 1240. *f.* 540. says, that

Edw. II. thereof without exercising the Functions, and who moreover perpetually plagued those who had a dependance upon them, by the Credit which they had with the Pope, and by Citations and Appeals to his Court. For Example, the Deanery of *St. Paul's* in *London* was conferred by the Pope upon the Cardinal *de St. Marcel*, Archbishop of *Bourdeaux*, tho' it is a Benefice which absolutely required Residence, as appears by several Reasons mentioned in a

P. 134. Letter here from King *Edward* to the said Cardinal, dated at *Westminster*, *May* 12, 1309, persuading him to relinquish it.

It had been no great matter if the Pope had only disposed of *some* Benefices from time to time contrary to the Right of Patrons; but this was not enough, he sometimes challenged the Disposal of *all*; of which we have two Examples in this Volume. The first is of *Clement* V. who

while *Rubeus* and *Ruffinus*, two of the Pope's Factors, were very busy in *England*, collecting Money for the Pope; one *Mumelinus* comes from *Rome* with 24 *Italians*, and Orders to admit them to so many of the best Benefices as should next become void; and that in the same Year, the Pope made an agreement with the People of *Rome*, that if they would effectually aid him against the Emperor *Frederic*, their Children should be put into all the vacant Benefices in *England*: And thereupon Orders were sent to the Archbishop of *Canterbury*, and the Bishops of *Lincoln* and *Salisbury*, to make provision for three hundred *Romans* Children, to be served of the next Benefices that should fall; which, says the Historian, so astonished all that heard it, that it was feared they would have been drowned in the Abyss of Despair. And this made such an impression on the Archbishop, being a tender Man, to see the Church in that manner wounded, and so much Evil in his Days, that he disposed of his Affairs, and retired into *France*, where bewailing the deplorable state of his Country, he died not long after of Grief at *Pontiniac*. See *Godwin*, in this Archbishop's Life.

gave

gave all the vacant Benefices in the Province of *York* to Cardinal *Ademar*, who had the Title of St. *Anastasius*, on pretence of enabling him to support his Dignity; and not long after, he likewise gave him all those that became vacant in the Province of *Canterbury*: and because the King had conferred two Prebends out of the number of those Benefices so given by the Pope, and because the Cardinal had been summoned to Parliament, Pope *Clement* * wrote a very sharp Letter to the King in *November* 1311, from *Avignon*, wherein he calls the two Incumbents *Sons of Perdition*; and complains that it was a palpable Affront to God to hinder the said Cardinal from enjoying their Revenues. *A.* 1311. P. 284.

POPE *John* XXII. † went farther still; it was not enough for him to dispose of Benefices when vacant, but he aimed at the disposal of those that were not vacant, by revoking all the Dispensations granted by his Predecessors, for holding a Plurality of Benefices, and reserving to the Holy See the Disposal of such as should become vacant by such Revocation. Upon this, King *Edward* in a Letter dated from *Windsor* *January* 10, 1318. and signed by the King and Council, wrote so sharply to the Pope, that it is very probable the Pope let the Affair drop; at

* THIS Pope was swallowed up in sensual Pleasures, and so insolent, that he made *Francis Dandalo* a Noble *Venetian*, who had offended him by his Fidelity to the Republic, lie under his Table like a Dog. This was the Pope that condemned the Knights Templars, and removed the See to *Avignon*, where it continued seventy Years, and was for that reason called by the *Italians* the *Babylonish* Captivity.

† HE was Son to a Shoemaker, but a Man of great Wit and Learning; and when he died, which was in the 19th Year of his Reign, he left a greater Treasure behind him than any of his Predecessors. See *Platina*, *Atlas Histor.* and *Geog.*

Edw. II. least we hear no more of it in this Collection.

It would be too tedious to set down all the Examples which this third Volume is capable of furnishing upon the present Head; yet I must not forget to observe that the Pope never conferred a Bishoprick under any of those Pretexts I have mentioned, but the King opposed him vigorously to outward appearance, tho' I do not know one single Instance of his carrying his Point: so that after having made a great Outcry, and wrote Letters upon Letters to the Pope, or to the Bishop nominated, he was forced at last to truckle to the Pope's Authority. The whole Collection swarms with Complaints of this nature. It was *Edward* II. if I am not mistaken, who, when he could no longer refuse admission to a Bishop presented by the Pope, was the first that hit upon the expedient of obliging the Pope's Nominee to sign an Act before a Notary Public, by which he renounced the Clause in the Bull that assigned the Bishoprick to him, and owned that he held the same merely of the King's Favour. Of this we have many Instances in the present Volume, in the Case of the Archbishops of *Canterbury*, *Dublin*, *Armagh*, and the Bishop of *Winchester*. But the Pope, who would not seem to know any thing of these Renunciations, still continued to put the Clause in his Bulls.

P. 465, 273, 13, and 827.

Ecclesiastical Jurisdiction.

The second Article which relates to *Ecclesiastical Jurisdiction*, may be considered with respect to the inferior Clergy, or with regard to Bishops. As to the inferior Clergy, it does not appear that *Rome* acted with so much Vigor to maintain the Jurisdiction of the Ecclesiastical Court, as the Magistrates of *England* did to support the Rights of the Kingdom. The reason

ſon of it was, becauſe that on thoſe occaſions the Pope had to do with the Officers of Juſtice, who could not excuſe themſelves from executing the Laws of the Realm made in Parliament, without running a riſque of being puniſhed for their Negligence; whereas in the caſe of Biſhops, the Pope had only to deal with the King, who was not under thoſe Reſtraints of Fear. And we find that the Court of *Rome* was never backward to hinder Biſhops from pleading in the Temporal Courts. Of this we have ſome remarkable Inſtances in the preſent Reign, in the caſe of the *Scots* Biſhops of *Glaſgow* and *St. Andrews*, who being taken in Arms by *Edward* I. were detained in Priſon till *Edward* II. after having ſtood out againſt the Pope's Remonſtrances a long time, was obliged to ſet them at Liberty. The ſame thing happened in the Affair of the Biſhop of *Litchfield*, High Treaſurer in the Reign of *Edward* I. whom *Edward* II. had impriſoned for Miſdemeanor; which tho' it was a Crime within the Cogniſance of the Temporal Court, yet *Clement* V. pretended that the ſaid Biſhop could not be detained in the King's Priſons by reaſon of his Character, and at laſt obliged *Edward* to releaſe him.

A. 1292.

P. 73, 98, 118, 121, *&c.* and 710.

Citations to the See of Rome.

As to the third Article, *viz.* * Perſonal Citations to the Court of *Rome*, or before Judges delegated by the Pope, the *Engliſh* Magiſtrates ſpared no Pains to ſtop the abuſe thereof; but do what they could, they were not able to influence the Clergy, who from the Motives of Religion, or other Views, choſe to

* THIS and the foregoing Article are amply diſcuſſed by that great Oracle of Law and Divinity, Father *Paul* the *Venetian*, in one of his excellent Treatiſes, intituled, *The Rights of Sovereigns.*

Edw. II. obey the Command of the Pope, rather than the Laws of the Realm. This proved to be a Bone of perpetual Contention betwixt the two Courts; and in this Collection we find a great many Letters from the King to the Pope upon this Subject, with orders to the Archbishops not to admit of such Citations. *Nos volentes*, says *Edward* in a Letter from *Ely*, dated *Nov.* 3. 1314. to the Archbishops, *&c. hujusmodi dispendio & præjudicio, remedio quo poterimus obviare, & omnes jura coronæ nostræ impugnantium conatus illicitos refrænare, vobis omnibus & singulis mandamus, firmiter injungendo, ne prætextu alicujus Commissionis, aut Mandati vobis, aut alicui vestrum, per quemcumque facti, vel fiendi, quicquam in hac parte, per citationes, vel inductiones, aut alio quovis modo, nobis inconsultis, facere præsumatis*; i. e. We being inclined to obviate all Loss and Damage of that nature, by whatsoever Remedy is in our power, and to check all the illegal Attempts of those who impugn the Rights of our Crown, do command and firmly injoin all and every one of you, that under colour of any Commission or Mandate, given or to be given, to you or any of you by any one whatsoever, ye do not presume to do any thing in this Case by Citations or Persuasion, or by any other means whatsoever, without advising with us. We find also that the Parliament which was held at *Stamford* in *August* 1309, ordered a vigorous Letter to be written to the Pope to complain of these Grievances.

King's Letter to the Archbishops, &c. against them. P. 500.

Parliament's Letter to the Pope. P. 159.

It was plain that the Court of *Rome* gave little or no regard to all the King was able to say or write. This Prince, who thought he stood in need of the Pope, did not reckon it good Policy to push things too far; of which that Court was very sensible, and made an advantage,

vantage. But whenever the Parliament interfered, they were more upon the reserve, and paid greater respect to that Body than to the King. Therefore *Edward*, who perceived the Difference, often relied much upon the Credit of the Parliament, that his Instances might have the greater weight and effect; of which we have divers Instances in this Collection of Records. *Edward* writing to a certain Cardinal from *York*, *Oct.* 1. 1316, tells him, *Quod si nos nollemus facere, illas defenderet Communitas Regni nostri, ut jus nostrum hæreditarium ac nostræ Regiæ dignitatis:* i. e. Which, if we refused to do, the Commons of our Realm would defend them, as our Hereditary Right and Royal Dignity. And upon another occasion, the King writing to the Pope himself from *Newcastle* upon *Tine*, *August* 3, 1322, says, *Advertentes, si placet, quod, etsi dicti Clerici nostri a Jure, sibi in hac parte quæsito, seu Prosecutione ejusdem desistere vellent, nihilominus jus nostrum prædictum, in personis aliorum (vinculo juramenti prædicti Nos artante, & Magnatum Regni nostri Consilio perurgente, qui, etiam nobis dissimulantibus, toto Nisu contradicerent) prosequi cogeremur.* i. e. Considering, with submission, that altho' our said Clergy were inclined to depart from their Right in this Cause, or to desist from the Prosecution of it, yet should we be compelled to prosecute our Right aforesaid in the Persons of others, not only inasmuch as we are bound by our Oath aforesaid, but as we are strenuously urged to it by the advice of our Nobles, who, were we even to dissemble, would do their utmost to oppose it.

A. 1316. P. 573. P. 965.

As the *English* on the one hand complained of the Court of *Rome*, the latter on the other hand complained no less of the *English* Magistrates. We have a Letter from the Pope in P. 187.

No-

Edw. II. *November*, 1309. to the Bishop of *Worcester*, which enumerates all the Complaints of the Holy See against the King's Officers, or rather against the Laws of *England*, which ran counter to their Pretensions: but forasmuch as the Articles they relate to, are for the most part those which I have already glanced over, it is not material to insist upon them here; and therefore I dismiss them with this one Observation, that what the Pope was pleased to call the *Privileges and Immunities of the Church, the* English called the *Enterprizes and Usurpations of the Court of Rome*.

A MORE effectual Stand might have been made against the Pope perhaps in this Reign, if the King had but seconded his Parliament; but private Interests sometimes obliged this Prince not only to submit to the Pope's Pretensions, but also to corroborate them, by prompting him to exert his absolute Power. This he did in one particular Case, among many others, during the vacancy of the See of *Hereford*. The King had a mighty mind to place *Thomas Charlton* in that See; but being afraid that the Chapter would not elect him, he, by a Letter dated
P. 617. at *London*, *March* 28, 1317. desired the Pope to reserve to himself the disposal of that Bishoprick by the *Fullness of his Apostolick Power*; and having obtained his Request without much difficulty, he recommended *Charlton* to him. But hearing soon after, that the Pope had a Design to gratify *Adam Orleton* with the said Bishoprick, he desired him by a Letter from *Windsor* of *March* 30. following, not to place his Thoughts upon a Person so disagreeable to him; and assured *Or-*
P. 622. *leton* in a Letter from *Windsor* of *May* 30, that he
637. would never suffer him to be placed in that See.

THOSE

A. 1317.

Those who are ever so little acquainted with the History of this Century, know that the Period of Time, during which the Popes kept their See at *Avignon*, was not the most honourable for the Holy See. There is a Proof of the irregular Steps which the Court of *Rome* took at that time in a Letter from *Edward* II. dated at *Westminster*, *November* 22, 1317, and directed to the Cardinal St. *Cyriacus*; which sets forth, that when *Clement* V. conferred the Abbey of *Westminster* upon an Abbot named *Richard*, he exacted a Promise from him of six thousand Florins for himself, and another of two thousand for the Cardinals. P. 679.

Dispute between the Archbishops of Canterbury *and* York *about carrying the Cross.*

The Difference between the Archbishops of *Canterbury* and *York*, about carrying the Cross, still subsisted. The former pretended to the Right of having the Cross carried before him in the Province of *York*, but refused the same Privilege to the Archbishop of *York*, who had the same Pretension in the Province of *Canterbury*. This Quarrel was carried to such a height, that when both those Prelates happened to be in one and the same Province, which was always the case as often as the Parliament met, they were each attended by Guards. The King desires the Pope to make a Regulation for healing this Difference, by a Letter dated from *Nottingham*, *August* 6, 1317.

King's Letter about it to the Pope. P. 659.

The same Dispute in Ireland.

There was the very same Dispute betwixt the Archbishops of *Ireland*, as appears by a Letter to the King from the Archbishop of *Armagh* in the Year 1308, wherein he prayed his Majesty to excuse his attendance at the Synods which met in the Province of *Dublin*, and to give him leave to send his Proxy thither.

Article

Article IV. *Of the Knights Templars.*

History of the Knights Templars.

The Order of Templars was instituted in 1118, for defence of the holy Places of *Jerusalem*. Their first House being situate near the *Temple* of our Lord, gave occasion to their Name; and all the Houses which they liv'd in afterwards were call'd *Temples*. This Order was confirm'd in the Council of *Troyes* in 1127, according to Rules given by *St. Bernard*. The Fryars, or Brethren of this Order were divided into two Classes, one of Knights, and the other of Servitors.

After *Saladine* had conquer'd the Kingdom of *Jerusalem* from the Christians, this Order dispers'd itself into most parts of *Europe*, where it became very potent, and acquir'd vast Riches*, through the Liberality of the People, and the Bounty of Sovereign Princes, who had a high Esteem for the Virtues which were practis'd by these Fryars: but Riches made them as proud as they were before humble, and alter'd that exemplary Life of Piety which they led at first, to one that was execrably vicious; which render'd them odious.

The Author of their Ruin was *Philip the Fair*, King of *France*, to be revenged for a Tumult which some of them had rais'd in *Paris*. He had a Conference for this end with Pope *Clement* V. at *Poictiers*, where the entire Destruction of the whole Order was resolv'd on.

* *Matthew Paris* says they had 9000 rich Convents, tho' at first they lived upon Alms. Others say they had their subordinate Governors in all the Provinces of *Europe*, and no less than 16000 Lordships; the Greatness of which Revenue was not the least Cause of dissolving the Order.

Some

Some profligate Fellows, who were themselves Members of that Body, whether they did it of their own accord, or whether they were bribed to it by the *French* King, charged the whole Order with the grossest Crimes: whereupon *Philip* caused all of them who were in his Dominions to be apprehended, and fifty-seven of them to be burnt; but thinking this Revenge not severe enough, he proceeded to abolish the Order: and the Pope, who had engaged himself to favour the design, called a general Council at *Vienne*, in which the said Order was laid under an Interdict. *A.* 1307.

FORASMUCH as *England* was not a little affected by the Proceedings against the Knights Templars, because of the great Estates they possessed in that Kingdom, we find a great number of Acts upon the subject in this Collection, the chief of which we will just run over.

THE first Piece is an Answer from *Edward*, P. 18. dated at *Westminster*, *Oct.* 30, 1307, to *Philip the Fair*, wherein he tells him, that he can scarce give credit to that part of his Letter relating to the *abominable Heresy* spread in *Guienne*; but that he has ordered the Seneschal of *Agen* to inform himself of that Affair more particularly. Altho' the Templars are not so much as mentioned in this Letter, yet it is probable they were the Persons intended.

Pope's Letter to Edward about the Knights Templars.

AFTER this we have a Brief from Pope *Clement* to King *Edward*, dated *Nov.* 30, following, at *Poictiers*; in which he set forth, That upon Information given to the King of *France*, that the Templars, at their entrance into that Order, denied Jesus Christ, spit at a P. 30. Crucifix, worshipped an Idol in their Chapters, and committed other enormous Crimes, as the Grand Master himself had confessed; the said Prince

Edw. II. Prince had in one day caused all those in his Dominions to be apprehended, and all their Estates to be confiscated, in order to apply the same to the Service of the Holy War, if those Crimes were proved. He adds, that upon these Informations, of which *Philip* had given him an account, he had himself examined one of the Knights *magnæ generositatis & auctoritatis Virum*, a Man of great Generosity and Authority; who confessed that he himself had denied Christ as aforesaid, and that he had seen it done by another in the Isle of *Cyprus*, at the command of the Grand Master, in presence of above two hundred Brothers of the Order, of whom a hundred were Knights: And the Pope concludes with exhorting King *Edward* to follow the Example of the King of *France*.

King's Letters on the same Subject. *P.* 35. THERE'S a Letter from King *Edward* at *Reading*, *December* 4, 1307, to the Kings of *Castille*, *Arragon*, *Portugal* and *Sicily*, importing that a certain Clergyman came to him, who accused the Knights Templars of the most horrid Crimes, but that he could not give credit to it; and therefore he exhorts them to suspend their Judgment, if such an Accusation came before them. *P.* 37. And he sent another Letter to the Pope on the same Subject, dated at *Westminster* the 10th of the same Month, to vindicate the Templars, who, says he, bear a good Reputation in *England*. *P.* 34. And there is an Order placed in the *Fœdera* before those two Letters, enjoining all the Sheriffs to arrest all the Templars in the Kingdom upon the Feast of *Epiphany*, in 1308; which Order, tho' there is no date to it, *P.* 45. is signified in two Letters from the King, dated at *Byfleet*, *December* 20, 1307, and directed, the one to his Chief Justice and Treasurer

surer in *Ireland*, the other to the Lords of the Manors and Bailywicks in *Wales*. *A.* 1308.

IN pursuance of this Order, all the Templars in *England* were apprehended upon that day, and their Possessions seized into the King's hands. *Their Persons and Estates seized.*

AFTER this came a Bull from the Pope, dated at *Poictiers* in *August* 1308, and directed to the Archbishop of *Canterbury* and his Suffragans, to let them know what had been done with respect to the Templars: He there repeats almost the very same Facts which he had mentioned to the King, with this addition only, that he had caused seventy-two Knights and other Brethren of the Order to be examined by the Cardinals; who, after very strict Interrogatories, had reported to him, that the Persons accused had owned the Crimes with which they were charged, *viz.* the denying of Jesus Christ, and the spitting at the Crucifix; and that some of them had confessed Crimes which he was ashamed to mention. Then he tells them, that he has appointed a Committee of three Cardinals, four *English* Bishops, and certain Clergymen of *France*, to draw up the Informations, and to manage the whole Process that was to be carried on in *England* against the Templars. *Pope's Bull about 'em.* *P.* 101.

WHEN these Commissioners were arrived, the King expresly ordered the *English* Bishops of the Committee to attend every day at all the Proceedings, as appears by an Order he sent to the Bishop of *Lincoln*, dated at *Westminster*, *Sept.* 13, 1309, for fear, no doubt, of some Knavery on the part of the *Italians* and *French*. *P.* 168.

'TIS remarkable, that in all the Orders which this King granted to facilitate those Informations, we always meet with this Clause, *ob re-*

veren-

Edw. II. *verentiam sedis Apostolicæ*, out of respect to the Apostolic See. Perhaps, as this Process was managed in the name of the Pope, the King was afraid lest it might be brought into a Precedent.

WHEN this Examination was finished, a National Council was assembled at *London*, wherein the Knights Templars were condemned; but they were not treated with the same Severity as in *France*, for they were only confined to Monasteries instead of the common Prisons, and had small Pensions paid them for their Subsistance.

And the Council at Vienne.

THE General Council at *Vienne*, which was summoned partly for the Condemnation of the Templars, met in the Year 1311; but their Sentence was not published till the second Session, which was held in *May* 1312. It is the common opinion, that it was the Council which condemned them; but I think it safer to follow the opinion of those Historians, who seem to know more of the matter, and have asserted, that the Council did not think it just to abolish a whole Order for the Crimes of some of its Members; especially considering the Templars had been neither convicted, nor so much as summoned before the Council. These same Historians add, that the Fathers of the Council being intimidated, by the Presence of the Pope, who presided in Person, and of the King of *France*, who came to the second Session, did not dare to oppose the Bull of Condemnation, when read in their presence. 'Tis true, that in a following Bull from the Pope in this Collection, dated from *Vienne* in *May* 1312, *Clement* affirms, that the Council approved of what had been done in that affair; but it appears likewise in the very same Bull, that

P. 323.

A. 1312.

that becaufe the Proceedings againft the Templars had not been altogether according to the Forms of the Law, he could not intirely abolifh that Order, and that all he could do was to interdict it for ever. Thefe are his words, *Ejufdemque Ordinis ftatum, habitum atque nomen*——*Sacro approbante Concilio*, NON PER MODUM DIFFINITIVÆ SENTENTIÆ, *cum eam fuper hoc fecundum inquifitiones, & proceffus, fuper hiis habitos*, NON POSSEMUS FERRE DE JURE; SED PER VIAM PROVISIONIS, SEU ORDINATIONIS APOSTOLICÆ, *irrefragabili, & perpetuâ valiturâ fuftulimus fanctione; ipfum prohibitioni perpetuæ fupponentes. Univerfa etiam bona Ordinis prælibati, Apoftolicæ fedis ordinationi & difpofitione, auctoritate Apoftolicâ duximus refervanda.* i. e. We have by a Sanction irrefragable, which will for ever have Force, taken away the State, Habit, and Name of the faid Order, with the Approbation of the Sacred Council, *not by means of a definitive Sentence*, fince according to the Examinations taken, and Procefs made againft them, *we could not pafs fuch Sentence in Law, but by way of Apoftolical Precaution or Ordination*; fubjecting the fame under a perpetual Interdict. Alfo we have thought it fitting that all the Eftates of the faid Order be referv'd by Apoftolical Authority, to the ordering and difpofal of the Apoftolical See.

IT appears from hence, that tho' the Pope rely'd upon the Authority of the Council, yet he acted in his own Name, by virtue of his Apoftolical Authority. And we may venture to fay, that the Approbation of the Council mention'd by the Pope, feems very confiftent with the Explication we have of it from the Hiftorians; for it is not at all likely that Perfons chofe for Judges, in an Affair of fuch Confequence, fhould approve of a Sentence which they themfelves did not dare to pronounce. Befides, it is

Edw. II. very probable, that since the Pope had assembled that Council, principally for the Condemnation of the Templars, he would gladly have left that Work to the Council, if he had found that disposition in it which he wish'd for.

In the same Bull that I have just now quoted, the Pope declar'd that after having reserv'd the disposal of the Templars Estates to the Holy See, he had for a long time consulted with the Cardinals, Patriarchs, Archbishops, Bishops, Prelates, and others who were at *the Council* aforesaid; and that at length he had thought fit to assign those Estates to the Order of *St. John* of *Jerusalem*, by the Fulness of his Apostolical Power. Nevertheless he excepted the Estates which were situate in *Castile*, *Arragon*, *Portugal*, and the Isle of *Majorca*, still reserving the future disposal thereof to himself. Observe by the way, that he does not say it was a Resolution of the Council itself, but only that he had taken the Advice of those who were present at it. He added the Pains of Excommunication against all who detain'd the said Estates, and refus'd to deliver them to the Order of *St. John*, within a Month after the first Call.

P. 326. This Bull was follow'd in the next Month by a Letter to King *Edward*, exhorting him to submit to the said Disposition, and enjoining all the Earls and Barons of the Kingdom to deliver up the Templars Estates, which were in their Possession, to the Knights of *St. John*.

When *Edward* had contributed so readily to the Ruin of the Templars, he hoped to come in for his share of their Spoil, and had already degan to dispose of it; so that he was not a little surpriz'd, when he heard that he should be compell'd to quit his Hold. The Pope's Letter arriv'd

arrived at a time when that Prince was more A. 1313.
than ordinarily embarrass'd by domestic Quarrels; that is to say, very soon after the Death of *Gaveston*: yet he maintain'd himself in the possession of those Estates till the end of the Year 1313. But at last, the Prior of the Order of St. *John* in *England*, being furnish'd with a Letter of Attorney from the Grand Master, having presented a Petition to him upon this Subject, he did not dare to stand it out any longer, and granted him the Replevy of the Templars Estates that were in his power. Mean time being persuaded that great Injustice was done him, he made a Protestation before a Notary, in *December* 1313, in which he declared that the only reason of his dispossessing himself of those Estates, was the Fear of the Danger to which he should expose himself if he refus'd it; considering the short space of Time which the Bull gave him, according to a Clause the Prior had taken care to insert in his Petition. But he protested, that this should not be any Prejudice either to his own Rights, or those of his Subjects, which he reserv'd to himself to make the best of in due time.

THE *English*, who had received some part of those Estates from the King's Bounty, or who perhaps had purchas'd them, were very loth to obey; and we find some of them so long possessed of those Estates, as till the Year 1322, which was the occasion of a very severe Complaint made to King *Edward* that Year by Pope P. 956.
John XXII. in a Bull dated at *Avignon*, in the Month of *June*.

THOSE People thought themselves upon sure Ground, because the Parliament had not given their Consent to the King's Grant of the said Estates, which according to the Laws of the

 Realm,

Edw. II. Realm, ought to have been confiſcated to the Crown, and not to the Pope, or in favour of the Order of St. *John*. It ſeems alſo that the Knights of this Order were afraid, that ſooner or later the Parliament would bring this Queſtion upon the Stage; and therefore they preſſed the Pope not to let the King reſt till he had obtain'd his Parliament's Conſent to what had been done. And we find in the next Volume, that in the Year 1324, *Edward* wrote a Letter to the Pope dated at *Weſtminſter* the firſt of *April*, ſignifying that the Affair had been mov'd in Parliament, and that he hoped that the Order of St. *John* would remain in poſſeſſion of the Templars Eſtates *.

P. 46. in Vol. 4.

Thus you have what is moſt remarkable in this third Volume of the *Fœdera*, relating to the four general Articles, under which I endeavour'd to range the principal Affairs. There is a vaſt number of other Pieces upon Subjects that have no relation to theſe four Articles, to give an account of which would exceed our Bounds;

* The Curious who would know more of the original Rule and Nature of both theſe Orders, may conſult *Dugdale* of *Warwickſhire*, *Henry de Knighton's* Collection, *Thomas Walſingham's* Hiſtory, and *Stow's* Survey. As for the *Hoſpitallers*, or Knights of St. *John* of *Jeruſalem*, we ſhall find hereafter that King *Henry* VIII. diſſolv'd them, and ſeiz'd their Lands; that Queen *Mary* replac'd them in their ſhatter'd Manſion at *Clerkenwell*; and that Sir *Thomas Treſham*, who was made Prior of the Order, was call'd up by Writ to the Houſe of Lords as a Baron; but that they were finally diſſolv'd by Q. *Elizabeth*. It is ſaid that the Temple at *London* was antiently the chief Houſe of the Knights of this Order in *England*, and by them demiſed to ſome Students of the Law who came from *Thavies* Inn, for the yearly Rent of 10*l*. about the middle of the Reign of *Edward* III. and that the Lawyers held as Tenants to the ſaid Hoſpitallers till their Diſſolution by *Henry* VIII.

and

and therefore I ſhall only mention two or three of them. *A.* 1320.

'TIS remarkable that *German* Notaries were made uſe of in *England*, till the time of *Edward* II. which ſeems very odd; becauſe after the Reign of *Honorius*, none of the Emperors ever had any Juriſdiction in this Kingdom. But this King made an Order in Council at *Weſtminſter*, *April* 26, 1320. for ſuppreſſing all thoſe *German* Notaries, and forbidding any regard to be had to the Deeds or Inſtruments which they ſhould paſs for the future.

German Notaries put down.

P. 829.

WE find alſo that in 1317, there were marry'd Clergy in *Guyenne*; which is prov'd by an Order of *Edward* II. dated at *York*, *Sept.* 16, to the Conſtable of *Bourdeaux*, to make them pay the Cuſtoms for Wine, notwithſtanding their Privileges, which they had abus'd by ſelling of other People's Wine in their own Names, to cheat the King of his Duty.

Marry'd Clergy turn Wine-Merchants.

P. 666.

IT may perhaps be thought ſtrange that the Count of *Savoy* was once a Vaſſal to the King of *England*, and that he ſhould pay him Homage for ſome Lands in *Chablais*, as we find in an Act dated by this King at *Woodſtock*, *June* 24, 1318. But it muſt be obſerv'd, that it was a very common Cuſtom in that and the preceding Centuries, for petty Princes to receive certain Penſions from the great ones, for which they bound themſelves to pay Homage; and that very often, in order that they might have a foundation for thoſe Penſions, they mortgaged ſome part of their Dominions, and paid Homage for them as long as the Penſions were continu'd. Which appears from ſeveral places in the three firſt Volumes of the *Fœdera*, and alſo in the fourth.

P. 715.

IT appears that *Edward* I. was not very punctual in paying the Pope the annual Tribute of

Edw. II. 1000 Marks, which was establish'd by King *John*, because *Clement* V. demanded of his Son P. 187, 632 fifteen years Arrears, by a Brief dated in *Nov.* 1309. We have the Pope's Acquittance for the said Tribute for the Year 1317, dated at *Avignon*; and another for the Year 1318: but the rest remain'd in Arrears, for we find in the next Volume that the Pope demanded thirty years Arrears of *Edward* III.

We come now to the IVth Volume of the *Fœdera*, which begins with the four last Years of the Reign of *Edward* II.

History of the Spensers. The death of the Earl of *Lancaster*, and the Severities exercis'd towards all his Adherents, of whom some were executed, others banish'd, and a great many depriv'd of their Estates, seem'd to have put the *Spensers* in a fair way of enjoying their Fortune peaceably, without fear of any body's presuming more to oppose their Power. They wanted nothing now to make themselves perfectly easy, but to get some People out of the way, whom they look'd upon as private Enemies; and among these the Bishop of *Bishop of* Hereford, *and* Mortimer. *Hereford*, and young *Mortimer*, who was actually a Prisoner in the *Tower*. These were nevertheless still so formidable to the *Spensers*, that when they had contriv'd to ruin them, though their Credit was so great, they met with such opposition as they did not expect. The Bishop, whom they had charged with High Treason, was wrested from the King's Judges with a sort of violence by the Archbishops of *Canterbury* and *Dublin*, on pretence that a Lay-Court had no Power to judge him. This Action stopp'd some Prosecutions that were actually begun, and some that were intended against other Bishops who were in the same Circumstances; and the Affair was brought before the Parliament.

MOR-

MORTIMER indeed was more eaſy to become at, becauſe he had no Character to ſcreen him; and therefore he was try'd, and condemn'd to death, but the King changed that Sentence into perpetual Impriſonment. Not long after, this very *Mortimer*, tho' a cloſe Priſoner, laid a Plot to ſeize the *Tower*, and the Caſtles of *Windſor* and *Wallingford:* but his Conſpiracy being diſcover'd, he had the ſame Sentence paſs'd upon him again, and the King was ſo gracious as to give him his Life once more. If it be conſider'd that this Man had for his Enemies the two *Spenſers*, to whom (as was before obſerved) he had done as much Damage as amounted to 60,000 *l. Sterling*, it will not be diſputed that he had a very powerful Protection, ſince it was able to counterballance the Intereſt of two ſuch Favourites. This gives room to conjecture, that it was the Queen (*Iſabella* of *France*) who reſcued him from the Revenge of thoſe two potent Enemies. And what fortifies the conjecture, is the Paſſion which the Queen diſcover'd for him afterwards; from whence it may be inferr'd, that their good Underſtanding commenced before *Mortimer* was committed to the *Tower*. To this it may be added, that it was much about the ſame time that the *Spenſers* began to mortify the Queen, by abridging her of part of the Money that was aſſign'd her for her Maintenance; which made her complain to her Brother, *Charles the Fair*, that ſhe was treated like a Servant-Maid. As it does not appear that the *Spenſers* had any other Reaſon to complain of this Princeſs, 'tis very probable the Vexation they gave her was only to be revenged for the Protection which ſhe had granted their Enemy: but it was a Revenge that coſt them very dear, and involv'd the King him-

A. 1323.

Edw. II. himself in their Destruction. *Mortimer* had not only the good Luck to escape the Doom that was awarded for him, but he soon after found means to convey himself out of the *Tower*, and fled for refuge to *France*, notwithstanding all the Diligence that was us'd to retake him. These few Particulars were necessary, just to shew the Man who afterwards acted so considerable a part on the Theatre of *England*. 'Tis time now to give the Substance of the Events of the four last Years of the Reign of *Edward* II. which concluded with his being depos'd. Some Differences which happen'd betwixt *France* and *England*, touching *Guyenne*, furnish'd a Pretence for the late Troubles in *England*; but the Queen's Hatred of the *Spensers*, I will be bold to say, her Passion for *Mortimer*, and the Thirst after Revenge in those whom the *Spensers* had persecuted, were the real Causes; which must be a little explain'd, for the better understanding of the Acts contain'd in the beginning of this fourth Volume.

Breach betwixt the French *and* English *in* Guyenne.

AFTER the Treaty of *Montreuil*, between *Edward* I. and *Philip the Fair*, *France* and *England* had a very good understanding together, till about the beginning of the Reign of *Charles the Fair*, when an Accident happen'd, which, tho' inconsiderable in itself, made a Breach in the Union of the two Crowns. At a Town in *Agenois*, call'd *St. Sardos*, some Outrage was committed (what it was, the *Fœdera* does not explain) and King *Edward*'s Officers neglecting to bring the Offenders to strict Justice, the Persons aggriev'd appeal'd for it to the King of *France*, as sovereign Lord of *Guyenne*. Upon the said Appeal *Charles* issued an Arret, condemning some Gentlemen of *Gascoigne*, who were *Edward*'s Subjects, to Banishment, and confiscating their

their Eſtates to the Crown of *France*, particularly the Caſtle of *Montpezat*, on which the Town of *St. Sardos* depended. To prevent the execution of this Arret, thoſe who commanded in *Guyenne* for King *Edward*, put a Garriſon in that Caſtle; which obliged the King of *France*, who was reſolv'd to go thorough ſtitch, to raiſe Troops in *Perigord*, and other neighbouring Places, in order to beſiege *Montpezat*. At the ſame time he ſent a Summons to *Edward*, to come and pay him Homage for *Guyenne*, and the County of *Ponthieu*. This was a very unlucky Buſineſs for the King of *England*, or rather for the *Spenſers*, who could not endure to hear of a War, becauſe the whole Kingdom was full of Malecontents. They reſolv'd therefore to ſend Ambaſſadors into *France*, to endeavour to put an end to this difference by way of Negotiation; but the Ambaſſadors were not heard. *Charles* being reſolv'd to ſtrike while the Iron was hot, ſent his Uncle, the Count *de Valois*, to command his Army in *Guyenne*, where he made himſelf Maſter of the Diſtrict of *Agenois*, and ſome other Counties. *Charles* not content with theſe Advantages, threaten'd *England* itſelf with an Invaſion; which gave the *Spenſers* a Pretext for depriving the Queen of the County of *Cornwal*, of which ſhe was in poſſeſſion: as if they had thought that County ran too great a riſque, by lying in her hands. It would be too tedious here to give the Particulars of all the Negotiations upon this Subject; of the Projects that were contriv'd, but ill executed, to relieve *Guyenne*; and of the little Reſiſtance that was made by the Earl of *Kent*, the King's Brother, who was ſent into that Country, to oppoſe the Progreſs of the Count *de Valois*: It will be ſufficient to obſerve, that *Edward* finding himſelf in no condition to carry

A. 1314.

Edw. II. carry on the War, was resolv'd, cost what it would, to put an end to the Difference by a Treaty. Therefore he dispatch'd the Bishop of *Norwich*, and the Earl of *Richmond*, into *France*, with the necessary full Powers, to make what Concessions soever they thought fit, with respect to the Difference in question. After King *Charles* had drill'd them on for some time, he signify'd to them by the Pope's Nuncios, That if the King of *England* would send his Queen to *Paris*, it was not to be doubted but she would obtain favourable Terms from the King her Brother. *Edward* accepted of the Proposal, and sent his Queen over to *France*, where she concluded a Treaty, importing in substance, That all *Guyenne* should be deliver'd up to the King of *France*; but that if *Edward* would come to *Beauvois*, and there do him Homage, then *Charles* out of love to his Sister, would restore that Province to the King of *England*, except the District of *Agenois*, and other late Conquests in that Country; as to which, *Edward* might form his Demands in the Court of Peers. *Edward* ratify'd this Treaty, and made Preparation to go and pay his Homage: but before the time stipulated by the Treaty was come, an Expedient was agreed on to excuse him from that ungrateful Drudgery; which was, that he should give up *Guyenne*, and the County of *Ponthieu*, to Prince *Edward* his Son, who was then thirteen Years of Age; and that *Charles* should receive the Son's Homage, and restore him those two Provinces, on the payment of 60000 Livres *Tournois*.

Treaty betwixt Edward *and* Charles *of* France.

EDWARD, without any hesitation, clos'd with an Expedient which suited well with his Inclination, and yielded those Lands to his Son, who set out immediately to pay his Homage for them. That was the fatal Term or Period of

that

that ſhort Calm which *Edward* enjoy'd, after he had ſubdued the Barons. As ſoon as the young Prince was got to *Paris*, the Queen his Mother, who, in all probability, had manag'd the whole Intrigue, that ſhe might have him under her own Wing, began almoſt openly to take Meaſures for putting the Deſigns ſhe had before concerted in execution. She held ſecret Councils, to which ſhe admitted none but *Mortimer*, and the other *Engliſh* Exiles, who had conſtant Acceſs to her; while the Biſhops of *Wincheſter* and *Exeter*, who were *Edward*'s Ambaſſadors, were excluded. At this time, ſo great were her Familiarities with *Mortimer*, and ſo little her Caution to conceal the Paſſion ſhe had for a Man whom ſhe ought to have baniſhed from her Preſence, as an Enemy to the King her Husband, that ſhe gave the whole Court of *France*, and eſpecially *Edward*'s Servants, reaſon to ſuſpect that not only ſome dangerous Conſpiracy, but ſomething yet more criminal, was carried on under the Cloak of their ſecret Conferences. The Biſhop of *Exeter* could not but be ſcandaliz'd to ſee it. He thought it was his Duty to inform the King his Maſter of it, as well as of the Suſpicions he had that ſome Miſchief was hatching againſt him; as it was eaſy to conjecture from the ſecret Conferences which the Queen held with the Exiles: and for this purpoſe he ſtole away from *Paris*, without taking his leave, in order to inform the King of all Paſſages. *Edward* had already begun to think it ſtrange, that the Queen ſhould make ſo many frivolous Pretexts to delay her Return, after he had wrote to her ſeveral times to come back, and bring her Son with her. And the Information he received from the Biſhop of *Exeter* oblig'd him to repeat his Orders, which were no better obey'd. At length, when *Iſabella* could form

A. 1326.

His Queen's Proceedings in France.

Edw. II. form no more Excuses upon the score of the Affairs that brought her to *Paris*, she sent word to *Edward* by the King her Brother, that she was not willing to expose her self any more to the ill Treatment of young *Spenser*, who hated her. Mean time her Friends in *England*, especially the Bishop of *Hereford*, endeavour'd to debauch the King's Subjects, and to form a Party, which in a short time became very considerable; and no wonder, considering how odious the *Spensers* were to the People, and how contemptible the King. The Queen, on her part, was no less industrious to gain Friends: She had got a Promise of considerable Assistance from (*William*) the Earl of *Hainault*, by granting young *Edward* in Marriage to *Philippa* that Earl's Daughter. When she had maturely concerted all her Measures, she left her Brother's Court, from whence it was pretended that she was expelled, and took the Road of *Hainault*, where she found Troops ready, the Command of which the Earl of *Hainault* gave to *John* his Brother, Lord of *Beaumont*, whom *Isabella* was glad to own for her Knight.

Her Invasion of England.

She embark'd with her Troops, and landed * in the County of *Suffolk*, where all her Friends came to join her, being headed by the Earl of *Kent*, the King's Brother, *Henry* Earl of *Lancaster*, Brother to him who was beheaded, the Bishops of *Lincoln* and *Hereford*, and many others, who brought her Forces, which they had mustered privately for that Occasion.

EDWARD flatter'd himself all along, that he should be able to lay this Storm, by the Letters which he wrote to the Pope, the Cardinals, the King of *France*, his Wife, and his Son; not considering, that while he tried those fruitless Reme-

* *At* Orewell, *near* Harwich, *on* Sept. 22, 1326. *See* *Dr.* Kennet's *History of* England.

dies,

dies, he gave the Queen and her Friends time to strengthen their Party. They had ſuch good Succeſs, that no body had the Courage or Inclination to declare for the King, when he went about to raiſe an Army to oppoſe the Invaſion. The cold Reception he met with, almoſt whereever he came, oblig'd that unhappy Prince to retire to the Weſtern Counties, where he hoped to find more Friendſhip. But the People of thoſe Parts were as diſaffected as their Countrymen; the Queen having given out every where, by her ſelf and her Friends, that ſhe only aim'd at the Favourites, for whom the People had no great Affection. When ſhe was at *Wallingford*, ſhe publiſh'd a Manifeſto to this very purpoſe, and continu'd her March to the Weſt, in purſuit of the King. In this Extremity, *Edward* being deſtitute of Friends, Troops and Money, reſolv'd at laſt to ſubmit to his ill Fortune; and having left *Spenſer* the Father in *Briſtol*, embarked on board a ſmall Veſſel, with a deſign to retire to *Ireland:* but the contrary Winds drove him on the Coaſt of *Wales*, where he was obliged to land, and not knowing which way to turn himſelf, lay hid for ſome time in the Abbey of *Neath*. Mean time the Queen came before *Briſtol*, which making no great Reſiſtance, *Spenſer* the Father was there taken, and hang'd without any of the Forms of Law, at the Age of fourſcore and ten *. The King being not to be found, and there being certain Advice that he was gone beyond Sea, the Lords who accompanied the Queen met at *Briſtol*, and named for Guardian, or Regent, of the Kingdom, young

A. 1326.

Edward *leaves the Kingdom.*

Old Spenſer *taken and hanged.*

* He was drawn and hanged in his Coat Armour, upon the common Gallows, ripp'd up before he was dead, and was beheaded and quarter'd. *Kennet*'s Hiſtory of *England*.

Edward,

Edw. II. Edward, who took upon him the Administration. This done, the Queen march'd to *Gloucester*, where she put forth a Proclamation, inviting the King her Husband to come and resume the Government; though according to all Appearance, and as the Sequel plainly demonstrated, she did not design he should. A Rumour being now spread, that the King lay hid in *Wales*, the Earl of *Lancaster* made such strict Search after him, that he found him; and having secured both him, and the Companions of his Fortune, *viz.* Young *Spenser*, *Buldock* * the Chancellor, and *Simon Reading*, he brought them to *Monmouth*. Upon this News the Queen went to *Hereford*, where she sent for *Spenser*, and caused him to be hanged on a Gallows fifty foot high †. Then she summon'd a grand Council, wherein it was resolved, That as the Commission of Guardian was expir'd by the King's Return, the Bishop of *Hereford* should be sent to the King, to demand the Great Seal, without which they who were then at the Helm could do nothing that was valid. *Edward* being a Prisoner, delivered it with a good Grace, and authorized his Wife and Son to make use of it as they should think proper, even in Affairs of meer Grace and Favour. As soon as the Queen had the Great Seal in her possession, she there-

The young one executed in like manner.

* Sir *Roger Baldock* was also Bishop of *Norwich*. He was committed first to the Bishop of *London*'s Prison, from whence he was pull'd out by the common People, to be carried to *Newgate*; but they beat him so cruelly by the way, that he died of his Bruises, in great Torment. *Walsingham's Chronicle.*

† He was at this time Earl of *Gloucester*, and hanged in his Coat Armour, with these Words writ on it, *Quid gloriaris in malitia?* Why boastest thou thy self in Mischief? *Psalm* 52. *Simon Reading* was hanged with him. *Daniel's History of Edward* II.

with

with seal'd all the Acts she thought necessary, in the King's Name, and especially an Order for calling the Parliament. This was one of the last Orders that was passed in the Name and by the Authority of the King, tho' he had no hand therein, and concludes the Acts of the fourth Volume of the *Fœdera*, so far as they relate to his Reign. There being a small Chasm in this Collection, between the Calling of the Parliament, and the Beginning of the Reign of *Edward* III. I shall just observe, for the sake of connecting the History, that the said Parliament, which met towards the End of *January*, 1327, resolved unanimously to depose *Edward* II. and to set his Son upon the Throne: which Resolution would have been executed without any other Formality, if the young Prince had not protested upon Oath, that he would never accept the Crown, without his Father's Consent. Upon this unexpected Resolution, the Parliament sent Deputies to *Kenelworth* (Castle, in *Warwickshire*) where the King was then in custody, to require him to resign the Crown; which the wretched state of his Affairs did not permit him to refuse. Nevertheless this Resignation passed for voluntary; and it was upon this Foundation that young *Edward*, who was but fourteen Years of Age, accepted the Offer of the Crown.

A. 1327.

P. 242.

King Edward's *Resignation to his Son.*

WE proceed now to those Acts of this fourth Volume, which relate to the Events abovementioned: but as it would be a Task too tedious, to undertake to shew the Usefulness of every one of those Acts in particular, I shall therefore only single out some of the most remarkable, by which one may judge of the Use that may be made of the others.

IN

Edw. II.

A Mistake of Mezeray, *about* Mortimer, *rectified.* P. 7, 8, 9.

IN the first place, we find several Orders here, dated in *August*, 1323. and issued by the King, at *Kirkham* and *Pickering*, for apprehending *Mortimer*, who escaped out of the *Tower*; which shew that *Mezeray* was mistaken, when he asserted that *Mortimer* made his Escape in 1325, and went to wait on (Queen) *Isabel* at *Paris*, since it appears, that he was there near two Years before her.

Hue and Cry against Roger Mortimer. P. 22.

THE next we come to, is a remarkable Piece, because it makes mention of *Mortimer*'s being twice pardon'd. It was issued by the King at *Nottingham*, *Nov.* 14, 1323. and has this Title, *De hutesio & clamore*, which undoubtedly is understood by very few. It is a Translation of the *English* Words *Hue and Cry* *, which come from the *French Huer* and *Crier*. The *English* have a way sometimes to find out lurking Criminals, which is practis'd no where else. The Constables, assisted by all the People of the Village or Parish, make strict search in the Houses and Fields, with great Cries, or *Huées*, which they call Hue and Cry, which is carried from Parish to Parish, till they come to the Sea side: and as no body can excuse themselves from assisting the Constables, who have Power to search every where, it is a very hard matter for the Malefactor to escape. Nevertheless *Mortimer* was not to be found, which shews he was already gone beyond Sea.

THE several Pieces we have in this Collection, relating to the Affair at *St. Sardos* (abovemention'd) make us perfectly acquainted with the Cause and Original of the Disputes between *England* and *France*; which no Historian that I

† SEE Sir *Thomas Smith*'s Commonwealth of *England*, cap. 23.

know

know of, either *French* or *English*, has clearly explain'd. *Mezeray* says, that the ground of the Quarrel betwixt the two Kings, was *Edward*'s refusing to assist at the Coronation of *Charles the Fair*, and the putting of a Garrison by the Seneschal of *Bourdeaux*, into a Castle which the Lord of *Montpezat* had built in the Territories of *France*. But the Historian was certainly mistaken in both; for in the first place, as to the Coronation, there is not a single Act in this Collection, tho' there are a great many upon the Subject, which makes the least mention of this first cause of Quarrel: but there is a full account of the Homage which *Edward* deferr'd, because he pretended that the Summons was not made in due form. As to the second Particular, he is as much out in that as in the other; for the Dispute was not about a Castle newly built, but about the Confiscation of *Montpezat*-Castle, on account of a thing that happen'd at *Sardos*, which was a Village that belong'd to it. This Affair is perfectly well explain'd in several Pieces that we find in this Collection, both in the Reigns of *Edward* II. and *Edward* III.

A. 1324. *Another Mistake of* Mezeray.

THERE's an Order from the King, dated *Sept.* 18. 1324, for taking the County of *Cornwal* into his own Possession again, because of the risque there was in leaving it in the hands of the Queen.

King's Order about the County of Cornwal. *P.* 84.

AND here we have a Letter from K. *Edward* to the Pope, dated *March* 8, 1325, at the *Tower* of *London*: which is a Piece the more remarkable, because it shews that the first Proposal of sending *Isabella* into *France* came from that Kingdom; that some eminent Members of King *Charles*'s Council open'd the Matter first to the Pope's Nuncio's; and that the latter propos'd the Expedient to the *English* Ambassadors: Whereupon

His Letter to the Pope about sending his Queen to France. *P.* 140.

Edw. II. on the Bishop of *Exeter* was dispatch'd into *England*, to make the Proposal.

The Treaty with the French King. P. 153.

THE Treaty which *Isabel* made with the King her Brother, is inserted here at large; a Treaty so disadvantageous to the King of *England*, that surely the *Spensers*, who govern'd him, were terribly afraid of a War, or else they would never have advis'd him to ratify it: for he not only engaged to deliver up all *Guyenne* to the King of *France*, without any other Security for the Restitution of it besides *Charles*'s bare word, a Security which his Father *Edward* did not like in the Case of *Philip the Fair*, but he also consented that *Charles* should keep the Territory of *Agenois*, only saving to himself the liberty of having his Right to it discuss'd in the Court of Peers: And finally, in case he should happen to carry his Cause in that Court, he engaged to pay a certain Sum towards the Charge of the War. By all which it is evident that *Isabel* was not very mindful of her Husband's Interests. This Treaty is dated *May* 31, 1325.

Queen's Conspiracy against her Husband.

QUEEN *Isabel*'s Conspiracy against her Husband has been, I may venture to say, but lamely explain'd by the Historians. It is perfectly surprizing to see this Queen, who had made no great figure in *England* before she went to *France*, return a Year after at the head of an Army, and dethrone the King her Husband, without any previous sign of her Intrigues. *Mezeray* only says, that her Brother *Charles* promis'd her Assistance against the *Spensers*: but that afterwards when he heard of her Conduct with *Mortimer*, he turn'd her out of his Dominions, and forbad his Subjects to assist her: Whereupon this desolate Queen took shelter in *Hainault*, where *John*, Brother to the Earl of that name, gave her a welcome Reception, de-

declared himself her Knight of Honour, and assembled 300 Knights to conduct her into *England*. This Collection gives abundance of light upon this head, and shews, if I am not deceiv'd, that this Conspiracy was form'd before the Queen went into *France*, and was carry'd on all the time she was at *Paris*. *A.* 1323.

I will not here repeat what I have already said, touching the Probability there is that her Correspondence with *Mortimer* began in the Year 1323, or sooner; and that it was owing to her Protection that the Life of that Man was sav'd, which brought upon her all the Uneasiness she suffer'd from the *Spensers*. This being premis'd, it may be inferr'd that the Queen herself was the Author of her Journey to the King her Brother, since it is evident, as we have already seen, that the first Proposal of it came from him. It is equally probable that it was the Queen who was the Contriver of the Expedient for the Cession of *Guyenne* and *Ponthieu* to her Son, for the use she made of it shews that she was very much concern'd to bring it about; whereas it could not be imagin'd what Advantage the same would have been to the King of *France*, if it had not been only to do his Sister a Favour. The *French* Historians say that *Charles* had no hand in his Sister's Conspiracy, and that he even expell'd her his Dominions. But this Collection, I think, shews very clearly that he enter'd very far into the Secret: for besides that *Mezeray* makes no Scruple to own, that the King had promis'd his Sister a Supply both of Men and Money, the desire the King express'd to see her, and his readiness to come into the Alteration or Exchange of *Edward* the Father's Homage into that of *Edward* the Son, could proceed from no other Cause but a desire to serve her;

Another Mistake in History discover'd.

Edw. II. her; otherwise it would have been more honourable for him to receive Homage from the
King of *England*, than from his Son. He had
so few Objections to make to this Alternative,
that the Negotiation was concluded in less than
a Fortnight: for the Acts of this Volume shew
P. 163. that on the 21st of *August*, 1325, *Edward* thought
even of going himself to pay the Homage; but
that on the 24th he wrote to the King of *France*
from *Langedon* near *Dover*, to desire to be excused, on pretence of his being suddenly taken
ill upon the Road: That by Letters Patent
P. 164. dated at *Langedon*-Abbey aforesaid, on the second of *September* following, he made over the
County of *Ponthieu* to his Son; that the Letters Patent by which King *Charles* consented to
P. 165. it, are dated the 4th of *September*; that on the
10th *Edward* made a Conveyance of *Guyenne*
(according to a Form which had been sent him
P. 168. from *France*) by an Instrument dated at *Dover*;
and that on the 12th his Son *Edward* embark'd
for *France*. If to this we add, that the King
of *France* kept his Sister at Court almost a whole
Year after he had receiv'd the Homage of the
young Prince, maugre all the Sollicitations of
Edward, who press'd him many times to send
her home again; that the said Princess was still
P. 226. in *France* on the 4th of *September*, 1326, as
appears by a Letter from *Edward* of that Date
to the Inhabitants of *Bayonne*; and that she
landed in the County of *Suffolk* on the 22d *ditto*;
we must be of opinion that all Affairs were
concerted before she left the Court of the King
her Brother, and by consequence that she was
not expell'd, as is pretended, till it was time for
her to enter upon Action.

Here is *Edward*'s Anſwer dated at *Weſtminſter*, *December* 1, 1325, to *Charles the Fair*, who had ſignify'd to him that the Queen could not return into *England*, becauſe ſhe was ſo much hated by *Spenſer* the Son. In this Anſwer *Edward* juſtifies *Spenſer*, and aſſures the King of *France* that he had never been wanting in his due Reſpect to the Queen; and that if he had, he ſhould not have eſcaped Puniſhment: *for by God*, ſays he, *there is neither* Hugh, *nor any Man living in our power, who means her any harm, but if we knew it, we would puniſh in ſuch a manner that others ſhould take warning; and this is, was, and always ſhall be our Will, and God be thanked we have the power in our own hands.* He added, that he could not conceive what made his Wife complain of *Spenſer*, conſidering how extreme civil ſhe was to him when he took his leave of her, and the very affectionate Letters ſhe had ſent him ſince her departure.

A. 1325. P. 180. *King* Edward's *Letter to the King of* France, *about his Queen and* Spenſer.

He wrote a Letter the ſame day to his Queen, preſſing her to return, and told her that the Biſhop of *Wincheſter* had aſſured him, that in his preſence the King her Brother had proteſted that he would not detain her contrary to the Tenor of her Paſſport. The Letter begins with the word *Dame*, which I know not whether it was the ordinary Style, or whether he gave her ſo dry a Title by reaſon of the Matters of Complaint he had againſt her.

Another to his Queen. P. 181.

The next day he alſo wrote a Letter to his Son, which by reaſon of its brevity, and to give an Idea of the *French* Language at that time, I ſhall here inſert intire.

And to his Son. P. 182.

Treſcher Fiutz, tot ſoiez vous joeſue, & de tendre age, remembrez bien ceo que nous vous chargeaſmes, & commandaſmes, a veſtre departir de nous, a Doure,

Edw. II. *& de ceo que vous nous respondistes lors, dount nous vous savions molt bon gre, & ne trespassez, ne contravene, en nul poynt, ce que nous vous chargeasmes adounque pur nully.*

Et puis qu'il est ensi, que vestre Homage est resceu, esploitez vous devers notre trescher Frere le Roy de Fraunce vestre Uncle, & parnez vestre conge de lui, & venez, par devers nous en la compaignie, nostre treschere compaignie, la Roine, vestre Mere, si ele veigne tantost.

Et si ele ne veigne, venez vous, oue tote haste, sanz plus longe demoere; car nous avoms tresgrant desir de vous veer, & parler: Et ceo ne lessetz, en nulle manere, ne pur Mere, ne pur autri, sur nostre beneizon.

i. e. Most dear Son, remember in your Youth and tender Age what we charged and commanded you when you left us at *Dover*, and what you said to us in Answer, with which we were mightily pleas'd; and do not trespass or contravene what we then charged you in any point, upon any account.

And since your Homage has been receiv'd, go to our most dear Brother the King of *France*, your Uncle, and take your leave of him; and then come away to us in the company of our most dear Companion the Queen, your Mother, if she comes so soon.

And if she does not, come you with all haste without longer stay, for we have a very great desire to see and speak with you. And hereof fail not by any means, neither for Mother, nor for any other Person, as you tender our Blessing.

MANY

MANY Historians, even of the *English*, have affirm'd, that *Edward* being provok'd at the Disobedience both of his Wife and Son *, banish'd them both by a Proclamation: but this has no other foundation than a Report which had been current in *France*, as appears by a Letter which King *Edward* wrote to the Pope on this subject, dated *April* 15, 1326, from *Kenelworth*; wherein he complain'd of those who were the Propagators of those false Reports, and assures him, that such a Thought never came into his head, for that instead of hindering their Return he did all that lay in his power to bring them home. *Et idem filius noster*, said he, *erga nos non deliquit, nec permittit ætatis teneritudo ut sibi offensa aliqua possit, aut debeat imputari. Propter quod inhumanum foret, nec fœdus permitteret naturale, tantæ crudelitatis sævitiam contra eos exercere.* i. e. And as for our said Son, he has not offended us; and indeed the Tenderness of his Age is such, that he cannot be chargeable, either with the doing or intending any harm. Wherefore it would be both inhuman and unnatural to treat them with so much Rage and Cruelty.

A. 1326.

A Mistake in many Histories, confuted by the King's Letter to the Pope, about his Wife and Son.

P. 200.

EDWARD no sooner heard the News of the Queen's being landed, but he publish'd a Proclamation from the *Tower* of *London*, on the 27th of *September*, 1326, for pursuing and destroying all the Invaders of his Kingdom; but he excepted the Queen, his Son, and the Earl of *Kent*, his Brother. And by another Proclamation from thence next day, he put a Price upon *Mortimer*'s Head, promising to the Person who brought it, the Pardon of all his Crimes, and

His Proclamation against the Invader Mortimer, *&c.*

P. 231, 232.

* WE find it particularly in the *Compleat History of* England.

Edw. II. a Reward of Three Pounds † Sterling; which was such a Trifle for so notable a Service, that I cannot help thinking there has been some Mistake in the Transcript.

Manifesto against the Spensers. *P.* 236.

HERE is also the Manifesto of the Queen, of *Edward* the Son, and of the Earl of *Kent*, against the *Spensers*, in the usual Style of Pieces of this nature, where the main business is to shew that nothing is aim'd at but the Good of the Publick: It is dated at *Wallingford*, *October* 15, 1326.

Edward *the Son appointed Regent.* P. 237.

THERE is likewise a Memorandum, dated the 26th of the same Month, at *Bristol*, of the Nomination then and there made of *Edward* the Son, for Guardian or Regent of the Kingdom; and of the sending the Bishop of *Hereford* to the King, to demand the Great Seal. In it are these words, *Et idem Dominus Rex, habitâ inde aliquali deliberationi penes se, respondebat, Quod placuit sibi, mittere dictum magnum sigillum suum, præfatis consorti suo, & filio; & quod iidem consors & filius, dictum sigillum, sub privato sigillo suo tunc clausum, aperiri facerent, & non solum ea quæ pro jure & pace essent facienda, sed etiam quæ gratiæ forent, sub dicto magno sigillo, fieri facerent.* i. e. And the said Lord the King, after having deliberated within his own Breast, made answer, That he approv'd of the sending of his said Great Seal to his Consort and Son aforesaid; and of their causing the said Seal, then included in his Privy Seal, to be open'd; and that under the said Great Seal they should transact not only those Things which might be done both by Law and for the sake of Peace, but also those Things which were Acts of mere Grace and Favour.

† MR. *Daniel*, in this King's Life, in the History aforesaid, makes it 1000 *l.*

THIS

THIS Great Seal was made uſe of to procure the Payment of ſome of the Queen's Debts, for reſtoring the Eſtate of the Earl of *Richmond*, which the King had cauſed to be confiſcated, becauſe the ſaid Earl had had a hand in the Treaty of *Paris*; and laſtly, it was made uſe of to aſſemble in the King's Name and Authority, that very Parliament which was to depoſe him.

A. 1324.

P. 239, &c.

THESE being the moſt remarkable Pieces in the Beginning of this fourth Volume, which relate to the domeſtic Affairs of *England*, we proceed now to the

Affairs of Scotland.

DURING the four laſt Years of the Reign of *Edward* II. we find nothing remarkable in this Collection with reſpect to *Scotland*, but a Letter dated at *Avignon*, in *January* 1324. from Pope *John* XXII. to this Prince; wherein he informs him of his Reaſons for giving *Robert Bruce* the Title of King of *Scotland*, which he had till then refuſed him; which ſaid he, can be no Prejudice to the Rights of *Edward*.

Pope's Letter to Edward *about* Robert Bruce. P. 28.

FROM thence it may be inferred, that the Excommunication againſt the Perſon of *Robert* was taken off; but it was not ſo with reſpect to the Interdict on the Kingdom of *Scotland*, which lay under it till the Peace that was made in the Beginning of the Reign of *Edward* III.

Affairs Eccleſiaſtical.

THE Collation to Biſhopricks bred freſh Quarrels from time to time between the Pope and the King, and by conſequence gave the latter freſh Mortification; a very great Inſtance of

Edw. II. of which was the Case of the Bishoprick of *Winchester*, which I shall explain in a word or two, because it was one of the principal Subjects of the Acts of these four Years. *Edward* had sent Ambassadors to the Pope, *Rigand* Bishop of *Winchester*, and *John Stratford* Archdeacon of *Lincoln*. The former dying at *Avignon*, *John* XXII. according to the Usage already establish'd, being to dispose of that Bishoprick, and the King at last acknowledging the Pope's Right, which he had before in vain oppos'd, he immediately gave Orders to *Stratford*, to desire that Bishoprick for *Robert Baldock*, who was afterwards Chancellor. *Stratford* acted his Part so well, that he procur'd it for himself; which put *Edward* into such a Passion with his Ambassador, that he called him a Prevaricator. He wrote several Letters to the Pope, to get this Nomination revoked: but it was in vain; for *John* stood by what he had done and sent home the new Bishop, with a Letter of Recommendation, in which he assured *Edward*, that *Stratford* did all that was in his power to get *Baldock* promoted to the Bishoprick, but that *Stratford*'s own extraordinary Merit had determined him to gratify him with it, in which he hoped he had done the King a pleasure. When this Bishop was returned, *Edward* was resolved to prosecute him for several matters charged upon him relating to the other Articles of his Embassy; but he could not carry his Point so far as to get him condemned: and this Affair came just to the same Conclusion as those of this nature generally did, that is to say, the new Bishop was approved by the King, after having renounced the Article of the Pope's Bull which assigned him the Temporality.

Dispute between the King and the Pope, about the Bishop of Winchester.

EDWARD

A. 1324.

EDWARD undertook another Affair, in which he succeeded no better. He would fain by the Pope's Authority have deposed the Archbishop of *Dublin*, the Bishops of *Lincoln*, *Bath* and *Wells*, *Hereford*, and *Condom* in *Guyenne*; or, at least, have transported them out of his Dominions. This occasioned a great Number of Letters, which this Prince sent to the Pope, but were of no Availment.

Edward's *Complaint of the* Conservatiæ, *P.* 25, 26, 27.

IN *January*, 1324, we find *Edward* complaining to the Pope, *&c.* in 3 Letters dated from *Kenelworth*, of a certain Prerogative called *Conservatiæ*, which was pleaded by a certain Cardinal, Archdeacon of *Ely*, when he summoned the Bishop of the said Diocess to appear before him. I know not what those *Conservatiæ* meant which *Edward* in his Letter called *Novæ adinventiones, quæ à tramite juris communis exorbitant*; i. e. New Inventions, which ramble wide from the Path of Common-Law *. It seems to have been some Privilege granted to the Cardinals with respect to the Benefices they held in *England*; but I only give this by way of conjecture.

As the Pope took care to maintain his Authority, he was no less diligent to augment his Revenues. We find here, that *John* XXII. after having granted the King a Tenth upon the Clergy, for the War against *Scotland*, reserved to himself for the Time to come, by another Bull, the fourth Part of the said Tenth, for the pressing Necessities of the Holy See. *Edward* refused for a while to pay the Pope the said fourth Part, because Reservation had not been

* IT is particularly remarked of this Pope, that he was fond of Novelties, always changing the old Dignities and Societies in the Church for new ones.

made

Edw. II. made thereof in the first Bull: upon which the Pope wrote him a very severe Letter from *Avignon*, in *October* 1323.

Pope's Letter to Edward, about the Tenths. P. 19.

NEVERTHELESS *Edward* did not flinch till 1326. when finding himself in very great Perplexities, he wrote to the Pope, that he referred himself intirely to his Discretion upon that Head.

THE Obligation which the Archbishops of *Canterbury* were under, to go and receive the Pall in Person from the Pope's own Hand, was so established, that from the time of *Honorius*, who was the third Archbishop of that See, no body had been excused from it. And we find that in the Reign of *William the Conqueror*, *Lanfranc*, tho' he was in such high Esteem at the Court of *Rome*, could never obtain this Dispensation. *Walter Reynolds*, who was elected in 1313, had better fortune; for he received the Pall at *Canterbury*, and obtained from *Clement* V. a Delay of five Years, which, we shall find in the Acts of this Collection, was often renewed.

THIS Pall was become so necessary to the Archbishops, that it was reckoned such an essential Mark of their Dignity, that they could not exercise their Functions without it: For we find here, that some Thief having stole away the Archbishop of *York*'s Pall, the King wrote a Letter to the Pope, from *Kenelworth*, *April* 1, 1326, to desire him to send his Grace another *.

* THE *Pallium*, or Pall, was a sort of Mantle, worn by the Emperors, as an Ensign of Power, and by them in the 4th Century imparted to the Prelates, as a Mark of their Authority over the inferior Orders. At first it reach'd from Neck to Heel, covering all the Body, resembling a Priest's Cope, but that it was close before. Afterwards it became

became a kind of Stole, which hung before and behind, with four scarlet Crosses, one on the Breast, another on the Back, and one on each Shoulder. The Popes gave it at first to Primates and Apostolick Vicars only; but not to any Western Prelate, before the 6th Century. In the 8th they granted it to all Metropolitans, or Abbats, and afterwards to several considerable Bishops, who received this Pall at Consecration, till when they could not exercise any Function. It was used only at the Altar, in the Celebration of solemn Mass, when they put it about their Necks, above their other Pontifical Ornaments. Dr. *Howel* says, It is made of Lambs Wool, without any artificial Colour, spun by a peculiar Order of Nuns: that it is adorned with little black Crosses, having two Labels hanging down before and behind; and that on certain Days it is cast into St. *Peter*'s Tomb. We read that they sometimes put it upon the Corps of Patriarchs and Archbishops when they are buried.

THE *Romish* Prelates pay a great Rate for this Pall; insomuch that Dr. *Howel* tells us, That Dr. *Gray*, when chose Archbishop of *York*, in the Reign of King *John*, gave for his no less than 1000 *l*. By the superstitious Order of the Church of *Rome*, it should be made of the Wool of those two Lambs, which being offered at the High Altar, upon St. *Agnes*'s Day, are, after the hallowing of them, committed to the Sub-Deacons of that Church, and kept by them in a particular Pasture. It must be noted, that the whole Garment is not of the Woollen Manufacture, but only that List or Plaite of it, which falls down before and behind, and goes round the Neck. *Claude Villette*, a Canon of St. *Marcellus*, relates this whole Affair at large, in his Book called *Raisons de l'Office & des Ceremonies de l'Eglise Romaine*.

WE

Edw. III.

We come now to the Martial Reign of Edward III. *of which Mr.* Rymer *gives the following general Account, in his Dedication of this fourth Volume to the late Queen, in the Year* 1707.

General Character of his Reign.

'THIS Book, may it please your Majesty, 'gives a Prospect into the Reign of your 'most noble Progenitor, King *Edward* III. a 'Time of great War and great Successes.

'Some Years from the Beginning of his 'Reign, he wrote himself King of *FRANCE*; 'and before the End of his Reign, he saw his 'younger Son (that was born at *Gaunt*) saluted King of *SPAIN*.

'His CONFEDERATES, the Counts 'of *Holland* and *Zealand*, the Marquesses of *Cleve* 'and *Juliers*, the Dukes of *Brabant* and *Guelder*, 'of the *Nassau* Family, the then Emperor, and 'other *German* Princes; Names (till now from 'your Archives reviv'd and rais'd to light) long 'buried in Oblivion. These his Confederates seem much-what of the same Mould 'with Your Majesty's Allies.

'In the 20th Year of his Reign was the 'Battle of *Cressy*.

'In the 30th was the Battle of *Poictiers*.

'In the 41st Year of his Reign was that total Rout given to the United Forces of *France* 'and *Spain*; whereby King *Pedro* was set upon 'the Throne, his Rival forc'd to quit the Kingdom, and flee into *France* for Shelter, &c. '&c.

The

N. B. Dr. *Nicholson*, late Bishop of *Carlisle*, and now of *Londonderry*, speaking of this Prince, calls him the Greatest in Europe, of his time, and the Glory of our English Throne. And Mr. *Joshua Barnes*, whose Account

THE Acts in the *Fœdera*, which relate to the Reign of *Edward* III. take up the far greatest part of the 4th Volume, all the 5th and 6th Volumes, and part of the 7th. To make an Extract of every Piece in those Volumes, would be a Work too tedious and voluminous; therefore we shall confine our selves to those Acts which are of most Importance, and which are most capable of giving any light into this Reign, one of the most considerable in the *English* History.

THE chief Transactions of this 4th Volume, which takes in the eleven first Years of *Edward* III. may be reduc'd to four principal Heads.

Account of his Reign is the best that can be consulted, in the Opinion of that Learned and Right Reverend Antiquary, gives this general Character of *Edward* III. in his Preface.

'THE Subject Matter of 'my Discourse is the Ho-'nour of my Country, the 'Life and Actions of one of 'the greatest Kings that per-'haps the World ever saw.— 'It is an old Observation, '*That Subjects usually con-'form themselves to their 'Prince*: And here certain-'ly, if ever any great and 'Martial Monarch was Lord 'of any like himself, we shall 'find this King to have been 'so: Many great and re-'nowned Heroes and Cap-'tains, bold in Attempts, 'wise in Conduct, and for-'tunate in Success, being 'thick almost in every Page 'of this History: wherein 'will appear the greatest Va-'riety of Adventures, the 'most hazardous Enterpri-'zes of War, the most exact 'Counsels, and politick Ne-'gotiations, and the most 'frequent instances of Cou-'rage, Piety, Generosity, and 'Princely Conduct; with 'the most wholesome Laws 'and Rules of Government, 'that perhaps the whole 'World can furnish us with-'al, in so short a Period of 'Time.'

AND the Reverend Mr. *Eachard*, in his Introduction to this Reign, says, The *English* Nation not only recover'd Vigour and Strength in it, but also Beauty and Glory.

I. DOMES-

Edw. III

I. Domestic Affairs.

II. Those common to *England* and *Scotland.*

III. *EDWARD*'s Quarrels with *France.* And,

IV. Affairs Ecclesiastic or Religious.

To give an account of the numerous Acts foreign to these four Articles, would swell this Work to a much greater Bulk than the *Fœdera* it self.

Article I. Domestic Affairs.

King Edward III. *enters on the Government.* P. 243.

EDWARD III. was but fourteen Years of Age when he came to the Crown; which tho' his Father had been forced to resign, yet in the very first Proclamation that was published in the Name of the new King, dated at *Westminster, Jan.* 29, 1327, his Ministers make him say in the Preamble, that he took the Government of the Kingdom upon him, not only by the Consent of his Father, but in Obedience to his Orders*. By this, and many other Acts

* Mr. *Daniel,* in his History of this Reign, remarks, that this Preamble was intended to palliate the wrong done to the Father, but that it made it more apparent.

Dr. *Kennet,* in his Notes upon this Historian, would have the Reader observe, that he was no Friend to the Barons and their Cause.

Bishop *Nicholson* has a remarkable Note with respect to those Barons, *viz.* That the Barons who join'd with the Earl of *Lancaster* against *Edward* II. being too great and powerful to be named Rebels, had the softer Name of *Contrarients* bestowed on them; and he takes notice of a Roll of Records in the *Tower*, which is from them called *Rott. Contrarientium.*

Mr. *Barnes* says, a General Pardon was proclaim'd at his Accession, which gave occasion to succeeding Kings to follow the Example of so great a Precedent.

of

of the like nature, 'tis manifest that the Declarations of Princes are not always the safest Vouchers for the Truth of History. *A.* 1327.

THE same Parliament which depos'd *Edward* II. caus'd *Edward* III. to be proclaim'd, and chose him twelve Guardians or Governors, of whom *Henry* Earl of *Lancaster* was to take care of his Person: But this was a Nomination intirely useless, for the Queen, who had the Power in her own Hands, seiz'd the Government, and left the Guardians appointed by Parliament nothing more than the Shadow of Authority, while *Roger Mortimer* govern'd under her with absolute Power. But the Parliament, far from resenting it vigorously, seconded the Designs of the Queen and her Minister, Designs which had no other End but to run down the late Government. The Exiles were recall'd, the Conduct of the late Earl of *Lancaster* was approv'd of, and the Judgment given against him revers'd, as contrary to the Laws of the Kingdom. The Bishops of *Winchester*, *Norwich*, *Lincoln* and *Hereford*, were restor'd to their Temporalities, and had the chief Management of Affairs under the Direction of the Queen and *Mortimer*. And all the Sentences pass'd against the Adherents of the Earl of *Lancaster* were revers'd, upon a Supposition that they had been extorted by the Credit of the *Spensers*. This is the main Subject of the first Acts of this Volume, which contain the Petitions presented to the Parliament by those who had been disgrac'd in the late Reign.

His Guardians mere Cyphers.

Queen and Mortimer *govern all.*

ISABEL had a Dowry settled upon her, which swallow'd up two Thirds of the Revenues of the Crown; and she paid the very Debts that she had contracted in *France*, out of the publick Treasury. Moreover, she made an Assignment

Queen's Revenue.

Edw. III. ſignment of a yearly Penſion of 1000 Marks to *John* Earl of *Hainault*, who had accompany'd her to *England*.

From P. 249, to P. 262.

All the Meaſures taken by the Queen, *Mortimer*, and the Parliament, were to render the late King's Conduct odious, in order to juſtify what they had done to him. When *Iſabel* undertook her Expedition againſt her Husband the King, ſhe relied chiefly on the Support of the Adherents of the late Earl of *Lancaſter*, who was beheaded at *Pontefract*; and it was they, properly ſpeaking, that depos'd King *Edward* II. and plac'd his Son upon the Throne. Therefore, in order to give ſome Colour for the exceſſive Rigour with which the late King had been treated, it was neceſſary, not only to juſtify that Earl's Conduct, but even to cry up his Merit, and ſet it in oppoſition againſt the pretended Injuſtice of *Edward* II. And the People being at that time ſo prepoſſeſs'd in favour of the Earl, that they went even to St. *Paul*'s Church to worſhip his Picture, as I have already mention'd; they did not let the favourable Conjuncture ſlip, but thought proper to write to the Pope in the Name of the King, deſiring him to canonize *Thomas* Earl of *Lancaſter*: And theſe were ſome of the Expreſſions made uſe of in the Letter dated at *London*, the laſt Day of *February* 1327.

Inſtance made for canonizing the Earl of Lancaſter.

Quadam floruit prærogativâ conſtantiæ ſingularis. Nam ſtatutis & ordinationibus Regni Angliæ, ſecundum Deum, pro utilitate Reipublicæ & defenſione libertatis Eccleſiæ, digeſto Regni Conſilio, rationaliter promulgatis, juratus corporaliter & adſtrictus, promiſſam Deo fidem inviolabiliter tenuit, & inſurgentes ex adverſo Regis & Regni perfidos ſeductores, zelo juſtitiæ corripuit magnanimiter & contrivit. *Poſt*

Post plurima, atque longa, quæ sic in puritate Spiritus, & spe cælestis retributionis, peregit, certamina, justus ab injustis capitalem devote subiit sententiam, & sic in Domino feliciter obdormivit. Qui jam velut fluvius de loco voluptatis ad irrigandum egregiens Paradisum, in partes divisus, terram Angliæ sancti sui sanguinis effusione, rubricatam rore cælesti, temperat salubriter & fœcundat, dum ad piam ejus invocationem, tot gloriosa, suprà naturam, divinitus fiunt miracula & infinita salutis remedia, favente Deo, per ipsius preces & merita conceduntur. A. 1327.

i. e. HE was eminent for his singular Constancy, which he retain'd as a Prerogative; for having corporally sworn, and bound himself before God, to keep the Statutes and Ordinances of the Realm of *England*, promulged by Order of the Council of the Realm, for the Benefit of the Republick, and the Defence of the Liberty of the Church, he inviolably kept his Oath to God; and out of his Zeal for Justice, magnanimously check'd and crush'd the perfidious Seducers who rose up against the King and Kingdom. After many and tedious Conflicts which he went through, in the Purity of the Spirit, and the Hopes of a Reward in Heaven, the just Man devoutly suffer'd the Sentence of Death pass'd by the unjust, and so sweetly slept in the Lord: And now like a River descending from some pleasant Place to water Paradise, being divided into several Branches, gives a wholesome Temperature and Fruitfulness by its Celestial Dew to the Soil of *England*, which is dyed red with the Effusion of his sacred Blood; while through the pious Invocation of his Name, so many glorious supernatural Miracles are wrought by Inspiration, and while the infinite Remedies of Salvation

M 2

*Edw.*III. tion are by the Grace of God, granted through his Prayers and Merit.

'TIS no wonder at all, considering the then Circumstances of the Court of *England*, that those who govern'd in the King's Name, shou'd write such a Letter. But one cannot help thinking it strange, that *Edward* III. when he came of Age, and was perfectly acquainted with the Wrong that had been done his Father, should sollicit this Canonization more than once; particularly by two Letters he wrote to the Pope and Cardinals from *Winchester*, *March* 7. 1330; and by two others to the said Pope and Cardinals, dated from *Eltham*, the 3d Day of *April* 1331. Nevertheless, this new Saint was not plac'd in the Calendar till the following Reign. But tho' his Canonization was a long time a coming, yet he was reverenc'd before-hand as a Martyr: And we find a Permission from the King, sign'd at *York*, *June* 8. 1327. to make a Collection for building a Chapel on the very Spot where the Earl was beheaded.

P. 421. *and* 477. *King* Edward's *Letters for canonizing the said Earl.*

P. 291.

THUS the main Point was to blacken the Government of *Edward* II. The Condition of that depos'd King, as deplorable as it was, yet it gave Uneasiness to the Queen and *Mortimer*. *Henry* Earl of *Lancaster*, who had him in his Custody at the Castle of *Kenelworth*, had no reason to be fond of him; but his natural Generosity did not permit him to insult the Prince's Misery: and tho' he took care that his Prisoner should not escape, yet he paid his Devoirs to him; at which the Queen was alarm'd. This, added to some particular Reasons which that Lord had to be disgusted with *Isabel*, who had seiz'd the Government to his Preju-

Prejudice, made that Princeſs of opinion, that it was not ſafe to leave the King any longer in his Cuſtody. Therefore ſhe diſpatch'd an Order to Sir *John Maltravers*, and Sir *Thomas Gournay*, to take *Edward* from *Kenelworth* Caſtle, and carry him to that of *Berkley*, (in *Glouceſter-ſhire.*) Theſe two Gentlemen, the moſt brutiſh of the human Species, made that unhappy Prince ſuffer a thouſand horrid Indignities, enough to have broke his Heart; and thoſe who put him into their hands meant no leſs: but his Conſtancy was proof againſt all their Barbarities: So that theſe means failing, the two Guards had Orders to diſpatch him with all the Secrecy poſſible. They executed their Commiſſion in a manner the moſt ſhocking to human Nature, by thruſting up a hot Iron into his Fundament, through a Pipe or Horn, and burning his Entrails *: This was done immediately after the young King's Expedition againſt the *Scots*. But the Miſcreants, inſtead of receiving the Reward they expected, were forc'd to fly, after they had ſeen the very Perſons that had employ'd them, the firſt to diſown them, in order to ſmother that Part which they themſelves had in their Parricide.

A. 1327.

Murder of King Edward II.

* MR. *Barnes* ſays, this Murder was committed on the 21ſt of *September* 1327, at Midnight, not when he was about to disburden Nature, according to Dr. *Howel* and others, but as he lay faſt aſleep in his Bed: and that the Keepers being a little ſtartled at the Orders from the Queen and *Mortimer*, tho' they ſpar'd no other ill Uſage, ſent to the Biſhop of *Hereford*, a fit Caſuiſt, who was, it's thought, the Adviſer of it, to know whether it was lawful; to which the Biſhop ſent this Anſwer, according to Sir *Tho. de la More*, *Edwardum occidere nolite timere bonum eſt*; i. e. *To kill King* Edward *you need not to fear it is good*: which Anſwer, according to the placing of the Comma's, was either a Plea for himſelf, or an Incouragement for them.

*Edw.*III.

Edw. III's *Marriage with the youngest Daughter of* William *the good Earl of* Hainault. *P.* 306. *P.* 323.

Not long after, *Edward* III. ſolemniz'd his Marriage with *Philippa* of *Hainault*; which Match had been made up by his Mother before her Return to *England*. We have here the Pope's Bull of Diſpenſation for that Marriage, dated in *October* 1327, at *Avignon*; as alſo a Paſſport, dated by the King at *Clypſton* the 28th of *November* following, for the Earl of *Hainault* to bring over his Daughter to *England*, to conſummate the Marriage.

His unſucceſsful Expedition againſt the Scots.

Not long before the King's Marriage, he had made an Expedition againſt the *Scots*, in which he had ill Succeſs. *Robert Bruce* having broke the Truce, had ſent his Troops to ravage the Frontiers of *England*; which oblig'd the *Engliſh* to raiſe a great Army to drive them out of the Country. *Edward* put himſelf at the head of this Army: but after a great many fruitleſs Attempts to bring the Enemy to a Battle, he had the mortification to ſee them retire. This War was concluded by a Treaty of Peace, not the moſt advantageous to *England*: For, by the Advice of the Queen-Mother and of *Mortimer*, *Edward* quitted all his Pretenſions to *Scotland* for the Sum of 30000 Marks *Sterling*; and concluded the Marriage betwixt *Joan* his Siſter, and *David*, Son to *Robert Bruce*. The Service which *Mortimer* pretended to have done by negotiating this Treaty, was rewarded with the Title of *Earl of March*, which the King gave him in full Parliament*.

Mortimer *made Earl of* March.

Peace with Scotland.

The † ſcandalous Peace made with *Scotland*, without any Neceſſity, added to the Tragical Death

* He was made Earl of *March*, in the Parliament held at *Salisbury*, in *Auguſt* 1328.

† The Parliament which concluded that diſhonourable Peace with the *Scots*, was held at

Death of *Edward* II. and to the Insolence of the new-made Earl, made an Impression on the Populace, and much more on the great Men of the Kingdom. *Henry* Earl of *Lancaster* was one of those who were the most open in expressing their Disgust, which made the Queen and the Favourite take a Resolution to destroy him: They thought that the Protection he gave to a Gentleman who had kill'd the Lord *Holland*, furnish'd them with a good Pretence; for as he refus'd to deliver up that Gentleman to Justice, it was no difficult matter for them to persuade the young King, that there was a Necessity of chastising him for such a piece of Presumption; and Troops were rais'd for that End. *Lancaster* made Preparations on the other hand for his Defence, and brought over to his Interests *Edmund* Earl of *Kent*, the King's Uncle, with some other Lords; who being confederated, publish'd a Manifesto at large, exposing the Conduct of the Queen and her Mi-

A. 1328.

English *Lords provok'd to Arms by* Mortimer's *Insolence.*

at *Northampton*, in *March* 1328, when the King, by the Contrivance of his Mother, *Mortimer*, and Sir *James Douglas*, without the Privity of the Peers, surrender'd by Charter his Title and Sovereignty to the Kingdom of *Scotland*, restor'd many ancient Jewels and Monuments, among which one of great Value, call'd *The black Cross of* Scotland; also many Deeds, and other Instruments of their former Homage and Fealty, with the famous Evidence called the *Ragman Roll*, which was a Security and Memorial of the Fealty and Homage which the *Scots* ought to pay to the Kings of *England*; and besides, no *Englishman* was permitted to hold any Lands in *Scotland*, unless he would dwell there.

SEE Mr. *Barnes*'s History of this Reign; who says, that the Lady *Joan*, King *Edward*'s Sister, was marry'd to *David Bruce* the young King of *Scotland*, about the middle of *July* 1328; and that the *Scots* themselves afterwards, by way of Triumph, nicknam'd their Queen *Joan Make-Peace*; as if the Realm of *England* had made the Match out of fear, to rid their Hands of the War.

 nister.

*Edw.*III. nister. The Grievances therein set forth, were so flagrant, that the Queen, for fear the whole Kingdom wou'd be about her ears, consented to an Accommodation, which was concluded by the Intercession of the Archbishop of *Canterbury*. Tho' there is nothing of this in the *Fœdera*, yet it was necessary to speak of it, to shew the Cause of that Hatred which *Isabel* and the Earl of *March* had conceiv'd against the Earl of *Kent*; such a Hatred as nothing could satisfy but that Earl's Death. For this End they hatch'd a devilish Conspiracy, which it would be difficult to parallel. As *Edmund*, who was but 28 Years of Age, was of a frank generous Temper, and no doubt a little too credulous, he was easily persuaded by the Queen his Sister-in-law, that the Deposition of his Brother was absolutely necessary for the publick Good; and it was this that made him concur with her in the Execution of the Project already mention'd. But it was not long before his Eyes were open'd, when he saw that he had been engag'd in wrong Measures: His Expressions, and the Repentance which he discover'd, made it plainly appear, that he wish'd heartily the thing had never been done, and laid the Foundation of the Conspiracy which his Enemies form'd against him. Certain Persons were deputed to him, who made him believe that the King his Brother was still alive in *Corfe-Castle*, and who engag'd him in Measures to rescue him out of Captivity. It seems that *Edmund* was himself present at his Brother's Funeral; but the Strength of his Hopes that the pretended Secret now discover'd to him was true, made him easily believe that he had been deceiv'd by a Sham-Funeral: He fell therefore into the Trap that was laid for him, and went

Edmond *Earl of* Kent *trick'd out of his Life by a sham Plot.*

went to *Corse-Castle*; where being assur'd that *A.*1328.
his Brother was a Prisoner, he desir'd leave to see him. The Governor, who was properly instructed, excus'd himself upon account of the Orders he had to let no body see him; which thorowly confirm'd the Earl in his Opinion: who finding therefore that he could not be admitted, gave the Governor a Letter for the King his Brother, in which he assur'd him that he wou'd take Measures to gain him his Liberty. This Letter was carry'd to the Queen-Mother, who shew'd it to her Son, and obtain'd his Consent that his Uncle should be taken into Custody. It was at *Winchester*, where the Parliament was then assembled, that this unfortunate Nobleman was apprehended, condemn'd to lose his Head, and accordingly executed *.

IN this Volume we have the following Acts, relating either to *Edward* II. or the Earl of *Kent*.

TWO Assignments to *Barclay* and *Maltravers*, P. 287,
for subsisting the King's Father, then a Prisoner in *Berkley* Castle: One is dated at *Stamford*, 294.
April 24. 1327; the other at *Aldewerk* near *York*, the 5th of *July* following.

AN Order to take Bail offer'd by *William* P. 304.
Aylmere, charg'd with a Design of rescuing *Edward* from Prison: 'Tis sign'd by the King at *York*, *August* 20. 1327.

AN Order appointing anniversary Prayers for P. 312,
the Soul of *Edward* II. 'Tis dated in *October* 337.
1327, at a Place call'd *Crokesden*, in the King's Journey from *Lincoln* to *Nottingham*. There's another for celebrating his Obsequies, dated at *York* the 29th of *February* following.

* AT *Winchester*, *March* 19. 1330. See *Barnes's* History.

Edw. III. A Letter to the Pope from King *Edward* III. dated at *Reading*, the 24th of *March* 1330; wherein he tells the Pope, that the Earl of *Kent* had endeavour'd to foment Troubles in the Kingdom, by ſpreading a Rumour that the late King was ſtill alive; and that the ſaid Earl was the more juſtly puniſh'd, becauſe he himſelf was preſent at his Brother's Funeral. Nevertheleſs, 'tis not impoſſible but this Circumſtance, whether true or falſe, was added on purpoſe to prejudice the Pope againſt the Earl; for thoſe who were then at the Helm, were not very ſcrupulous of the Truth: Moreover, we find ſo much Diſſimulation in many Letters in this Collection, that 'tis not always ſafe to credit every Tittle.

P. 424.

P. 430. An Order from the King, dated at *Woodſtock* the 13th of *April* 1330, for proclaiming the Death of the Earl of *Kent* throughout the Kingdom, and for taking up thoſe who ſpread a Report that *Edward* II. was ſtill alive.

P. 447. Another Order, dated at *Clyve* the 8th of *Auguſt* following, for apprehending *Rice ap Griffin*, a *Welchman*, who was an Accomplice of the Earl of *Kent*, and rais'd a Diſturbance in *Wales*.

Edward being as yet but young, left every thing entirely to his Mother and the Earl of *March*, in whoſe favour he was ſtrangely prepoſſeſs'd; while they, on the other hand, made the moſt of his extraordinary Confidence, and borrow'd the King's Name to procure themſelves all manner of Advantages. *Iſabella* got a Grant under the King's Privy Seal, dated the
P. 410. 17th of *January* 1330, at *Oſeneye*, for 10000 Marks, part of the 30000 which were to be paid by the King of *Scotland*; and 'tis very probable, that the Earl of *March* finger'd the other

other 20000 Marks, as was afterwards charg'd upon him. *A.* 1330.

IT was by their Advice, that *Edward* was persuaded, tho' with a vast deal of Regret, to go over to *France*, to do Homage to *Philip de Valois*, whom he look'd upon as a Usurper of his Estate, as we shall find hereafter. 'Tis very probable that he was inform'd, during this Voyage, of many Particulars, which began to give him some Suspicion of his Mother's Conduct; for as soon as ever he was return'd, he wanted to have it fully explain'd to him. They who took care to inform him of it, remark'd those Errors to him which the Queen and the Earl of *March* had committed, as well in the first Expedition against the *Scots*, which was attended with ill Success, as in the scandalous Peace which they had caus'd him to patch up, without any Necessity, with *Robert Bruce*. He was inform'd of the Barbarity with which his Father was murder'd, and had the whole Conspiracy unravell'd to him, by which his Uncle the Earl of *Kent* lost his Head. His Friends fully convinc'd him of the Prejudice he had done himself, by going to perform Homage to *Philip de Valois*. They magnify'd the Wealth and Expences of the Earl of *March*, which were by far too great for a Subject. They insinuated to him, that it was very apparent that the Queen-Mother and her Favourite had a design to keep him always in a State of Minority; and last of all, to fill up the Measure of his Indignation, they told him, that his Mother was with Child by the said *Mortimer* *. These Informations had such an Effect upon his Mind, that he resolv'd to shake off the Yoke of his Managers, and to punish them. For this end he

The King incens'd against Mortimer.

* MR. BARNES observes, however, that no Effect of such Pregnancy appear'd afterwards.

went

*Edw.*III. went to *Nottingham*, where the Parliament was to meet, with a deſign there to put his Project in execution. He lodg'd in the Town with a ſmall Retinue, while the Queen his Mother, and the Earl of *March*, lay in the Caſtle, with a Guard of 180 Knights to attend them. It would have been difficult to have attack'd them with open force; ſo that *Edward* went another way to work: He gain'd the Governor, or Conſtable of the Caſtle, who introduc'd him in the dead of the Night, thro' a ſubterranean Paſſage, and gave him an Opportunity to enter into his Mother's Apartment, attended by ſome reſolute Perſons, to whom he had communicated his Deſign. The Earl of *March* was ſeiz'd in the Queen's Antichamber, and carry'd off, notwithſtanding the Tears and Cries of the Queen, who begg'd her Son, without ceaſing, to ſpare *the Gallant Mortimer*. Two of his Knights, who offer'd to make Reſiſtance, were kill'd. This done, the Earl was carry'd out of the Caſtle, the ſame way that the King enter'd, which was afterwards call'd *Mortimer*'s *Hole* *, and committed to the Tower of *London*. Next day *Edward* diſſolv'd the Parliament, and call'd a new one at *Weſtminſter*, wherein the King complain'd of the Queen's Male-Adminiſtration; and declar'd, that notwithſtanding his Minority, he would from this time forward govern by himſelf. Afterwards he caus'd Articles

Mortimer *taken Priſoner.*

* Our Hiſtorian quotes *Drayton*'s *Barons Wars*, to ſhew that this wonderful Paſſage was hewn and dug forth during the *Daniſh* Invaſions, by ſome of the *Saxon* Kings, for their further Security in caſe of a Siege. It ſeems that neither the Queen, *Mortimer*, nor any of their Attendants, knew of this Paſſage; a particular Deſcription of which, the Curious will find in *Barnes*'s Hiſtory, *p.* 48.

cles

cles to be drawn up against the Earl of *March*, who, without being heard in his Defence †, because his Crimes were so publickly notorious, was condemn'd to die the Death of Traitors, and suffer'd it accordingly, on the common Gallows at *Tyburn* *. Queen *Isabel* was stripp'd of her Estate and Authority, and confin'd to the Castle of *Risings* ††. *Mezeray*, and those who have copy'd after him, were mistaken when they said that this Prince hasten'd his Mother's Death in this Castle, since it is certain that she liv'd there 28 Years. *A.* 1330. *Condemn'd and hang'd.* *Queen* Isabel's *Confinement.* *A great Mistake of* Mezeray, *and other Historians.*

MANY are the Acts in this Volume relating to the Facts above-mention'd; the most material of which are,

A PROCLAMATION dated the 20th of *October* 1330, at *Nottingham*, containing the King's Reasons for apprehending the Earl of *March*: He declar'd also in this Proclamation, that being inform'd that those who had hitherto held the Reins of Government had been guilty of Male-Administration, he was resolv'd to govern himself, with the Advice of the great Men of the Realm. *P.* 453. Edward's *Proclamation against* Mortimer,

ANOTHER Proclamation dated at *Woodstock*, the third of *November* following, in which the King invites the Subjects to lay their Grievances before the Parliament, and complains bitterly of the last Assembly, saying, That the Members had been corrupted, and therefore *P.* 453. *His Proclamation for a new Parliament.*

† MR. *Barnes* observes, that in this respect he had the same Treatment as he had shewn before to the two *Spensers*, and to the Earl of *Kent* the King's Uncle.

* MOST of our Histories say this Execution was on the 29th of *November* 1330; but Mr. *Barnes* proves that it was on the 26th, and that he was bury'd on the 29th, after he had hung two Days and two Nights by the King's special Command.

†† MR. *Barnes* quotes *Holinshed* to shew that this was a Castle near *London*.

refus'd

Edw. III.

refus'd to hear the Grievances of the People. From thence he took occasion to exhort the Sheriffs to promote the Election of such Members, in their respective Counties, as were truly concern'd for the Welfare of their Country.

Another Mistake of Historians detected. P. 457.

THIS shews that *Edward* call'd a new Parliament, tho' several Historians affirm, that he only adjourn'd the old one from *Nottingham* to *Westminster* *.

Proceedings against the Earl of Lancaster, *&c. revers'd.*

AN Order, dated the 12th of *December* following at *Westminster*, reversing all Proceedings against *Henry* Earl of *Lancaster*, for taking Arms against the Earl of *March*.

A Permission to bury young Spenser. P. 461.

A Permission, dated at *Westminster* the 15th of the same Month, to interr the Remains of young *Spenser*, who was hang'd at *Hereford*.

King's Resumption of all Grants. P. 476.

A Resumption of all the Grants made since the King's Accession to the Crown: 'Tis dated at *Croydon* the 5th of *March* 1331.

A Pension settled on Sir John Nevil. P. 487.

AN Assignment of a Pension to Sir *John Nevil* †, for having arrested the Earl of *March*: 'Tis dated at *Havering Bower* the 10th of *May* following.

A Pardon to William Montague. P. 506.

A Pardon granted to *William Montague* on account of two of *Mortimer*'s Knights, who were kill'd when the Earl was arrested ‖: 'Tis dated at *Westminster* the 10th of *January* 1332.

* EVEN the accurate Mr. *Barnes* has fallen into this Mistake, *p.* 49.

† THIS was Sir *John Nevil* of *Herneby*; to whom, as *Barnes* says, the King granted 200 Marks in Tail special, and in his fifteenth Year he was Governour of *Newcastle* upon *Tine*; though Mr. *Drayton* and other Historians have ventur'd to say, that he was kill'd in the Arrest of *Mortimer*; and Mr. *Drayton* mistakes him for *Mortimer*'s Friend; an Error for which Mr. *Barnes* excuses him, because he was a Poet.

‖ THESE Knights were Sir *Hugh Turplington*, and Sir *Richard Monmouth*, according to the *Fœdera*; tho' Mr. *Barnes*, quoting *Knighton*, calls the latter Sir *John Monmouth*.

GOUR-

GOURNAY, one of the Assassins of King *Edward* II. having been apprehended at *Burgos* in *Castile*, by the diligence of *John Leynham*, Chamberlain to the King of *Castile*, *Edward* wrote several Letters about it, which we meet with in this Volume of the *Fœdera*, to the said *John Leynham*, (on whom he settled a Pension of 300 *l. Sterling*) to the King of *Castile*, and to the Echevins of *Burgos*. They are dated in *May* and *June* 1331, at *Havering Bower*, *St. Edmundsbury*, and *Norwich*. A. 1331. *Orders about* Gournay. P. 488, *to* 492.

AN Order to bring *Gournay* to *Bayonne*, dated at *St. Edmundsbury* the 28th of *May* 1331. P. 491.

ANOTHER dated at *Waltham* the 10th of *February* 1332, directed to the Mayor, &c. of *Bayonne*, for delivering *Gournay* into the hands of such Persons as the King should send to bring him over Prisoner to *England*. P. 509.

'TIS plain that our Historians are mistaken, who assert that *Gournay* was apprehended at *Marseilles* *, since 'tis very manifest from the *Fœdera*, that it was done in *Spain*. The Ruffian had his Head cut off aboard the Ship that was carrying him to *England*, which was probably owing to the Intrigues of those who were Accomplices in his Crime, that he might not discover who set him at work. *Another Mistake of Historians about* Gournay.

AN Assignment of the Revenues of the County of *Ponthieu*, (in *France*) to the Queen Mother, for her Subsistence, dated the 24th of *September* 1334, at *Westminster*. *King* Edward's *Settlement on the Queen-Mother*.

AN Order to carry to the Treasury 60,000 *l. Sterling*, which was found in *Wales*, being part P. 623. P. 697.

* AMONG others, we find this Error in *Daniel*'s History of this Reign, and that it has escap'd the Correction of the learned Annotator.

of

*Edw.*III. of the Treaſure loſt by *Edward* II. 'Tis dated at *Guildford* the 20th of *April* 1336.

The following are ſome looſe Acts concerning Domeſtick Affairs.

Charters in favour of foreign Merchants. P. 361, 516, 574.

THERE's a Charter dated at *York* the 8th of *Auguſt* 1328, confirming a former Charter in favour of foreign Merchants trading into *England*; and we find it further confirm'd by two other Acts of this King, *viz.* at *Stamford* the 13th of *April* 1332, and at *Knaresborough* the 16th of *Auguſt* 1333.

P. 344.

THERE are two Letters from the King, relating to the Marriage of *John* of *Eltham*, his Brother, with *Mary* of *Biſcay*: one of them is dated at *Lincoln* the 28th of *March* 1328, and directed to the King of *Caſtile*; the other, which is the ſhorteſt, I inſert, to give the Reader an Idea of the Language and Manner of Writing of that Age.

Le Roi, a noſtre Treſchere & Treſame, Marie, Dame de Biſcay, Salutz & bone affection.

Por ceo, que Parlaunce ad eſte faite devers Nous, de Mariage faire entre noſtre treſame Frere Johan de Eltham, & la File de veſtre Fiuz, que Dieu aſſoille.

Et nous ſerioms bien del aſſent, que le Mariage, ſe preigne iſſuit, que ceo fuſt a pleiſaunce de vous, & de noſtre Treſcher Coſyn, li Rois d'Eſpaigne; car nous entendoms que ceo purroit eſtre a honur & profit de nous & de vous, & aſſeuraunce de nos amis celes parties.

Vous prioms & requiroms affectuouſement, que vous voillez au dit Mariage bonement aſſentir, & nous certifier de ceo, que vous eut vodriez faire, a plus en haſt que vous purriez.

Don a Nicole le 28 jour de Marcz.

i. e. THE

A. 1328.

i. e. THE King to our most dear and well-beloved *Mary*, Lady of *Biscay*, Health and good Affection.

FORASMUCH as Proposal has been made to us of a Marriage between our dearly beloved Brother *John* of *Eltham*, and the Daughter of your Son, whom God bless:

AND whereas we are very willing that the said Marriage should take effect, with the Approbation of your self and our most dear Cousin the King of *Spain*; because we are convinced that the same may be of Honour and Profit both to Us and You, and to the Encouragement of our Friends, Parties thereunto:

WE affectionately intreat and request you, that you would please to give your hearty Consent to the said Marriage, and certify us of your Pleasure therein with all the speed that may be.

*Dated at** Nicole, *the 28th of* March 1328.

An Order for apprehending two Alchymists. *P.* 384.

AMONG the Acts in 1329, there is an Order dated the 9th of *May* at *Eltham*, to bring to the King, by fair means or by force, two Men who boasted of their Art to make Silver; and it seems that the King intended to set them at work for himself.

Pension settled on T. Priour. *P.* 497.

A PENSION granted to *Thomas Priour*, for the News which he brought to the King of the Birth of *Edward* his First-born Son: It is dated at *Westminster*, the 1st of *October* 1331.

Marriage Treaty of the King's Sister. *P.* 512.

A MARRIAGE Contract between *Eleanor* the King's Sister, and *Reynold* Count of *Guelderland*, dated at *Westminster* the 20th of *October*, 1332†.

ED-

* *Lincoln.*

† THIS *Eleanor* was King *Edward*'s younger Sister, who was about fourteen Years of Age

Edw. III

King's Demand of Money towards the said Marriage. P. 543, to 547. and 575.

EDWARD took occasion from this Marriage, to desire a Supply of his Subjects, which the Clergy refused him; and at last he was fain to make use of absolute Power to exact it, with a Promise that it should not be drawn into Consequence. This appears by several of his Letters to the Clergy, and by his Order to the Lords of the Treasury, dated at *Pontefract*, the 12th of *February*, 1333; where he mentions the Sums subscribed by the Clergy towards the Expences of his Sister's Marriage, and directs them to levy the said Sums, and carry them into the Treasury. See also the King's Letter to the Abbat of *St. Mary*'s at *York*, dated at St. *Edmundsbury*, the 28th of *August* following.

P. 649.

HERE we have the King's Approbation and Confirmation of the Grant of a Part of *Provence*, which was formerly given by *Eleanor*, Wife of *Henry* III. to *Thomas* and *Henry*, Sons of *Edmund* Earl of *Lancaster*: The said Approbation is dated at *Newburgh*, the 16th of *June*, 1335.

His Letter to the King of Armenia, p. 679.

THERE is also a Letter from *Edward*, dated at *York*, the 13th of *December* following, to the King of *Armenia*, wherein he promises him to go in Person and make War against the Infidels,

Age when married; and this *Reynold*, or *Reginald*, Earl of *Gueldre*, was a great Lover of King *Edward* and the *English* Nation. Her Portion was 15000*l.* which was no small Sum in those Days, when even the Marriages of the Daughters of *France* did not exceed 6000 Crowns ready Money. This Lady (who was the said Earl's second Wife) brought him two Sons, *Reginald* and *Edward*, both Dukes successively after their Father: For when this King *Edward* came to be made Vicar of the Sacred Empire, he created this Earl *Reginald*, Duke of *Gueldre*; since which that Earldom became a Dukedom. *Barnes's* Hist. of *Edw.* III.

dels, as soon as his Affairs would permit him. *A.* 1331.
This was putting the Day very far off, because he then began his Preparations for a War against the King of *France*.

Woollen Manufacture.

THO' there was a great Trade for Wool in *England* in the Reign of *Edward* III. it does not appear that the *English* knew as yet how to manufacture it into Cloth; as may be inferred from a Protection granted by the King at *Lincoln*, the 23d of *July*, 1331, to *John Kempe* of *Flanders*, a Weaver, who was come over to *England* to exercise his Art and Mystery, and to teach it to the *English*. P. 496.

AND we find the like Protection granted by the King at *Westminster*, the 3d of *May*, 1337, to fifteen Weavers of *Zealand*, who came to settle in *England* for the same purpose. P. 751.

Affairs of Scotland.

Acts relating to the Truce with Scotland.

THE thirteen Years Truce between *England* and *Scotland*, had been concluded about three Years when *Edward* III. came to the Crown. It was one of the first Cares of his Council to maintain this Truce, and, if possible, to change it to a lasting Peace. There are several Acts in the beginning of this Reign, which shew that this was then the Disposition of the Court of *England*.

THE first is an Order, dated at *Westminster* the 15th of *February*, 1327, for the strict Observation of the Peace with *Scotland*. P. 256.

THE second is a full Power granted to certain Commissioners to treat of a final Peace with the *Scots*: It is dated the 4th of *March* following, at *Westminster*. P. 270.

Edw.III THE third is *Edward's* Confirmation of the thirteen Years Truce. But *Robert* King of *Scotland* was otherwise inclined: He wanted to take an advantage of *Edward's* Minority; and therefore, without any colour of Pretence, he broke the Truce *. His Generals, *Murray* and *Douglas*, advanced to the Frontiers with an Army of 25000 Men, almost all Horse, and committed some Ravages upon the Lands which the *English* still possessed in *Scotland*. This Invasion engaged the *English* to raise an Army of 60000 Men, including the 500 Men of Arms which *John* of *Hainault* brought from his own Country to *Edward's* assistance. As the King was on the point of setting out from *York*, where he had assembled his Troops, a Quarrel happened betwixt the Forces of *Hainault*, and the Archers of the County of *Lincoln*, in which a great deal of Blood was spilt on both sides †.

P. 271. King of Scotland *breaks it.*

Quarrel in the English *Army.*

No-

* ABOUT Easter 1327, *Robert Bruce* King of *Scotland* sent a short and brisk Defiance to King *Edward* and all his Realm, telling them, That he would shortly with his Power invade the Realm of *England* with Fire and Sword, and there do as he had done before in his Father's Reign, at the Battel of *Bannockbourn*. See *Barnes's* History.

† This Fray is particularly related by Mr. *Barnes*, who says, that *John* of *Hainault*, and his Foreign Auxiliaries, being very much favoured by the young King and his Mother, because they had formerly appeared in Defence of 'em against the *Spensers*, even when her own Brother the King of *France* had deserted her Quarrel; the King and Queen-Mother made a magnificent Feast, on purpose to do honour to the said Foreigners; but that their Servants, by their Insolence, so exasperated the *English*, that near 3000 of the Archers gathering together, many of the *Hainaulders* were slain, and the rest, with most of the Knights their Commanders, then at Court, forced to fly to their Lodgings in the Suburbs of *York*, where they fortified themselves the best they could. He says, that in the Tumult some part of the City

was

Nothing but Time could put an end to this Quarrel; and in the mean while, the *Scots* pass'd over the *Tine*, between *Carlisle* and *Newcastle*, and ravaged the Northern Counties of *England*. *A.* 1327.

WHEN the King was at *Nottingham*, he issued an Order, dated the 29th of *April*, 1327, for raising Troops; which is intitled, *De Arraiatione facienda*. This barbarous Word is form'd out of the old *French* Word *Arrayer*, which signifies *to adorn*, *prepare*, or *put in Order*; in Latin, *instruere*. The *English* have appropriated this Word to such Troops as they accoutre for War; and they call a Commission for raising Soldiers, a *Commission of Array*; and the Commissioners are called *Arrayers*.

King Edward's Commission of Array. P. 287.

THE Uproar being appeas'd, *Edward* marched towards *Durham* in quest of the *Scots*; but it was a long time before he could hear any Tidings of 'em: which made him so uneasy, that he promised a Pension of 100 *l.* Sterling, and the Honour of Knighthood, to the Man that should bring him in sight of the Enemy. He was informed, not many days after, that they were encamped but two Leagues from him, over against *Stanhope Park*, on the other side of the River *Were*. He posted thither with the Army immediately, on purpose to give them Battel; but they were so advantageously posted,

P. 296. *He offers a Reward to any that could bring him in reach of the* Scots *Army.*

was fired; that 80 Archers, most of 'em *Lincolnshire* Men, were killed that day, which was *Trinity-Sunday*; and that at Night the Foreigners rose privately, and slew about 300 of the Archers of *Lincolnshire* and *Northamptonshire*, for which 6000 Archers had combin'd and vowed a desperate Revenge; but that the King, to secure the Strangers from their Fury, set strong Guards about them, and displaced the Archers from their former Quarters, who by the King's Authority, and the earnest Endeavours of the great Men, who charitably took the Strangers part, were in some time pacified.

 that

Edw. III that he had no opportunity of attacking them: and the two Armies faced each other for a whole Fortnight, with only the River between them, without coming to a Battle. At last, the *Scots* retired in the Night-time, and by precipitant Marches returned to their own Country, whither the *English* did not think fit to pursue them. Thus ended this first Expedition of *Edward*; the ill Success of which was afterwards charged upon *Mortimer*, who was accused of having favoured the Enemies Retreat.

The Scots *Army returns home.*

The confused Accounts of this Expedition.

THE Particulars which Historians relate of this Expedition are a little confused, but they may be explained by having regard to the Dates of the several Orders which *Edward* issued during the Campaign, and which are to be met with in this Volume of the *Fœdera*. It would be too tedious to shew the Mistakes which some modern Historians have committed in this Affair; therefore this Remark shall suffice, in order to direct the Curious who would know more of the Matter, to consult the Volume it self.

A Pension settled on Rokesby *for bringing the King's Army to the sight of the* Scots.

THE King's Order for settling a Pension on *Thomas Rokesby*, for bringing him to the sight of the Enemy, is dated at *Lincoln*, the 28th of *September*, 1327 *.

QUEEN

* MR. *Barnes*, who says the King knighted *Rokesby* with his own Sword before the whole Army, gives us the remarkable Speech he made to the King, as follows.

'MAY it please your Majesty, I have now brought certain Tidings of the *Scots* your Enemies: They are not above three Miles from hence, lodg'd strongly on a great Hill in *Weredale* beyond the River *Were*, where they have been these eight Days expecting our coming. Dread Sir, What I say I'll maintain for Truth; for I ventured so near to take the better View of them, that falling into their hands, I was carried before their Leaders, where being question'd, I declar'd how

QUEEN *Isabel* and *Mortimer*, who sat at the Helm of Government in *England*, did not think a War for their Interest, and shewed a very great Inclination for Peace. The King of *Scotland* finding them thus disposed, laid hold of the Opportunity, and caused a Proposal to be made to them of a firm and lasting Peace between both Nations, which was immediately accepted. This Treaty (*as has been partly observed already*) was altogether to the advantage of *Scotland*; for by it *Edward* quitted his Right to the Sovereignty of that Kingdom, as well as all his other Pretensions, and restored to *Robert* all the Deeds on which they were founded, with all the Jewels taken at *Edinburgh* by *Edward* I. his Grandfather. Thirty thousand Marks, which *Robert* was to pay in three Years time, were reckoned a valuable Consideration for all these Restitutions; and the Peace was sealed by the Marriage of *Joan*, *Edward*'s Sister, with *David* Prince of *Scotland*, who was but seven Years of Age. Thus was *England* a Sufferer thro' the Minority of its King, and the Male-Administration of those who govern'd in his Name. In this Volume we have the authentic Act which *Edward* delivered as his Resignation of all his Pretensions upon *Scotland*. It is dated at *York* the first of *March*, 1328.

A. 1328.

Scandalous Peace with Scotland.

King's Resignation of his Superiority over Scotland.

P. 337.

'how desirous your Majesty 'has been all along to find 'them out; but when I mentioned the Estate your Majesty had promised, besides 'the Honour of Knighthood, 'as a Reward to him that 'should first bring Tidings 'of them to your Majesty, 'the Lords that command 'their Army having made 'me promise to discover 'where they were to your 'Majesty, freely quitted me 'my Ransom, and gave me 'full Liberty: For they said, 'they were every whit as desirous to fight with you; and 'if it please your Majesty, I 'shall shew you the Faces of 'them presently.'

Edw. III

King Robert Bruce's Death. P. 400.

KING *Robert* died in 1329 (the 9th of *July*) and there is a Passport of King *Edward*, dated at *Gloucester* the first of *September* following, which was granted to *James* Earl *Douglas*, who set out with his Heart for *Jerusalem* *.

IN a very little time the Face of Affairs was changed, *Edward* became of Age, or at least assumed the Reins of Government; and *Scotland* in its turn happened to be under a Minority, by the Death of *Robert Bruce*, who left his Son a Minor. The Fall of Queen *Isabel*, and the Punishment of the Earl of *March*, gave the *English* liberty to complain of the scandalous Peace which had been made with *Scotland*: And it was no difficult Task to persuade young K. *Edward* that he was not obliged to observe a Treaty so disadvantageous to *England*, and which had been made before he came of Age. He resolved therefore to set it aside, but was obliged to stay till he had made an end of some Affairs with *France*; so that he did not enter into Measures for the Execution of his Project till the Year 1331. He did not intend an open Rupture with *Scotland*, because the *Scots* gave him no Cause for it; but was resolved upon another Method to carry his Point, which was to excite Troubles in *Scotland*, that might furnish him with the Pretext he wanted. For this End he sent for *Edward Baliol*, the Son of *John Baliol*, whom *Edward* I. placed upon the Throne of *Scotland*, and afterwards depos'd, to come into *England*. It was now 32 Years since the *Baliol*

* THIS gallant Nobleman, whom the deceas'd King had conjured on his Deathbed to carry his Heart to the Holy-Land, to assist the Christians against the Infidels, was killed on his way to *Jerusalem*, in a Battel against the *Moors* in *Spain*, in the Year 1330. For his Death and heroic Character, *vide Buchanan*.

Family

Family had renounc'd the Crown: *John* was dead, and his Son did not so much as once think of reviving his Pretensions. Mean time, as he was necessary to King *Edward*, he caress'd him to a very great degree, and made him believe that the Kingdom of *Scotland* properly belong'd to him: And to these Persuasions he added a positive Promise of Assistance to enable him to recover his Right. As Men are very apt to close with what seems to tend to their advantage, *Baliol* thought that *Edward* only acted out of pure good Will to him, and therefore embraced his Offer without hesitation; whereas nothing was farther from *Edward*'s Thoughts, whose only view was to make a Tool of him to serve his own Purposes. He left *Baliol* therefore to build his Castles in the Air, and engaged him in the Undertaking, from which himself expected to reap all the Profit.

A. 1331.

Conference betwixt King Edward *and* Edward Baliol.

THIS Affair being thus settled, *Edward* took care to acquaint his Subjects privately, that they would do him a pleasure by assisting *Baliol* in his Design to recover his Kingdom. This was a sufficient hint to engage several Persons who had old Claims to Lands in *Scotland*, which they had obtain'd by the Bounty of *Edward* I. but lost by the Revolution that happen'd in Affairs after the Coronation of *Robert Bruce*. They rais'd Troops therefore, and went and offer'd them to *Baliol*, who was resolv'd to transport them by Sea to *Scotland*: Just as he was putting them aboard, *Edward* publish'd Proclamations, expressly forbidding his Subjects to assist *Baliol*; but this was not done till it was too late to hinder it. We find this Proclamation dated the 9th of *August*, 1332, at *Wigmore*; with an Order of the same day to all the Inhabitants of the Northern Counties, strictly to observe the Peace with

P. 529.

Edw. III. with *Scotland*. He had publish'd an Order of the like nature the Year before, which was dated at *Windsor* the 16th of *February*, at the same time that *Baliol* was making his Preparations; but it seems to have been done only to lay the *Scots* asleep. Upon these several Orders, and the Proclamation which I have just now mention'd, some Historians ground *Edward*'s Justification; and from hence they pretend to demonstrate, that he had no hand in *Baliol*'s Undertaking. But besides that it is not always safe to trust to the Declarations of Princes, it is manifest that *Edward* was privy to *Baliol*'s Designs from the very Beginning; because the latter did not come into *England* without two good Passports from the King, the one dated the 20th of *July*, 1330, at *Woodstock*, and the other on the 10th of *October* following, at *Nottingham*. But that they had such a Correspondence and Concert, will appear yet farther by the Sequel.

P. 470.

A Mistake of several Historians discover'd with respect to Edward *and* Baliol.

His Passports for Baliol, *p.* 445, 452.

EDWARD's Proclamation did not hinder *Baliol* from embarking his Troops to the number of 2500 Men, with whom he sail'd to *Kingborn*, where he had scarce put them ashore, but he was obliged to stand a Battel with the Lord *Seaton*, who was advanc'd with 10000 Men to hinder his landing. The necessity which the *English* were under of getting the Victory in an Enemy's Country, where they had no place of Retreat, made them fight desperately, so that they routed the *Scots* Army. This first Success procured *Baliol* fresh Succours, which were brought to him by the antient Friends of his Family. With this Reinforcement he had the Courage to face the Earl of *Fife*, who follow'd at the heels of the Lord *Seaton* with a powerful Army, which he beat as heartily as he

Battles betwixt Baliol *and Lord* Seaton, *the Earl of* Fife, *and* Nigel Bruce.

he did the former, and put to the rout. Two days after he defeated another Army commanded by *Nigel Bruce*, which was augmented by the broken Remains of the preceding; and finally, he routed the Earl of *Fife* a second time, who advanc'd with a burning Thirst of Revenge, but carry'd off a double Mortification. Four Battels thus gain'd in a few days, put *Baliol* in a Condition to fear no considerable Opposition any longer: He advanced therefore farther into the Country, took *Perth* or *St. Johnstoun*, and *Edinburgh*; after which he went to *Stoon*, where he was crown'd, if not with the Consent of all the *Scots*, yet at least without Opposition *.

A. 1331.

Baliol's *Coronation*

WHILE these Things were transacting in *Scotland*, *Edward* artfully made use of some Troubles that happen'd in *Ireland*, for a Pretence to arm: For this end he assembled his Parliament, and told them the necessity of his carrying an Army into *Ireland*, to settle the Affairs of that Island. His Design was approv'd, and the Parliament granted him a considerable Subsidy. He rais'd Troops therefore, and sent them towards the West, as if he intended to embark them on that Coast: While they were on the March, he told the Parliament, That the Troubles in *Scotland* demanded his Presence in the North, and that it was not safe to let the Frontiers lie naked while their Neighbours were up in Arms. His Voyage to *Ireland* was broke off therefore, and his Troops design'd for that Island had Orders to advance towards the Frontiers of *Scotland*. *Edward* began from that time to complain that the *Scots* had broke the Peace,

Edward's *Connivance to assist him.*

* Mr. *Burnet*, who gives a particular Account of all these Battles, says the Coronation was on the 27th of *September*, 1331.

and

Edw.III. and pretended Advice from good hands, that they had a design to invade *England*. Tho' this was a very shallow Complaint, considering the sad state of the *Scots* Affairs at that juncture, yet it was upon this Pretext that he rais'd fresh

P. 533. Troops, as appears by a Commission which he issu'd for that purpose on the 7th of *October*, 1332, from *Nottingham*.

K. David *retires to* France.

MEAN time King *David*, after all his Losses, was retired with his Wife into *France*, leaving a Regent in *Scotland*, who did all that Man could do to retrieve his Master's Affairs, which were at a very low ebb. This Regent seeing

King Edward's *Commission to treat with the Envoys of the Regent of* Scotland.

Edward advancing to the Frontiers, sent to know what was his design. *Edward* amus'd his Envoys for a while, by appointing Commissioners to treat with them, as appears by his full Powers, dated at *York*, the 26th of *October*, 1332; but to conclude any thing, was far from his intention: for at the same time he made

P. 535. a Treaty with *Baliol*, whereby he own'd him for King of *Scotland*; on which Condition, the

He makes a Treaty at the same time with Baliol, *who does him Homage for the Realm of* Scotland.

latter yielded him the Town and County of *Berwick*, and engaged for himself and his Successors, to perform Homage and Allegiance to the Kings of *England* for the Crown of *Scotland*. The Act is dated at *Roxburgh*, the 23d of *November* following; and plainly shews the secret understanding there was betwixt *Edward* and *Baliol*. 'For the latter therein declared,

P. 537. That he had been crown'd by the Permission of *Edward*, and by the Assistance of the good People of *England*. He added, moreover, in this Act of Cession, that he had perform'd Homage and Allegiance for all *Scotland*, and for the Isles thereon depending; and that he had taken the Oath of Fidelity to him, in quality

P. 539. of his Vassal. By another Act of the same Date,

Date, *Baliol* engaged to succour *Edward* with all his Forces, as often as he should be required; and openly acknowledg'd, that he had been crown'd by his assistance. It must be observ'd, that these Acts are dated the 23d of *November*; that is to say, three Months after *Baliol*'s entrance into *Scotland*. Can any body imagine therefore, that *Baliol* could in so short a space of Time, and immediately after his Coronation, without any apparent Cause, take a resolution to become a Vassal to *Edward*, and to yield *Berwick* to him, if there had not been a previous Agreement for that purpose before he engaged in the Undertaking? Vain therefore are the Efforts of certain Writers to justify *Edward* upon this Article, since it is manifest that he was the first Author of this Expedition. *A.*1332.

Another of Edward's *Commissions to treat with the Envoys of the Regent of* Scotland. *P.* 540.

YET, for all this, *Edward* continu'd to dissemble the Part he was acting, and to amuse the Regent of *Scotland* by Negotiations, as appears by another full Power which he granted to Commissioners to treat with him, dated at *York*, the 14th of *December* following.

His Apology to the Pope. *P.* 540.

BUT this Disguise being seen thro' by the Publick, the Pope wrote to him, reproaching him for his Injustice to *Scotland*: and here we have *Edward*'s Answer, dated the 15th of the same Month, at *York*; wherein he endeavours to justify himself from the Suggestions of his Enemies, and for this end makes use of the same Argument we have already mention'd, *viz.* by giving the Pope to understand, that just as he was setting out for *Ireland*, he was inform'd that the *Scots* had a design to invade his Dominions, and that this was the only reason which engaged him to march towards the Frontiers. The Date of this Answer of his

Edw. III. his to the Pope, is three Weeks after he had receiv'd *Baliol*'s Homage.

It was not long neither before the Regent of *Scotland* suspected *Edward*'s Designs, who he imagin'd would not have brought so powerful an Army upon the Frontiers, if he had not had some ill Intention. Therefore he spent the whole Winter in raising an Army in those Counties which continu'd to declare for King *David*. This was enough to furnish the King of *England* with Matter of Complaint that the *Scots* intended to break the Peace, and to invade *England*; which, says *Edward*, obliged him to be before-hand with them; and he himself actually began the Hostilities: and when the *Scots* prepared to defend themselves, the Lord *William Douglas*, who had the misfortune to be taken Prisoner by the *English*, was laid in Irons, as if he had been guilty of Rebellion or High-Treason.

His Apologies to the King of France, *and the Earl of* Flanders, *for the War with* Scotland. *P.* 556, 557

The War being begun, *Edward* still pretended that the *Scots* were the Aggressors, and endeavour'd to make the King of *France* and the Earl of *Flanders* believe as much, by two Letters; that to the Earl of *Flanders* being dated at *Newcastle* upon *Tine*, the 27th of *April*, 1333, and that to the King of *France* dated at *Belford*, the 7th of *May* following. This plainly shews what Precaution is necessary in the reading of the Letters of this and many other Princes, wherein we find the Truth so often disguis'd.

He besieges and takes Berwick. *P.* 564.

All the Motions of *Edward* ended at last in the Siege of *Berwick*, which he attack'd in *July* following, the 15th of which Month is the Date of its Capitulation. The Governour of it being inform'd that the Regent was advancing to raise the Siege, thought he should run

run no hazard by engaging to surrender the Place, if it was not reliev'd before the 20th instant. No sooner was the Capitulation sign'd, but *Edward* heard that the Enemy was just at hand, and therefore he went to receive them upon *Halydown* Hill; where he gain'd one of the most signal Victories that the *English* ever obtain'd over *Scotland*. And here we have the King's Orders, dated at *Berwick* upon *Tweed*, the 22d and 28th of *July*, 1333, for Thanksgivings for the said Victory, which was won, if I mistake not, upon the 18th of that Month *.

A. 1333.

Victory at Halydown *Hill.*

King's Orders for Thanksgivings for it.

Berwick thereupon surrender'd; and the *Scots* being quite dispirited by so many Losses, one upon the neck of another, left *Edward* and *Baliol* to congratulate each other on their Success; while a few, who still retain'd their Fidelity to King *David*, lay conceal'd about the Bogs and Mountains, waiting for better Times.

P. 568, 571

IN *February*, 1334, *Baliol* held his first Parliament at *Edinburgh*, and not at *Perth*, as many Historians have affirm'd †; for Mr. *Rymer* has given us the Acts of the said Parliament, dated at *Edinburgh*, in the Month aforesaid. The Homage perform'd by *Baliol* was therein approv'd; *England*'s Sovereignty over *Scotland* re-establish'd, and the Surrender of *Berwick* confirm'd. Moreover, all the Acts passed in the Reign of *Robert Bruce*, were therein repeal'd, as having been made by illegal Authority.

A Mistake of Historians about Baliol's *first Parliament.*

P. 590, to 595.

ON the 12th of *June* following, *Baliol* thinking he had not done enough for King *Edward*, was desirous to give him a farther Testimony

Baliol's *Grants to King* Edward.

* According to *Henry de Knighton*, and *Joshua Barnes*, the Battle was fought on the 19th.

† *Walsingham* and *Barnes* are both guilty of this Error, whose Authority, no doubt, misled many others.

of

Edw. III. of his Gratitude, by an Instrument dated at *Newcastle* upon *Tine*, whereby of his own Accord and free Will, he gave him the Grant of *Edinburg*, *Roxburg*, *Jedworth*, *Selkirk*, and some other Towns, Castles, and Districts, which lay convenient for *England*; of all which Places *Edward* immediately took possession, as we find by two Acts of his, dated at the same Place, on the 15th, which was but three days after the Date of the Grant.

P. 614.

Edward *takes possession of them.* P. 616, 617.

THE *Scots* finding themselves thus betray'd by their new King, began to take new measures, and resolv'd to perish, rather than be any longer in subjection to the King of *England.* They perceiv'd, without much difficulty, that *Edward* was in reality King of *Scotland* more than *Baliol*; and that the latter was but a Tool to serve the Purposes of the King of *England.* Therefore they secretly assembled some Troops, with which they went and surpriz'd *Baliol* when he thought nothing of the matter; and by that unexpected Attack entirely defeated him, and obliged him to mount a Horse without a Saddle, and fly to *Carlisle*, from whence he sent his Protector an Account of his Disaster.

Baliol *defeated merely by a Surprize.*

EDWARD was too deeply engaged in his Affair, to leave his Work unfinish'd and imperfect; therefore he march'd into *Scotland*, where he ravaged several Counties, and then return'd into his Dominions. The *Scots* assembled again in the following Winter, in order to make head against another Invasion, which they apprehended from *Edward*; but the King of *France* procured a Truce for them to the end of *June*, which gave them some Respite. As soon as it was expired, *Edward* ravaged *Scotland* a second time, but could not bring the

King Edward *revenges it by an Excursion into* Scotland, *and after a short Truce ravages it again.*

Scots

Scots to a Battle, because they were afraid to expose the few Troops they had left. Mean time the Earl of *Namur*, who serv'd *England*, was taken by the *Scots*, but set at liberty by *Murray* the Regent of *Scotland*; who, to extend his Generosity to him yet further, thought fit to accompany him to the Frontiers, and had the Misfortune to be taken Prisoner himself by the Garison of *Roxburg*, upon the 13th of *August*. After *Edward* had done all that he listed in *Scotland*, at the Request of the Pope and the King of *France*, he granted a Truce till the Feast of *Easter*, 1336; as appears by several Instruments of his, dated the 1st of *November*, 1335, at *Dodington*; the 8th *ditto* at *Alnwick*; the 16th and 23d at *Newcastle* upon *Tine*; and on the 22d and 26th of *January* following, at *Berwick* upon *Tweed*.

A. 1336. *Earl of* Namur *taken by the* Scots, *and the Earl of* Murray *by the* English.

Edward *grants another short Truce.* P. 674, 675, 676, 681, 684, 685.

DURING this Truce, King *David*, who was all the while a Refugee in *France*, had the liberty of sending Ambassadors into *England* to treat of an Accommodation, but it all came to nothing. Those Negotiations are the subject of several Acts in this Collection, which are of the less Importance, because they were of no effect. Tho' *Baliol* still bore the Title of King of *Scotland*, he had no more Authority there; for *Edward* was Lord of all, and he only allow'd *Baliol* five Marks a day for his Subsistence.

Baliol *but a Cypher, and kept at short Allowance by* K. Edward

As soon as the Truce was expir'd, *Edward* march'd a third time into *Scotland*, as appears by divers of his Orders, dated at *Perth*, or *St. Johnstoun*, from the 3d of *July* to the 3d of *September*, 1336.

Edward's *3d March into* Scotland. P. 700, 708

THE Remainder of the Year was spent in divers Negotiations in favour of the *Scots*, at the Sollication of the King of *France*, who

Edw. III. suffer'd *Edward* to trifle with him, as appears by several of *Edward*'s Acts, dated at *Perth*, as aforesaid, in *July* and *August*. King *Edward* had left the Command of his Troops to the Earl of *Athol*, who had the ill Luck to be surpriz'd by the *Scots*, and kill'd in Battle *.

P. 704 to 707.

Orders for subsisting the Earl of Murray, *a Prisoner in the Tower.*

P. 729, 735

AMONG the Acts of the Year 1337, there is an Order of the 24th of *January*, for the Payment of twenty Shillings a Week for the Subsistence of the Earl of *Murray*, then Prisoner in the Tower; which Allowance we find augmented afterwards, by an Order of the 16th of *March* following, to twenty six Shillings and eight Pence *per* Week, because of the Dearness of Provisions.

Edward'*s fourth Expedition to* Scotland.

AFTER many fruitless Negotiations which were carry'd on about the beginning of the Year 1337, *Edward* went again, in the Month of *June*, to *Scotland*; and in this fourth Expedition made cruel Ravage of that unhappy Kingdom: after which he return'd home to his own Dominions, because he found no Enemies to oppose him. In the next Article we shall find the Motive which inclin'd that Prince to give the *Scots* some Respite; tho' he would not have given over his Enterprize nevertheless, if he had not thought them sufficiently reduced. Here end the Acts of this fourth Volume, which relate to *Scotland*.

IN our Account of the second Volume of the *Fœdera*, the Foundation of the King of *England*'s Pretensions to *Scotland* is stated at large,

* MR. *Barnes* says, this Battle was fought in the Fields of *Kilblain*, upon the last day of *December* 1335; and that the Earl of *Athol*, who fell in it, *viz.* *David Strabolgi*, (and not *Cumin*, as *Hector Boetius* and *Buchanan* erroneously call him) was also a Baron of *England*, where he had large Possessions.

and

and it is left to the Reader to judge whether Edward III. was justifiable in reviving them, after they had been so solemnly renounced, and whether the ways and means he made use of for this end were regular. They who have endeavour'd to justify him upon this Article, have rather given proofs of their Prepossession than of their Sincerity: the Prepossession, I mean, of *England*'s Sovereignty over *Scotland*, which has been for a long time the favourite Passion of the *English* Politicians, and is so still with some; for not many Years ago, Books were publish'd upon this very subject with as much Earnestness as if the Affair was a new subject of Controversy: but it is to be hoped that the Union of the two Kingdoms has now almost entirely quash'd this Contention, which has already been of too long standing. *A.* 1337.

Article III. *Affairs of* France.

FEW People are Strangers to the great and famous Quarrel between *Edward* III. and *Philip* of *Valois*, concerning the Crown of *France*, and the War that broke out betwixt those two Princes upon that occasion. This fourth Volume contains only the Preparations for this bloody War; such Preparations as lasted eight or nine Years before *Edward* declared actual War. Tho' the Transactions during those nine Years may seem of little importance at first, yet several Instructions may be gather'd from the Acts which this Volume furnishes for that *Period*, or rather *Parenthesis* of Time. They let us in a great measure into *Edward* the Third's Character, whose Enterprizes were attended with such great and happy Successes, that Historians have slightly pass'd over the minutest of his Ac-

 tions,

Edw. III. tions, in order to expatiate upon the most considerable. In the Narrative of his Victories they have taken vast delight to extol his Valour, his Prudence, Generosity, and the Sublimity of his Genius; and every body must acknowledge that the Encomia they gave him were his due. But all this is not sufficient to make up the compleat Character of this Prince; which, to be perfectly acquainted with, the Reader should know his Suppleness in Negotiations, and some other Circumstances attending his Actions of a lower Class; which shew that his Virtue was not of the most rigid kind, or at least that he was convinc'd that Dissimulation was not incompatible with the Virtues of a great King. This was a Fault which he was guilty of in common with many great Princes, who were as careless as he of the Reputation they left to Posterity; tho' such a Care or Regard ought to be as great a Constraint and Check to them, as the Fear of the Laws is to private Persons. We have seen a remarkable instance of this Insincerity in *Edward*, in the Designs which he form'd against *Scotland*; and the remaining Part of this Volume furnishes us with some other Proofs of it in his Conduct to *Philip de Valois*, before he formally enter'd upon that War, which he had long been contriving against him.

King Edward's Character.

As soon as *Edward* was seated on the Throne, the Queen his Mother, and *Mortimer*, who govern'd all Affairs, and as much dreaded a War with *France* as with *Scotland*, consulted how to put an end to all the Differences which *England* had with *France*. The last Treaty which *Isabel* concluded at *Paris* had left some things undetermin'd, which were capable of producing Quarrels between the two Crowns, and which it was therefore necessary to prevent, especially

during

during *Edward*'s Minority. Accordingly Ambassadors were sent to *France* about a Month after the King's Coronation, in order to settle all the Matters in dispute. Their full Powers are dated at *Westminster*, the 22d of *February*, 1327, and they concluded a Treaty the 31st of *March* following, at *Paris*; by which it was stipulated, among other things, that *Edward* should pay *Charles the Fair* 50,000 Marks *Sterling*, for the Charges of the preceding War, and demolish the Castles of the condemn'd Lords of *Gascoigne*, who were moreover pardon'd as to Life and Member, provided that they obey'd the Ban, *i. e.* submitted to Banishment. Tho' *Edward* did not much mind the execution of this Treaty, yet the two Kings liv'd in Peace all the rest of this Year.

A. 1327. *Ambassadors sent to* France. P. 264, 267. *Treaty with* Charles the Fair *of* France. P. 279.

ABOUT the beginning of 1328, a fresh Quarrel broke out between the two Crowns, of much greater importance than that which was lately accommodated. *Charles the Fair* happen'd to die on the first of *February*, without Male-Issue; but *Blanche*, his Queen, was seven Months gone with Child. It was given out, that before his death he nominated his Cousin-German, *Philip de Valois*, to be Regent till the Queen was brought to bed. On the other hand, *Edward* demanded the Regency, as the nearest Relation of the deceas'd King, to whom he was Nephew; whereas *Philip*, as has been said, was no more than Cousin-German. This was a Question which the States of the Kingdom were assembled to decide. *Philip* founded his Plea upon the *Salic* Law; which, said he, excluded all Women and their Descendants from the Crown, and by consequence from the Regency. *Edward* argu'd on the other hand, that the *Salic* Law only excluded Women from the Crown on ac-

A fresh Quarrel breaks out between the two Nations, about the Regency of France.

Edw. III. account of their Sex, and not the Male-Iſſue, deſcended from ſuch Women, becauſe they had not that Imbecillity of Sex. The States however adjudg'd the Regency to *Philip de Valois*, during the Queen's Pregnancy; who being brought to bed of a Daughter on the firſt of *April* that ſame Year, *Philip de Valois* was own'd King of *France*, and crown'd the 28th of *May* following.

BEFORE we proceed further, it is neceſſary to obſerve, that the ſubject in debate has been attended with ſome Difficulties which were never fully clear'd up, and which ſome Acts in this Volume may help to elucidate or reſolve. The firſt Difficulty is to know whether *Edward* ſent Ambaſſadors into *France* to demand the Regency immediately after the death of *Charles the Fair*. 2. Whether the States of *France* made two Decrees, one for aſſigning the Regency to *Philip*, another for adjudging the Crown to him. 3. Whether *Edward*'s Ambaſſadors demanded the Crown for their Maſter, after Queen *Blanche*'s Delivery; whether they were heard; and whether the States determin'd for *Philip*, after conſideration of the Arguments brought by both Claimants. 4. It will be neceſſary to examine where the Knot of the Queſtion between the two Claimants chiefly lay; a Diſpute which the *French* Hiſtorians ſeem to have hurry'd over in too general a manner, and with very great Confuſion, as if they were afraid to loſe ground by a cloſe diſcuſſion of Particulars. I hope therefore it will not be unacceptable, if I make a ſhort pauſe upon each of the ſeveral Queſtions, becauſe the great Conſequences with which this famous Proceſs was attended, render this Subject one of the moſt con-

considerable Articles in the Histories of *France* and *England*. *A.* 1328.

Dispute betwixt Edward *and* Philip de Valois *about the Regency of* France.

1. ALL the *French* Historians unanimously affirm, that *Edward* sent Ambassadors to *France* to demand the Regency; and they mention the very Speech which they made to the States of that Kingdom, with their very Allegations, and the Answer return'd to them by *Robert* of *Artois*, who was then a great Stickler for *Philip*. But among all the *English* Historians, I know not one who mentions this Embassy: And in all the Acts of this fourth Volume, which contains a multitude of others that are of less importance, there is not a single Sentence to be found which gives room to believe that *Edward* sent any Ambassadors upon this Errand. It is likewise to be suppos'd, that Queen *Isabel* and the Earl of *March*, who managed all the Affairs of the Realm, would not have offer'd at any such thing, for fear of engaging themselves in a War with *France*, since the said Queen and Earl, for the sake of avoiding a War with *Scotland*, had presum'd visibly to betray the Interests of their Pupil. These Reasons make it shrewdly suspicious, that the Speeches of the *English* Ambassadors, and of *Robert* of *Artois*, were invented by *Paul Emilius*, who publish'd them, or by some other Historian. Nevertheless this is but a negative Proof, which cannot entirely be depended on, since all the *French* Historians agree in the contrary. But be it as it will, whether *Edward* did or did not send Ambassadors to demand the Regency, it is certain that he look'd upon the States Determination in favour of *Philip de Valois*, as a piece of Injustice done to himself, being very sensible of the Advantage which his Competitor might reap

Edw.III. reap from the Regency, in caſe the Queen Dowager ſhould be brought to Bed of a Daughter. This appears from the Letters which he wrote during the interval between the Decree made about the Regency and the Queen's Lying-in, who was not brought to Bed till the Month of *April*. Theſe Letters, directed to ſeveral Noblemen of *Guyenne*, to the Univerſities, Biſhops, Priors, Abbats, Knights, and Gentlemen of eighteen Towns of *Navarre*, to twenty nine Noblemen of *Foix* and *Languedoc*, and to nineteen Towns of this latter Province, imported that he intended to recover his Inheritance by one means or another, when he ſaw it a proper Time. One would be apt to think, that by his Inheritance he meant *Guyenne*, if in ſome of thoſe Letters he did not plainly talk of the Inheritance of his Mother: This ſhews that he ſpoke of the Kingdom of *France*, as well as of *Navarre*, which was in the ſame Caſe, and not of *Guyenne*, to which his Mother had no Right. Theſe Letters are dated at *Lincoln*, the 28th of *March*, 1328, before the Queen's Lying-in.

King Edward's Letters to the Nobility, &c. in France.

P. 344, *to* 347.

II. The ſecond Difficulty to be ſolv'd, is to know whether the States that had given the Regency to *Philip de Valois*, immediately after the death of *Charles the Fair*, did by a ſecond Sentence decree the Crown to him likewiſe, after the Queen Dowager's Delivery. Here we find a mighty Confuſion in the *French* Hiſtorians, who jumble theſe two Queſtions together, which they ought by all means to have ſtated ſeparately. They ſay indeed, that the States ſettled the Regency on *Philip*; and they affirm likewiſe, that the States ſet the Crown upon his Head: but when they talk of the

Confuſion in the French *Writers.*

the latter Decree, it looks as if they meant A. 1328. the former, relating to the Regency, because they there bring in the *English* Ambassadors, and put the very same Speech into their Mouths which they made when they demanded the Regency for their Master; and they make *Robert* of *Artois* return just the same Answer. 'Tis impossible that the same Things should happen on those two different Occasions: The Reason is plain, for supposing that the Ambassadors of *England* were present at the first Decree of the States about the Regency, which I am loth either to affirm or deny, for the Reasons mention'd in the foregoing Article; it is however certain, that they were not present when the Crown was decreed to *Philip*; and that they did not demand it, because they had not yet received Orders about it. What I have now mention'd, is evident from two decisive Pieces in this Collection. The first is a full Power granted by *Edward* to his Ambassadors, to demand the Crown of *France* in his Name; which full Power is dated at *Northampton*, the 16th of *May*, 1328, only twelve Days before *Philip*'s Coronation.

King Edward's *Demand of the Crown of* France, *p.* 354.

Now that the *English* Ambassadors could get to *Paris*, or supposing them there already, that they could receive their Commission, and execute it; that a Question so important should be examin'd and determin'd in an Assembly of the States, where, according to *Mezeray*, Parties ran very high; and finally, that the Preparations for the Coronation, and the Ceremony it self, should be perform'd in the space of twelve Days; that so short a space of Time, I say, should be sufficient for all those Things, is a Matter almost past belief. The second Piece is a sort of Manifesto by King *Edward*, which we meet with in the 5th Volume of

Edw. III. the *Fœdera*: In the ſaid Manifeſto, *Edward* expreſly complains, that his Ambaſſadors had not been heard, and that they had even run the hazard of their Lives. All this gives room to believe, that there was no ſolemn Sentence given touching the Crown, and that when *Philip de Valois* had obtain'd the Regency, he never troubled his Head about a ſecond Deciſion, but caus'd himſelf to be crown'd; imagining that the ſame Reaſons which made him a Regent, conſtituted him King. It muſt be own'd, at leaſt, that if there was a ſecond Decree, it was made with very great Precipitation, and without the Intervention of the *Engliſh* Ambaſſadors.

III. The third Difficulty is explain'd under the ſecond Head, and therefore it is not neceſſary to inſiſt on it.

IV. Tho' *Edward* ſeem'd tacitly to acquieſce in the Decree of the States, yet he never abandon'd his Deſign to aſſert his Right when a fair Opportunity ſhould offer; but his Age, the Subjection in which he was kept by his Mother and *Mortimer*, and the War with *Scotland* which enſu'd, hinder'd him from openly diſcovering his Deſign, till the Year 1337, as we ſhall ſhew preſently. But as this Affair was attended with terrible Conſequences, and was, as it were, the Beginning and Cauſe of the moſt remarkable Tranſactions mention'd in the Hiſtories of *France* and *England* for above a Century, it is neceſſary to explain the fourth Difficulty, which is to know exactly upon what Plea *Edward* grounded himſelf, when he undertook to wreſt the Crown of *France* out of the Hands of *Philip*. It ſeems as if the main View of the *French* Authors, was to render this Matter obscure, by treating it in a general way, and insinuating that *Edward* disputed with the *French* the Authority of their *Salic Law*, of which they had been in Possession near a thousand Years: By this means, if I may venture to say it, they have misled their Readers, and prejudic'd a multitude of People against *Edward's* Pretensions.

A. 1328.

A just Reflection on the French *Authors.*

THE *Salic* Law, according to which the *French* exclude Women from the Crown, is only founded upon Tradition; for never was any Original, or authentick Copy of it produc'd. The Author of it and its Vouchers are alike unknown; for they only quote an old Chronicle without giving us either its Date or Author, which ascribes the Glory of it to *Pharamond*, the first King known among the *French*. From *Pharamond* to the Death of *Lewis Huttin*, that is to say, for almost 900 Years, it was not put in practice, at least we know of no publick Act, or any Fact related in ancient Histories, to prove beyond dispute that the *French* govern'd themselves by this Law in the Disposal of their Crown. This will no doubt be thought very strange, by those who are already prepossest in its favour; therefore 'tis necessary to enter into a short Detail upon this Subject, and briefly to run over the three Races or Families of the *French* Monarchs.

Salic Law.

WHILE the Family of *Meroveus* was upon the Throne, there are but three Instances that can be produc'd to prove the Practice of this Law; and all three too weak to support the Inferences which some would fain deduce from them. The first is taken from the Settlement which was made of the Crown after the Death of *Childebert* King of *Paris*, whose two Daughters were depriv'd of their Father's Succession. See what *Mezeray* says upon this Subject, in his Abridgment.

The Merovingian *Race of* France.

Edw. III. Abridgment. *Their Uncle* Clotaire, *either in hatred of their Father, or for fear lest they should pretend to the Succession, detain'd them in Prison till he was sure of the Kingdom. This is the first Instance of the* Salic *Law in favour of the Males.* Is it possible to bring a more silly Allegation than that to prove the Authority of this Law, since it manifestly discovers that it was Force only which depriv'd those Daughters of *Childebert* of their Father's Inheritance! The second Instance may be fetch'd from the History of the Succession after the Death of *Cherebert* King of *Paris*. This Prince had left three Daughters, of which the two eldest were Bastards and Nuns. *Bertha*, who was the youngest, and was afterwards the Wife of *Ethelbert* King of *Kent* in *England*, was hinder'd from succeeding her Father, by her three Uncles, *Gontran*, *Sigebert* and *Chilperic*: But this was likewise by Force, and not by virtue of the *Salic* Law, of which no History makes mention in this Place. In order to prove that this Succession was by virtue of the *Salic* Law, the said Law should either be produc'd in due Form, or at least it should be prov'd that it had been put in Practice before: But the Instance I gave just now is the only one that precedes this; and, as I have before shewn that to be insufficient, there's no making use of it upon this Occasion. The third Instance is taken from the Succession of *Gontran*, which his Brothers shar'd betwixt them, because he had left only one Daughter: But this Daughter was a Nun, and by consequence not capable of succeeding. Besides, History says no where, that *Gontran*'s Brothers succeeded to him by virtue of the *Salic* Law, but only that they shar'd the Succession; which they were like enough to do, as well by Force as by legal Right; the rather, because 'tis well known that the *French* Princes were not

over

A. 1328.

over ſcrupulous at that time. All who underſtand any thing of the Hiſtory of *France*, know full well that in thoſe Days Force had a greater Share than the Laws, in the Diſtribution of the Kingdoms into which that Monarchy was divided. Towards the Concluſion of this Race, the * Mayors of the *Palace* took upon them to place ſuch Princes of the Royal Family upon the Throne as they thought fit, without troubling themſelves with the Laws of the Country, Laws which are moreover very much unknown to us.

The Carlovingian *Race.*

IN the *Carlovingian* Race, which ſucceeded next to the Throne, we don't find that the Daughters were depriv'd of the Crown by virtue of the *Salic* Law; nor am I certain that there was ever any occaſion to put it in Execution. Be this as it will, we learn on the contrary, that, towards the end of this Race, the Deſcendants of *Charlemagne*, by the Female ſide, diſmember'd that potent Monarchy, as *Mezeray* ſomewhere obſerves; and all the while it does not appear that the *Salic* Law was ſo much as once oppos'd to their Pretenſions.

The Capetian *Race.*

AS to the Third, namely the *Capetian* Race, 'tis certain that there was no occaſion to put that pretended Law in Execution for above 300

* Theſe *Maires du Palais*, as the *French* call 'em, were Officers, whoſe Authority was ſo exorbitant, that they were not only the Guardians, but Governors of ſome of their ancient Kings, and either inthron'd or dethron'd 'em at their Will and Pleaſure. Hiſtory tells us, that *Clovis* II. and the ten Kings that follow'd him, to the concluſion of the *Merovingian* Race, were call'd *Faineans*; *i. e.* Idle Drones, becauſe inſtead of minding the Government themſelves, they left all to theſe *Mayors*, to whom every body made their Court, while the Princes ſpent their Time in Pleaſures, and were in a manner kept Priſoners in their Palaces, with ſuch Servants as the *Mayor* pleas'd, who were rather Spies upon 'em, than Attendants: And this very *Clovis* marry'd a Slave belonging to the *Mayor* of his Palace. *Vid.* Mezeray.

Edw. III. Years: And if any ſhould offer to object that never any Woman ſucceeded to the Crown from the beginning of the Monarchy, that's ſaying nothing to the purpoſe; for by the ſame Reaſon it may be prov'd, that there's a Law which excludes from the Crown thoſe that are born blind, becauſe ſince *Pharamond* no one that was born blind ever aſcended the Throne. To this we may add, that if the *Salic* Law had been eſtabliſh'd and own'd in *France*, *Hugh Capet*, who diſtributed among the Grandees of his Realm thoſe Lands, of which Dutchies, Earldoms, and Lordſhips were afterwards form'd, would not have fail'd to ſubject thoſe Lands to that ſame Law; becauſe no body could have taken it ill, if he had ſubjected the Parts to the ſame Law to which the Whole was ſubject. Nevertheleſs he did not do it, for on the contrary, 'tis certain that the great Fiefs belonging to the Crown deſcended to the Females, as is poſitively affirm'd both by *Paſquier* and *Mezeray*. But I do not pretend by this to combat the Right of the Males as for what relates to the Time preſent; the States of the Realm having thus eſtabliſh'd it, being a ſufficient Conſideration to put it out of all manner of Diſpute: Neither do I propoſe to treat of any thing but what paſs'd down to the firſt Deciſion of the States of the Realm, made after the Death of *Lewis Huttin*; which was not many Years before the Proceſs now in queſtion. To this Enquiry into the *Salic* Law in general, it is neceſſary to add another for the ſake of particular Caſes which have reſpect to that Law, by ſhewing what regard was had to it from the Death of *Lewis Huttin*, to that of *Charles the Fair*.

A farther Enquiry into the Salic Law.

Lewis Huttin, who dy'd in 1316, only left one Daughter nam'd *Joan*; his Queen Dowager being

ing then with Child, the States chose to stay till A. 1316.
she was deliver'd before they dispos'd of the Crown: For if she had been brought to bed of a Son, this Son must have succeeded the Father; not by virtue of the *Salic* Law, but by virtue of a Law common to all States where the Males are preferr'd before the Females in the same degree of Kindred. Till the said Queen was brought to Bed, *Philip*, Brother to the deceas'd King, was declar'd Regent; an Honour which young *Joan* his Niece was not in a Condition to dispute with him, because she her self was under the necessity of having a Guardian. But *Mezeray* observes, that the Duke of *Burgundy*, *Joan*'s Uncle by the Mother's side, made Preparation to assert his Niece's Right in case the Queen Dowager miscarry'd, or was deliver'd of a Daughter. Mean time the Queen was brought to Bed of a Son nam'd *John*, who was immediately recogniz'd for King, but did not live above eight Days; whereupon a great Quarrel arose about the Succession. *Charles* Count *de Valois*, Uncle to the deceased King, and the Duke of *Burgundy*, declar'd openly for *Joan* against her Uncle *Philip*; in which they both set up against their own Interests, because as they were Princes of the Blood, the *Salic* Law was advantageous to their Families. This shews that the said Law was not yet firmly establish'd, because the first Princes of the Blood, and the chief Peers of the Realm, made no Scruple to maintain a Right which was directly against it. Be that as it will, the States decided in Favour of *Philip*, who was surnam'd *the Long*, and was the fifth King of *France* of that Name. This now was the first clear, exact and undisputed Decision that the States of *France* ever made in Favour of the *Salic* Law, which was 900 Years after the Foundation of the *French* Monarchy. *Philip the*

Edw. III. *Long* dying after a short Reign, and leaving only three Daughters, his Brother *Charles the Fair* succeeded him without Opposition, to the Prejudice of his Nieces. This again was a second incontested Decision in Favour of the Males. Lastly, after the Death of *Charles the Fair*, who left his Queen also with Child, the Dispute now in question arose between *Edward* III. and *Philip de Valois* for the Regency, or rather for the Crown of *France*. Thus have I given you the most material Passages, with respect to the *Salic* Law, from the very Foundation of the *French* Monarchy.

A State of the Question between Edward *and* Philip de Valois.

Now, in order to give a true State of the Controversy between *Edward* and *Philip de Valois*, it must be consider'd that they both laid down the *Salic* Law for the Basis of their Pretensions. The only difference between them was, that *Philip* would have it to extend to the Descendants of the Females; whereas *Edward* insisted, that it ought to extend only to the Females, because of the Imbecility of the Sex; and not to their Male-Descendants, who had not that Incapacity. 'Tis therefore plain, that those who have asserted that *Edward* directly oppugned the *Salic* Law, have not stated the Question as it ought to be; for *Edward* was too wise a Prince to reject a Law which was the only Basis of his Right.

An Oversight of some Historians detected.

For without the *Salic* Law what Right had *Charles the Fair* to the Crown, when his elder Brother had left three Daughters? And if *Charles* had not had a Right to the Crown, how could his Sister *Isabel*, who was *Edward*'s Mother, come by any Right to it? Besides, if the *Salic* Law had not taken Place, *Edward* himself would have had no Right to the Crown; because the Daughters of *Philip the Long*, the Daughters of *Charles the Fair*, and his own Mother, who

was ſtill alive, would have come in before him. *A.*1328.
Therefore he was far from diſputing the Authority of this Law, which, whether true or not, was ſo much for his Advantage; but he maintain'd that it extended to the Females only, and not to their Deſcendants: From whence he inferr'd, that as he was the neareſt Male Heir to the deceaſed King, the Crown devolv'd to him by Right of Affinity; and not to *Philip de Valois*, who was not ſo near a-kin by one Degree. *Philip* on his part maintain'd, that the Law excluded not only the Females, but their Deſcendants; and this was properly the very Queſtion now to be decided by the States of the Realm. In order to form a Judgment of this Proceſs by the ordinary Rules of Juſtice, it were neceſſary to have recourſe to the Law it ſelf, or to Precedents; but neither the one nor the other is to be found. The *Salic* Law was no where in being, and in all the Hiſtory of *France* there was not a ſingle Inſtance to be met with that match'd the preſent Caſe: For the two foregoing Deciſions of the States, with reſpect to *Philip the Long* and *Charles the Fair*, and which at the ſame time were the only ones to be met with in the Hiſtory of *France*, did in no Senſe come up to it: 'Tis true, they eſtabliſh'd the Authority of the *Salic* Law, but they had no View to the Excluſion of the Deſcendants of Females, the only Point in controverſy. This by the way, confirms me in my Opinion, that the Harangues inſerted by *Paul Emilius*, I mean the Speech of the *Engliſh* Ambaſſadors, and the Anſwer of *Robert of Artois*, are ſpurious; becauſe neither the one nor the other enters into the Knot of the Queſtion. If it was a difficult Matter to prove the Exiſtence of the *Salic* Law, as I have already demonſtrated, it was no leſs difficult to explain it, for want of conſidering its Terms and Circumſtances.

Edw. III. cumſtances. Nevertheleſs there was a neceſſity of giving Judgment one way or another; and the States decided the Matter in favour of *Philip de Valois*, to which they were determin'd probably by four Reaſons. 1. That *Iſabel* could not convey a Right to her Son, which ſhe had not her ſelf. 2. That *Edward* was a Foreigner, born out of the Realm. 3. That he was ſtill a Minor: And, 4. That they were afraid of a Civil War if they ſhould award the Crown to that Prince; and that if a War ſhould be the Conſequence, they had rather expoſe themſelves to the Hazards of a Foreign one. But theſe are Reaſons which this is not a Place to enquire into. 'Tis ſufficient to obſerve, that the Deciſion of the States was new and unprecedented; that it was not taken from the Law it ſelf, and that it was purely grounded upon Reaſons of State. From hence therefore, I cannot help concluding, that *Edward*'s Pretenſions were not ſo extravagant as the *French* Authors would have them commonly underſtood. A grand Deciſion, which is ſupported neither by the Law it ſelf, nor any preceding Decree, is neceſſarily ſubjected, which way ſoever we turn it, to the Reproaches of the Party who loſes the Cauſe, without any Reflection upon the weakneſs of the Reaſons urg'd by the Complainant. *Edward* therefore might complain, that the Affair had been wrong decided, as to the Matter of it; and that the Award was null and void as to the Form of it, becauſe it had been paſs'd with too much Precipitancy; and particularly becauſe his Ambaſſadors had been deny'd a Hearing. And if to all this we add, that 'tis extremely probable there was no other Decree of the States than that which awarded the Regency to *Philip*, it will naturally be ſuppos'd that *Edward* did not complain without Reaſon; and it was this very Con-

Deciſion of the States of France *in favour of* Philip de Valois *conſider'd.*

A Vindication of Edward's *Pretenſions.*

Consideration that made him take a Resolution to maintain his Right by Force of Arms. I hope to have Pardon for this Digression, tho' 'tis not borrow'd from the Acts of the *Fœdera*, where nothing is to be found that sets forth *Edward's* Right in particular; for in all the Acts where any mention is made of it, the said Right is all along suppos'd as devolv'd to *Edward* by the Death of *Charles the Fair*, without entring into the Merits of the Cause. *A.* 1328.

BUT tho' the Acts of the *Fœdera* do not give us the particular Reasons on which the said Prince founded his Pretensions to the Crown of *France*; yet they plainly discover that he intended some time or other to assert his Right; contrary to the Opinion of those Writers who affirm that he was put upon it by *Robert* of *Artois*, and of others, who pretend that he never design'd it till the Year 1339, when he was provok'd by the *Flemings*, which we shall take notice of in the Account of the next Volume.

IT was with this View that in *June* 1328, King *Edward* form'd the Project of a League against *France*, with the Duke of *Brabant*, and all the Towns and People of that Province, as well as all those Noblemen in particular, who were inclin'd to engage in his Service, as appears from several Commissions which he dispatch'd that very Year. *His League with the* Brabanters *against* France.

WE find in a full Power which he gave to his Commissioners, dated the 22d of *August* 1328, at *Pontefract*, that he order'd them to demand of the Duke of *Brabant*, and all that wou'd enter into his Service, that they shou'd engage to serve him as well in Peace, as in a time of War, against any King or Prince whatsoever. This is a manifest Indication, that the Person aim'd at was the King of *France*, with whom he was then at Peace, and against whom he nevertheless P. 366.

Edw.III. verthelefs intended a War; for if this League had a View to the *Scots*, he needed not to have been fo careful in the wording of his Commiffion.

P. 366. THERE is another full Power to his Envoys of the fame Date, to treat with the Count *de Loos*, and all manner of Perfons that were difpos'd to engage in his Service.

P. 367. THERE's one of the like Nature, dated at *Wisbich*, the 15th of *September* following, to the Senefchal of *Gafcoigne*, and the Conftable of *Bourdeaux*, impowering them to treat upon the fame Foot with the Count *d'Armagnac*, the Vifcount of *Lomagne*, the Lord of *Albret*, and with all manner of Perfons of what Rank or Condition foever. Shall it be faid then, that all thefe Preparations were made againft *Scotland*, with which Nation his Majefty had but juft concluded a Peace? No; for it appears on the contrary, that they were defign'd againft

P. 368. *France*, by certain Letters Patent, dated at *Wifbich* aforefaid, the 16th of the fame Month, by which his Majefty engag'd himfelf to make neither Peace nor Truce with *France*, without including the Towns and Nobility of *Gafcoigne*. Nor can it be faid that he had a mind to go to War with *France* for any Interefts or Views lefs than for the Crown it felf, becaufe he had fettled all his other Difputes with that Kingdom but the very Year before.

PHILIP of *Valois*, who was engag'd in a War againft the *Flemings* from the beginning of his Reign, was in no great Hafte to demand King *Edward*'s Homage for the Dutchy of *Guyenne*, and Earldom of *Ponthieu*; for it was not till *March* 1329, that he fummon'd him to go over and pay it in Perfon. *Edward* was very loth to go and humble himfelf to a Prince, whom he look'd upon as no better than an Ufurper;

A. 1329.

ſurper; but his Council was of another Opinion, and it was agreed that he ſhould go and pay the Homage himſelf. Our Prince was as yet under the Guardianſhip of his Mother and of the Earl of *March*, who thought a War extremely prejudicial to their Intereſts, as plainly appear'd by the Peace which they had made with *Scotland*. 'Tis very probable, therefore, that it was by their Intereſt that the aforeſaid Opinion was carry'd in Council, on purpoſe to avoid a War, which wou'd have been inevitable if this Homage had been refus'd. Mean while *Edward*'s Compliance was ſorely againſt the Grain, tho' he had not Reſolution enough as yet to reſiſt thoſe to their Faces who had the Management of his Affairs. Mr. *Barnes*, who wrote the Hiſtory of his Life, avers, that he made an open Proteſtation before all his Council, againſt the Homage which he was to pay, that his Pretenſions to the Crown of *France* might not be thereby prejudic'd. And tho' we have nothing like this in the *Fœdera*, yet all the Meaſures taken by this Prince, both before and after the Homage, render this Circumſtance very probable. All we have in that Collection upon this Subject is a Letter from King *Edward* to *Philip*, in which he acquainted him, that he had for a great while reſolv'd to pay his Duty to him, but that ſeveral Affairs had interven'd to hinder him. This Letter is dated the 14th of *April* 1329, at *Wallingford*. He went over to *France* on the 15th of *May*, and perform'd his Homage at *Amiens* on the 6th of *June* following. The Inſtrument, or Deed of Homage, containing all the Particulars which paſs'd upon that occaſion, diſcovers ſome which may ſerve to clear up Facts that have been wrong explain'd by certain *French* Hiſtorians.

King Edward'*s Letter to* Philip de Valois, *about his Homage.* P. 381.

The Inſtrument of his Homage. P. 389.

PHILIP

Edw. III.

The History of it.

PHILIP claim'd * Liege Homage of *Edward* for the Dutchy of *Guyenne*, and the Earldom of *Ponthieu*; but in the Conferences which were held upon that Subject before the Ceremony, *Edward* protested, That he was not certain whether he ought to render Liege Homage, and therefore he refus'd to perform it otherwise than in general Terms. Nevertheless he promis'd upon his Honour, That if it should appear to him, after he had consulted his own Archives, that the Homage ought to be Liege, he would recognize the same by Letters Patent under his Great Seal. And upon this Condition he was admitted to perform only a Verbal Homage.

THE Instrument above-mention'd imports, that *Edward* appearing before *Philip*, *Miles de Noyers*, Viscount of *Melun*, Great Chamberlain of *France*, said to him, SIRE, *The King would have you understand, that he does not admit you to Homage for the Lands which he possesses, and ought to possess in* Gascoigne *and the* Agenois; *as to which Lands the late King* Charles *protested, that he never meant to receive Homage*. Then the Bishop of *Lincoln* protested on his part for *Edward*, That the Homage he was performing should not prejudice his Right to all *Guyenne*, and all its Dependencies; and that *France* should not thereby acquire a new Right. After this he deliver'd a Schedule to the Chamberlain, containing the Form of the Homage; upon the receiving of which Schedule the Great Chamberlain said to the King of *England*. 'SIRE, You become Liege-man to my Lord

* Homage Liege is done by the Vassal ungirt and bareheaded, with join'd Hands laid on the Evangelists, and a Kiss receiv'd in the taking of his Oath. *See* Cotgrave.

'the

'the King, for the Dutchy of *Guyenne* and its 'Dependencies, which you acknowledge to hold 'from him, as Peer of *France*, and Duke of '*Guyenne*; according to the Form of the Peace 'made between his and your Predecessors, the 'Kings of *France* and *England*; and according 'as you and your Ancestors, the Dukes of '*Guyenne*, have perform'd for the said Dutchy 'to his Ancestors the Kings of *France*.' The King of *England* answer'd, *Yes*. Then the Chamberlain proceeding said, SIRE, *The King of* France *receives you according to the Protestations already made:* to which the King of *France* said, *Yes*. This done, *Edward* putting his Hands between those of *Philip*, the latter receiv'd him by a Kiss of the Mouth. The same Ceremony was repeated by way of Homage for the Earldoms of *Ponthieu* and *Monstrevil*. The Schedule above-mention'd, was exactly agreeable to the Words of the Chamberlain just now repeated. 'Tis certain, therefore, that *Edward* paid only a Verbal Homage at that time, and in general Terms, tho' *du Tillet*, *de Serres*, and some other *French* Historians, have asserted the contrary.*

A. 1329.

Mistake of French *Historians.*

IT

* MR. *Barnes* also quotes *Mezeray*, and the King of *England*'s own Letters afterwards, to shew that this was a Mistake; and it deserves the more to be taken notice of, because it stands uncorrected in the *General History of* England, where Mr. *Daniel*, Penman of this Reign, seems to have taken it upon trust from those careless Writers above-mention'd, That when the King appear'd before *Philip*, he consented to put off his Crown, Sword, and Spurs, and to kneel down before him on a Cushion. Mr. *Barnes* observes what a mighty Disappointment our King's Stiffness in this Point was to *Philip* of *France*, who expected a very formal and full Homage, and invited the Kings of *Bohemia*, *Navarre* and *Majorca*, that he might

have

Edw. III.

P. 390.

It appears by a *Memorandum* in the *Fœdera*, that *Edward* return'd to *England* on the 11th of *June**. Before he went, he agreed with *Philip*, that as to their reciprocal Demands and Pretensions, he would send Ambassadors to *Paris*, to put an end to all Disputes. The rest of this Year was spent in various Negotiations, as well about the reciprocal Demands made at *Amiens*, as on the Proposals of marrying *Edward's* Brother and Sister to the Children of *Philip*. The King's full Powers for negotiating the Marriages are dated at *Canterbury* the 16th of *June*, and at *Gloucester* the 24th of *September* 1329. *Edward*, as had been agreed on, sent as Ambassadors to *Paris*, *Henry* Earl of *Lancaster* and the Bishop of *Norwich*. Their Instructions are dated at *Kenilworth* the 3d of *December*, and at *Eltham* the 27th of *January* following.

Marriage Treaty betwixt the Families of England *and* France.

P. 392, 403.

P. 407, 411.

Early next Year *Edward* had Intelligence that *Philip* intended to press him to a categorical Answer, about the Nature of the Homage perform'd at *Amiens*; and therefore he sent a full Power to his Ambassadors to discuss all his

have the more noble Witnesses of it. There came also, says our Author, all the chief Nobility of *France*, as if they had resolv'd to out-rival the *English* Nation, from whom they expected no more than 600 Horsemen; but our King carry'd over with him four Bishops, four Earls, of whom two were his Uncles, eight other Lords, above forty Knights, and a thousand Horse of War.

* The Reason of the King's hasty Departure seems a Circumstance too material to be omitted, taking for granted what Mr. *Barnes* says, *viz.* That *Philip* inwardly fretting that the King had not paid him the Obeisance he expected, laid a Plot to seize his Person when he was most separated from his Attendants, which being whisper'd to the King, he took Shipping with his Company on a sudden, and sail'd for *England*, before any Man knew the Reason of his Haste.

his Rights at the *French* Court: But all this was only to gain time; and *Philip*, who perceiv'd it, sent Ambassadors to him, requiring him to send over the Declaration which he had promis'd by a Letter from *Eltham*, dated the 5th of *February*. Those very Ambassadors did *Edward* amuse almost a whole Year, without giving them a positive Answer, by starting Proposals from time to time, which, tho' perfectly trifling, occasion'd divers Negotiations that we find in the Acts of the Year 1330. *A.*1330. *P.* 411.

KING *Edward* continued all the while to make sure of extraordinary Assistance from the Lords and Towns of *Guyenne*, as appears from several full Powers issued for that purpose from *Woodstock*, on the 27th of *April*; to one of which is added a List of 118 Lords, which shews that the King had great Designs that were not bounded by *Guyenne*. Mean time, as *Philip* still teaz'd him, and as *Edward*'s Affairs were not yet ready, a Treaty was concluded at *Bois de Vincennes*, on the 1st of *May* *; by which *Edward* engag'd to pay *Philip* 50000 Marks Sterling, according to the Agreement made with *Charles the Fair*; and 60000 Livres of *Paris*, which he ow'd for the Conveyance of *Guyenne*, which his Father had made over to him. He engag'd likewise to demolish the Castles of the Lords of *Gascoigne*, who were under Condemnation. His Ratification of this Treaty is dated at *Woodstock* the 8th of *July*; but *Philip* was not pleased with it, as appears by two Letters from *Edward*, the one to the Pope, the other to the Seneschal of *Guyenne*, both dated at *Nottingham* the 20th day of *Sep*- *P.* 432; 433. *Treaty betwixt* Edward *and* Philip. *P.* 437. Edward's *Ratification.* *P.* 443. *P.* 449; 450.

* EVEN the accurate Mr. *Barnes* seems to have been mistaken here, in dating this Treaty *May* 30.

Q *tember.*

Edw.III. *tember*. *Philip* had no reason indeed to be satisfy'd with a Treaty which did not procure him any new Advantage, and which took no manner of notice of the principal Article of his Pretensions, *viz*. The Declaration of the Homage. But his Refusal to ratify this Treaty, was not at all disagreeable to the King of *England*, who was glad to keep Affairs embroil'd, that he might have a Colour for making Preparations against *Philip*, without giving him any room to suspect that he aim'd at his Crown. Therefore he sent a Commission to the Seneschal of *Guyenne*, to treat with the Counts *de Foix* and *de Cominges*, and others; which Commission is dated the 20th of *September*, as above. P. 451.

He granted the like full Powers to make Treaties with the Duke of *Brabant*, the Earls of *Flanders*, *Guelderland*, *Loos* and *Chiny*, and with all that were inclin'd to join with him; we find them dated the 11th of *October*, 1330, at *Nottingham*. Ibid.

While these things were transacting, *Philip*, being out of Patience because his Ambassadors receiv'd no Answer, sent his Brother the Count *d'Alencon* into *Guyenne*, where he took and demolish'd the Castle of *Xaintes*, and plunder'd that of *Bourg*. *Edward* was then laying that Scheme with *Baliol*, which was mention'd in the foregoing Article; and to prevent the Interruption of his Projects, he resolv'd to give the King of *France* Satisfaction, and accordingly sent him the Letters Patent which he promis'd about the Homage. In those Letters he declar'd, That the Homage which he had perform'd, ought to be deem'd Liege; and that for the future those which he and his Successors should pay, should be perform'd after the same

Edward's *Letters Patent for his Homage to* Philip *of* France.

manner, and with the same Circumstances as *Philip* demanded; of which there was a Pattern in those same Letters, which were dated the 30th of *March*, 1331, at *Eltham*. *A.* 1331. *P.* 477.

FIVE Days after, *Edward* went to *France*, on pretence of fulfilling a Vow; there he had an Interview with *Philip*, and made an Agreement with him, dated the 10th of *April*, whereby *Philip* gave him 30000 Livres *Tournois* for the Damage done at *Xaintes* and *Bourg*. At *Edward*'s Request he also pardon'd the Lords of *Gascoigne*, by an Amnesty dated the 13th of the same Month, and consented that their Castles should not be demolish'd. An Historian, who wrote the Life of *Edward*, pretends that he went over to *France* in a Disguise, and without *Philip*'s Knowledge, in which he is certainly mistaken*.

His Interview and Treaty with him in France. *P.* 483. *Gets a Pardon for the Nobility of* Gascoigne. *P.* 485. *An Error in History.*

ONE wou'd have thought that a firm Peace shou'd have been establish'd between the two Kings; but *Edward* had no design to keep it; and therefore he endeavour'd, in all the Treaties which he made with *Philip*, to leave some Handle or other, that he might always have a Pretence for taking Arms when he saw a proper time: Then was not a favourable Conjuncture, because he was engag'd in a War against *Scotland*; and instead of being in a Condition to fall upon *Philip*, he had reason to fear the latter's giving powerful Assistance to the *Scots*. Therefore he was under a Necessity, during this War, to amuse him with the Appearances

* MR. *Barnes* is guilty of this Mistake, who mentioning his Voyage to *France*, to perform a Vow which he had made to visit some Holy Places there, for his Deliverance from former Troubles and Dangers, says he went over privately, with no more than fourteen in Company, all disguis'd like Merchants.

Edw.III. Edward *artfully deludes* Philip.

of a sincere Desire to live in Peace with him, and yet to leave Affairs in such a Condition, that a Pretext for a Rupture might not be wanting on a proper Occasion. That was manifestly the Aim of all *Edward's* Negotiations with *France*, during the Term of five Years, which the War with *Scotland* lasted. And for this purpose, knowing that *Philip's* Heart was entirely set upon an Expedition, which he had engag'd in, to the *Holy Land*, he made him believe he would go with him, and sent Ambassadors to him to regulate all things proper for their Voyage. But as this Affair would perhaps, have been settled too soon for him, he affected to spin out the Time, by renewing some old Pretensions, which the Treaties of *Monstrevil* and *Perigueux*, made between his Grandfather and *Philip the Fair*, had left undetermin'd: And under pretence of deciding these Differences, before they set forward to the *Holy Land*, *Edward* trifled with *Philip* while he push'd on his Conquests in *Scotland*. And the better to decoy the King of *France*, at his Sollicitation, he granted the *Scots* several Truces from time to time, on purpose to make him believe that he really design'd to continue his Friend and Ally. And this was the Drift of all the Acts we meet with on this Subject, from the Year 1332 to 1335, which are no more than full Powers to treat with *Philip*, sometimes upon the Expedition to the East, sometimes upon Projects of Marriages between the Princes and Princesses of the two Families, and at other times upon the Treaties of *Monstrevil* and *Perigueux*, and other Particulars which it wou'd be needless to mention.

Mean while, tho' *Philip* did not suspect that *Edward* had any Thoughts of reviving his Pretensions

tensions to the Crown, yet he was sensible that *A.* 1336.
it was not his Interest to suffer him to be absolute Master of *Scotland*; and therefore he declar'd his Design to assist that afflicted Nation, whose King was come to his Court for Refuge. *Edward* laid hold on this Handle as a Pretext to make Preparations on his part. For this end he call'd a great Council at *London*, to consider of those which *France* was making against *England*. *Edward* took it for granted, that the Assistance given by *France* to *Scotland*, was a Breach of the Peace with *England*; but he wou'd not have it understood, that the War which himself carry'd on against *Scotland*, an Ally of *France*, was any Breach of the Peace at all. This seem'd to be the reason of that Quarrel, which grew every Day hotter between the two Kings: And the happy Success which *Edward* had been bless'd with against *Scotland*, made him talk with the greater Confidence, because he saw the Day at hand when he might be able to bring all his Designs to light. This was the State of Affairs during the Years 1332, 1333, 1334 and 1335. that is to say, the most part of the time that *Edward* was engag'd in the War with *Scotland*.

IN 1336, when he expected little or no Opposition from the *Scots*, he press'd the Conclusion of his Foreign Alliances, especially those with the Duke of *Brabant*, the Earl of *Guelderland*, and the Marquis of *Juliers*. And to incline his Subjects to raise him great Supplies he pretended that the Kingdom was threaten'd with an Invasion from *France*, and order'd all his Subjects from 16 to 60 Years old to bear Arms, by a Proclamation dated at *Walsingham* the 16th of *February*, 1336. At the same time he demanded the Restitution of some Lands which *Philip* detain'd

King Edward'*s Policy to get Money for the* French *War.*

His Proclamation for arming his Subjects.

P. 687.

Edw. III. detain'd from him in *Guyenne*; and by a Writ dated *June* 20 at *Newcastle* upon *Tine*, call'd a Great Council to consider of Ways and Means for opposing the pretended Invasion from *France*; which was with an apparent View, to have a Pretext for desiring the greater Supply from his Subjects. Nevertheless he sent Ambassadors again to *France*, to treat with *Philip* about the Voyage to the *Holy Land*, as appears by his Letter dated at *St. Johnstown* the 6th of *July* following; from whence it may be suppos'd by the way, that he was not under the least Apprehension of an Invasion. Mean time he did not send this Embassy with a View to engage in that Undertaking, but only to avoid the Reproach of his having hinder'd the holy Voyage, of which *Philip* made a Handle to the Pope. With this View he gave a Commission to his Ambassadors, at the same time, to treat with *Philip* for the adjusting of all the Differences that remain'd betwixt them, on purpose to make him believe that his only Aim was Peace. But he took care not to leave the old Pretensions, with respect to the Treaties of *Monstrevil* and *Perigueux*, out of the number; which so perplex'd the Treaty, as render'd the Conclusion of it exceeding difficult; which was what he wanted.

He summons a Council. P. 701, 705.

He sends Ambassadors to Philip *to treat about the Voyage to the* Holy Land. P. 703.

P. 704.

The Invasion which *Edward* pretended to be so much afraid of from *Philip*, came to nothing more than an Embassy which the latter sent to *England*, to sollicit some Accommodation in favour of King *David*; as appears by the Protection which *Edward* granted to his Ambassadors, dated at *St. Johnstown* the 3d of *September*, 1336. But all this was to no purpose, for *Edward* had no other View than to amuse the King of *France*, and so nothing was concluded.

Philip's *Embassy to* Edward *in favour of King* David. P. 707.

Edward

Edward found the *Scots* were so exhausted, that he saw the War on that side drawing to a Period; and therefore, as is said before, he us'd double Diligence to conclude his Foreign Alliances, that he might be in a Condition to attack *France* as soon as that War was ended. This is evident from all the Acts in the Year 1336, in which we find his full Powers to conclude Alliances with several Princes of *Germany* and the *Netherlands*, while he was compleating the Reduction of *Scotland*. 'Tis probable that he wou'd not have made a Secret of his Designs against *France* so long, if the Disgrace which happen'd in *Scotland* to his General the Earl of *Athol* had not carry'd his Arms into that Country a fourth time*. Therefore he made as if he was for an Accommodation with *Philip*, and also with *David Bruce*, and receiv'd the Ambassadors whom both those Princes sent him, as appears by his Protections granted to the *French* Ambassadors at *Langely* the 28th of *January*, 1337. and by the full Powers granted to his own Ambassadors to treat with them, dated at *Windsor* the 18th of *April* following. Mean time he continu'd to negotiate with Foreign Powers; and not only with Princes, but with all manner of Persons that were dispos'd to engage in his Service, as appears by his full Powers, dated at *Windsor* the 19th of *April*.

A. 1336.

P. 730, 745.

Edward's *full Powers to treat with Foreigners.* *P.* 746.

ROBERT Earl of *Artois*, who was at variance with *Philip* of *France*, was already in *England* in *April* 1337†, as appears by a Warrant,

* IT appears from Mr. *Barnes* that this Battel wherein the Earl of *Athol* fell, was fought the last Day of *December*, 1335. in the Fields of *Kilblain*, near the Castle of *Kildrummy*; and to him we refer for the Particulars.

† ACCORDING to Mr. *Barnes*, this Earl fled hither in Disguise so early as the latter end of the Year 1332, about the time that King *Edward* held his first Parliament at *York*.

Edw. III. rant, which King *Edward* gave him to hunt in his Forests, dated the 23d of that Month at *Westminster*. Most Historians say that this *Robert* of *Artois* put it first into *Edward*'s Head to go to War with *Philip* for the Crown of *France*: but the Measures which *Edward* had concerted before that Earl's Arrival, make it apparent, that the most he did was to confirm him in the Design which he had already form'd.

His Warrant to Robert *of* Artois *to hunt in his Forests.*

P. 747.

A Mistake of Historians concerning Robert *of* Artois.

The following is a List of the chief Princes and Noblemen with whom *Edward* negotiated a Treaty, during the War against *Scotland*.

List of K. Edward's *Allies.*

The Count *d'Armagnac*.
The Count *de Foix*.
The Viscount *de Lomagne*.
The Viscount *de Tartas*.
The Lord of *Albret*.
The Duke of *Austria*.
The Duke of *Brabant*.
The Count Palatine of the *Rhine*.
The Earl of *Holland*.
Lewis of *Savoy*.
Lewis of *Bavaria*, Emperor.
The Marquis of *Brandenburg*.
The Archbishop of *Cologn*.
The Marquis of *Juliers*.
The Earl of *Hainault*.
The Earl of *Gueldre*.
The Earl of *Zealand*.
The Earl of *Mons*.
The Earl of *Marlia*.
Edward Son to the Earl of *Limburgh*.
The Earl of *Geneva*.
Hugh of *Geneva*.
The Count *de Loos*.
The Earl of *Chiny*.
Herman of *Blankard*, Dean of *Aire*.

William

William of *Duyvenvorde*. *A.* 1337.
The Lord of *Chalanck*.
Andrew of *Peyteyr*.
Nicholas of *Dort*.
Robert of *Tocburgh*.
Lambert of *Deppy*.
Croye of *Hochstraet*.
John of *Quatre Mars*.
Henry of *Geminith*.

To whom might be added a great Number of other private Gentlemen of *Guyenne*, *Almaine*, and the *Netherlands*, and especially of the Towns of *Flanders*, who made a League with him afterwards, by the Intrigues of *Jacob van Arteveld*, or *Arteville* *. Every one of which Allies

* Mr. *Barnes*, who gives an extraordinary Account of this Man, says, that tho' he was but of mean Birth at *Ghent*, being no more than a Refiner of Honey, or as some call'd him a Brewer, yet he rose to that excessive Wealth and Power, by his great Wit and Courage, that he render'd himself more absolute than ever any Earl of *Flanders*; for undertaking to be the Patron of the People, he had all things entirely at his Command; and those who wou'd not appear to be his Friends, were treated as Enemies to the Public. He never walk'd the Streets without sixty or eighty lusty Yeomen at his Heels, among whom were three or four of his secret Council, who upon a Sign given from him, kill'd every Man they met with upon the Spot, be he who he wou'd, if he was one that *Jacob van Arteveld* fear'd or hated. He collected every Groat of the Earl's Rents and Profits, and spent them at Pleasure, without taking or making any Account; and banish'd all the Lords and Gentlemen whom he suspected to be the Earl's Friends; of whose Lands he levied one Moiety for his own Use, the other for the Use of the Exiles Wives and Children. And in every Town he had Soldiers and Servants in pay, to spy and give him notice if any Person had a Design against him, whom he never left till he had banish'd or destroy'd.

Edw. III. lies engag'd to furnish him with a certain Number of Troops on Consideration of so much Money.

His Convention with the Earl of Hainault. *P.* 783.

In the Conventions which he made with the Earl of *Hainault*, dated at *Stamford* the 12th of *July* 1337, it appears, that the said Earl, tho' he was his Brother-in-law, wou'd not engage with him but upon Condition that *Edward* shou'd have the Title of the Emperor's Lieutenant or Vicar. This shews the reason why *Edward* courted that Dignity, which the Pope reproach'd him for afterwards, as being beneath him.

His Letter to the Emperor, urging him to be reconcil'd to the Holy See. P. 799.

In a Letter dated from *Westminster* the 26th of *August*, 1337, to *Lewis* of *Bavaria*, the Emperor, *Edward* sollicited him to be reconcil'd to the Holy See. And it appears by this Letter, that the Emperor had engag'd to come in Person to *Edward*'s Service with 2000 Men at Arms, for which he was to receive 300,000 Florins.

All the World now plainly saw that *Edward* was resolv'd upon a War with *France*, but no Declaration had as yet been made that it was to enforce his Right to the Crown. This was a Secret which *Edward* kept still in his own Breast. The Pretence he made use of for arming, was to put himself in a Posture of Defence against *Philip*, who had made an Alliance with the *Scots*, and threaten'd, as he said, to

destroy'd. From hence the *English* were under a Necessity of making him their Friend, which in the Course of Providence afterwards prov'd his Downfal: for on the 17th of *July*, 1345, he was murder'd by the Populace in his own House at *Ghent*, who were exaspera-ted by his endeavouring to establish King *Edward*'s Son Count of *Flanders*, in prejudice of the right Line; and by his squandering the Treasures of *Flanders*, and conveying them to *England*.

invade

invade *England*. In order to make his Subjects believe with what Regret he took Arms, he put forth a Proclamation from *Westminster* the 28th of *August*, 1337, in which he notify'd to his People all the Steps that he had taken to prevent this War, of which these were the chief.

A. 1337.

His Proclamation of his Reasons for taking Arms against France.

P. 804.

His Offers to France.

1. He had offer'd his Son the Duke of *Cornwal* in Marriage to a Daughter of *Philip*, without desiring any Dowry.

2. He had made an Offer of his Sister *Eleanor*, Countess of *Gueldre*, in Marriage to *John*, *Philip*'s eldest Son, with a very great Sum of Money.

3. He had offer'd *Philip* as much Money as he should reasonably demand, to make him Satisfaction for Damages.

4. He had propos'd to accompany him to the Holy Land, on condition that he wou'd restore him one Moiety of the Lands which he kept from him.

5. He had made him the same Offer, if *Philip* wou'd but engage to make him that Restitution after their Return.

6. At *Philip*'s Request he had granted the *Scots* a Truce, during which they had kill'd the Earl of *Athol*.

7. And, notwithstanding this Instance of the *Scots* Treachery, he had, at the Request of the King of *France*, granted them another Truce.

The Reader will judge of the Importance of these Offers, and whether they were not liable to such Constructions as might have easily furnish'd *Edward* with a Pretext for revoking his Promise. Accordingly *Philip* did not regard 'em. The Ruin of the *Scots* (the only thing that *Philip* was then afraid of) was too prejudicial to his Interests, to suffer him to abandon

Edw. III. don that Nation, as *Edward* demanded of him in Purſuance of thoſe Offers, which were not near ſo advantageous to *Philip* as to the King of *England*.

His Letter on the ſame Subject to the Pope. P. 807.

EDWARD wrote much in the ſame Strain to the Pope, on purpoſe to arm him, as he ſaid, againſt the falſe Suggeſtions of his Enemies; as appears by his Letter dated *September* the 1ſt, 1337, at *Weſtminſter*. But not a Word yet of his Pretenſions to the Crown of *France*. On the contrary, he granted full Powers to his Commiſſioners, dated the 3d of *October*, at *Weſtminſter*, to treat with the King of *France* on all Points whatſoever, without making the leaſt Mention, all the while, of the Crown.

P. 812.

YET the very ſame Day he gave a Power to his Envoys beyond Sea, to yield to thoſe who were inclin'd to engage in his Service, certain Lands and Fiefs belonging to him, whether he was in Poſſeſſion thereof or not, as well in the Kingdom of *France*, Dutchy of *Aquitain*, and other parts abroad, as in *England*, *Ireland*, &c.

P. 815.

He makes a formal Demand of the Crown of France. P. 818.

BUT four Days after this he quite pull'd off the Mask, which he had wore ſo long, and gave a Commiſſion to the Duke of *Brabant*, the Marquis of *Juliers*, and *William Bohun* Earl of *Northampton*, to demand the Crown of *France*, and to take Poſſeſſion of it in his Name. This full Power is dated the 7th of *October*, 1337, at *Weſtminſter*.

Ibid. *Appoints a Lieutenant or Vicar General, and challenges the Obedience of the* French. P. 819.

THE ſame Day he ſent a Patent to the Duke of *Brabant*, conſtituting him his Lieutenant or Vicar General in *France*: And alſo,

AN Order, enjoyning all *Frenchmen* to pay the ſame Obedience to the Duke of *Brabant* as to himſelf.

THESE three laſt-mention'd Pieces are a deciſive Proof, that he did not ſtay till 1339 before

fore he publickly declar'd his Pretensions to the Crown, as some *French* Historians affirm, to satisfy a Scruple of the *Flemings*; of which we shall take Notice in our Account of the next Volume of the *Fœdera*.

A. 1337.

An Error of French *Historians detected.*

EDWARD having taken this Step, wrote to the Pope, desiring he would excuse him for his having made an Alliance with the Emperor, then under Excommunication; the Letter is dated the 17th of *October*, at *Westminster*.

Edward *sends to the Pope to excuse his making an Alliance with the excommunicated Emperor.* P. 826.

BENEDICT XII. who then fill'd the See of *Rome*, and was inclinable to favour *France*, hearing of *Edward*'s Preparations, sent two Cardinals to him, to endeavour to prevent the Effusion of Christian Blood. Their Passport granted by *Edward* is of the same Date as the Letter.

His Passport for two Cardinals. P. 827.

UPON News of the Legates coming, *Edward* assembled his Parliament to consult about the manner of their Reception, and the Motives of their being sent: The Writ for calling it was dated at *Westminster* the 20th of *December*.

He calls a Parliament upon their Arrival. P. 832.

EDWARD mightily caress'd the Legates, and in pure Complaisance to them, engag'd himself not to commence a War against *France* before the 1st of *March*, 1338. But this was no such great Favour as he wou'd have them think it to be, since the Engagement was dated at *Guilford* the 24th of *December*, 1337. 'Tis true that it was prolong'd afterwards to *Midsummer-day*.

His Truces with the French *previous to the War.* P. 833.

THUS end the Acts of this fourth Volume of the *Fœdera* that relate to *France*. My chief View in dwelling so long upon this Volume, which in the main has little more in it than the Preparations for a War with *France*, was to shew the Genius, and part of the Character of

Edw. III. *Edward* III. and I cou'd not poſſibly have made a ſhorter Abridgment of it without loſing my Aim.

Article IV. *Affairs Eccleſiaſtical.*

THERE are fewer Pieces in this Volume, relating to Eccleſiaſtical Affairs, than in any of the three preceding; and ſuch as we find here are of no great Moment, or properly ſpeaking, but a Repetition of what has been already publiſh'd in the other Volumes. Here are the very ſame Diſputes between the Popes and the *Engliſh*, touching the Collations to Benefices, Appeals, and Citations to the Court of *Rome*. Therefore I think it will be needleſs to enter into any Particulars upon this Head, ſince we have ſeen what it treats of in the preceeding Volumes. It muſt only be remember'd, that in all the Diſputes that happen'd between the King and the Pope about the Collation to Benefices, the King was always worſted, becauſe the Clergy took part with the Pope. This made the Popes endeavour every Day to augment the Number of Benefices, and to claim the ſole Diſpoſal of 'em to themſelves. For Example, we find in this Volume, that when the See of *Worceſter* became vacant, by the Tranſlation of its Biſhop to that of *Ely*, the Pope immediately fill'd the vacant See, without any regard to the Nomination of the Chapter. The Reaſon he gave for it was not borrow'd from Scripture, nor from the ancient Canons, but from his mere Will and Pleaſure: *For*, ſaid he, *before the Vacancy of the See of* Worceſter, *we had made an Order, that all Biſhopricks, which became vacant by the Tranſlation of Biſhops to another See, ſhou'd be*

at

at our Diſpoſal. At this rate if he had taken a Fancy to order before-hand, that all the vacant Benefices, no matter how, ſhould be at the Diſpoſal of the Holy See, it would have been a ſufficient Reaſon to deprive all the Chapters, and all the Patrons of their Right. But we ſhall ſee in the Sequel of this Reign, that the King and Parliament gave a Check to this Uſurpation. *A.* 1330.

HERE are in this, as well as in the other Volumes, ſeveral Orders of the King againſt Appeals and perſonal Citations to the Court of *Rome*, and againſt other of the Pope's Vexations; but as they contain nothing new, or particular, we ſhall paſs them by.

A LETTER from *Edward* to Pope *John* XXII. dated at *Woodſtock* the 12th of *April*, 1330, ſhews, that this Pope did not forget himſelf when he granted the King the Tenths upon the Clergy, becauſe of thoſe which he granted to this Prince, for the Term of four Years, he reſerv'd one Moiety to himſelf.

King's Letter to the Pope about the Clergy paying Tenths. P. 428.

WE find alſo the very ſame Pope demanding 30 Years Arrears of the Tribute eſtabliſh'd by *John Lack-land*, deducting only what *Edward* II. had paid. The King, whoſe Intereſt it was at that time to humour the Court of *Rome*, promis'd to pay 500 Marks every Year till the whole was paid, reckoning four Florins of Gold for every Mark; but he was not ſo good as his Word, and we ſhall ſee hereafter that at laſt he aboliſh'd this Tribute.

EDWARD having given leave to a certain Cardinal, who had Benefices in *England*, to ſummon his Debtors into the Spiritual Court; the Parliament pray'd him to revoke that Order, as contrary to the Laws of the Kingdom: which

Edw. III. which he did accordingly, by another Order of the 28th of *June*, 1328, at *Evesham*.

P. 356. *His Letters to the Pope for canonizing certain holy Men.* IN this Volume are several Letters from *Edward* to the Pope to obtain the Canonization of the Earl of *Lancaster*, *viz.* one dated at *London* the last Day of *February*, 1327, another at *Winchester* the 7th of *March*, 1330, and a third from *Eltham* the 3d of *April*, 1331. A Letter
P. 268.
421. also for the Canonization of *Robert* of *Winchel-*
478. *sea*, Archbishop of *Canterbury*, dated at *Westmin-*
272. *ster* the 8th of *March*, 1327. Two others for
275. canonizing *John* of *Dalderby* Bishop of *Lincoln*,
336. one dated at *Westminster* the 11th of the same
375. Month; the other at *York* the 20th of *February*, 1328; and one for canonizing *William de la Marche* Bishop of *Bath* and *Wells*, which is dated at *Westminster* the 20th of *February*, 1329.

Pope Benedict*'s Letter notifying his Election to King* Edward. HERE we have also a Brief, or Letter, from Pope *Benedict* XII. in which he notify'd his Election to *Edward* before any other Christian Prince: 'Tis dated at *Avignon* the 5th of the Ides of *January*, 1335.

P. 633. *Pope's Bull against certain Heretics of* Bavaria. *P.* 315. THE chief thing in this fourth Volume, with respect to Religion, is a Bull of Pope *John* XXII. against certain Heretics of *Bavaria*, who taking part with the Emperor against the Pope, had written a Book containing certain Propositions which the Pope condemns in this Bull; and not only condemns, but particularly confutes by such Arguments as were furnish'd him, or were approv'd, says he, by a great Number of Cardinals, Archbishops, Bishops, and Doctors both of Divinity and Law. If the Account given of this Volume were not too long already, I would here add every one of the Pope's Arguments at large: But to be short, I shall content my self with mentioning the five condemn'd Propositions,

and ſome of the moſt remarkable Proofs by *A.*1327.
which the Pope confutes them. This Bull is dated at *Avignon* the 10th of the Calends of *November*, 1327.

PROPOSITION I.

WHEN Jeſus Chriſt *paid Tribute* * *to the* Emperor, *by means of a Piece of* Money † *taken in the Mouth of a* Fiſh, *he did not do it out of Complaiſance, but mere Neceſſity.*

JESUS CHRIST, *ſays the Pope*, being the Son of *David*, was not oblig'd to pay Tribute; therefore 'tis falſe to aſſert, that he was under a Neceſſity to pay it. The Hereticks reaſon falſly when they ſay, that the Temporalities of Jeſus Chriſt, and by conſequence Church Livings, were ſubject to the Emperor's Juriſdiction; becauſe Jeſus Chriſt paid for his Perſon, and not for his Eſtate.

PROPOSITION II.

St. PETER *had no more Authority than the other* Apoſtles, *and* Jeſus Chriſt *has eſtabliſh'd no Head over the Church.*

AMONG other Arguments which the Pope brings to confute this Propoſition, he ſays, that Jeſus Chriſt gave the other Apoſtles a limited Power, when he ſaid to them, *Whoſeſoever Sins ye remit*, &c. and when he ſaid, *Go forth and baptize:* But that the Authority which he gave

* 'Tis call'd *Didrachma* in the Original; which was in value 15*d*.

† In the Original 'tis *Stater*, which is half an Ounce of Silver, in value 2*s*. and 6*d*.

Edw. III. to *Peter* was unlimited, *Feed my Sheep*; and elsewhere, *I will give thee the Keys*, &c. which he says to no other Apostle in particular.

Moreover he said to St. *Peter*, *Launch out into the Deep*, meaning that he alone was to define the most important Doubts and Disputes in Matters of Faith; whereas he said to the other Apostles, *Leave your Nets*.

PROPOSITION III.

IT belongs to the Emperor *to make a* Pope, *to depose him, and to punish him.*

Among the Arguments which *John* XXII. makes use of to combat this Proposition, he says, That St. *Peter* was establish'd by Jesus Christ, and not by any Temporal Lord; that the Emperors before *Constantine* made no Popes; and that *Constantine*, far from having acquir'd such Right by his Conversion, became on the contrary a Son and a Disciple subject to the Pope. He adds, that this Emperor transferr'd the Seat of his Government to *Constantinople*, because he thought it impracticable to exercise his Power in a City which was the Residence of the Head of the Christian Church.

After many other Arguments, which have nothing in them more than common, he falls upon the Hereticks for maintaining, that *Pilate* in quality of Judge Ordinary caus'd Jesus Christ to be crucify'd. Upon this he says, that these Words are capable of a double Sense, to mean either that *Pilate* crucify'd Christ *de jure*, or that he did it *de facto*; if *de jure*, this is false, for no Man can be condemn'd by Law till he is found guilty; now Jesus Christ was innocent:

innocent: If we understand it *de facto*, no other Inference can be drawn from it, but that the Emperor may unjustly put the Pope to Death, and not only the Emperor, but any other private Person. A. 1327.

PROPOSITION IV.

ALL Priests, whether Popes, Archbishops, or Bishops, have an equal Jurisdiction according to the Institution of Jesus Christ: *And if any one has more Authority than the others, they have receiv'd it from the* Emperor, *who, as he gave it, can also revoke it.*

AMONG many other Arguments, the Pope makes use of the following, to shew that the Distinction of several Degrees of Power in the Church, is by the Institution of Jesus Christ. He by whose Authority any thing is done, seems to do it himself. Now *Peter*, the Vicar of Jesus Christ, and the Head of his Flock, considering, that as the Flock increas'd, it wou'd be necessary to increase the number of Shepherds, instituted various Degrees of Power in the Church: Therefore such Distinction being made by the Authority of St. *Peter*, it is the same as if it had been made by Christ himself.

As to the Question, *Whether all Priests are equal?* he says, that as to the Dignity of their Order they are all equal, but not as to Power. Yet he acknowledges, that when an inferior Priest celebrates the Eucharist, the same Effect follows as if it had been done by a superior; because 'tis one and the same internal Priest, *viz.* Jesus Christ, who produces Transubstantiation.

PROPOSITION V.

THE whole Church join'd together can punish no Man in a compulsive Way, unless it be by Authority from the Emperor.

JOHN XXII. pretends that the Power of Excommunication is a compulsive Power; and that the Power of Excommunication being granted to the Church by Jesus Christ, the Church has therefore a compulsive Power. To prove that Excommunication is compulsive, he argues, that the major Excommunication not only deprives the Person excommunicated of the Sacraments, but excludes him also from the Communion of Believers. Now adds he, the Imperial Laws say that 'tis reckon'd worse to converse with Men, and be depriv'd of their Suffrage, than to be totally separated from Mankind; therefore Excommunication is worse than temporal Punishment, from whence it follows that the Church has a compulsive Power.

As a farther Proof that the Power of the Church is compulsive, he mentions the Power which *Peter* exerted with respect to *Ananias*; and that Passage of St. *Paul* to the *Corinthians*, *Shall I come unto you with a Rod?* and that other Passage, *The Weapons of our Warfare are not carnal, but mighty through God, to the pulling down of strong Holds.*

WE

A. 1329.

WE proceed now to the fifth Volume of the Fœdera, *which is a Continuation of the Acts of* Edward III. *a Reign of so much Glory to the* English *Nation, that Mr.* Rymer *cou'd not help introducing this Volume, as he did the fourth, with a triumphant Character of it in his Dedication to the late Queen, which we hope will not be deem'd an improper Preface to our Account of it.*

May it please, &c.

'THIS Volume is a Continuation of the 'publick Acts and Treaties in the most 'active and prosperous Reign of *Edward* III.

'IN course of Time it brings to that memo'rable Day, the Battel of *Poyctiers*, where *Ed'ward* of *Woodstock* (otherwise call'd the *Black 'Prince*) took the *French* King Prisoner.

'THE Battel of *Cressy* in the 20th, and this 'of *Poyctiers* in the 30th Year of his Reign, 'were two the most famous Actions (of any 'Ages by-past) that have the Honour to live 'in Story.

'THE Fight of *Cressy* brought into *English* 'Hands the fair Town of *Calais*.

'FROM *Poyctiers*, besides the *French* King, 'were brought over into *England* (What Pri'soners! What Hostages!) the Duke of *Or'leans*, the Duke of *Anjou*, the Duke of *Ber'ry*, the Duke of *Vendosme*, the Duke of *Bour'bon*, and *James* of *Bourbon*, Progenitor of 'your Majesty's now Adversary of *France*.

'THOSE were Times of Triumph! those 'were shining Days!

'YET add 20 great Names more; and throw 'in the Obligations of three Millions for the '*French* King's Ransom, &c.

THIS Volume contains a great many Pieces which may be of vaſt uſe for illuſtrating the ſeveral Events of the Reign of *Edward* III. one of the moſt conſiderable in the *Engliſh* Hiſtory. But as the numerous Acts are not all of equal Importance, I ſhall confine my ſelf to ſome of thoſe which may ſerve to illuſtrate any Fact that is obſcure or doubtful in it ſelf, or diſguis'd by Hiſtorians.

KING *Edward*'s Affairs with *France*, being as it were the Center to which all his Negotiations tended, it is neceſſary to begin with this Article, as being of the greateſt Importance, and that on which all the others do in ſome meaſure depend.

King Edward'*s Affairs with* France *from the Beginning of* 1338, *to the end of* 1356.

THO' *Edward* was ſeveral Years preparing for a War againſt *Philip* of *Valois*; and tho' he diſcover'd his Deſign of wreſting the Crown from him laſt Year, (*viz.* 1337.) yet he was not able to put himſelf at the Head of his Army till the Month of *September*, 1339. As it was his Intention to attack *Philip* by *Flanders*, ſo he made it his chief Care to fortify his League by Alliances with the Princes of *Germany* and the *Netherlands*. The Emperor *Lewis* of *Bavaria*, the Dukes of *Brabant* and *Gueldre*, the Earl of *Hainault*, the *Flemings*, who were then govern'd by *Jacob van Arteveldt*, and the *German* Princes their Neighbours, were thoſe whoſe Alliance was likely to be of the greateſt Service to him in his Enterprize. He had already made ſome Treaties with ſeveral of them, as we have mention'd elſewhere. And now it

King Edward's *Alliances.*

was neceſſary that he ſhould go himſelf into the *Netherlands* to confirm all thoſe Alliances, and to take juſt Meaſures with his ſaid Confederates for the Execution of his Deſign. He ſet out therefore from *England* in *July* 1338, for *Antwerp*, where he ſtay'd above a Year to ſettle all his Affairs. But ſoon after his Arrival, he went to *Cologn* to confer with the Emperor, who gave him the Title of Vicar of the Empire*. We have already taken notice that the Earl of *Hainault* wiſh'd that *Edward*

A. 1338.

His Journey to Flanders, *and to* Cologn, *where he confers with the Emperor, who makes him Vicar of the Empire.*

* THIS Interview was truly glorious and magnificent; two Thrones being erected in the open Market-place, one for the Emperor, the other for the King; the Emperor took his Place firſt, and King *Edward* ſat down by him. There were for Aſſiſtants, 4 great Dukes, 3 Archbiſhops, and 6 Biſhops, 37 Earls, and according to the Eſtimation of the Heralds 17000 Barons, Banerets, Knights and Eſquires. The Emperor having his Scepter in his Right Hand, and the Globe in his Left, and the Knight of *Almain* holding over his Head a naked Sword, his Imperial Majeſty did then and there declare the Diſloyalty, Falſhood, and Villany of the King of *France*; and thereupon defy'd him, and pronounc'd, that he and his Adherents had forfeited the Protection and Favour of the Empire. And then he conſtituted King *Edward* his Deputy, or Vicar General of the Empire; granting unto him full and abſolute Power over all on this ſide as far as *Cologne*; whereof he gave him his Imperial Charter, in ſight of all that were preſent. Mr. *Barnes*, to whom we are oblig'd for this Account, mentions a Report of ſome, that at the firſt Meeting, the Emperor took it ill that King *Edward* refus'd to ſubmit himſelf to the Kiſs of his Feet, (as it ſeems Kings were wont to do to the Emperors) but our *Edward* gallantly anſwer'd, 'That he himſelf 'was a King Sacred and Anointed, and had Life and 'Limbs in his Power, being 'accountable to none but 'God, as ſupreme and independent of all others; 'being alſo Lord of Sea and 'Land, and wearing no leſs 'than an Imperial Crown: 'wherefore he ought not to 'abaſe himſelf to any mortal Potentate whatever.' Which Anſwer was accepted.

Edw. III. was invested with that Dignity; and undoubtedly the King himself was of opinion, that it wou'd be serviceable to him for engaging several *German* Princes in the League.

His March into France. P. 124.

These Affairs having employ'd him till *September* 1339. it was not till that Month that he put himself at the Head of his Troops, to enter into the Territories of *France*. We find by one of the Acts of this Volume, that on the 26th of that Month he was at *Marchienne*, between *St. Amand* and *Doway*, from whence he advanc'd into the *Cambresis*, where he heard that *Philip* of *Valois* was drawing near with a numerous Army. Notwithstanding their Superiority *Edward* pass'd over the *Schelde* to meet them, so that the two Armies were quickly near enough to engage. *Philip* even sent *Edward* a Challenge, which was accepted on the Spot, and the Day and Place actually settled for deciding the Quarrel by a general Combat; but *Philip* retir'd on a sudden without offering to strike a Blow. They say he was intimidated by Letters from *Robert* King of *Naples*, a great Astrologer, who told him he wou'd have bad Success. Be it as it will, *Edward* seeing no Prospect of coming to a Battel, retir'd on his part into *Hainault*. Thus ended this first Campaign without any Bloodshed.

Philip *challenges, and runs away.*

EDWARD spent the rest of this Year at *Antwerp*, where important Affairs detain'd him till the Month of *February* 1340. That which took up most of his time, was the Negotiation which he had on foot to bring the Towns of *Flanders* into the League. In the Year 1331 he had made a Treaty with them, by which they were only engag'd to observe an exact Neutrality; but at last he gain'd the *Flemings* on his side, upon condition that he wou'd take the Title

A. 1340.

Title of King of *France*, because *Philip*'s Emissaries had inspir'd them with such a Scruple, that they look'd upon it as a high Crime to bear Arms against the Sovereign Lord of *Flanders*; and they thought they should be skreen'd from this Reproach by recognizing *Edward* in that Quality. Ever after *Edward* took the Title of King of *France*, and caus'd his Arms to be quarter'd with those of *France* and *England**. 'Tis not strange that *Edward* was prevail'd on to take this Title, since he ceas'd to give it to *Philip*, after he had manifested his Design to prosecute his own Claim to the Crown, as we shall see hereafter.

Edward *assumes the Title and Arms of King of* France.

THE time that *Edward* spent at Home, till the next Campaign, was employ'd in Preparations for the War; borrowing Money on all Hands, and taking Precautions to maintain his Allies in the League, and his Subjects of *Guyenne* in their Allegiance. After having taken all these Measures, he sail'd from *England* on the 22d of *June* for the *Netherlands*, carrying with him a Fleet of 300 Sail. Two Days after his Departure he met the *French* Fleet in the way to *Sluys*, consisting of 500 Sail, waiting to intercept him in his Passage: Notwithstanding the Enemy's Superiority, he began a Battel with 'em, which lasted all Day, and in which the *French* Fleet was so entirely ruin'd, that only 30 Ships e-

P. 195.

English *Fleets beats the* French *before* Sluys.

* EITHER at this time, or soon after, the King set at the Foot of his Shield, beneath the Arms of *France* and *England*, thus quarter'd, this *French* Motto, which is continu'd to this Day, DIEU ET MON DROIT, *i. e.* *GOD AND MY RIGHT*, declaring thereby his Confidence to be only in God and the Equity of his Cause. *See Mr.* Barnes.

scap'd

Edw. III. ſcap'd. This Fight happen'd on the 24th of *June*, 1340 †.

Siege of Tournay.

After this Victory *Edward* put himſelf at the Head of his Army, which was 150000 Men ſtrong, of whom he detach'd 50000 under *Robert* of *Artois* to *St. Omer*, while himſelf went with the reſt to beſiege *Tournay*. The Succeſs of this Campaign was far ſhort of anſwering ſuch great Preparations. *Robert* of *Artois*, after having receiv'd a Shock near *St. Omer*, ſaw his whole Army diſpers'd, which conſiſted chiefly of the Militia of *Flanders*, while *Philip* of *Valois*, who was advanc'd near *Tournay*, gave ſuch Interruption to the Siege, that *Edward* was three Months before the Place without any proſpect of taking it; nor was it even poſſible for him to give Battel, tho' he ſent a * Charter of Defiance to *Philip*, becauſe he would not accept it. As *Edward* ſaw no probability of making himſelf Maſter of *Tournay*, and as he could not raiſe the Siege without Diſgrace, he was extricated out of this Difficulty by *Joan* Counteſs Dowager of *Hainault*, his Mother-in-law, and Siſter of *Philip* of *Valois*, who coming out of a Convent to which ſhe was retir'd, negotiated with ſuch Succeſs, that ſhe made the two Kings conſent to a Truce, in which all their Allies were comprehended. The ſaid Truce was to laſt till the 25th of *June* next following.

Truce with France.

† Mr. *Barnes*, who relates the Particulars of this Fight, ſays the *French* loſt 25000 or 30000 Men, among whom were two of their Admirals; and that the *Engliſh* took 230 Sail of their Ships, beſides thoſe they deſtroy'd.

* *EDWARD* challeng'd him to fight at ſingle Combat, or to end the Diſpute by a Battel of 100 of the ſtouteſt Soldiers on each Side. Mr. *Barnes* has inſerted the Challenge at large.

EDWARD,

EDWARD, after ſuch mighty Preparations for War, was very much mortify'd when he ſaw he was oblig'd to make a Truce which broke all his Meaſures, and render'd all the Expence he had been at till then entirely fruitleſs. He had the more reaſon to lament the ill Succeſs of this Campaign, becauſe he ſaw himſelf on the point of loſing all his Allies. The Duke of *Brabant* had already withdrawn his Troops, during the Siege of *Tournay*; the *Flemings* ſeem'd to be ſorry that they had enter'd into the Alliance; and the Emperor, being diſguſted that the Truce of *Tournay* was made without his Privity, threaten'd to abandon the Confederates, which he did; and his Defection drew that of the *German* Princes along with it. To this add a Conſideration which fretted *Edward* as much as any one thing, *viz.* How to raiſe Money to pay off his Debts, and a Supply to enable him to renew the War when the Truce was expir'd. He had enter'd on this War by the Advice of the Archbiſhop of *Canterbury*, his Prime Miniſter, and upon the Promiſes he had made him that nothing ſhould be wanting. Nevertheleſs he was no ſooner engag'd in the Siege of *Tournay*, but the Archbiſhop, being ſway'd, as 'tis thought, by Pope *Benedict* XII. who was very partial to *France*, not only fail'd to ſend the Money which he had promis'd him, but alſo oppos'd the raiſing of a Subſidy which had been granted to the King by Parliament. This Breach of Promiſe oblig'd *Edward* to engage in conſiderable Loans, and to pay great Intereſt for Money, which diſabled him from making due Preparations for renewing the War. In 1341, when he return'd to *England*, he took the Archbiſhop of *Canterbury* to task, whom he accus'd of having

A. 1341.

Edward's *Allies begin to fall off.*

Edward *ſuffers by the Archbiſhop of* Canterbury's *Breach of Promiſe.*

Edw. III. ving maliciously thwarted the Execution of his Design. Mean time, as he stood in need of the Clergy, he was afraid to push that Prelate to the utmost; so that he came off with making some Submissions, after he had in vain try'd to set the People at Variance with the King. In these Straits *Edward* took care to get the Truce prolong'd to the 24th of *June*, 1342. He sadly wanted so much time to set his Affairs in order, which were very much unsettled by the want of Money, and the Infidelity of his Allies. 'Tis very probable that this Truce wou'd have been succeeded with a final Peace, if the Death of the Duke of *Bretagne*, which happen'd at this Juncture, had not been attended with such Consequences as flush'd *Edward* with Hopes that he should be able to attack *Philip* on that Side with better Success. As *England* was very much interested in the Quarrel that happen'd on account of the Succession of the Duke of *Bretagne*, 'tis necessary just to explain the Origin of this Quarrel, and the Occasion which *Edward* had to meddle in it.

Death of the Duke of Bretagne.

Quarrel about his Succession.

ARTHUR II. Duke of *Bretagne*, had Children by two Wives; by the first, *John* II. who succeeded him, *Guy*, who was Earl of *Pentebria*, and *Peter*, who left no Issue; and by the second, *John*, who was Earl of *Montfort* in *France* by Right of his Mother. *Guy*, the second Son of *Arthur*'s first Wife, died in 1331, and left but one Daughter, nam'd *Jane*, whom *John* II. her Uncle, gave in Marriage to *Charles* of *Blois*. This *John* II. dying in *April* 1341, *Bretagne* was disputed between *John* Earl of *Montfort*, and *Charles* of *Blois*; the former maintaining that the said Dutchy ought to revert to him, as the nearest Heir of his Brother *John* II. and *Charles* of *Blois* insisting upon the Prerogative which

which gave *Jane* his Wife the same Right as Guy her Father wou'd have had if he had been living. This Affair being carry'd into *France*, and referr'd to the Court of Peers, *Bretagne* was awarded to *Charles* of *Blois*, who was Nephew to *Philip* of *Valois*. *John* of *Montfort* pretending that Injustice had been done him, had Recourse to *Edward's* Protection; and after having done him Homage he went into *Bretagne*, where he made some Progress; but his Happiness did not last long, for at the Approach of *John* Duke of *Normandy*, whom his Father King *Philip* had charg'd with the Execution of the Arret pass'd in favour of *Charles* of *Blois*, the Earl of *Montfort* was oblig'd to retire to *Nantes*, where he was immediately besieg'd, taken, carry'd to *Paris*, and committed to the great Tower of the *Louvre*.

A. 1342.

Earl of Montfort *pays Homage to* Edward *for* Bretagne.

He is taken, and committed to Prison.

NEVERTHELESS his Imprisonment did not put an end to the Affair: *Margaret* of *Flanders*, his Wife, who manag'd Affairs for her imprison'd Husband, renew'd an Alliance with *Edward* in the Name of her Son, but four Years of Age, and promised to deliver up all the Places of *Bretagne* to him, which were at her Disposal. In Consequence of this new Treaty, *Edward* sent Troops to *Bretagne* under the Command of the Earl of *Northampton*, to take Possession of the said Dutchy. Not long after he sent *Robert* of *Artois* thither, who after having made himself Master of *Vannes*, was besieg'd there, and dy'd of the Wounds he receiv'd in the Defence of the Place, which was carry'd by Storm. The Earl of *Northampton* having not Forces enough to maintain himself in *Bretagne*, *Edward* resolv'd to go thither himself with powerful Succours; and arriving in the Dutchy in the Year 1342, he there caus'd four

Edward *sends Troops to* Bretagne.

Goes himself with a great Reinforcement.

Edw. III. Places to be besieg'd at once. But at the Approach of the Duke of *Normandy*, who advanc'd at the Head of a numerous Army, *Edward* was oblig'd to muster all his Forces in one Body, which when all was done was still inferior to the *French* Army; therefore he chose to intrench himself, which he did in such a manner, that the Duke did not once dare to attack him. In fine, after both Armies had spent great part of the Winter, as it were in sight of each other, with great Inconvenience to both, two of the Pope's Legates mediated a general Truce, in which all the Allies and Adherents of the two Kings were comprehended. This Truce, which was sign'd the 20th of *February*, 1343, at *London*, was to last till *Michaelmas* 1346. It was likewise agreed that the two Kings shou'd send their Plenipotentiaries to *Avignon*, to negotiate a Peace there before the Pope as a private Person, which Negotiation was to begin upon such a Day, and to last so long: That the Pope shou'd send a Nuncio to *Bretagne*, to see to the Observation of the Truce: That the City of *Vannes* shou'd be put into the Nuncio's Hands, to keep it in the Pope's Name till the end of the Truce; and that *John* of *Montfort* shou'd be set at Liberty.

Another Truce with France. *P*. 357.

THO' King *Edward* appointed his Plenipotentiaries for the Peace, by a Commission dated the 20th of *May* 1343, at *Westminster*, and gave them their Instructions, and their full Powers, yet an unthought-of Accident retarded their Departure. *Nichol de Flisco*, who was *Edward's* Envoy at the Pope's Court, being taken from his House in the Night-time, and carry'd into *France*, *Edward* was resolv'd to have Satisfaction for this Affront before he sent away his Ambassadors, as appears by his Letter to the Pope

P. 366.

dated

dated *July* the 6th, 1343, at *Clarendon*; and at the ſame time demanded a Paſſport to protect them from the like Acts of Violence. But the Pope having not yet taken one Step to puniſh thoſe who had carry'd off the King's Envoy, and being moreover unwilling to grant a Paſſport, contrary to the uſual Form, the *Engliſh* Plenipotentiaries ſtay'd in their Iſland; which was the reaſon that the Term fix'd for the Treaty was often prolong'd.

A. 1344.

P. 375. Edward *demands Satisfaction for the Arreſt of his Envoy.*

IT was now the Year 1344, yet *Edward* did not care to enter into any Negotiation before he had Satisfaction as well for the Seizure of his Envoy, as the extraordinary ſafe Conduct which he demanded for his Ambaſſadors. To this was added another Cauſe of Complaint, *viz.* for the detaining of *John* Earl of *Montfort*, whom *Philip* ſtill kept in Priſon, contrary to an expreſs Article of the Truce, on Pretence that the ſaid Prince cou'd not find Sureties in *France*. Yet 'tis probable that all theſe Obſtacles wou'd have been remov'd, had it not been for another Accident, which was the Occaſion of the Breach of the Truce. *Oliver de Cliſſon*, a Lord of *Bretagne*, and 10 other Lords and Gentlemen of that Province, or *Normandy*, having been arreſted in *Bretagne* by Order of the King of *France*, were conducted to *Paris*, where the ſaid Prince caus'd them to be beheaded without any Form of Law. The *French* Hiſtorians pretend that thoſe Lords were Friends and Partiſans of *Charles de Blois*, and that they went voluntarily to *Paris* to aſſiſt at a Tournament: but we ſhall find by the Sequel that their Account has not one Word of Truth in it, and that on the contrary they had declar'd for *John* Earl of *Montfort*, and were apprehended in *Bretagne*. Be this as it will, *Edward* demanded Satisfaction for

And for other Acts in Violation of the Truce.

A Miſtake of French *Hiſtorians, about ſome Gentlemen who were taken up and beheaded by their King, without any Form of Tryal.*

Edw. III. for this Violation of the Truce, and sent Ambassadors to the Pope for that very Purpose. This Affair spun out the Remainder of this Year and part of the next, without the Pope's giving or procuring *Edward* the Satisfaction he demanded. On the contrary, it appears from several Acts in this Collection, that he press'd him to make Peace without including his Allies, and that he endeavour'd to render him responsible for the Violation of the Truce, by laying all the Blame of it upon him. In fine, after *Edward* had waited a whole Year for the Satisfaction which he demanded of *Philip*, perceiving there was no Likelihood of obtaining it, he, by a Declaration dated the 24th of *April* 1345, at *Westminster*, notify'd that the Truce was broke. But as this was what he did not expect, he cou'd not be in a Condition to renew the War till towards the middle of the Year 1346.

P. 448.

King of France *sends his Son into* Guyenne.

THIS Delay had like to have cost him dear, because *Philip* took that Opportunity to send his Son, the Duke of *Normandy*, into *Guyenne*, with an Army of 100,000 Men, who threatned to drive the *English* entirely out of the Province. But it was owing to *Edward*'s good Fortune, that the Progress which the Duke made fell short of what might be expected from so great an Armament; for he only took a few paltry Towns along the *Garonne*, and then laid Siege to *Aiguillon*, where the brave Resistance of the Besieged made him lose a great deal of Time. Mean time *Edward*, who saw *Guyenne* in great Danger, resolv'd to go thither himself with some Succours. With this View he embark'd the second of *July* 1346, with an Army of about 30,000 Men, among whom were 4000 Men of Arms. As impatient as he was to go and

King Edward *sails to the Relief of his Subjects in* Guyenne, *but lands in* Normandy.

P. 518.

and relieve his Subjects in *Guyenne*, it was not possible for him to execute his Design, the contrary Winds having drove him back twice upon his own Coasts; and at last, seeing that he cou'd not pursue his Voyage to *Guyenne*, he resolv'd by the Advice of *Godfrey* of *Harcourt*, a *Norman* Lord who had fled to him for Refuge, to make a Descent into *Normandy*. Pursuant to this Resolution he caus'd his Troops to land at *La Hogue* in the *Coutantin*; and as *Philip*'s Forces were a great way off at that time, he had Leisure to ravage *Normandy* without any Opposition, but from the Count *d'Eu*, Constable of *France*, who offering to stop his Progress with the Militia of the Country, was routed and taken Prisoner. After this *Edward* advanc'd to *Poissy*, from whence he sent a Challenge to *Philip* to fight him under the Walls of the *Louvre*. Upon the very first Advice of *Edward*'s landing, *Philip* us'd extraordinary Diligence to assemble an Army, which very soon amounted to above 100000 Men; and with this Army he form'd a Design to shut up the *English* between the *Seine* and the *Oyse*, in order to cut off their Retreat. *Edward* perceiving this at last, tho' late, resolv'd to retire into the County of *Ponthieu*, but found great Difficulties in the Undertaking for want of a Passage over the *Soame*: However he was fortunate enough to discover and force the Pass of *Blanquetaque*, tho' guarded by 12000 Men under the Command of *Gondemar du Fay*; and that very Night after he had pass'd his Army over the River, he went and encamp'd at *Cressy*, where he was resolv'd to stay for *Philip*, who next Day came up with him; and upon the 26th of *August* 1346, happen'd the famous Battel of *Cressy*, where *Philip* was entirely routed,

A. 1346.

Sends a Challenge to the King of France.

Edw. III. *The Battel of* Cressy *won by* Edward *the* Black Prince.

routed, after the Loss of 30000 Men, 1200 Knights, the Earl of *Alencon* his Brother, the King of *Bohemia* his Ally, and 15 Princes, or Noblemen of the greatest Quality in the Kingdom. It may be said that *Edward*'s eldest Son the Prince of *Wales*, who was but 15 Years of Age, gain'd this Victory, the King his Father standing off at a Distance with a Body of Reserves, to have supported him in case of Need, without offering to strike a Blow, that he might not rob the Prince his Son of any part of the Glory.*

AFTER

* Mr. *Barnes*, who gives the Detail of this glorious Fight and complete Victory, mentions one or two Particulars which deserve to be taken Notice of in this Place. He remarks it as a signal Instance of the Divine Favour to *Edward*'s Arms, that not one of the *English* Nobility fell in the Action, and that only three of their Knights and one Esquire were kill'd. He says, that the *French* King brought with him from *St. Dennis* the great and holy Standard of *France*, which being by the *French* held as sacred as if it came down from Heaven, was originally only us'd in the Wars against the Infidels; That *Philip* being secure of the Victory, and resolv'd to make an end of the War at one Blow, notify'd, by erecting this hallowed Banner in the Field of Battel, that all the *English* shou'd be put to the Sword, except only King *Edward* and his Son the Prince of *Wales*: And that King *Edward* hearing of this cruel Resolution, caus'd also his Burning Dragon to be erected, which signify'd as little Mercy to be shew'd to *Frenchmen*. From hence our Author very judiciously apologizes for *Edward*'s keeping at a Distance all the time of the Battel, because if the Victory shou'd have declar'd against him, all wou'd have been utterly lost; and to those Declarations our Author ascribes it that so many of the *French* were put to the Sword, and not one of 'em taken Prisoner. Mr. *Barnes* adds, that in this Battel the Prince of *Wales* took and won the Arms of the King of *Bohemia* (being

AFTER this great Victory *Edward* caus'd *Calais* to be invested on the 5th of *September*, and continu'd the Siege eleven Months, so as that *Philip*, who advanc'd about the end of that Term at the Head of an Army of 150000 Men, cou'd not find an Opportunity to attack him in his Intrenchments, much less to bring him out to a pitch'd Battel.

A. 1348. *Siege of* Calais.

IN 1347, while *Edward* was employ'd in the Siege of *Calais*, he receiv'd News that *David* King of *Scotland*, who had enter'd *England* with 60000 Men, was defeated and taken Prisoner. At length on the first of *August* 1347, *Edward* made himself Master of *Calais*, and turning out all the Inhabitants put an *English* Colony into the place.

David *King of* Scotland *taken Prisoner.*

Calais *taken.*

TWO Months after the taking of *Calais*, the Pope's Legates mediated a Truce from the 28th of *September* to the end of *June* 1348; after which *Edward* return'd to *England* in Triumph. In this Truce as well as in the former it was agreed, that the two Kings shou'd send their Ambassadors to *Avignon*, there to negotiate a Peace in the presence of the Pope as Mediator. But the same Difficulties which occurr'd before, with relation to the sending of the *English* Ambassadors, still subsisting, there was a Necessity for frequent Prolongations of the Term fix'd for the Negotiation, and by consequence the Truce was several times renew'd. A terrible Plague with which *France* was afflicted in 1348, and *England* in 1349, did un-

Pope mediates a Truce.

Plagues both in France *and* England.

(being the Ostrich Feathers with the Motto ICH DIEN, *i. e. I SERVE*) which have ever since been worn by all the Princes of *Wales*, eldest Sons to the Kings of *England*. He observes, that ever after this Victory the *French* call'd this Heroic Prince of *Wales*, *Edward le Noir*, or the *Black Prince*.

Edw. III. doubtedly contribute not a little to the cooling of the Passion of both Kings to renew the War, so that the Truce was prolong'd, time after time, to the 1st of *August* 1350.

Death of Philip *of* France.

KING *Philip* dying the 22d of that Month, his Successor *John* was mightily for renewing the Truce, and found no great Difficulty in obtaining it, the Plague having made such a Havock in *England*, that it had carry'd off almost half the People. Therefore the said Truce was farther prolong'd to the 1st of *August* 1351, and a Treaty resolv'd on. But as *Avignon* was too far distant from *England*, and *Edward* moreover not well pleas'd with the Pope, the two Kings agreed that a Peace should be negotiated in some place which was nearer at hand to both. For this end they sent their Ambassadors in 1351, the one to *Calais*, and the other to *Guesnes*; and between those two Towns Tents were erected, under which the Plenipotentiaries of both Parties conferr'd together, in order to settle the Preliminaries of a good Peace.

A Treaty set on Foot between the new King and Edward.

THE first thing they agreed upon was to prolong the Truce to the 12th of *September* 1352; but this being too short a Term to adjust all the Differences, it was farther prolong'd to the 1st of *August* 1353, and finally to the 1st of *April* 1354.

DURING this last Prorogation King *John* seem'd inclinable at length to conclude a Peace on condition of yielding up *Guyenne*, and the Counties of *Artois* and *Guisnes*, with the City and Territories of *Calais*, in full Sovereignty to *Edward*. This is very clear from the *English* Historians, tho' *Mezeray* makes no mention of it. Mean time, as several Acts in this Volume of the *Fœdera* make it manifest, that *Edward* thought the Peace as good as made; and as it is hardly

A material Omission in the French *Historian* Mezeray.

I

hardly to be ſuppos'd he wou'd have come into it without finding ſome Advantage in it; what the *Engliſh* Hiſtorians have advanc'd on this Point ſeems to be out of all manner of Diſpute. *A.* 1354

NOTWITHSTANDING the Diſproportion there was between *Edward*'s firſt Pretenſions, and the Offers now made to him, he accepted the latter. There remain'd nothing to be done, but to conclude this Treaty in a ſolemn manner; for which end the two Kings thought they cou'd not do better than to get it confirm'd by the Pope, whom they empower'd to bind both of 'em by Eccleſiaſtical Cenſures to the Obſervation of the ſaid Treaty, and the ſame was to be ſign'd in his Preſence. Purſuant to theſe Conventions *Edward* ſent his Ambaſſadors to *Avignon* with very ample Powers, dated at *Weſtminſter* the 28th of *Auguſt* 1354, to ſign the Treaty, and to ſubmit himſelf to the Pope's Juriſdiction, with reſpect to the Obſervation of it. But the Proſpect of this Peace ſoon vaniſh'd, becauſe *John*'s Ambaſſadors refus'd to confirm before the Pope what had been agreed on between *Guiſnes* and *Calais*. *P.* 794.

War with France *breaks out again.*

THIS Refuſal occaſion'd a freſh Rupture: for notwithſtanding all the Pope's Inſtances with *Edward* to renew the Negotiation, he wou'd hear no more Talk of Peace; but having taken a Reſolution to begin the War again with Vigour, he gave the Government of *Guyenne* to his Son the Prince of *Wales*, and ſent him into that Province to ſtrike the firſt Blow, while himſelf made Preparations for a ſecond Invaſion of *France* elſewhere.

Edward *the* Black Prince *ravages* Languedoc, *&c.*

THE Prince of *Wales*, then but 25 Years of Age, arriving in *Guyenne*, put himſelf at the Head of a ſmall Army, and therewith ravag'd

Edw. III. *Languedoc*, where he took *Carcassonne* and *Narbonne*, and carry'd off a great Booty, which he plac'd for Security in *Bourdeaux*. After having refresh'd himself a little in that City, he set out from thence with an Army of 12000 Men, of whom only 3000 were Natives of *England*; travers'd the Countries of *Perigord* and *Limousin*; and entring into *Berry*, went and shew'd himself at the Gates of *Bourges*, where he heard that King *John* was advancing at the Head of 60000 Men. This News obliging him to think of a Retreat, he was inclinable to take a Compass, and retire into *Guyenne* thro' *Poictou*; but *John* made such haste that he came up with him at last at *Maupertuis* near *Poictiers*, where Prince *Edward* was oblig'd to intrench himself in a Post embarass'd with Vines and Hedges, which gave him great Advantage. Tho' it had been easy for *John* to have starv'd this little Army, shut up as it was in an Enemy's Country, yet his Impatience to be reveng'd for the Ravages which the *English* had committed in *France*, did not permit him to stay so long, and he resolv'd to attack the Prince in his Intrenchments: but he had the Misfortune to be entirely defeated by this handful of *English*, and to fall himself into the Enemy's Hands, with his fourth Son *Philip* (afterwards call'd the *Hardy*) about 15 Years of Age, and a great many other Lords of the best Quality in the Kingdom *. In this Battel,

Battel of Poictiers.

* This Battel was fought the 19th of *September* 1356, the *French* had 50000 Horse, and as many Foot; and the *English* but 8 or 9000 Men in all, according to the Report of the Lord *Riboumont*, who was sent by King *John* to view Prince *Edward*'s Army before the Battel: And the *English* are said to have taken more *French* Prisoners, than they had Men to guard 'em. Mr. *Barnes* gives an ample Account of the Battel, for which we have not room, but

Battel, which was ſo fatal to *France*, there were only 6000 *French*-Men kill'd, but in that Number were 800 Gentlemen, beſides the Duke of *Bourbon* Prince of the Blood, the Duke of *Athens* Conſtable of *France*, the Marſhal *de Neſle*, and above 50 other great Lords. After this glorious Victory the Prince of *Wales* quietly led his Priſoners to *Bourdeaux*, and ſent the great News to the King his Father, who order'd Thankſgivings to God for eight days together in all the Churches of *England*. With this Victory end the Acts of this Volume relating to *France*. We ſhall ſee what were the Conſequences of this famous Battel, in our Account of the next Volume. *A.* 1331.

but cannot omit an Obſervation of his upon the Sur-name of this *French* King's young Son and Fellow Priſoner *Philip*, which moſt Authors have deriv'd from his Courage and Valour in War; but Mr. *Barnes* thinks this the moſt probable Account of any that he had ſeen, *viz.* That when his Father, then a Priſoner in *England*, was dining one Day with King *Edward* at his Table, this young Prince *Philip* was with others of the *French* Nobility appointed to wait; and that a young Nobleman of *England*, who likewiſe attended, ſerving King *Edward* firſt, and then King *John*, this *Philip* gave him a Box o'th' Ear, ſaying, *What, dare you ſerve the King of* England *firſt when the King of* France *is at the Table?* The offended Nobleman thereupon drew his Dagger, but King *Edward* forbad him to ſtrike; and commending the noble Spirit of the young Prince, ſaid to him in *French*, *Vous eſtes Philippe le Hardi*, i. e. *Thou art* Philip *the* Hardy, *or* Bold.

WHAT we have hitherto given is in general the Subject of the Acts of the fifth Volume which relate to France. *'Tis time now to glance over the most important of them; and as it is not possible to mention all without running into too great a length, we shall only point out some of them, and insist upon none but such as may serve to illustrate any Passage of the* English *History. And for the Reader's Conveniency we shall range them according to the Dates of the Years, that in case of need he may have recourse to what is mention'd in the foregoing Account under those Years.*

An Account of the Acts in the fifth Volume of the Fœdera, *relating to the Affairs with* France.

Truce with France. *P.* 2.

1. A Prorogation to the 24th of *June* 1338, of the Truce which *Edward* had granted to *France* at the Instance of the Pope's Legates to the Festival of *Easter*, dated at *Westminster February* 24, 1338*.

Edward's *Letter to the Emperor, for granting the Title of King to the Dauphin of* Vienne. *P.* 10.

2. *EDWARD*'s Letter to the Emperor, praying him to grant the Title of King to the Dauphin of *Vienne*, dated at *Westminster March* 3, 1338. Probably the Dauphin had promis'd upon this Condition to engage in *Edward*'s Cause.

His Letter to the two Archbishops, desiring their Prayers, &c. P. 20.

3. A Letter from *Edward* to the Archbishops of *Canterbury* and *York*, desiring the Fa-

* It may be a Question which is most chargeable, such kind of Truces, or some Campaigns? for Mr. *Barnes* says, that these Christian Peace-makers cost the Church of *England* 50 Marks a Day all the time they stay'd here, which was from the middle of *December* 1337, to the 21st of *March* following.

your

vour of their Prayers; and that they wou'd excuse him to his People on account of the great Taxes which he was oblig'd to lay upon them*, dated at *Berwick* upon *Tweed*, *March* 28, 1338. *A.*1338.

Edward's Order for the Defence of the Isle of Wight. *P.* 24.

4. AN Order for the Inhabitants of the Isle of *Wight* to take Arms against a Descent then threaten'd by the *French* Fleet, dated *April* 15, 1338. at *Havering Bower* in *Essex*. 'Tis likely that this gave occasion to the following Act, *viz.*

His Repeal of the Suspension with France. *P.* 35.

5. A REPEAL of the Suspension granted to *France*, because *Philip* first began Hostilities; dated at the Tower of *London*, *May* 6, 1338†.

* WHAT these Taxes were we may partly guess by the Account which Mr. *Barnes* gives, who tells us, that the Laity granted to the King the one half of their Wools throughout the whole Realm for the next Summer, which he receiv'd graciously; and of the Clergy he also levied the whole, causing them to pay nine Marks of every Sack of the best Wool; but after the rate of one half he took, in whose Hands soever it was found, as well Merchants as others, according to the foresaid Grant: So that of the Abby of *Leicester* only, as *Knighton*, one of that House, witnesses, he had no less than 18 Sacks. After this he took a Fifteenth of all the Commonalty of his Realm in Wool, the Price of every Stone, rated at 14 Pounds *per* Stone, at two Shillings. And yet in *November* last he had sent the Bishop of *Lincoln*, and the Earls of *Northampton* and *Suffolk* with 10000 Sacks of Wool into *Brabant* to make Retainers in *High-Germany*; and there at the same time they sold all their Wool, every Sack for 40 *l.* which amounted in all to 400000 *l.* Besides all this, he is said about this time to have seiz'd on the Wealth of the *Cluniacks* and *Cistercians*, Aliens, and of the *Lombards*, and all the Triennial Tythes, which were first intended for the Holy War.

† MR. *Barnes* says, that immediately upon this, *Edward* seeing that the *French* King refus'd to give Security for observing the Truce inviolably, not only revok'd the latter Prorogation of it, but set out for *Flanders*, there to confer personally with his Allies in pursuance of his Designs against *France*.

6. THE

Edw. III.

Edward's Treaty with the Flemings. P. 55.

6. The Treaty between King *Edward* and the Provinces and Towns of *Flanders*, dated at *Antwerp* the *Wednesday* after Trinity, 1331.—— In this Treaty the *Flemings* only engag'd themselves to observe an exact Neutrality between the two Kings; but the Date of it so far back as the Year 1331 is remarkable, because it is a Proof that even at that time *Edward* had form'd a Design to recover the Crown from *Philip*; as I have already observ'd. Tho' it was scarce two Years that he had perform'd his Homage to *Philip*, and had not hitherto made any Discovery of his Pretensions; yet in this Act he calls *Philip* the *Pretended King of* France. This Treaty was not ratify'd by *Edward* till the 26th of *June* 1338, at *Walton*.

His Ratification of it. P. 59.

His full Powers to treat with Philip. P. 56.

7. His full Powers to the Archbishop of *Canterbury* and others to treat with *Philip de Valois*, in one of which he only styles him *Consanguineum nostrum Franciæ*, i. e. *Our Cousin of* France, without giving him the Title of King; and in the other, the most excellent Prince and illustrious Lord *Philip* King of *France*, dated at *Westminster* and at *Walton*, the 21st of *June* 1338.

Letter to the Emperor. P. 59.

8. His Letter to the Emperor, acquainting him that he was just ready to embark for the *Netherlands*, dated *June* the 21st 1338, at *Walton*.

9. A Memorandum of the Day of his going on board, *viz.* the 16th of *July* 1338*.

A Recal of the full Powers, in which Philip *is styl'd* King of France. P. 66.

10. A Recal of all the full Powers in which *Philip* of *Valois* is styl'd King of *France*, dated at *Antwerp July* the 22d 1338.

* He went with a Royal Navy of 500 Sail, and many great Lords of *England* in his Company, who are mention'd by Mr. *Barnes*.

In

A. 1338.

The Emperor makes Edward *Vicar General of the Empire.*

IN a few Days after *Edward* set out for *Cologn*, where the Emperor gave him the Style and Title of Vicar General of the Empire. I am surpriz'd that this Charter is not to be met with in the *Fœdera* †.

II. A BRIEF or Letter from Pope *Benedict* XII. in which he reproaches *Edward* for his Alliance with *Lewis* of *Bavaria*, styling himself Emperor, then under Excommunication; and excuses himself for granting the Tenths to *Philip*, pretending he had no View to

Pope's Letter to Edward, *upbraiding him for his Alliance with the excommunicated Emperor, P.* 88.

† MR. *Barnes* gives the Oath sworn to *Edward*, next Day, by the Emperor and all his Barons, *viz.* 'That they 'wou'd help him against the 'King of *France* and all his 'Adherents, both to live 'and die with him for seven 'Years, if the War shou'd 'continue so long. That 'all the Barons of *Almaine*, 'from *Cologn* and on this 'side, shou'd immediately 'enter the King of *England*'s 'Service, and be always 'ready to come unto him 'as often as summon'd a'gainst the King of *France*, 'as well where the King of '*England* shou'd be in Per'son, as to any other place 'to which he shou'd assign 'them. And that if any of 'the said Lords shou'd re'fuse to obey the said King 'of *England* in the Premi'ses, then all the other 'Lords of *High-Germany* 'shou'd rise in Arms against 'that Man till they had de'stroy'd him.

MR. *Barnes* says that King *Edward* held a Parliament about *November* the 11th in *Brabant*, where being deck'd in his Royal Robes, with a Crown of Gold on his Head, and seated on a stately Throne five foot higher than any other, the Emperor's Charter was then and there openly read, declaring, 'That King *Ed*'*ward* of *England* was made 'Vicar General, or Lieu'tenant for the Emperor, 'and as such had full Power 'to make Laws, and to ad'minister Justice to every 'Person in the Emperor's 'Name, and to coin Money 'both Gold and Silver at his 'pleasure with his own 'Stamp and Inscription. It 'was also therein command'ed, that the Lords, and o'ther Subjects of the Em'pire, shou'd yield Obe'dience and pay Homage to 'the King of *England*, his 'Vicar, as to himself.

support

support him against *Edward*, but against the *Germans* only, who threaten'd *France* with an Invasion. For a Proof of this he is pleased to quote the very Terms of his Grant; as if the Expressions of it could possibly weaken the Force of the Supply against *Edward*. This Letter is dated at *Avignon*, the Ides of *November*, 1338.

Edward *forbids to give* Philip *the Title of King of* France. *P.* 93.

12. A PROHIBITION to the *English* Plenipotentiaries to give *Philip de Valois* the Title of King of *France*. Dated at *Antwerp*, *Nov.* 16, 1338.

His full Powers to treat with Philip. *P.* 92, 95.

13. His full Powers to the said Ambassadors to treat with *Philip*, whom he only stiles *Philippum de Valesio*, *consanguineum nostrum*, *i. e.* *Philip* of *Valois*, our Cousin: Dated at *Antwerp*, *Nov.* 15, 1338. And at the Pope's Request the King granted new Powers to his said Ambassadors, immediately after, at the end of which is this Memorandum, *Iidem archiepiscopus*, *episcopi*, & *alii suprascripti*, *habent consimile procuratorium ad tractandum cum excellentissimo principe domino Philippo rege Franciæ illustri. i. e.* The said Archbishop, Bishops, and others above-mention'd, have the like full Powers to treat with the *most excellent* Prince and Lord, *Philip*, the *Illustrious King* of *France*.—— Probably this was a Form to be made use of, in case they should happen to agree upon Articles of Peace. This shews at the same time, that *Edward* would then have been contented with less than the Crown of *France*.

He excuses the Earl of Hainault *from giving the Empire Succours.* *P.* 122.

14. *EDWARD*'s Letters Patent, whereby he declares, in quality of Vicar of the Empire, that the Earl of *Hainault* is not oblig'd to furnish it with any Succours; dated at *Brussels August* 20, 1339.

15. AN Order dated at *Markoyn* (*Marchienne*) *infra marchiam Franciæ*, the 26th of *September*, 1339. for remitting ſmall Debts owing to the Crown.

A. 1339

He remits ſmall Debts owing to the Crown.

P. 124.

16. HIS Promiſe to the Marquis of *Juliers*, to make him a Peer of *England*, dated at *Antwerp*, *Nov.* 28, 1339. which was upon his Return from the Campaign.

Promiſes to make the M. of Juliers *an* Engliſh *Peer.*

P. 139.

17. A BULL of *Benedict* XII. wherein he offers to be Mediator between the two Kings of *France* and *England*, dated at *Avignon*, the 10th of the Calends of *January*, 1339.

Pope offers to mediate between England *and* France.

P. 146.

18. A FULL Power to treat with the *Flemings*, who had reſolved to enter into the League againſt *France*; dated at *Antwerp*, *January* 4, 1340. In purſuance hereof a Treaty was made with the *Flemings*, by which they engag'd to enter into the League, on condition that *Edward* ſhould take the Title of King of *France*. The Treaty is not printed in the *Fœdera*, but there is the Ratification of it, dated at *Ghent*, the 28th of *January*, 1340.*.

Edward'*s full Powers to treat with the* Flemings.

P. 153.

Treaty ratify'd.

P. 155.

19. ED-

* IT was part of the Convention, according to our truſty Hiſtorian Mr. *Barnes*, that *Edward* ſhould take upon him the Arms as well as Title of King of *France*, which he did, and thereupon receiv'd the Homage of the *Flemings*. Our Author ſhews, that though this Prince afterwards, perhaps to gratify the *French* Nation, or becauſe that was the more ancient and greater Monarchy, plac'd the *Flowers de Lis*, in the dexter and moſt honourable Quarter, yet it was not ſo at their firſt intermingling. And he confirms his Opinion from what King *Philip* ſaid upon this occaſion to ſome *Engliſh* Agents employ'd at his Court. 'Our Couſin, ſays he, doth 'wrongfully quarter the 'Arms of *England* and *France*, 'which notwithſtanding doth 'not ſo much diſpleaſe us, 'becauſe indeed he is deſ-'cended (tho' by the weaker 'Sex) of our Kin; and there-'fore as being a Batchelor, 'we cou'd eaſily be content 'to allow him part of the 'Arms of *France*; but where-

'as

Edw. III. His Answer to the Pope's Letter. P. 156.

19. *EDWARD*'s Answer to a Letter from the Pope, beginning *Sanctissimo, &c. Edwardus rex Franciæ & Angliæ, &c.* and dated at *Ghent*, the 30th of *January*, 1340.

It appears by this Answer, that tho' *Edward* pretended a Right to the whole Kingdom of *France*, he would have been contented with a great deal less, if *Philip* could have prevail'd on himself to have made him any Offers. *Pro certo tamen, de voluntate tamen partis adversæ, nec per dictos Cardinales, nec per alios huc usque scire nequivimus, quod idem Philippus nobis quidquam facere voluerit, vel offerre. Et re vera si nobis oblationem etiam mediocrem, tunc fecisset, ad vitandum guerrarum discrimina, & expensarum profluvia, super ea responsionem rationabilem fecissemus. Sed jam non vidimus quid per viam pacis ulterius cum honore nostro facere valeamus. i. e.* Neverthelefs, certain it is, that thro' the Humour of the adverse Party, we could never know by the said Cardinals, nor any others, to this Day, that the said *Philip* had any Inclination to transact any thing with

'as in his Seals and Letters 'Patent, he styles himself K. 'of *England*, and of *France*, 'in the one, and sets the 'Quarter of his Arms with 'Leopards, before the Quarter charg'd with Lillies, 'in the other, this is that 'which we disdain exceedingly; for thereby it shou'd 'seem he prefers that inconsiderable Isle of *England*, 'before the mighty Kingdom of *France*.' To this Complaint, Sir *John Shoreditch* made Answer, "That 'it was the Custom of *England* to set the Title and 'Arms of their Progenitors 'before those of a Right 'deriv'd from the Mother. 'And thus, *said he*, doth my 'Lord the King of *England* 'prefer his paternal Coat, 'both out of Duty and Reason.' But it appears they were alter'd soon after, even as they stand now, only that when *Charles* VI. of *France*, with design to shew a difference, chang'd the *Semee Flowers-de-Lis* into three, our King *Henry* V. also did the like, and so it hath continu'd ever since.

us,

us, or to make us an Offer. And indeed, if he had at that time made us a ſmall Offer, we ſhould, for avoiding the Hazards and Expences of a War, have returned a reaſonable Anſwer. But now we don't ſee what we can do farther in a way of Peace, conſiſtent with our Honour. *A.* 1340.

Order for payment of Money to Nich. de Fliſco. *P.* 156.

20. AN Order to pay a certain Sum of Money to *Nichol. de Fliſco*, who went to *Avignon* upon the King's Buſineſs; dated at *Ghent*, *Jan.* 30. 1340. in the firſt Year of our Reign as King of *France*, and the fourteenth as King of *England*.

Edward's *Declaration, inviting the* French *to own him their King.* *P.* 158.

21. KING *Edward*'s Declaration to the *French*, notifying that the *Flemings* had recogniz'd him for King of *France*, and inviting them to follow their Example; dated at *Ghent*, *Feb.* 6. 1340. In this Declaration he ſaid, That he might not be thought to neglect the Favours of God, and that he might conform himſelf to his Will and Pleaſure, he had reſolved to take upon him the Government of the Kingdom of *France*, which was devolv'd to him by the Death of *Charles the Fair*, and which, during his Minority, *Philip* had ſeiz'd unjuſtly, and with Violence. He alſo promis'd to govern the ſaid Realm according to the Laws and Cuſtoms in uſe at the time of his Predeceſſor St. *Louis*.

Declaration of Philip's *ill Returns to* Edward's *Advances.* *P.* 160.

22. ANOTHER Declaration ſetting forth all the Overtures and Advances he had made from time to time to *Philip*, and the ſeveral Injuries he had received from him. Dated as above.

Day of his Return to England. *P.* 174.

23. A MEMORANDUM of the Day of *Edward*'s Return to *England*, *viz.* the 21ſt of *February*, 1340.

24. A LETTER to the Archbiſhop of *Canterbury*, ſummoning him to come to the Parliament, and about his taking the new Title of King of *France*,

Edw.III. *France*, dated at *Harwich*, the 21st of *February*, as aforesaid. *Non mirantes ex hoc quod stylum nostrum consuetum mutavimus, & regem Franciæ nos facimus nominari; nam diversæ subsunt causæ, per quas hoc facere necessario nos oportet, & quas vobis, ac aliis prælatis & magnatibus, necnon communitatibus ejusdem regni Angliæ, ad dictum parlamentum plenius exponemus, &c. i. e.* Wonder not that we have alter'd our usual Style, and that we have taken the Title of King of *France*; for various are the Reasons for which it necessarily behov'd us to do it, and which we shall explain more at large to you and the other Lords Spiritual and Temporal, and also to the Commons of our said Realm of *England*, at the said Parliament.

Letter to the Archbishop of Canterbury, *requiring his Presence in Parliament, to hear the Reasons of his taking the Style and Title of* France. *P.* 174.

Pope's Letter, dissuading him from using that Title. P. 173.

25. A LETTER from *Benedict* XII. exhorting *Edward* to quit the Title of King of *France*; dated at *Avignon*, the third of the Nones of *March*, 1340. *Nuper excellentiæ regis literis*, says the Pope, *nostro apostolatui præsentatis, & contentis in ipsis plenius intellectis, novus in eis descriptus titulus, & impressio sigilli Franciæ armis & Angliæ sculpti, ut prima facie videbatur, stuporis & admirationis magnam nobis materiam ministrarum. i. e.* Upon certain of your Excellencies Letters lately presented to our Apostleship, and upon fuller Discovery of the Contents thereof, the new Title described in it, and the Impression of the Seal engraved with the Arms of *France* and *England*, no sooner appeared to our View, but it gave us great Cause of Astonishment and Admiration.— In the remaining Part of the Letter the Pope endeavours by all the Arguments that he could think of, to persuade the King to lay aside that Title.

M. of Julier's *Peerage and Pension. P.* 184.

26. THE King's Patent for creating *William* Marquis of *Juliers*, a Peer of *England*, by the Style

Style and Title of Earl of *Cambridge*, with a Penſion of 1000*l. per Annum:* Dated at *Weſtminſter, May* 12, 1340 *. *A.* 1340

It appears from ſeveral Acts in this Volume, that *Edward* had pledg'd his Hereditary Crown, which he calls *Hæreditarium & præcellentiorum*, to the Archbiſhop of *Triers*, for 50000 Florins. The Convention for this Purpoſe is dated the laſt Day of *February*, 1338. He alſo pledged his Queen's Crown, and another leſſer, to ſome Merchants at *Cologn*, as appears by Letters of Pledge and Redemption, dated at *Weſtminſter*, the 17th of *May* 1340, the 10th of *March* 1344, and the 10th of *April* 1345.

K. Edward *pawns his Crowns.* *P.* 101, 185, 409, 447.

27. *EDWARD*'s Letter to the Pope, complaining that *Nichol. de Fliſco*, his Envoy, was carry'd away by Night from *Avignon* into *France*. 'Tis dated at *Clare*, the 1ſt of *June*, 1340. He demands Satisfaction for this Affront, and tells the Pope in plain Terms, that he cannot expect to have any Ambaſſadors from him, till he has done him Juſtice for that Violation of the Law of Nations †.

His Letter to the Pope complaining of his Envoy's being carry'd into France. *P.* 188.

28. *ED-*

* Here Mr. *Barnes* obſerves a miſtake of the Learned Antiquary Mr. *Camden*, who ſays in his *Britannia*, that King *Edward* III. for the Love he bore to Queen *Philippa* his Conſort, created the Lord *John* of *Hainault* her Uncle, Earl of *Cambridge:* and that upon his Revolt to the *French* he diveſted him thereof, and conferr'd it upon *William* Marquis of *Juliers*, Siſter's Son to that Queen: whereas the Truth is, that the ſaid Lord *John* was not now, nor for ſome Years after, revolted to the *French*, as is alſo own'd by the diligent and accurate Sir *William Dugdale*.

† Mr. *Barnes* ſays, that while *Nichol. de Fliſco*, and his Son *Andrew* were at *Avignon*, under the Pope's Protection, certain wicked Perſons, to curry Favour with the King of *France*, about Midnight, on *Good Friday* Eve, enter'd his Houſe by Violence, broke open his Chamber, and hardly giving him

T

Edw. III.

His Letter to his Parliament about his Victory at Sea, and the March of his Forces by Land.

28. *EDWARD*'s Letter to his Parliament, acquainting them with the Victory he had gain'd at Sea. 'Tis dated at *Bruges* the 9th of *July* 1340. He alſo gave them Advice that he was marching to *Tournay* with 100000 Men, and that *Robert* of *Artois* was advancing at the ſame time to *St. Omer* with 50000.

P. 197.

A Miſtake of Mezeray *in relation to* Philip's *Anſwer to King* Edward's *Challenge.*

MEZERAY ſpeaking of the Charter of Defiance which *Edward* ſent to King *Philip*, ſays, that the latter return'd only an Anſwer by word of Mouth, that a Sovereign never accepts any Challenge from his Vaſſal. But that was not *Philip*'s Anſwer*. Here follow both the Charter, and the Anſwer.

him time to put on one thin Garment, hurry'd him and his Son, and one young Gentleman away; and carried them down the *Rhoſne* to a certain Tower, from whence they convey'd them into *France*. For which Injury, the Pope not only thunder'd out the moſt heavy Edicts againſt the Authors and Accomplices of that Crime, but put the whole Kingdom of *France* under an Interdict; which obliged *Philip* to ſend the Priſoners back to the Pope, who then took off the Interdict, and hang'd all thoſe of his own Family, who had a hand in the Matter, before the Doors of the Houſe which they had broken open, not excepting his own Maſter of the Horſe (who kill'd himſelf in Priſon for Anguiſh and Shame) whoſe Body he order'd to be expos'd on a Gibbet, to be devour'd by the Birds of the Air.

* Mr. *Barnes*, who charges both *Mezeray* and *du Cheſne* with this Abſurdity, thus confutes it. 'How know they, '*ſays he*, what King *Philip* 'ſent by Word of Mouth? 'And how could King *Philip* 'imagine that his Word 'ſhould be taken in a matter of ſuch conſequence, 'when all Challenges ought 'to be confirm'd by Hand 'and Seal, unleſs made in 'the hearing of the Defendant? And how was 'this an Anſwer to King '*Edward*'s Challenge, when 'as King *Philip* in his Letter profeſſes he would not 'anſwer him, becauſe he 'took not the Letter to be 'directed to him?' Truth needs no ſuch pitiful Salvo.

29. *PHILIP*

A. 1338.

29. *PHILIP* of *VALOIS*,

Edward's *Challenge to* Philip *of* Valois. *P.* 198.

'We have long and often, peaceably demanded of you by our Ambassadors, and otherwise, in the most reasonable manner we could devise, that you would please to restore unto us our lawful Inheritance of *France*, which you have a long time detain'd from us, and wrongfully possess'd. And whereas we plainly see that you intend to persevere in your injurious Detention thereof, without returning us any satisfactory Answer to our Demand; we give you to understand, that we are enter'd into the Province of *Flanders* as sovereign Lord thereof, and are now passing thro' the Country.

'And we farther signify to you, that by the Help of our Lord Jesus Christ, and our righteous Cause, with the Forces of the said Country, and with our Subjects and Allies; considering the Right we have to that Inheritance you wrongfully detain from us,

'We are now approaching towards you, to make a quick Decision of this our rightful Challenge, if you also will draw near.

'And forasmuch as so great an Army as we bring with us on our part, supposing you also on your part to do the like, cannot subsist long in the Field without great Destruction, both of the People and Country; which thing all good Christians ought to avoid, especially Princes, and others who are the Governors of the People: We are desirous that,

'By as short a Dispatch as may be, and to prevent the Mortality of Christians, since

*Edw.*III. ‘ the Quarrel apparently belongs to you and ‘ me,

‘ THAT the Controversy between us may be ‘ decided by our own Persons, Body to Body; ‘ to which thing we offer our selves, for the ‘ reasons aforesaid, and according to the good ‘ Opinion we have of your great Nobility, ‘ Sense and Wisdom.

‘ AND in case you shall not vouchsafe this ‘ way; that then the Disputes may be ended by ‘ the Battel of one Hundred of the most suffi- ‘ cient Persons of your Party, and as many of ‘ my Liege Subjects.

‘ AND if you will not admit, either of the ‘ one or of the other way; then that you will ‘ assign unto us a certain Day, before the City ‘ of *Tournay*, to combat both of us, Power a- ‘ gainst Power, within ten Days next after the ‘ Date of this our Letter.

‘ AND we would have all the World to know ‘ that we offer you the Conditions above-men- ‘ tion'd, not out of any Pride or Malice, but ‘ for the Causes aforesaid, to the intent that the ‘ Will of our Lord Jesus Christ being declar'd ‘ between us two, Peace may grow more and ‘ more among Christians; and that thereby the ‘ Enemies of God may be resisted, and Chri- ‘ stianity enfranchis'd.

‘ AND which soever of our said Offers you ‘ will chuse, please to send a speedy Answer by ‘ the Bearer of these Presents.

‘ GIVEN under our Privy Seal, at *Chyn*, in ‘ the Fields of *Tournay*, the 26th Day of *July*, ‘ in the first Year of our Reign as King of ‘ *France*, and the 14th as King of *England*.

30. *PHILIP's*

A. 1340

30. *PHILIP*'s Anſwer.

'*PHILIP* by the Grace of God, King of 'France, to *Edward* King of *England*. We have 'ſeen your Letters brought to our Court, and 'ſent on your part to one *Philip* of *Valois*; 'wherein are contain'd certain Requeſts which 'you make to the ſaid *Philip* of *Valois*. P. 199.

'AND,

'BECAUSE the ſaid Letters came not unto 'us, and the ſaid Requeſts were not made unto 'us, as it clearly appears by the Tenor of the 'ſaid Letters;

'WE do not return you any Anſwer to the 'Premiſes: Nevertheleſs, foraſmuch as we have 'underſtood by the ſaid Letters, and otherwiſe, 'that you are enter'd into our Kingdom, and 'have invaded our People, more thro' Preſump-'tion than Reaſon; and not conſidering the 'Duty which a Liege Man oweth unto his 'Lord:

'FOR you are enter'd contrary to your Liege 'Homage, when you acknowledg'd our ſelf, as 'Reaſon is, King of *France*, and promis'd the 'faithful Obedience, which a Liege Man ought 'to promiſe to his Lord; as more plainly doth 'appear from your Letters Patent, ſeal'd with 'your Great Seal, which we have in our Cu-'ſtody, and which you ought to have always 'before your Eyes.

'OUR Intention is, as ſoon as we think fit, 'to drive you out of our Kingdom, for the 'Honour of us, and our Realm, and the Profit 'of our People: And this to do, we have firm 'Hope in Jeſus Chriſt, from whom we derive 'all our Power.

'For by your Enterprize, proceeding more 'from Presumption than Reason, the Holy 'Voyage beyond Sea hath been hinder'd, a 'great Number of Christians put to Death, the 'Divine Service diminish'd, and Holy Church 'less reverenc'd,

'And as touching that which is noted, that 'you expect to be assisted by the *Flemings*; we 'firmly trust that the good People and Com-'mons of that Country, will so behave towards 'our Cousin, the Earl of *Flanders* their Lord, 'that it may not be to their Dishonour: and 'that to us, their Sovereign Lord, they will 'preserve their Honour and Loyalty.

'And as for what Mistakes they have hither-'to committed, that have been occasion'd by 'the evil Counsels of such Persons, who nei-'ther had any Regard to the publick Welfare, 'nor to the Honour of their Country, but only 'to their own private Advantage.

'Given in the Fields, near the Priory of 'St. *Andrew*, under our Privy Seal, in the Ab-'sence of our Great Seal, the 30th Day of *July*, 'in the Year of our Lord 1340.

A Truce between the two Kings. P. 205.

31. A Truce concluded between the two Kings, from the 25th of *September* 1340, to the 24th of *June* 1341. It was sign'd on the Day aforesaid, in the Church of *Espechin* or *Spetelin*.

Day of Edward's *Return to* England. P. 216.

32. A Memorandum of the Day of *Edward's* Return to *England*, which was the 30th of *November* 1340*.

His Letters of Complaint to the Pope and English *Bishops against the Archbishop of* Canterbury. P. 225, 236, 240.

33. Several Letters from *Edward* to the Bishops of *England*, and to the *Pope*; signifying his Grounds of Complaint against the Arch-

* He came over privately, and landed at the Tower, at one a Clock in the Morning, to prevent any Rumour.

bishop

bishop of *Canterbury*, and that Prelate's Misdemeanours: One is directed to the Bishops of *London*, *Chichester*, *Worcester*, *Salisbury*, *Bath* and *Wells*, *Exeter*, *Norwich*, &c. and dated at *Langley*, the 10th of *February*, 1341. That to the *Pope*, is dated there the 14th of *March*: and there's a third to the Bishop of *London*, dated from the Tower of *London* the 31st *ditto* †. *A.* 1341.

34. A LETTER from the Emperor, wherein he offers himself to be Mediator between the two Kings; and says, that *Philip* has already accepted his Mediation. He excuses himself for coming to an Accommodation with the King of *France*; pretends to be displeas'd with *Edward* for making a Truce without his Privity; and in short, revokes the Charter, whereby he constituted *Edward* Vicar of the Empire: It is dated at *Frankfort* the 25th of *June*, 1341.

The Emperor's Defection from Edward, *and Revocation of his Vicarship.* P. 262.

35. *EDWARD*'s Answer to the Letter aforesaid, wherein he begs the Emperor's Excuse for not accepting his Mediation, his Pre-

Edward'*s Answer to it.* P. 264.

† THE Archbishop being by chance gone from *Lambeth* when the King came home, heard of his Majesty's Indignation, and wisely kept out of the way till the Storm was over. Mr. *Barnes* accuses him of being as cold at last in the Affair of the War with *France*, by the Pope's Threats and Persuasions, as he was at first a great Promoter of it. He had govern'd the Realm, during the King's Absence in *Flanders*; and when an account was demanded of him, he guarded himself after the manner of those Times, by publishing Articles of Excommunication with the then dreadful Ceremony of Bell, Book and Candle, against all that should lay violent Hands on the Persons and Goods of the Clergy; the Bells ringing dolefully all the while, and the Candles being suddenly extinguish'd with a Stench. The Reader may see a particular State of the Archbishop's Case, and his Defence, in *Barnes*'s History, where we find that upon his Submission he was fully pardon'd, and receiv'd to Favour.

tensions being so clear, that he was not willing to refer them to doubtful Arbitration. And as to the Truce, he desires him to remember, that according to their Conventions, he was authoriz'd to make a Truce when he thought fit, tho' not a final Treaty of Peace. He adds, that he admires at the Revocation of his Charter; because according to their Treaty he was to enjoy the Title of Vicar, 'till he was in peaceable Possession of the Kingdom of *France*, or the best part of it: 'Tis dated the 14th of *July*, 1341, at *Westminster*.

Prolongation of the Truce with France. *P.* 281.

36. A PROLONGATION of the Truce to the 24th of *June* 1342. It is dated at *Westminster*, the 27th of *September*, 1341.

Edward's *Grant to* John *of* Montfort. *P.* 280.

37. A GRANT of the Earldom of *Richmond* in *England*, to *John* Earl of *Montfort*, to make him amends for his Earldom of *Montfort*, which was confiscated by the *French* King. It appears by this Act, which is dated at *Westminster* the 24th of *September* 1341, that there had been a Treaty of Alliance betwixt *Edward* and the said Earl.

His Commission to Walter de Manny *to take possession of* Brittany. *P.* 301.

38. A COMMISSION to *Walter de Manny*, to take Possession in the King's Name, of the Towns, *&c.* in *Brittany*: It is dated at *Westminster* the 10th of *March* 1342. This was after the taking of *John* of *Montfort*, and by Virtue of a new Treaty with *Margaret* his Wife.

And to E. Northampton. *P.* 304.

39. AN Order for the Earl of *Northampton*'s Passage into *Brittany*: Dated at *Eltham* the 27th *ditto*.

His Letter about the new Pope. *P.* 314.

40. A LETTER concerning the Election of Pope *Clement* VI. Dated the 22d of *May* 1342, at *Westminster*.

Robert *of* Artois *goes for* Brittany. *P.* 326.

41. AN Order to make Provision for the Passage of *Robert* of *Artois* into *Brittany*: Dated at the *Tower* of *London*, *July* 3, 1342.

42. THE

42. THE King's Letters Patent, constituting the Earl of *Northampton* his Lieutenant in *France* and *Bretagne*; and giving him a Power to confer Titles and Honours in the Kingdom of *France*: Dated at *Windsor*, *July* 20, and 22, 1342.

A. 1342.

E. Northampton *made the King's Lieutenant in* France. *P.* 330, 332.

43. *EDWARD*'s Letter to one of the Legates, complaining of *Philip*'s having broke the Truce, by Hostilities on the Sea, and in *Guyenne*; dated at the Tower of *London* the 8th of *August* following.

Edward's *Letter to the Pope's Legat.* *P.* 337.

44. A MEMORANDUM of the Day of the King's Departure for *Bretagne*, viz. *October* 4. 1342.

He goes for Bretagne. *P.* 342.

45. SEVERAL Acts, dated from *Rosere* in *Bretagne*, *November* 12, 1342.

P. 346.

46. AN Order to the Sheriffs of *England*, to proclaim a Truce till *Michaelmas*, 1346. Dated at *London* the 20th of *February* 1343.

A three Years Truce. *P.* 357.

47. A MEMORANDUM of the Day of the King's Return to *England*, viz. *March* 2. 1343.

King's Return to England. *P.* 357.

48. A BRIEF of *Clement* VI. wherein he acquaints the King that according to the Conventions of the Truce, *Philip* has promis'd to send his Ambassadors to *Avignon*, and desiring *Edward* to send his thither also. He tells him moreover, that *Philip* has offer'd to set *John* of *Montfort* at Liberty, provided he give security for his Return, but that the said Earl had not yet been able to find any: 'Tis dated at *Avignon* the 14th of the Calends of *June* 1343.

Pope's Letter to the King. *P.* 365.

49. *EDWARD*'s full Power to his Ambassadors, dated at *Westminster*, *May* 20. 1343. to go and treat before the Pope, *Non ut Judice, sed ut privata Persona, & Tractatore, & Mediatore communi: Non in Forma nec Figura Judicii, sed extrajudicialiter, & amicabiliter*, i. e. *Not as a Judge, but as a private Person, and common Negotiator*

Edward's *full Power to his Ambassadors to treat before the Pope.* *P.* 366.

Edw.III. *tiator and Mediator: Not in the Form or Figure of Judgment, but extrajudicially and amicably.*

And to others to excuse him to the Pope. *P.* 367. 50. An Order of the same Date for sending other Ambassadors to the Pope, to complain that the Truce was not executed in all its Articles by *Philip*, and to excuse *Edward* if he did not send a solemn Embassy till he had receiv'd Satisfaction.

His Letter to the Pope, about his Envoy de Flisco. *P.* 374. 51. *EDWARD*'s Letter to the Pope dated *July* the 6th 1343, at *Clarendon*, complaining, that those who had carry'd off his Envoy *Nicol. de Flisco*, were but too easily pardon'd. He freely tells him, that the great Men of his Kingdom oppose the Departure of his Ambassadors, till he had Satisfaction given him upon this Article; and from thence takes occasion to demand an extraordinary safe Conduct, specifying the particular Clauses necessary for securing his Ambassadors from the like Injuries.

His full Powers renew'd. *P.* 381. 52. A Renewing of the full Power for the solemn Embassy to *Avignon*, dated the 29th of *August* 1343. at *Westminster*.

Another of his Letters to the Pope. *P.* 394. 53. Another Letter to the Pope, complaining of several Infractions of the Truce. He consents to the Prolongation of the Term fix'd for the Treaty, and demands a safe Conduct for his Plenipotentiaries, in the Form already prescrib'd; 'Tis dated *November* the 29th 1343, at *Westminster*.

Another about safe Conduct. *P.* 419. 54. Another Letter demanding the safe Conduct, dated the 3d of *August* 1344, at *Rising*.

Instructions to the Bishop of Norwich. *P.* 420. 55. A Full Power of the same Date to the Bishop of *Norwich*, to complain to the Pope of the Infractions of the Truce.

Pope's Letter about Edward's *Ambassadors.* *P.* 433. 56. A Brief of Pope *Clement* VI. desiring *Edward* to send him the solemn Embassy he talk'd of; and that according to the Conventions,

tions, one or more of the Ambaſſadors might be *A.* 1341.
ſome Prince of his Royal Family. He deſires alſo that one of them may be charg'd with his Secrets, and order'd to communicate the ſame to him, which he promiſes to keep as carefully *quaſi Confeſſionis Sigillo*, as if it were under the Seal of Confeſſion. This Letter is dated at *Avignon* the 8th of the Ides of *December* 1344.

King's Anſwer to two of the Pope's Legates. *P.* 439.

57. THE King's Anſwer to two Legates who had writ to him from *Lyons*, to inform him that they were ſent to him to exhort him to Peace. He tells them that he cannot treat without the Participation of his Allies; that he had already, by the Advice of his Council, return'd the ſame Anſwer to the Pope's Nuncio, and that he cannot depart from it. 'Tis dated at *Weſtminſter* the 28th of *January* 1345. It ſeems by this Letter that the Pope importun'd him to abandon his Allies, which had undoubtedly a View to *John* of *Montfort*.

His Letter to the Pope on the Violation of the Truce of Bretagne. *P.* 453.

58. *EDWARD*'s Letter to the Pope concerning the Violation of the Truce of *Bretagne*, by the beheading of certain Noblemen of that Country at *Paris*: 'Tis dated at *Weſtminſter May* the 26th 1345. In this Letter, which is very long, *Edward* makes a brief Recapitulation of all that had paſs'd from the beginning of the War, to the Concluſion of the Truce in *Bretagne*; after which he adds, *Et cum ſic, ſpe Pacis arridente, ſub dictarum Treugarum fiducia redeuntes in Angliam, dimiſſis paucis Miniſtris noſtris in Britannia, pro regimine dictarum Partium, & Coadjutorum noſtrorum ibidem, ordinaſſemus Nuncios noſtros ad Sanctitatis veſtræ præſentiam, pro Tractatu Pacis, prout condictum fuerat tranſmittendos; ſupervenerunt nobis nova certa non leviter pungentia mentem noſtram, de morte*, (*videlicet*) quorundam Nobilium, nobis Adhærentium, captorum in Britan-

 nia,

Edw. III. nia, *& de speciali præcepto dicti Philippi, Parisiis ignominiose morti contra formam dictarum Treugarum tyrannicæ traditorum; nec non de strage, & depopulatione magna Fidelium, & locorum nostrorum in Britannia, Vasconia, & alibi, ac Tractatibus subdolis & occultis cum Alligatis & subditis nostris, habitis, quos sic a nobis auferre & sibi attrahere nitebatur; ac aliis, de facili non numerandis, injuriis & flagitiis contra dictas Treugas, per partem præfati Philippi, tam in terra quam in mari factis, & attemptatis, per quæ dictæ Treugæ noscuntur, per partem dicti Philippi, notorie dissolutæ.* He adds a little lower, *Ut taceamus de excessibus per Nuncium Sanctitatis vestræ, pridem pro conservatione Treugarum prædictarum missum in Britanniam, perpetratis, qui quod sedasse debuit dissidium, propensius excitavit, non Conservatorem Treugarum, sed partem contra Nos & Nostros potius se ostendens; super quo Sanctitas vestra (salve pace sua) remedium non adhibuit licet super hoc fuisset, ut decuit, requisita.*

i.e. ‘And when thro' a smiling Hope of ‘Peace, in confidence of the said Truce, re‘turning into *England*, having sent a few of ‘our Servants into *Bretagne* for the Govern‘ment of those Parts, and of our Coadjutors ‘there, we had design'd to send our Ambassa‘dors to your Holiness in order for a Treaty ‘of Peace, according to Agreement, there came “unto us certain News not a little provoking, ‘*viz.* of the Death of certain Noblemen, our ‘Adherents, who were taken in *Bretagne*, and ‘by the special Command of the said *Philip*, ‘contrary to the Form of the said Truce, shame‘fully and tyrannically put to death at *Paris:* ‘And also of the great Slaughter and Devastation ‘of our Liege People and Places in *Bretagne*, ‘*Gascoigne* and elsewhere; and of his subtle and ‘secret

A. 1341.

'secret Treaties held with our Allies and Subjects, whom he therefore endeavour'd to take off from us, and to bind unto himself; and of other Injuries and Offences, not easily to be number'd, against the said Truce on the part of the said *Philip*, done and attempted both by Land and Sea; whereby the said Truce, on the part of the said *Philip*, is notoriously known to be dissolv'd. —— Not to say any thing of the excessive Enormities of your Holiness's Legate lately sent into *Bretagne* for the Preservation of the said Truce, who more earnestly rais'd the Contention which he ought to have allay'd; not approving himself a Conservator of the Truce, but rather a Party against Us and Ours: Concerning which your Holiness (with your leave) apply'd no Remedy, although (as was fitting) you was thereto requir'd.

A Mistake of Mezeray, *and other Historians, about the Imprisonment of certain Lords in* Bretagne.

THIS Letter plainly discovers a Mistake in *Mezeray* and other *French* Historians, who assert that the Lords of *Bretagne*, who were beheaded at *Paris*, were of the Party of *Charles* of *Blois*, and that they were actually apprehended at *Paris*, whither they went voluntarily to assist at a Tournament; for on the contrary 'tis evident, that they were of *John* Earl of *Montfort*'s Party, and that they were apprehended in *Bretagne*. *Quorundam Nobilium*, says *Edward*, *nobis Adhærentium*, *captorum in Britannia*, i. e. *Certain Noblemen our Adherents who were taken in* Bretagne. This Error, whether a wilful one or not, is of the more importance, because the Death of those Noblemen being the principal Foundation of the Breach of the Truce, if what those Historians advance were true, *Edward* cou'd not be justify'd for having unsea-

Edw. III. unseasonably broke the Truce: For what reason could he possibly have had to take offence at the Death of any Lords of the contrary Party, even tho' as *Argentre*, an Historian of *Bretagne*, affirms, they had maintain'd a Correspondence with him? Was it not lawful for *Philip* and *Charles* of *Blois* to punish their own Subjects? But if those Lords were of *John* of *Monfort's* Party, and if they were apprehended in *Bretagne* during the Truce, how can *Philip* be excus'd for such a Breach of it?

John *of* Montfort's *Escape.*

It seems that *Philip* was willing to give *Edward* some satisfaction, by releasing *John* of *Montfort* from the Tower of the *Louvre*, and leaving him in *Paris* upon his Parole: but *John* of *Montfort* did not think himself bound to keep his Parole; and therefore escaping out of *Paris*, he went to find out *Edward*, to whom he perform'd new Homage in these Terms: 'I own 'you rightful King of *France*; and to you as my 'Liege Lord, and natural King of *France*, I 'perform my Homage for the Duchy of *Bretagne*, which I claim to hold from you my 'Lord, and become your Liege-man in Life, 'and Member, and earthly Honour, to live and 'die against all your Enemies.' It was perform'd at the Archbishop's Palace at *Lambeth* the 20th of *May* 1345.

His new Homage to King Edward. *P.* 452.

Edward's *Manifesto.* *P.* 459.

59. *EDWARD's* Declaration of the Causes of the War, and Justification of his Conduct. 'Tis dated at *Westminster* the 14th of *June* 1345.

Godfrey *of* Harcourt's *Homage.* Ibid.

60. The Act declaring the Homage perform'd to *Edward* by *Godfrey* of *Harcourt*, the *Norman* Lord, who fled to *England* for Refuge. 'Tis dated at *Westminster* the 13th of *June* 1345.

Pope's Letter to Edward *taxing him with the Breach of the Truce.* *P.* 465.

61. A Bull of Pope *Clement* VI. in answer to *Edward's* Letter of the 6th of *May*. This is a remarkable Bull, in that it makes *Edward* only

only blameable for the Breach of the Truce. A. 1343. This put me upon examining the principal Articles of the Charge, because on such inquiry depends the Illustration of this Fact, which the Historians have left in great Obscurity. At the same time this may serve as one among the numerous Examples I shall bring, to shew the vast Service that is done to Truth by the Acts printed in the *Fœdera*.

PORRO, says the Pope, *quia illi qui dictas tuas nobis missas Litteras dictitarunt, rei veritatem forsitan ignorabant, multa posuerunt in eis, & aliqua tacuerunt, in quibus erraverunt notabiliter, factum taliter recitando*: i. e. Moreover, because they who dictated your Letters to us, perhaps not knowing the Truth, have inserted many things, and omitted others in which they have err'd remarkably, by reciting the Fact after such a manner.

Now the Proofs which the Pope brings to convince *Edward*, that he was the Infractor of the Truce, are these.

1. He upbraids him for not executing the Conventions, by which he engag'd to send Ambassadors to him, one of whom was to be a Prince of the Blood Royal; both which Articles, says he, *Philip* has perform'd.

Vindication of Edward's Conduct.

In answer to this Objection, it may be observ'd, that amongst the Ambassadors nominated by *Edward*, were *Henry* of *Lancaster* Earl of *Derby* his Cousin, and *Hugh Spenser* Son to one of his Cousin-Germans. The Nomination of these Ambassadors is prov'd by the full Power which was given them, dated at *Westminster* the 29th of *August* 1343. 'Tis true, that before this solemn Embassy was sent away, he dispatch'd other Ambassadors to the Pope, to complain of some Infractions of the Truce, and of the carrying off of *Flisco*, as also to demand an effectual safe Con-duct. P. 381.

Edw. III. duct. From hence the Pope takes occasion to object, that not one of the Ambassadors sent to him was a Prince of the Royal Family. But who does not see that this Objection is perfectly captious, since those Ambassadors were not sent to treat of Peace? On the other hand, if *Edward* did not send his Plenipotentiaries, it was because no Satisfaction was given him, as to the carrying off of his Envoy, and that the Pope had even absolv'd those who committed that Violence without his Participation. In the second place, *John* of *Montfort* was detain'd in Prison, contrary to the Conventions of the Truce. And finally, the Pope refus'd to grant the *English* Plenipotentiaries their safe Conduct, in the Form wherein *Edward* demanded it. Therefore the Pope could blame none but himself for the Delay of the *English* Ambassadors, till the time that the Lords of *Bretagne* were put to death.

2. As to the Execution of those Lords, the Pope excuses it thus. He says, that when he wrote about it to the King of *France*, *Philip* return'd for Answer, that he had caus'd them to be put to death for divers Crimes which they had committed, and particularly for having broke the Truce of *Bretagne*: That besides, those very Gentlemen had affirm'd, that they had no manner of Confederacy with *Edward*, but only with *John* of *Montfort*; and that the said Earl, then a Prisoner at *Paris*, affirm'd on his part, that he had made no Alliance with *Edward*. But nothing is more evident than the Weakness of this Excuse. Cou'd *Philip* be ignorant that the Truce was made in *Bretagne* upon account of the War which *Edward* carry'd into that Province in favour of *John* of *Montfort*? Besides, there's no manner of probability that *Montfort* shou'd declare he had made

made no Alliance with *Edward*, ſince it was by virtue of the ſaid Alliance that his Liberty was ſtipulated in the Articles of the Truce, and to that alone in all likelihood he ow'd his Life; for had it not been for *Edward*'s Protection he wou'd have been expos'd to the Severity of the Laws, for having taken up Arms againſt his Sovereign. He was not ſo weak therefore to deprive himſelf of that Protection, by declaring that he had made no Alliance with his Protector. 'Tis alſo worthy of remark, that *Philip* own'd that the Lords who had been beheaded were of *John* of *Montfort*'s Party; and that he did not diſown their being apprehended in *Bretagne*, as *Edward* affirm'd in his Letter to the Pope. 'Tis therefore evident, that ſince all the Allies and Adherents of the two Kings were included in the Truce, *Philip* was the Man that broke it, by cauſing the Lords of the contrary Party to be taken up in *Bretagne*, and put to death at *Paris*. *A.* 1343.

3. THE Pope ſays to *Edward*, that as he complain'd of certain Infractions of the Truce, *Philip* made the like Complaint on his part. In this 'tis poſſible that both Parties were to blame.

4. AS to *Edward*'s Complaint that *Charles* of *Blois* broke the Truce, and that *Philip* aſſiſted him; the Pope makes anſwer, that the King of *France* had aſſur'd him, that he gave that Prince no manner of Aſſiſtance. He adds, that *Charles* of *Blois* repairing in Perſon to *Avignon*, had declar'd in his Preſence, that he was not included in the Treaty, that he was not once nam'd in it, and that he was not ſo much as requir'd to ſign it. But this again is an evaſive Anſwer, becauſe the Truce made in *Bretagne* between the two Kings, included all their Subjects and Allies, as may be ſeen in this Volume of the *Fœdera*,

Edw. III. *Fœdera*, in the Order for proclaiming the three Years Truce, seal'd at *London* with the great Seal the 20th of *February* 1343, tho' they were not therein nominated, and that none but the Ambassadors of the two Kings sign'd the Treaty. And if, under pretence that *Charles* of *Blois* had not sign'd the Truce, and was not therein mention'd, it was lawful for him to continue the War in *Bretagne*, it was equally lawful for *Montfort*'s Party to have done the same: Consequently this Truce, which had been chiefly made for the sake of *Bretagne*, wou'd have been a mere Delusion.

Order for proclaiming the three Years Truce with France. *P.* 357.

5. As to *Edward*'s Complaints to the Pope about his Nuncio, *Clement* contents himself with denying the Fact, and with barely saying that he wou'd have punish'd his Nuncio, if he had observ'd the least Partiality in his Conduct.

6. It is not so easy, indeed, to excuse *Edward* upon the Pope's Complaint that the *English* had by force made themselves Masters of the City of *Vannes*, after having turn'd out the Pope's Troops, who ought to have kept it till the Expiration of the Truce. This perhaps might be by way of Reprisal for some Place which had been taken by *Charles* of *Blois*. By the way, this may serve to let us into the Secret how *Vannes* came into the Hands of *John* of *Montfort*, which is a Fact whereof the Historian of *Bretagne* was ignorant.

These were the Arguments on which *Clement* laid the greatest Stress, in order to convince *Edward* that it was he who first broke the Truce. He did not mention one Word in this Bull about the carrying off of *Flisco*, and 'tis probable he had nothing to say to excuse it. *Edward* therefore might justly say to the Pope upon this Article as well as the foregoing, that

those

those who had dictated his Bull had paſs'd over some important Articles in Silence, and diſguis'd the Truth of others. Several other Obſervations might be made upon this Bull, only I am afraid of running out into too tedious a Diſcuſſion of it: And I am of opinion that what has been ſaid may be ſufficient to ſhew which of the two Kings was chargeable with the Breach of the Truce. *A.* 1346.

62. *EDWARD*'s Letter to the Pope dated at *Weſtminſter* the 11th of *November* 1345, wherein he acquaints him that he is preparing ſuch an Anſwer to the above-mention'd Bull, as he doubts not will be ſatisfactory to him. Edward's *Letter to the Pope.* *P.* 483.

THE Anſwer is not inſerted in the *Fœdera*, neverthelefs we find that afterwards he ſent a Man to the Pope with Inſtructions upon this Subject, dated the 8th of *January* 1346, at *Woodſtock*. *P.* 489.

63. A PROCLAMATION, or Manifeſto, dated at *Weſtminſter* the 15th of *March* 1346, juſtifying the War againſt *Philip* of *Valois*. What is very remarkable in this Proclamation is *Edward*'s ſaying, that immediately upon the Death of *Charles the Fair*, he conſulted the Lords Spiritual and Temporal, and the Civilians of his Kingdom; and that by their Advice he ſent Ambaſſadors into *France* to demand the Crown. He adds, that they cou'd not obtain Audience; and that after having left their Proteſts, they were oblig'd to retire for fear of their Lives. This is a Confirmation of what was ſaid upon this very Particular in our Account of the fourth Volume of the *Fœdera*. *His Proclamation, ſetting forth the Reaſons of his War with* France. *P.* 496.

64. CONVENTIONS between *John* Duke of *Normandy*, Son to *Philip de Valois*, and the *Normans*, by which the latter oblige themſelves to *The* Normans *deſign to invade* England. *P.* 504.

Edw. III. to follow the Duke into *England* with 40000 Men, to make a Conqueſt of that Kingdom, on certain Conditions ſpecify'd on both ſides, in caſe the Undertaking ſhou'd be crown'd with Succeſs. 'Tis dated at *Bois de Vincennes, March* the 23d, in the Year 38; which is ſuppos'd to be a Miſtake of the Preſs in this Collection for 1346*.

Regent's Letter to the chief Cities, upon the Victory at Creſſy. *P.* 525.

65. A LETTER from the King's Son *Lionel*, then Regent in *England*, to the Mayors and Bailiffs of the chief Cities of the Kingdom, and to the Sheriffs of the Counties, acquainting them with the Victory gain'd by the King's Forces at *Creſſy*. 'Tis dated the 6th of *September* 1346, at *Windſor*.

Order to ſend the King Forces to ſupport the Siege of Calais. *P.* 527.

66. AN Order to ſend great Succours to the King, to make head againſt *Philip*, who was aſſembling all the Forces of *France* to raiſe the

* MR. *Barnes* ſays this was call'd the *Ordinance of* Normandy; and that a Copy of it was produc'd in the *Engliſh* Parliament in *January* 1337, according to which the Duke of *Normandy* was to paſs as Chief, with other Nobles of that Province, into *England*, with 40000 Men of Arms, Knights, Eſquires, and Perſons of good Eſtate, and 40000 Foot-men; Methods being there preſcrib'd for keeping the Sea; and an Order was alſo added, That the ſaid Duke ſhould remain in *England* with the ſaid Forces for ten Weeks: That if the Realm of *England* ſhould be conquer'd, the Duke ſhould not only have all the Honour and Advantage of it, but all that the King of *England* was then poſſeſs'd of ſhould remain entirely to the ſaid Duke, and the Knights and Lords with him: That all which belong'd to the Nobles and Laity of *England*, ſhou'd be beſtow'd on the Churches and famous Towns of *Normandy*, only of the Revenues of the Church of *England* the *French* King ſhou'd receive 20000 *l.* a Year, ſaving the Rights of the Pope; and that every thing taken from the *Scots* at any time, and annex'd to the Crown of *England*, ſhould be reſtor'd.

Siege

Siege of *Calais*. 'Tis dated the 3d of *October* 1346, at *Windsor*. *A.*1348.

67. A TRUCE concluded near *Calais*, from the 28th of *September* 1347, to the 9th of *July* 1348. *Truce near* Calais. *P.* 588.

68. SEVERAL Prolongations of it till the 1st of *August* 1350. and full Powers to make a Treaty of Peace. *Edward*'s Prorogations of the Truce; and the full Powers he gave to his Ambassadors to repair for a Treaty of Peace to the Apostolic See, are dated the 13th of *February*, the 15th of *May*, the 6th of *August*, the 11th and 25th of *September*, and the 18th of *November* 1348; and the 10th of *March*, the 2d and 15th of *May*, the 28th of *August* 1349; and the 13th of *June*, the 1st and 28th of *July* 1350. *Prolongations of it, and full Powers for a Treaty of Peace.* *P.* 608. 623. 629. 640. 642. 649. 657. 660. 664. 671. 672. 676. 678

69. A LETTER from Pope *Clement* VI. on the Death of *Philip de Valois*, exhorting *Edward* to make a Peace with *John* his Son and Successor. 'Tis dated at *Avignon* the 3d of the Nones of *September* 1350. *Pope's Exhortation to* Edward *on* Philip'*s Death.* *P.* 680.

70. FULL Powers to renew with *John* the Truce made with *Philip* his Father. They are dated at *Westminster*, *November* the 2d 1350. *Truce renew'd with his Successor.* *P.* 690.

71. SEVERAL Prolongations of the Truce, in order to negotiate a Peace. They are dated at *Westminster* the 27th of *June*, at the Tower the 26th and 27th of *July*, and the 4th of *September*, the 11th *ditto* at the place of Treaty between *Guisnes* and *Calais*, and at *Westminster* the 1st of *October* 1351. *Prorogations of the Truce.* *P.* 711. 714. 715. 722. 725. 727.

72. *EDWARD*'s Letter to the Pope, in which he signifies his Resolution to conclude a Peace with *John*; *Ita quod ex parte nostra, non reperietur, per Dei gratiam, dissimulatio, dilatio vel defectus, quod de nobis sentire velit vestra Moderatio circumspecta*: *i. e.* Insomuch that on our Edward'*s Letter to the Pope.* *P.* 772.

 part

Edw. III. part there shall not be found, by the Grace of God, any Dissimulation, Delay or Deficiency, &c. 'Tis dated at *Westminster* the 8th of *November* 1353. This was when *John* made such Concessions as to offer *Guyenne*, *Artois*, *Guisnes* and *Calais* to *Edward* in full Sovereignty.

Another to the new Pope, Innocent VI. *P.* 753.

73. A LETTER to Pope *Innocent* VI. upon his Advancement to St. *Peter*'s Chair, dated the 20th of *June* 1353, at *Westminster*.

His full Powers to his Ambassadors to renounce France. *P.* 779.

74. *EDWARD*'s full Power to his Ambassadors, more ample than the preceding, for concluding a Peace, and for renouncing the Crown of *France* in his Name, dated the 30th of *March* 1354, at *Westminster*.

Prorogation of the Truce. *P.* 781.

75. A PROROGATION of the Truce from the 6th of *April* 1353, to the 1st of *April* 1354, dated *April* the 6th aforesaid, under the Tents before *Guisnes*.

King submits his Rights in France *to the Pope's Jurisdiction.* *P.* 794.

76. A POWER given to the Ambassadors, more ample than all before granted, whereby it manifestly appear'd that *Edward* thought the Peace as good as concluded. 'Tis dated the 28th of *August* 1354, at *Westminster*; these are the Words of it, *Dantes & Concedentes eisdem Procuratoribus, Auctoritatem & Mandatum speciale Tractandi cum dicto Adversario nostro, seu Deputatis & Assignatis per eum, de pace finali inter Nos & ipsum feliciter, per Dei gratiam ineunda, & super omnibus Debatis, Litibus & Controversiis, inter Nos & dictum Adversarium Nostrum exortis: Specialiter super Jure quod habemus, vel habere poterimus, ad Coronam & Regnum Franciæ, & pertinentias eorundem, vel in eis Transigendi, Componendi, Pacificandi, & etiam Juri nobis in hac parte competenti ex causa Transactionis, seu Compositionis ac Recompensationis nobis propter hoc faciendæ renunciandi,* &c. *Et cum inter Nuncios utriusq; partis sic transactum fuerit & finaliter concordatum, ut*

sic

ſic concordata, quantum ad Nos attinet, fideliter obſerventur, ſubmittendi Nos, Hæredes & ſubditos Noſtros ac Terras & Dominia & omnia quæcunque quæ jam habemus in Regno Franciæ, Et quæ, virtute hujuſmodi Concordiæ in eodem contigerit nos habere, *juriſdictioni dicti Domini Summi Pontificis, (videlicet) ut ipſe per Cenſuras Eccleſiaſticas, & alias vias legitimas, ad obſervationes præmiſſorum Nos, & Hæredes & Subditos noſtros, compellere valeat & artare, & omnia ſic concordata, autoritate Apoſtolica confirmare, omologare, & quacum firmitate vallare: i. e.* Giving and granting to the ſaid Plenipotentiaries full Power and ſpecial Command to treat with our ſaid Enemy, or ſuch as are deputed and aſſign'd by him, happily to negotiate a Peace betwixt Us and Him, by the Grace of God, and to treat of all Debates, Diſputes and Controverſies ariſen betwixt us and our ſaid Adverſary; eſpecially concerning the Right which we have, or may have, to the Crown and Kingdom of *France*, and their Appurtenances; even to tranſact, compound, or bargain therein; and alſo to renounce our competent Right for the ſake of the Tranſaction or Compoſition, and Recompence to be made to us on that Account, *&c.* And when it has been ſo tranſacted and finally agreed between the Ambaſſadors on both ſides; that the Articles ſo agreed on, as far as appertains to us, may be punctually obſerv'd, we give them the Power to ſubmit Us, our Heirs and Subjects, Lands, Dominions, and all things whatſoever are ours in the Kingdom of *France*, and which we ſhall happen to have there, by virtue of ſuch Agreement, to the Juriſdiction of our ſaid Lord the Pope, (*viz.*) That he may compel and bind Us, our Heirs and Subjects by Eccleſiaſtical Cenſures, and other legal Methods, to the Obſervation of

*A.*1354.

Edw. III. the Premises, and confirm, ratify and fortify the said Agreement in all its Articles.

'Tis evident from this full Power, that such Offers had been made to *Edward* as he thought fit to accept; which confirms what the *English* Historians have advanc'd on this Head, tho' *Mezeray* has thought fit to pass it over in silence.

Mezeray *convicted of wilful silence in a material Article.*

77. The Power given by the Archbishops and Bishops of *England* to five Civilians to consent in their Name to the Treaty which was to be sign'd in Presence of the Pope, desiring the Pope to confirm it by his Authority, and to oblige to the Observation of it by the severest Censures; dated at *Westminster August* the 28th 1354.

The Bishops Power to certain Civilians for signing the Treaty. *P.* 796.

78. The Power given by *Lionel* and *John*, Sons to King *Edward*, and by 85 *English* Noblemen, of the same Tenor and Date as the former.

The like from the Princes and Nobility. *P.* 797.

This Negotiation being spun out to the end of the Year 1354, *Edward*'s Expectations were frustrated by King *John*'s Refusal to confirm what had been agreed upon before *Guisnes*.

K. John's *Refusal to ratify the Treaty near* Guisnes.

79. *EDWARD*'s Letter dated at *Westminster, June* the 1st 1355, to the Bishops of *England*, informing them that the Ambassadors of the two Crowns assembled between *Guisnes* and *Calais* had concluded Articles of Peace, and agreed to go to the Pope to get them confirm'd by his Authority; but that his Ambassadors, after having waited a long time, had been oblig'd to return home, those of *France* having refus'd to confirm what had been agreed to.

Edward's *Letter on that Subject to the Bishops of* England. *P.* 816.

80. The

80. THE Commiſſion by which *Edward* ſent the Prince of *Wales* in Quality of his Lieutenant to the Province of *Gaſcoigne*; dated *July* the 16th at *Northfleet*. *A.* 1355. *Prince of* Wales's *Commiſſion as Lieuten.* Gaſcoigne. *P.* 823.

81. THE Patent appointing *Henry* of *Lancaſter* the King's Lieutenant in *Bretagne*; dated at *Portſmouth*, *September* 14th 1355. *D. of* Lancaſter's *as Lieuten. in* Bretagne. *P.* 826.

82. THE King's Anſwer to a Letter from the Pope preſſing him to renew the Negotiations of Peace, wherein *Edward* tells him, that after having been ſo groſly deluded by his Enemy, he has taken up Arms again, and cannot think of renewing the Negotiations upon ſuch very uncertain Hopes. 'Tis dated *May* the 2d 1356, at *Weſtminſter*. Edward's *Letter to the Pope, declaring he cannot enter into a new Treaty with* France. *P.* 851.

NEVERTHELESS to give ſome Satisfaction to the Pope, who inceſſantly teaz'd him to make Peace, *Edward* empower'd his Son the Prince of *Wales*, then actually in *Guyenne*, to treat with *France*: which Power is dated at *Weſtminſter*, *Auguſt* 1ſt 1356. *His full Power to his Son to enter on a Treaty.* *P.* 858.

'TIS very probable that *Edward* referr'd the Affair to the Prince his Son, who was at that time ravaging the Provinces of *France*, for no other end but to get rid of the Pope's troubleſome Sollicitations.

83. *EDWARD*'s Letter to the Prelates of his Kingdom, acquainting them of the great Victory the Prince of *Wales* had gain'd near *Poictiers*, and of the taking of King *John*; dated *October* the 10th 1356, at *Weſtminſter*. *His Letter to the Biſhops on the Victory at* Poictiers. *P.* 869.

84. HIS Letters Patent appointing *Philip* of *Navarre* Governor of *Normandy*; dated at *Weſtminſter*, *October* 30th 1356. *He appoints* Philip *of* Navarre *his Governor in* Normandy. *P.* 871.

THIS Prince was Brother to *Charles* King of *Navarre*, whom King *John* detain'd in Priſon

Edw. III. ſon at the Caſtle of *Arleux* in the Diſtrict of *Cambray*.*

EDWARD's *Affairs with* Scotland.

WHEN we clos'd our Account of the fourth Volume of the *Fœdera*, we left *Scotland* in a very unhappy State. *Edward* being Maſter of the chief Places, reign'd there, while *Edward Baliol* had the Title indeed of King, but no more than the Shadow of Sovereignty, ſo long as King *David* was a Refugee at the Court of *France*, which ſought rather to prolong the War in *Scotland*, than to put an end to it by any powerful Succours. After the time that *Edward* had made known his Deſigns againſt *France*, *Philip* of *Valois* wou'd have been very glad if he could have made a powerful Diverſion in *Scotland*; but it was too late, for then he had enough to do to oppoſe a League form'd againſt him, while *Edward* amus'd him with the falſe Hopes of Peace, as was obſerv'd in the Account of the preceding Volume. For this Reaſon the Succours with which he was able to furniſh the *Scots*, were not very conſiderable. Mean time *Robert Stuart*, who was Regent in *Scotland* for King *David*, perceiving that *Edward* would have Work enough cut out for him in *Flanders*, flatter'd himſelf with the Hopes of making his Advantage of this Diverſion; and therefore, after having aſſembled ſome Troops, as ſoon as he heard that *Edward* was gone beyond Sea, he renew'd the Hoſtilities in *Scotland*. The little Oppoſition he met with from *Baliol*, with

Robert Stuart's *Progreſs in* Scotland.

* MR. *Barnes* ſays that King *John*, who was his Father-in-law, impriſon'd him for privately correſponding with his Enemies.

whom

whom *Edward* had left but few Forces, and ſome little Succeſs which attended his Arms at the Beginning, giving him a fair Opportunity to augment his Army, he reſolv'd to beſiege *Perth*, which he did accordingly next Year, *viz.* 1339, juſt about the Time that *Edward* began his firſt Campaign in *Flanders*. The taking of this Place, which coſt him a Siege of three Months, having oblig'd *Baliol* to retire towards the Frontiers of *England*, the Regent improv'd his Advantages, and attack'd the ſtrong Town of *Sterling*, which he took by Compoſition, after he had likewiſe made himſelf Maſter of *Edinburgh* by a Stratagem. *A.* 1341.

EDWARD being too buſy in his Preparations for the Campaign which he was to make in *Flanders* in the Year 1340, to have any Thoughts of *Scotland*, *Steuart* took that Opportunity to make an Incurſion into *Northumberland*, from whence he carry'd away a great Booty. Afterwards, while *Edward* was before *Tournay*, the Regent of *Scotland* made himſelf Maſter of *Roxborough*, and in ſhort of all other places which the *Engliſh* held in *Scotland*, ſo that *Berwick* only remain'd in their Hands.

THE *Scots* being expreſly included in the Truce which was made before *Tournay* in the Year 1341, as ſoon as it was expir'd, *Edward* reſolv'd to go once more and ravage *Scotland*, while the Truce which he had prolong'd with *France* ſtill ſubſiſted. With this View he went to *Newcaſtle*, where he waited in vain for his Fleet which was to bring Proviſions for his Army. A violent Storm which diſpers'd that Fleet having broke his Meaſures, he was oblig'd to grant the *Scots* a Truce, on condition that they wou'd ſubmit to his Authority, if King *David* did not return to *Scotland* by a certain time

Edward's *Truce with the* Scots.

Edw. III time with an Army ſtrong enough to give Battel. *Buchanan* ſays, that *David* was already in *Scotland incognito*, and that he likewiſe made an Incurſion into *Northumberland*. Be this as it will, *Edward*, whoſe Head was full of the Affair of *Bretagne*, mention'd in the preceding Article, granted a new Truce to King *David*, and then retir'd.

It was during this Truce, towards the latter end of the Year 1342, that *Edward* went to carry the War into *Bretagne*, where in *February* 1343, he made a Truce which was to laſt till *Michaelmas* 1346, and in which *Scotland* was included. It was obſerv'd in the foregoing Article, that this Truce was broke ſo far as related to *France*, in the Year 1345, and that *Edward* made a Deſcent in *Normandy* in 1346.

K. David *invades* England.

While *Edward* was that Year ravaging *Normandy*, and the Neighbourhood of *Paris*, *David* broke the Truce on his part, by ſending Forces to make an Incurſion into *England*, while himſelf was preparing to give a more powerful Diverſion. This evidently appears from an Act in the *Fœdera*, which I ſhall mention hereafter.

EDWARD laying Siege to *Calais* after the Battel of *Creſſy*, *Philip* who was not in a Condition to come ſoon enough to raiſe it, engag'd King *David* to make a powerful Diverſion in *England*, in hopes that *Edward* wou'd be oblig'd to haſten home to the Relief of his own Subjects. By this time *David* could not but be very well prepar'd to receive him, becauſe he had been in *England* ſix Weeks after the Battel of *Creſſy*, at the Head of 60000 Men, and was even advanc'd as far as *Durham*. The Diligence of the *Engliſh* to oppoſe this Invaſion was ſo great,

great, that by the Care of the Archbishop of York, and some Lords in the North, they were soon in a Condition to give the Scots Battel; which they did near Durham, where the Scots Army was entirely routed, with the Loss of 15000 Men, and King David himself taken Prisoner.

A. 1354.

He is routed and taken Prisoner.

THE Loss which the Scots suffer'd, together with the Imprisonment of their King, would have put them out of a Capacity to stop the English Arms, if France had not taken care to get them included in the Truce of Calais, and in the frequent Prolongations thereof to the Year 1354, as was observ'd in the preceding Article. During these Truces, Endeavours were us'd for procuring King David his Liberty by several Negotiations, which after having lasted many Years, were at length consummated in a Treaty made in the Year 1354, by which Edward engag'd to set David at full Liberty for a Ransom of 90000 Marks Sterling, payable in nine Years; for which David was oblig'd to give good Sureties. This happen'd at the very Juncture when Edward made sure of concluding a Peace with King John, according to the Articles agreed on betwixt Guisnes and Calais: But as John had no design to confirm those Articles, he engag'd the Scots to renew the Hostilities, by sending 40000 Crowns to be distributed, as Buchanan says, among the leading Men in Scotland: Therefore just as David was going to be set at Liberty, Stuart took Berwick by Surprize, and set Fire to it*. This unexpected Rupture forcing Edward to take other Measures, he caus'd David to be more closely confin'd in the Castle of Odiham,

K. David's Ransom.

Scots fed with Money from the French King.

Berwick taken by surprize, fir'd and then abandon'd by the Scots.

* MR. Barnes says this happen'd on the 6th of November 1355.

and

Edw. III. and march'd towards the Frontiers of both Kingdoms to recover *Berwick*; which was no difficult matter for him to do, because the *Scots* had abandon'd it.

Edward's *Ravages in* Scotland.

EDWARD's Expedition did not end with *Berwick*, but he likewise made himself Master of *Edinburgh* and *Roxburgh*, and ravag'd some of the Counties of *Scotland* without Mercy; and if it had not been for a Breach of the Treaty, then begun with *France*, 'tis very likely that *Edward* would have made himself Master of all *Scotland*. At least there is no doubt but he intended it, when 'tis consider'd, that at that time he began his Negotiations with *Baliol*, whereby the latter was to make over to *Edward* all his Right to that Kingdom, as appears by some Acts in this Volume. The Negotiations for this Purpose, which probably were interrupted by the Preparations that *Edward* was oblig'd to make for renewing the War against *France*, were begun again in the Year 1356. 'Till then *Edward* made use of *Baliol*'s Name in the War with *Scotland*; but at length he took off the Mask, and determin'd to act in his own Name. For this end he got *Baliol* to yield him the Kingdom of *Scotland*, with all its Dependencies, on the Payment of a yearly Pension of 2000 *l. Sterling*, which he gave him as a Compensation for that imaginary Crown. And with this the Acts of the fifth Volume relating to *Scotland* conclude: We will just run thro' the chief of them.

Baliol *resigns his Claim to* Scotland *to* Edward *for a Pension.*

Edward's *Nomination of a Governor of* Perth. *P.* 70.

1. An Act declaring *Baliol*'s Dependance upon *England*, dated at *Northampton* the 4th of *August* 1338, *Teste Custode Angliæ*. 'Tis a Request, or rather an Order to *Baliol* to give the Government of *Perth* to *Thomas Ughtred*, in these Terms; *Cum, pro reipublicæ, ac vestrorum & nostro-*

nostrorum subditorum, commodo & utilitate, de Concilio nostro, ordinaverimus, quod Dilectus & Fidelis noster, Thomas Ughtred habeat custodiam villæ Sancti Johannis de Perth in Scotiâ.—Vestram amicitiam requirimus & rogamus, quatenus eidem Thomæ custodiam villæ prædictæ, per Literas vestras Patentes, in forma debita, committi faciatis: i. e. Whereas, for the publick Good, and for the Profit and Advantage of your and our Subjects, we have order'd that our trusty and well-beloved *Thomas Ughtred* shall have the Government of *Perth*, or *St. Johnstown* in *Scotland*——We require and expect from your Friendship, that you commit the Government of the said Town to *Thomas Ughtred*, as aforesaid, by your Letters Patent dispatch'd in due Form.

A. 1340.

2. AN Order to pay *Baliol* thirty Shillings a Day for his Subsistence in time of Peace, and fifty Shillings a Day in time of War. 'Tis sign'd *Teste Custode*, and dated at *Berkhampstede*, *May* the 3d 1339.

Order for Baliol's *Subsistence Money.* *P.* 109.

3. A PARDON granted to *Thomas Ughtred* for having surrender'd the Town of *Perth* to the Enemy; dated *October* the 29th 1339, at *Kenington*, *Teste Custode*.

Thomas Ughtred's *Pardon.* *P.* 131.

4. AN Allowance to *Baliol* of forty Shillings a Day in time of Peace, and three Pounds in time of War; dated at *Westminster*, *May* the 20th 1340.

A farther Allowance to Baliol. *P.* 186.

5. SEVERAL Furloughs for the Earl of *Murray*, a Prisoner in *England*. They are dated at *Kenington*, *July* the 18th; at *Billibrig*, *August* the 1st; at *London*, *August* the 20th; at *Berkhampstede*, *August* the 25th; at *Andover*, *September* the 25th; at *Wallingford*, *October* the 25th and 26th 1340; at *Westminster*, *February* the 8th, and *May* the 28th; at *Langley*, *July* the 1st; and at the *Tower* of *London*, *July* the 21st 1341.

Furloughs to the Earl of Murray. *P.* 197, 200, 202, 205, 213, 214, 224, 250, 262, 268.

6. A

Edw. III.

6. A POWER granted to *Henry* Earl of *Lancaster* to make a Peace or Truce with the *Scots*; dated at *Westminster*, *October* the 10th 1341.

Power to E. *of* Lancaster. *P.* 285.

7. AN Order to assemble an Army against *Scotland*; dated *November* the 4th 1341, at *Newcastle* upon *Tine*.

Order to assemble an Army. P. 290.

8. A PASSPORT for certain Envoys coming into *England* from *David Bruce* to treat with the King; dated *March* the 20th 1342, at *Westminster*.

Passport for David's *Envoys. P.* 303.

9. AN Order for the exact Observation of the Truce concluded in *Bretagne* with the *Scots*; dated *May* the 20th 1343, at *Westminster*.

Order for observing the Truce. P. 367.

10. AN Order to assemble Troops to make Head against the *Scots*, who after having made an Incursion into *England*, were withdrawn, and muster'd all their Forces to make a fresh Invasion; sign'd *Teste Custode*, the 20th of *August* 1346, at *Westminster*. The Date of it is remarkable, because it shews that King *David* had begun Hostilities even before the Battel of *Cressy*, which was not fought till the 26th of the same Month.

Another Order to assemble Troops. P. 524.

11. A LETTER from the Regent of *England* to the Archbishop of *York*, thanking him for the Victory at *Durham*; dated at the *Tower* of *London*, *October* the 20th 1346. It appears by this Letter that the said Prelate did not only raise Forces to make Head against the *Scots*, but that he was also in the Battel; *Vestras, insuper fidelitatem & strenuitatem probatissimas, pro honore nostri nominis, & tuitione Rei nostræ publicæ Anglicanæ, contra hostiles invasiones Scotorum, Inimicorum & Rebellium nostrorum, Modernis temporibus præexpertas, sudoribus Bellicis, præsertim in nostra absentia, claras factas, cum intimis gratiarum actionibus in Domino commendamus: i. e.* Moreover, We heartily commend in the Lord your

Regent's Thanks to the Archbishop of York *for the Victory at* Durham. *P.* 528.

your approv'd Fidelity and Valour for the Honour of our Name, and the Defence of our Government of *England*, against the Hostile Invasions of the *Scots*, our Enemies and Rebels, which you have lately signaliz'd in the Toils of War, especially in our absence. *A.* 1350.

IN another Act dated at *Westminster*, *November* the 18th 1350, for the Pardon of the Archbishop of *York*, the King says, *Attendentes grata & laudabilia obsequia, quæ venerabilis Pater Willielmus de la Zouche Eborum Archiepiscopus, multipliciter nobis fecit, nec non locum magnum, quem nobis & toti Regno Angliæ, pro defensione ejusdem Regni, præsertim in conflictu Dunelmensi, noscitur tenuisse: i. e.* In Consideration of the acceptable and commendable Acts of Obedience of many Kinds, which the most Reverend Father, *William de la Zouche* Archbishop of *York* has perform'd to us; and also the great Share which 'tis known to us, and to the whole Kingdom of *England*, he has had in the Defence of the said Kingdom; especially at the Battel near *Durham*, &c.

An Act for the Pardon of the Archbishop of York. *P.* 692.

12. AN Order to bring *David Bruce* to the *Tower*; dated *December* the 15th 1346, at *Eltham*.

Order to commit David *to the* Tower. *P.* 537.

13. THE Honour conferr'd on *John Coupland*, who took *David Bruce* Prisoner; King *Edward* made him a Knight Banneret for his Service, and settled 500 Pounds a Year on him and his Heirs for ever, as appears by the Patent dated at *Eltham*, *January* the 20th 1347.

Coupland's *Reward for taking him.* *P.* 542.

14. AN Order for the Prosecution of the Earls of *Menteith* and *Fife*, who revolted from *Edward*'s Interest, and were taken in the Battel of *Durham*. 'Tis dated at *Windsor*, *February* the 22d 1347.

Order for prosecuting the Earls of Menteith *and* Fife. *P.* 549.

Edw. III.

Judgment pass'd on them. *P.* 550.

15. THE Judgment by which Sentence of Death is pass'd upon those Earls, and a Reprieve granted to the Earl of *Fife*, the King's Cousin; dated as above.

Treaties for the Release of David. *P.* 618, 625, 632, 634, 645, 646, 647, 657.

16. SEVERAL Acts relating to the Negotiations set on Foot for the Enlargement of *David Bruce:* They are dated at *Westminster*, *April* the 16th and *July* the 3d; at *Odiham*, *August* the 8th; at *Westminster*, *August* the 12th; at *Odiham*, *August* the 12th; at *Westminster*, *October* the 10th, 18th, and 23d 1348; and at *Langley*, *February* the 25th 1349.

Edward's *Acceptation of* Baliol's *Protest.* *P.* 699.

17. *EDWARD*'s Acceptation of *Baliol*'s Protest that the Treaty on Foot with *David Bruce* shou'd not prejudice his Rights; dated *March* the 4th 1351, at *Westminster*.

David's *Passport to* Scotland. *P.* 722.

18. A PASSPORT for *David Bruce*'s going to *Scotland* with the King's Permission; dated *September* the 4th 1351, at the *Tower* of *London*.

More Treaties for his Liberty. *P.* 723, 724, 725, 727, 728, 733, 736, 737, 746, 756, 758, 761, 787.

19. CONTINUATION of the Negotiations for *David*'s Liberty; dated as above, the 4th, 5th, and 6th of *September*, and at *Westminster* the 3d of *November* 1351; at *Westminster* the 1st of *February*, and the 18th of *March*; at *Windsor* the 28th of *March*, and at *Westminster*, *December* the 6th 1352; at *Westminster*, *July* the 7th and 13th, and *October* the 15th 1353; and at *Westminster*, *June* the 18th 1354.

Edward's *Concession to* Baliol's *Protest.* *P.* 748.

20. A CONCESSION to *Baliol*, that the Treaty on Foot with *Scotland* shall not prejudice his Rights; dated *March* the 8th 1353, at *Westminster*.

Another Concession. *P.* 788.

21. *EDWARD*'s Letters Patent, by which he consents that all the Overtures whatsoever which *Baliol* shou'd make in the Treaty then negotiating with him, relating to the Cession of the Kingdom of *Scotland*, shall not do him any

Prejudice

Prejudice in case the Treaty be not concluded; dated *June* the 30th 1354, at *Westminster*. *A.* 1354.

22. CONVENTIONS betwixt the *English* and *Scotch* Commissioners for the Liberty of *David Bruce*; dated at *Newcastle* upon *Tine*, *July* the 13th, 1354. The Conditions were, 1. That he should be at entire Liberty to go where he pleas'd: 2. That he should pay King *Edward* 90000 Marks *Sterling*, in nine Years time, payable at the rate of 10000 *per Annum*: 3. That there should be a Truce between *England* and *Scotland* till the whole Sum be paid: 4. That *Edward Baliol* should be included in the Truce: 5. That *David* should deliver up 20 Hostages. The rest of the Articles relate to the Character of the said Hostages, and the Security for the Payment. *Conventions for David's Liberty. P.* 793.

23. *EDWARD*'s and the *Black Prince*'s Ratifications of it; dated *October* the 5th 1354, at *Westminster*. *Ratifications of it by the King and Prince of* Wales. *P.* 799, 800.

THESE Conventions were reduc'd into the Form of a solemn Treaty, which was sign'd at *Berwick* the 12th of *November* following. 'Tis surprizing that no *English* or *Scotch* Historian has made mention of it. *Treaty about it. P.* 812.

IN Pursuance of this Treaty, *David* was conducted to *Newcastle*, to be put into the Hands of the *Scots*; and it appears from several Acts of this Year, that they only waited for the Arrival of the chief Hostages to be exchang'd with the said Prince: but the above-mention'd Treaty not being executed by reason of the Surprize of *Berwick*, which happen'd towards the middle of *December*, 1354, *Robert Steuart*, Regent of *Scotland*, had a mind to renew the Negotiation in 1356, as appears from a full Power granted by the said Regent to his Envoys, dated the 17th of *January* 1356, at *An Omission of our Historians. Regent of* Scotland's *Power for a new Treaty. P.* 822.

 Perth.

Edw. III. *Perth*. This Affair was spun out till the Year 1357, that *David* was at length releas'd, as we shall find when we come to the next Volume of the *Fœdera*.

Baliol's *Cessions to* Edward, *P.* 832, 833, 834, 838, 839, 840, 842, 845.

24. *BALIOL*'s Cession of the Kingdom of *Scotland*, and all its Dependencies, *&c.* to *Edward*; dated at *Roxburgh* and *Banbury*, *January* the 20th, 25th and 27th; and at *Westminster*, *March* the 12th 1356.

Conventions betwixt him and Edward. *P.* 836.

25. Conventions between *Edward* King of *England* and *Edward Baliol*, by which the former engag'd to pay the latter in lieu of the Crown of *Scotland* a yearly Pension of 2000*l.* *Sterling*, payable at four Terms; dated at *Banbury*, *January* the 20th 1356.

Edward's *Proclamation for maintaining the Laws of* Scotland. *P.* 846.

26. *EDWARD*'s Proclamation, wherein he promises to maintain the Laws and Customs of *Scotland* without Variation; dated *March* the 15th 1356, at *Westminster*.

P. 859.

We find by an Instrument dated at *Westminster*, *August* the 6th 1356, that *Edward* desir'd time of *Baliol* for the Payment of the second Quarter of his Pension, by reason of the great Expences he had been oblig'd to.

Commission to treat about David's *Liberty*. *P.* 847.

27. A Commission to treat with the *Scots* concerning the Liberty of *David Bruce*; dated *March* the 25th 1356, at *Westminster*.

Passport for the Scots *Envoys*. *P.* 875.

28. A Passport for the *Scots* Envoys; dated at *Westminster* the 13th of *December* 1346.

Other Foreign Affairs.

During the nineteen Years to which the Acts of this Volume relate, *Edward* had a Multitude of Negotiations with several Princes, especially with respect to his grand Affair, I mean the War with *France*. But as it would run me to too great a length to account for all these

these Negotiations, I shall but just mention the Princes and others with whom he had to treat during that Term, to the end that such as shall happen to want Recourse to any of those Articles may consult the *Fœdera* it self. *A.* 1351.

Summary of Edward'*s Negotiations.*

HERE are Negotiations therefore with the Emperor *Lewis* of *Bavaria*, the Towns of *Flanders*, the Duke of *Gueldre*, the Marquis of *Juliers*, and the Duke of *Brabant*, particularly the latter, about a Marriage which was propos'd between *Edward*, eldest Son to the King, and a Daughter of that Duke. It seems that the Pope refus'd a Dispensation for this Marriage, tho' it was often desir'd of him.

Dispute betwixt his Queen and her Sister.

THERE's also a Treaty with the Earl of *Hainault*, *Edward*'s Brother-in-law. After that Earl's Death there was a Difference between his two Sisters, the eldest of which, *Margaret*, was Widow to the Emperor *Lewis* of *Bavaria*, and *Philippa* the youngest had marry'd *Edward* III. They both laid Claim to the Succession of *Hainault*, *Holland*, and *Zealand*, as appears by several Acts in this Volume.

Marriage of his Daughter.

HERE we also find certain Negotiations with *Alphonso* IX. King of *Castile*, chiefly relating to the Marriage of *Joan*, *Edward*'s eldest Daughter, with *Peter*, afterwards surnam'd the *Cruel*, who was *Alphonso*'s eldest Son. The Match being at last concluded, after tedious Negotiations, that Princess died at *Bourdeaux* in her way to her Spouse.

Truce of 20 Years with Spain. *P.* 717.

IN this Volume we likewise find some Acts which make mention of a certain *Spanish* Fleet that committed great Disorders in the Channel, and which *Edward* went in Person to attack. The Advantage he gain'd in the Action, procur'd a Truce of 20 Years with the *Spaniards*; which is dated at *London*, *August* the 1st 1351.

Edw. III. HERE are Treaties alſo with the Kings of *Arragon*, *Portugal* and *Majorca*, *Philip* of *Navarre*, Brother to *Charles the Bad*; the Duke of *Auſtria*, the Marquis of *Brandenburgh*, the Emperor *Charles* IV. the Count of *Geneva*, the Dauphin of *Viennois*, *Godfrey* of *Harcourt*, and ſeveral Lords of *Guyenne*, and particularly with the Lord *de le Bret* or *d'Albret*.

Ranſom of Charles *of* Blois. *P.* 862.

THERE are alſo ſeveral Acts in this Volume which relate to *Bretagne*, and to the Alliance with *John* of *Montfort*; and a Treaty made with *Charles* of *Blois*, who having been taken Priſoner at the Battel of *Rein* in 1347, was brought to *England*, where he ſtay'd till 1356, when he obtain'd his Liberty for a Ranſom of 700000 Crowns, payable at ſundry Terms, of which *Edward* forgave him one half, on Condition that he would pay the other punctually at the Terms agreed on. The Act for this Purpoſe is dated at *Weſtminſter* the 10th of *Auguſt* 1356.

HERE are moreover ſeveral Propoſals for the Marriage of *Edward*'s Children; all which Articles furniſh Matter for an infinite Number of Acts which it wou'd be too tedious to give an Account of.

Domeſtick Affairs.

ENGLAND having enjoy'd a profound Peace during theſe 19 Years, there happen'd no Event at home of any Conſequence. Therefore all the Contents of this Article may be rang'd under ſome looſe Acts, of which theſe that follow are the moſt material.

Order for ſeizing the Tin of Cornwall, *&c.* *P.* 39.

1. AN Order to ſeize all the Tin of *Cornwal* and *Devonſhire*, to help defray the Expences of the War, by giving Security to the Proprietors;

tors; dated *May* the 10th 1338, at the *Tower* of *London*. *A.* 1341.

2. LOANS made to the King by Abbeys, consisting of several Pieces of Plate belonging to Churches; in the Months of *May* and *June* 1338. *Loans to the King by Abbeys. P.* 48, 49, 50, 59, 60.

3. A PERMISSION to dig in the County of *Devon* for Mines of Gold and Silver, on Condition that the Proprietors of the Lands should be at the Expence, and that the King should have one third of the Gold or Silver when refin'd; dated at *Northampton*, *August* the 4th 1338, *Teste Edwardo Duce Cornubiæ*, &c. *Custode Regni*. *Permission to search for Gold and Silver Mines in* Devon. *P.* 71.

4. A PROHIBITION to pay either the King's Creditors, or the Assignments payable out of the Revenues, 'till the King's Return; dated *May* the 6th 1339, at *Antwerp*. *Payment of the King's Debts stopt. P.* 109.

5. A LICENSE to the Weavers of *Bristol*, *&c.* to make Woollen Cloth without being liable to any Molestation from the King's Officers; dated at *Langley*, *November* the 25th 1339. *License for making Woollen Cloth. P.* 137.

6. AN Order for erecting a Staple of Wool, *&c.* at *Bruges*; dated at the *Tower* of *London*, *August* the 8th 1341. *A Wool Staple at* Bruges. *P.* 273.

7. A REPEAL of a Statute made in Parliament by the King's single Authority, pretending that he had not given his Consent to it, if he had not been afraid that the Parliament would break up without finishing the publick Affairs; dated *October* the 1st 1341, at *Westminster*. *King's Repeal of a Statute made by himself. P.* 282.

8. AN Act for reversing the Attainder of *John Maltravers*, because contrary to the Laws of the Kingdom he had never been heard in his own Defence; dated *December* the 28th 1347, at *Guilford*. *Attainder of* Maltravers *revers'd. P.* 600.

Edw. III. 'Tis very probable that this was the same *Maltravers* who was charg'd with the Murder of *Edward* II. for 'tis said in this Act that he came to wait on the King at *Sluys* in *Flanders*. But this Reversal was only a matter of mere Form, because *Edward* granted it on Condition that he should appear in Court when summon'd.

A Wool Staple at Calais. P. 618.

9. An Order for erecting another Wool Staple at *Calais*; dated at *Westminster*, *April* the 5th 1348.

Offer to elect the King Emperor of Germany. P. 622.

10. The King's Credentials to his Ambassadors, to answer those sent from the *German* Electors to make him an Offer of advancing him to the Empire: 'Tis dated *May* the 10th 1348, at *Westminster*.—We don't meet with this Answer in the *Fœdera*, but 'tis very well known from other Authorities that he refus'd this Dignity.

Order not to depart the Kingdom on account of the Plague. P. 668.

The Plague which ravag'd *England* during the Year 1349, gave Occasion for several Acts, of which there are these two remarkable.

The first is a Prohibition to leave the Kingdom upon account of the Pestilence; dated *December* the 1st 1349, at *Westminster*.

Order relating to Servants in time of the Plague. P. 693.

The second is an Order whereby both Men and Women, who had no Estates or no Profession to maintain themselves, were oblig'd to enter into Service, for the Wages common to the Places where they liv'd, on pain of being imprison'd till they could find Sureties for their Obedience. What gave Occasion to the Order was this: The Plague having carry'd off most of the Domestics in the Kingdom, it was a hard matter to get any; and those that were inclin'd to go to Work, or Service, took that Opportunity to exact upon their Masters.

Affairs

*A.*1341.

Affairs with the Court of Rome, *or relating to Religion.*

THE Uſurpations of the Popes in the matter of Collations to Benefices, and ſome Differences between the Archbiſhops about carrying the Croſs, are the chief Subject of the few Pieces in this Volume relating to Religion. Theſe that follow may be deem'd the moſt material.

1. AN Order to the Archbiſhop of *Canterbury* to revoke certain Cenſures, which he had denounc'd againſt the Commiſſioners charg'd by the King to make Enquiry into the Miſdeameanors of his Miniſters, of whom this Prelate was the chief. *Order againſt Ecclesiaſtical Cenſures. P. 234.*

QUOD ſi facere non curaveritis, ad vos tanquam Inimicum, & Rebellem noſtrum, & pacis Regni noſtri perturbatorem, quantum de jure poterimus, capiemus: i. e. Which if you do not take care to do, we ſhall proceed againſt you by Law as an Enemy, a Rebel, and a Diſturber of our Peace: 'Tis dated at *Weſtminſter*, *March* the 6th 1341.

2. A NOTIFICATION to two Chaplains and Commiſſioners of the Pope, of certain Articles relating to the Regal Rights and Prerogatives, to the end that they may not infringe upon them in their Judgment of ſuch Cauſes as are brought before them: 'Tis dated at the Tower of *London*, *July* the 28th 1342. *Notifications of the K's Prerogatives to the Pope's Commiſſioners. P. 335.*

3. A LETTER wherein *Edward* earneſtly intreats the Pope to revoke certain Orders contrary to the Prerogatives of the Crown, which, he ſays, he is reſolv'd to maintain: 'Tis dated at *Weſtminſter*, *May* the 12th 1343. *K. deſires the Pope to revoke ſome Orders. P. 363.*

Edw.III. 4. An Order to arrest all that came into the Kingdom with Provisions or Bulls from the Pope, for Benefices depending on the King's Collation; dated at *Westminster*, *June* the 15th 1343.

Order against those that came for Benefices. *P.* 371. *Another.* *P.* 377.

5. A Prohibition, pursuant to a Resolution of Parliament, to execute the Pope's Mandates, touching the Provision or Grant of Benefices to Strangers; dated at *Clarendon*, *July* the 23d 1343.

Another. *P.* 378. 6. An Order to arrest all that brought Bulls into the Kingdom; dated as above *July* the 30th.

K's Letter to the Pope *P.* 382. 7. The King's Letter to the Pope on this Subject; dated at *Westminster*, *August* the 30th 1343, in which are these Words: *Novit igitur Deus Veritatis, esse verum quod tam Proceres, & Nobiles, quam Communitas Regni nostri Angliæ, nuper in Generali Parliamento nostro apud Westmonasterium congregati, attendentes* Provisorum exercitum qui Regnum nostrum Angliæ in excessiva multitudine jam invasit, *& perpendentes ac dolentes dampnum & præjudicium intolerabilia, quæ dicto Regno, ex hujusmodi Provisionibus, provenerunt, & provenire timentur per amplius in futurum, & impatientes dictorum doloris & præjudicii; proposuerunt querelose & clamose unanimiter, & dixerunt quod talia diutius tolerare non poterant, nec volebant.*

i. e. The God of Truth therefore knows it to be true, that not only the Lords, but the Commons of our Realm of *England*, in our Parliament at *Westminster* assembled, considering *the Army of Provisors which has already invaded our Kingdom of* England *in excessive numbers*, and weighing with Sorrow the intolerable Loss and Prejudice which the said Realm has already sustain'd, and has cause to apprehend yet more here-

hereafter, and being impatient under the ſaid Loſs and Damage, have loudly complain'd and declar'd one and all, that they cannot and will not bear ſuch things any longer. *A.* 1343.

8. ANOTHER Letter to the Pope on the ſame Subject, but much ſtronger: 'Tis dated at *Weſtminſter*, *Sept.* 10. 1343. and has theſe Words in it: *Sed (quod dolendum eſt) ipſius vineæ propagines degenerant in labruſcas, & exterminant illam apri de ſylva, ſingulareſque feræ depaſcunt eam, dum per impoſitiones & proviſiones ſedis apoſtolicæ (quæ ſolitò graviùs invaleſcunt) ipſius peculium, contra piam voluntatem & ordinationem donatorum, manus occupant indignorum, & præſertim exterorum; & ejus dignitates & beneficia pinguia perſonis conferuntur alienigenis, plerumque nobis ſuſpectis; qui non reſident in dictis beneficiis, & vultus commiſſorum eis pecorum non agnoſcunt, linguam non intelligunt, ſed animarum curâ neglectâ, velut mercenarii, ſolummodo temporalia lucra quærunt: & ſic diminuitur Chriſti cultus, animarum cura negligitur, ſubtrahitur hoſpitalitas, eccleſiarum jura depereunt, ruunt ædificia clericorum, attenuatur devotio populi. Clerici dicti regni, viri magnæ literaturæ, & converſationis honeſtæ, qui curam & regimen animarum poſſent ibi ſalubriter peragere, & forent pro noſtris, & publicis conſiliis opportuni, ſtudium deſerunt, propter promotionis congruæ ſpem ablatam, quæ divinæ ſcimus non eſſe placita voluntati.*—— *Nos autem Anglicanæ depreſſionem eccleſiæ, & exhæredationem coronæ regiæ, & mala prædicta, quæ diſſimulata diutiùs adjicerent veriſimiliter graviora, patulo cernentes intuitu, ad vos, ſucceſſorem apoſtolorum principis, qui ad paſcendum non ad tondendum oves dominicas, ac ad confirmandum, & non deprimendum fratres ſuos mandatum à Chriſto ſuſcipit, iſta deferimus, votivis affectibus ſupplicantes, quatenus,* &c. *Another.* *P.* 385.

Edw. III.

i. e. BUT what is matter of Grief is, that the Slips of this very Vine are degenerated into a wild Vine, and the Boars out of the Wood do waste it, and every wild Beast devours it, while by the Impositions and Provisions of the Apostolic See (which now grow more insupportable than ever) its own Substance, contrary to the pious Intent and Order of the Donors, is detain'd in the Hands of the unworthy, and especially Foreigners; and its Dignities and fat Benefices are conferr'd upon Strangers, who for the most part are Persons whom we suspect, and who neither reside on the said Benefices, nor know the Face nor understand the Voice of the Flock to them committed; but wholly neglecting the Cure of Souls, like Hirelings, only seek temporal Gain; and so the Worship of Christ is impair'd, the Cure of Souls neglected, Hospitality withdrawn, the Rights of the Church lost, the Houses of the Clergy dilapidated, the Devotion of the Laity decay'd; the Clergy of the said Kingdom, who are Men of great Learning and honest Conversation, and are able to perform the Cure of Souls effectually, and would also be fit for Ours and the publick Service, forsake their Studies, because the Hopes of any reasonable Preferment are thus taken away, which we know is not pleasing to the Divine Will.—— We therefore by this their Representation plainly beholding the Depression of the Church of *England*, and the Disinherison of our Crown, with all the foresaid Evils, which, if longer dissembled, would probably very much increase, do now refer them unto you, who are the Successor of the Prince of the Apostles, who receiv'd Command from Christ to feed, not to shear the Lord's Sheep, and to *strengthen*, not to *oppress* his Brethren, heartily intreating that, *&c.*

9. A ME-

9. A MEMORANDUM concerning a Man who was taken up the 4th of *November* 1344, with nine Bulls of Provision to Benefices in his Custody. *A.* 1346. *A Person arrested with Bulls.* P. 843.

NOTWITHSTANDING all the Remonstrances that *Edward* made to the Pope, it seems the latter had no Regard to them, so that the King was oblig'd to get satisfaction by some other means. For this end he seiz'd all the Revenues of the Benefices possess'd by Foreigners, in order to help defray the Charges of the War; and wrote a Letter of Excuse to the Pope for so doing, which he dated from *Westminster* the 12th of *February* 1346. *Benefices enjoy'd by Foreigners seiz'd.* P. 490.

THE Popes did not only nominate to vacant Benefices, but also reserv'd to themselves, under various Pretexts, the Collation to Archbishopricks, Bishopricks, and all the best Benefices; and granted Letters of Provision before they became vacant, for fear of being forestall'd. Here are several Bulls in this Collection containing such Provisions, particularly, *Popes fill up the best Livings before vacant.*

1. A BULL enjoining that the Bishop of *Worcester* be put in possession of the Archbishoprick of *York*, as soon as it shall become vacant; dated at *Avignon* the 16th of the Calends of *November* 1352. *Bulls for Bpks before vacant.* P. 744.

2. ANOTHER to fill the See of *Worcester*, when it shall become vacant by the Translation of the Bishop to the Archbishoprick of *York*; dated as before at *Avignon* the 11th of the Calends of *November*. P. 745.

3. A BULL of Provision for a Canonship of the Cathedral of *Litchfield*, tho' there was none vacant, and for the first vacant Prebend: *Non obstantibus de certo Canonicorum numero, & quibuslibet aliis Statutis, & Consuetudinibus ejusdem Ecclesiæ contrariis, juramento, confirmatione Apostolicâ,* *For a Canonship and Prebend.* P. 513.

Edw. III. *licâ, vel aliâ quâcumque firmitate roboratis*: *i. e.* Notwithstanding the certain number of Canons, and all other Statutes and Customs of the said Church whatsoever to the contrary, whether bound by Oath, Apostolical Confirmation, or any other Security whatsoever. 'Tis dated at *Avignon* the 8th of the Ides of *June* 1346.

King's Injunction about Procurations. *P.* 558. 4. THE King's Prohibition to the Prelates to suffer the raising of Money in their Dioceses, under the Title of *Procurations*, for the Cardinal Legates employ'd in *France* in the Negotiations of Peace; dated at *Reading*, *April* the 12th 1347, *Teste Custode.*

P. 630, 635. 5. A PERMISSION to raise those *Procurations*, by reason of the good Services which the Legates had done the King; dated at *Westminster*, *August* the 6th 1348, and at *Clarendon*, *September* the 5th following.

Order about the ABp. of Armagh's *carrying the Cross.* *P.* 666. 6. AN Order to hinder the Archbishop of *Armagh*, pretending to be Primate of *Ireland*, from having the Cross carry'd before him in *Dublin*; dated at *Westminster*, *November* the 20th 1349.

His Quarrel thereupon with the ABp. of Dublin. *P.* 743. 7. A PERMISSION to the said Prelate to be absent from the Parliament assembled at *Dublin*, because of the Quarrel betwixt him and the Archbishop of that See about carrying the Cross: This Act is dated at *Westminster*, *September* the 12th 1352.

Pope's Nuncio forbid to raise first Fruits, &c. *P.* 747. 8. A PROHIBITION to the Pope's Nuncio to raise the first Fruits of the Benefices for the Pope under pretence of the Collations, or Reservations of the Court at *Rome*; dated at *Hertford*, *January* the 20th 1353.

K's Letter to the Pope. 9. A LETTER to Pope *Innocent* VI. upon his Exaltation to St. *Peter*'s Chair; dated at *Westminster*, *June* the 20th 1353.

10. A PRO-

10. A PROHIBITION to moleſt the Archbiſhop of *York* for bearing the Croſs in *London*; dated at *Weſtminſter*, *April* the 1ſt 1353.

A. 1353.

ABp. of York *carries the Croſs in* London. *P.* 753.

11. ANOTHER againſt moleſting certain Clergymen at *Bourdeaux*, who were marry'd, notwithſtanding they had had the Tonſure; dated at *Sandwich*, *July* the 25th 1355.

Marry'd Clergy. P. 824.

12. A LICENSE to *John Blome* of *London*, to go to the Monaſtery of *Glaſtenbury*, and dig for the Corpſe of *Joſeph* of *Arimathea*, according to a divine Revelation which he ſaid he had had upon that Subject in the Year 1344. 'Tis dated at *Weſtminſter*, *June* the 10th 1345.

Permiſſion to ſearch for the Corpſe of Joſeph *of* Arimathea. *P.* 458.

WE

Edw. III.

WE come now to the fifth Volume of the Fœdera, *which we ſhall introduce, as we have done the two former Volumes, with ſuch part of Mr.* Rymer'*s Dedication of it to Queen* Anne, *as opens a farther View of the glorious Reign of King* Edward III.

May it pleaſe your Majeſty,

'AFTER the many Leagues and Alli-
'ances in former Volumes, in the laſt
'(that was preſented to your Majeſty) ap-
'pear'd the Operations of War, and a won-
'derful Succeſs in Battels.

'IN this Book TWO CAPTIVE KINGS
'(whom God had given into the Hands of
'your moſt noble Progenitor *Edward* III.) are
'ranſom'd and ſet at Liberty.

'THEREUPON enſu'd (that commonly
'call'd) THE GREAT PEACE; a
'Treaty the moſt ſolemn, and the moſt memo-
'rable that ever had been form'd between two
'contending Nations.

'THIS furthermore contains, beſides the
'Peace with *France*, one Exploit of War on the
'other ſide of the *Pyreneans*, one deciſive Blow
'at *Nazara*.

'IN ſhort, your Majeſty, with this Volume,
'gives to the World a Partition of *France*, and
'the Conqueſt of *Spain*, &c.

[*To return to Mr.* Rapin.] THIS ſixth Volume of the *Fœdera* contains ſixteen Years of the Reign of *Edward* III. *viz.* from the beginning of the Year 1357, to the end of 1372. Foraſmuch as *Edward*'s Affairs with *France* are the principal Subject of this Volume, I ſhall inſiſt chiefly on this Article, the reſt containing little remarkable. *A.* 1357.

I. *The Affairs betwixt* Edward *and* France.

Truce with France, *and King* John *brought Priſoner to* London.

IMMEDIATELY after the glorious Victory which *Edward* the Son gain'd near *Poictiers*, the ſaid Prince repair'd to *Bourdeaux*, whither the Pope ſent a Cardinal to him, to negotiate a Truce in favour of *France*. A Truce being accordingly concluded for two Years, the Prince of *Wales* ſet out in the Month of *April* 1357, to conduct King *John* to *London*, where * *Edward* receiv'd the Captive King with as much Honour as if he had come purely to pay him a Viſit.

His Son takes the Title of Regent.

NEVERTHELESS the Impriſonment of this Prince occaſion'd ſuch Troubles in *France*, that the Dauphin his Son, who took the Title of Regent, had no hopes of procuring his Father's Liberty. He had an Enemy, in the King of *Navarre*, who knew ſo well how to improve that fatal Conjuncture in order to ſow

* HE was met in *Southwark* by above 1000 of the chief Citizens of *London* on Horſeback: The Captive being mounted on a noble white Courſer in token of Sovereignty, and the Conqueror riding by his ſide on a little black Hobby, as if he ſhunn'd all Suſpicion of a Triumph. He was receiv'd by the Lord Mayor of *London*, &c. in all their Formalities, with the City Pageants; and in the Streets thro' which he paſs'd to *Weſtminſter*, the Citizens hung out all their Plate, Tapeſtry, and Armour, ſo that the like had never been ſeen before in the Memory of Man. King *Edward* receiv'd him on a Royal Throne in *Weſtminſter-Hall*, from whence he roſe haſtily and careſs'd him. He the ſame Day treated the *French* King, his Son *Philip*, and the reſt of the noble Captives at a Princely Rate; and till the Palace of the *Savoy* was ready for him, he lodg'd him in his own Court. *See* Barnes's *Hiſtory*, *p.* 526.

Edw. III. Discord in the State, that it was not possible for the Regent to make Preparations for renewing the War, as soon as the Truce should be expir'd. King *John*, who was thorowly inform'd of all those Disorders, and saw plainly that there was nothing to expect from the Sword, hop'd to procure his Liberty himself, by negotiating a Treaty of Peace with *Edward*. This Treaty, which cou'd not but be very advantageous to *England*, considering the Situation of Affairs, having been sent to *France*, the General Assembly of the States refus'd to ratify it, and promis'd the Dauphin to enable him to obtain Terms more advantageous, but were not as good as their Word.

King John *treats with* K. Edward *for his Liberty.*

EDWARD consequently despairing of such a Peace as he wish'd for, resolv'd to take up the Cudgels again; and as he thought that *John* meant nothing but to amuse him in the late Negotiation, he treated him with less Regard, and caus'd him to be shut up in the Castle of *Sommerton*. Mean time he made Preparations to carry the War into the very Heart of *France*, not doubting but he should be a vast Gainer by the Confusion which then reign'd in that Kingdom. He set out from *England* therefore in the Month of *October* 1359, with 1000 Sail of Ships, and an Army of 100000 Men. With this numerous Host he made himself Master of many Places in *Normandy*, where he put his Army into Winter Quarters; and in the Month of *March* 1360, he advanc'd towards *Champagne* with a Design to take in *Rheims*, where 'tis said he resolv'd to be crown'd. But missing his Aim, he caus'd the Gates of *Sens* to be open'd to him; and then turning towards *Burgundy*, he threaten'd that Province with entire Desolation. The Duke of *Burgundy*,

He is sent to a Castle in Lincolnshire.

K. Edward *sails with a mighty Army to* France.

His Progress in Normandy.

In Burgundy.

dy, who was not in a Condition to oppose him, resolv'd to capitulate upon the best Terms he could, in order to save his Dominions from being pillag'd; and obtain'd a particular Truce for three Years, on Condition of paying down 200000 Florins, and furnishing the *English* Army with Provisions. *A.* 1360.

As *Edward* quitted *Burgundy*, he march'd towards the Isle of *France* with a Design to draw the Regent to a Battel: But that Prince was too wise to hazard the Safety of *France* so rashly, and therefore lay close in *Paris*, so that all *Edward*'s Bravadoes could not fetch him out. The Siege of *Paris* seeming an Enterprize too difficult for the King of *England*, he turn'd back towards *la Beausse*, with a Design to go and refresh his Army on the Banks of the *Loire*. While he was encamp'd near *Chartres*, a terrible Storm arose, with Thunder and Hail of a prodigious Bigness, which kill'd 3000 Horses, and above 1000 of his Soldiers. This extraordinary Event, which seem'd to denote the Wrath of Heaven, struck this Prince with such a Terror, that turning towards the Steeple of the Church of *Chartres*, he fell on his Knees, and made a Vow to give Peace to *France* upon equitable Terms. With this Resolution he sent his Son the Prince of *Wales* to *Bretigny*, whither the Dauphin likewise repair'd; and in that very place those two Princes, after a Negotiation which lasted not above a Week, concluded a Treaty of Peace, which in all Appearance was much the same with what had been agreed on at *London* the Year before.

Great Storm of Thunder and Hail.

Treaty of Bretigny.

BY the Treaty of *Bretigny*, the Crown of *France* yielded to the King of *England* a great Number of Provinces in full Sovereignty, and, as it were, made a Partition of the Kingdom

Edw. III with the *English*. Besides this, King *John* engag'd to pay three Millions of Crowns of Gold for his Ransom, and to deliver up several Hostages, of whom five should be Princes of the Blood. In pursuance of this Treaty King *John* was conducted to *Calais*, where he was set at Liberty, after he had ratified the Treaty, and given all the other Securities that *Edward* was pleas'd to demand of him.

K. John ransom'd and releas'd.

WHEN he was arriv'd at *St. Omer*, he ratified every thing that he had done at *Calais*, swore to the Peace again, and made his eldest Son *Charles*, his other Sons, and twenty of the best Noblemen in the Kingdom take the same Oath. In fine, he did every thing that he cou'd to shew that what he had done was voluntary, although he was a Prisoner. And he made a greater Discovery of his Sincerity afterwards, by punctually executing the Treaty of *Bretigny*, two Articles excepted: The first related to the County of *Gavre* in *Gascoigne*, and to the Territory of *Belville* in *Poictou*, about which some Dispute arose: The second was with respect to his Ransom, which it was not possible for him to pay at the Terms prescrib'd, because of the ill State of his Kingdom.

MEAN time, the Non-Execution of these two Articles was the reason that *Edward* detain'd the Hostages in *England*. Among these there had been four that were call'd Lords of the *Flower de Lis*, *viz.* the Duke of *Orleans*, Brother to the King of *France*, the Dukes of *Anjou* and *Berry*, the King's Sons, and the Duke of *Bourbon*. As these Princes were quite weary of *England*, *Edward* was willing to set them at Liberty, on condition that the County of *Gavre*, and the Territory of *Belville*, which occasion'd his Quarrel with King *John*, should be deliver'd up to him. But juſt as they were *A.* 1360. at the point of executing this Agreement, which was ratified by the King of *France*, the Princes who were to be deliver'd being already conducted to *Calais*, the Duke of *Anjou* retir'd without Leave, and never return'd more: His ill Example was follow'd by four other Hoſtages of an inferior Rank; and by their Eſcape the Meaſures which had been concerted for the Liberty of the other Princes were entirely broke.

'TIS hard to gueſs the reaſon why *John*, who had acted ſo ſincerely in the Execution of the Treaty, did not oblige the Prince his Son to return into *England*, or why he did not ſend Prince *Philp* his fourth Son thither, or at leaſt ſome other Hoſtages, to ſupply the Place of the Duke of *Anjou*. Whatever Cauſe it was, his taking a Reſolution ſoon after to return to *England*, made ſome do him the Honour to ſay, that it was to throw himſelf again into Priſon, in order to make Reparation for his Son's Crime, and to ſhew that he was not conſenting to his Eſcape. But of this there's not the leaſt Shadow of Probability, becauſe by the Treaty he was only oblig'd to ſend back the Duke of *Anjou*, or to give the King of *England* ſome Satisfaction by ſending him other Hoſtages in the Duke's Room. Beſides, he had already executed the moſt important Articles of the Treaty, nothing remaining to be determin'd but the Affair of *Gavre* and *Belville*, and the reſidue of his Ranſom Money, of which he had already paid near a Million. Conſequently there was not the leaſt Neceſſity for his ſurrendring himſelf again a Priſoner to diſcharge his Faith. 'Tis ſtill more ridiculous to aſſert, as ſome have done, that his Love for a Lady at the Court of *England* made him return to *London*; for can it

Edw. III. be imagin'd that Prince of 50 Years of Age, should abandon a Kingdom in so bad a Condition as his was in then, to follow the Impulse of a foolish Passion*? They who tell us that he had a mind to settle with *Edward* the Expedition of a Croisado, of which the Pope had declar'd him General, seem to have more reason for what they say, though even this is at most but Conjecture. Whatever was the Motive of it, 'tis certain that he return'd to *London*, and that there he died some Months after, *viz.* on the 8th of *April* 1364.

King John *returns to* London, *and dies there.*

Battel of Avray, *and Treaty of* Guerande.

IN *September* following, the famous Quarrel between the Families of *Blois* and *Montfort* was decided by the Battel of *Avray*, where *Charles*

* MR. *Barnes* takes notice that many of our Writers indiscreetly surmise, as if one occasion of King *John*'s coming to *England* at this time, was for Love of the Countess of *Salisbury*: which Opinion, saith he, the noble Lord *Orrery* hath authoriz'd with his excellent Pen, in his Play call'd the *Black Prince*. But he wou'd have it consider'd that my Lord wrote a Poem for Delight, and not a History for the Establishment of Truth. Therefore he cannot pardon Sir *Richard Baker*, and others of his Character: For, says he, if they mean by the Countess of *Salisbury*, the first Earl of *Montague*'s Lady, who was *Catherine*, Daughter of the Lord *Grandison*, she had been dead above 12 Years: If they refer to the fair Lady of *Kent*, she was marry'd two Years before to Prince *Edward*, and was now with him in *Aquitain*, of which King *John* cou'd not be ignorant: And if they be forc'd to own the Lady *Elizabeth*, Daughter to the Lord *Mohun*, who was Wife to the second Earl of *Montague*, and the only Countess of *Salisbury* at this time; he desires them to bring the least Shadow of Authority for it. And upon the whole Mr. *Barnes* professes a great Resentment to see the Honour not only of a noble Lady, but also of two Kings, *John* and *Edward*, who are both said to have been in Love with her, thus shamefully traduced by Men of no Industry, or else of no Honesty.

of

of *Blois* was kill'd. This Battel was follow'd with the Treaty of *Guerande*, which put *John* of *Montfort* in Possession of *Bretagne*. *A.* 1366.

The Black Prince *made Prince of* Guyenne.

AFTER the Peace of *Bretigny*, *Edward* had in 1362, erected the Dutchy of *Guyenne* into a Principality, with which he had invested *Edward* his eldest Son. This Prince was gone to keep his Court at *Bourdeaux*, where he led an unactive Life, very unsuitable to his warlike Temper, the Peace giving him no manner of Opportunity to exercise his Valour. But in 1366, he was call'd out of this State of Inactivity by *Peter* surnam'd the *Cruel*, King of *Castile*, who having been drove out of his Dominions by *Henry* Count of *Trastemare*, his Bastard Brother, went to *Bayonne* to implore the Assistance of the Prince of *Wales*. As *France* naturally favour'd *Henry*, whom she had plac'd upon the Throne of *Castile*, this was a sufficient Reason to induce the *English* Prince to espouse the Interest of *Peter*. Therefore he assembled a powerful Army in his Principality; and after having made a Treaty with the King of *Navarre*, who gave him Passage into his Dominions, he repair'd to the Frontiers of *Castile*, where he met *Henry*, who was advanc'd to dispute his Entrance into that Kingdom. It was hard by the little Town of *Najara* that these two Princes fought a bloody Battel, in which the *Castilians* were entirely defeated. The Prince of *Wales*'s Victory was follow'd with the Restoration of *Peter*, who instead of making an Acknowledgment for so great a Piece of Service, suffer'd the best part of that Army, which had fought for him so valiantly, to perish with Hunger and Misery. This perfidious Action oblig'd the Prince of *Wales* to quit *Castile*, where he had contracted a Distemper he never

He restores Peter *King of* Castile *to his Dominions by the Victory at* Najara.

Peter'*s base Ingratitude.*

Edw. III. ver got rid of, in order to return to *Guyenne* with the rest of his Troops, who had reason to repent of their Expedition, glorious as it was.

Prince of Wales *forc'd to disband his Soldiers without Pay, who thereupon ravage all* Guyenne.

As soon as the Prince came to *Bourdeaux*, he disbanded his Army without paying it, having taken no Measures to find the Money, because he had depended upon the Faith of *Peter*, who had engag'd to bear the whole Expence of the War. The Troops, when thus disbanded without their Pay, thought they had Authority to get it where they could: Therefore they divided themselves into several little Bands, under the Conduct of some Officers of Reputation, and committed a multitude of Ravages in *Guyenne*. The Prince of *Wales*, who was not in a Condition to satisfy them, and who could not prevail on himself to push Soldiers who had serv'd him so well to the utmost Extremity, only intreated them to commit their Ravages elsewhere. Whether it was in respect to this Prince, or whether those Troops thought they could get more Booty in other Parts, they fell into the next adjacent Provinces of *France*, where they committed extravagant Outrages. *Charles* V. then upon the Throne, complain'd of it as a Breach of the Treaty; but he was answer'd that they were Persons unauthoris'd, and that he might fall upon them in what manner he pleas'd, without *England*'s taking their part. Mean time, to give him yet greater Satisfaction, *Edward* publish'd a Proclamation recalling all those Vagabonds, declaring them, in case of Refusal, Traitors and Rebels, and confiscating all their Estates. Tho', after such a Declaration, it was the Business of *France* to find Ways and Means to get rid of those Plunderers, yet the Prince of *Wales* was afraid lest the

Edward's *Proclamation against them.*

the Affair ſhould end in a War, of which he might be charg'd as the Author. To prevent this Inconvenience, he ſtudy'd Methods to ſatisfy thoſe Troops, by impoſing a Tax upon his Dominions, call'd *Fouage*, or Smoke-Money, becauſe it was laid upon every Hearth or Chimney. This Expedient bid fair for Succeſs, if after the Peace of *Bretigny*, the King his Father had not unhappily revok'd ſeveral Grants which he had made to the principal Lords of *Guyenne*, at a time when his Affairs requir'd him to make ſure of the Fidelity of the *Gaſcons*. This Revocation ſo incens'd thoſe Noblemen, that they reſolv'd to be reveng'd; and the new King of *France* was not wanting to incite them underhand. We ſhall find hereafter that this Prince had already form'd a Deſign to break the Peace, to have an occaſion to recover thoſe Provinces which *France* had loſt ſince the Treaty of *Bretigny*. The Nobility of *Guyenne*, who found themſelves ſupported by the King of *France*, incited their Vaſſals and Tenants to complain to them of the Chimney Tax newly impos'd; and having receiv'd their Complaints, they carry'd them to the Prince, by whom they were but ill receiv'd. Upon his Refuſal to redreſs this pretended Abuſe, they apply'd to the King of *France*, ſuppoſing that he was ſtill Sovereign of *Guyenne*, notwithſtanding his Renunciation of that Sovereignty; and begg'd him to grant them Letters of Appeal. *Charles* maintain'd them for a time at *Paris*, till his Affairs were ready; and at length granted them what they deſir'd. In conſequence of this Appeal, he caus'd the Prince of *Wales* to be cited before the Court of Peers, to vindicate himſelf againſt the Complaints of his Subjects. The Prince making Anſwer that he wou'd not fail to appear at the Head of 60000 Men,

A. 1343.

He impoſes a Chimney Tax.

His Subjects complain of it.

Charles *ſummons him to the Court of Peers.*

Edw. III. Men, *Charles* caus'd War to be declar'd againſt *Edward* by a Footman, becauſe the Prince had taken ſome pretext to arreſt thoſe who had brought him the Citation.

Declares War againſt him.

As we find but few Circumſtances of this War in our Collection of the publick Acts in the *Fœdera*, I ſhall content my ſelf with barely relating the Succeſs of it, which was very fatal to *England*. Immediately after the Declaration of the War, *Edward* ſaw himſelf robb'd of the County of *Ponthieu*, and heard at the ſame time, that the greateſt part of *Guyenne* was revolted. As he found himſelf under an indiſpenſable Neceſſity to renew the War, he reſum'd the Title of King of *France*, which he had dropp'd ever ſince the Treaty of *Bretigny*; but the Title procur'd him no manner of Advantage. *Bertrand du Gueſclin*, Conſtable of *France*, made great Progreſs in *Guyenne*, and the neighbouring Provinces; inſomuch that the Prince of *Wales*, whoſe Illneſs was turn'd into a perfect Dropſy, cou'd not oppoſe his Arms. On the contrary, after having ſeverely puniſh'd the City of *Limoges* for its Rebellion, he was oblig'd to return into *England* for the Recovery of his Health, leaving *John* Duke of *Lancaſter*, his Brother, in his place.

Edward *reſumes the Title of K. of* France.

His ill Succeſs, Sickneſs and Return to England.

Not long after, the Duke marry'd the eldeſt Daughter of *Peter the Cruel*, and immediately took the Title of King of *Caſtile*. This Enterprize oblig'd the Baſtard *Henry* to unite himſelf more cloſely with *France*, and to give the Conſtable powerful Aſſiſtance by Sea to beſiege *Rochel*. *Edward* did what he cou'd to relieve the place, by a Fleet commanded by the Earl of *Pembroke*, which was beat by the *Spaniards*, and *Rochel* was taken. Afterwards, *Du Gueſclin* advanc'd

Rochel *beſieg'd and taken.*

advanc'd into *Poictou*, and laid siege to *Thouars*, to which all the Nobility of the Province was retir'd. That Town being in no Condition to hold out long, the Noblemen of *Poictou* capitulated, and promis'd to own the King of *France* for their Sovereign, if the King of *England*, or one of his Sons, did not come into *Poictou* before *Michaelmass*, with an Army strong enough to give Battel. *Edward* hearing of this Capitulation, order'd a Fleet to be fitted out, on which he embark'd about the end of *August*, to save that Province; but the contrary Winds constantly opposing his Passage for above a Month, *Thouras* was taken from him, with all the rest of *Poictou*. *A.* 1375. *All* Poictou *reduc'd.*

IN one word, this War was so fatal to the *English*, that they had nothing left of all the Conquests they had made in *France*, but the single Town of *Calais*. Affairs being come to this Pass, the King of *France* consented to a Truce, which was concluded on the 11th of *February* 1375, and afterwards prolong'd to the 1st of *April* 1377. *Edward* died the 21st of *June* this same Year, three Months after the Expiration of the Truce. *Truce with* France.

THE most important Acts in this sixth Volume of the *Fœdera*, with respect to the Affairs of *France*, are these.

1. A TREATY of Truce made at *Bourdeaux*, *March* the 23d 1357, to last till *Easter* 1359. *Another. P.* 3.

2. A PASSPORT for a Cardinal coming to *England* to negotiate a Peace, with a Retinue of 100 Domesticks, and 150 Horses; dated at *Westminster*, *June* the 15th 1357. *P.* 21.

3. AN Order to conduct King *John* to the Castle of *Sommerton*; dated *January* the 2d 1358, at *Westminster*. This was after the States of *France* had refus'd to approve of the Articles of *Order to carry K.* John *to* Sommerton. *P.* 113.

of Peace agreed on at *London* betwixt the two Kings.

P. 117.

4. A PASSPORT for the Deputies of *Languedoc* going to wait on King *John* in *England*; dated *February* the 13th, at *Westminster*. This Province distinguish'd it self among the rest by its Zeal for its Sovereign.

The Truce prolong'd. P. 121.

5. A PROLONGATION of the Truce to the 24th of *June* following; dated at *London*, *March* the 18th 1359.

Edward's *Letter to the two ABps.* P. 134.

6. *EDWARD*'s Letter to the two Archbishops of *England*, wherein he complains of his being deceiv'd in the Negotiations of Peace; and as he is ready to take Arms again, he charges both those Prelates to appoint Prayers to God for the happy Success of his Expedition. They are dated *August* the 12th 1359, at *Westminster*.

His embarking for France. P. 141.

7. A MEMORANDUM of the Day that *Edward* embark'd for *France*, *viz.* the 28th of *October* 1359.

His particular Agreement with the D. of Burgundy. P. 161.

8. THE Agreement made with the Duke of *Burgundy*, containing a particular Truce of three Years for that Province, on the Duke's Payment of a Sum of 200000 Deniers of Gold *, call'd *Moutons*, within the Term of one Year; dated *March* the 10th 1360, at *Guillon* in *Burgundy*.

Pope's Bull to secure the Churches of France *from pillage.* P. 172.

9. A BULL of *Innocent* VI. to exempt the Churches of *France* from Pillage; dated at *Avignon* the 6th of the Calends of *May* 1360.

* AUTHORS are not agreed what this Sum was; *Mat. Villani* makes it 100000 Moutons, *Paradin* calls it 200000 Florins, *Walsingham* and an old *English* Manuscript in the Library of *Christ-Church-College* at *Cambridge*, make it only 70000 Florins; but *Mezeray*, *Hollinshed*, *Speed*, and *Barnes* call it 200000 Florins of Gold, or 35000 *l.* Sterling.

10. ORDER to carry King *John* to the Tower of *London*, *Teste Custode*, at *Reading* the 28th of *April* 1360. *A.* 1360. *K.* John *committed to the Tower.*

11. TREATY concluded at *Bretigny* near *Chartres*; dated *May* the 8th 1360. *P.* 173. *Treaty at* Bretigny. *P.* 178. &c.

NOTWITHSTANDING the length of this Treaty, which contains 40 Articles, 'tis absolutely necessary to make an Extract of it, because it serves as a Foundation for most of the Acts of this Volume, and many of the next: And it may be said, that 'tis almost impossible to understand the History of that time fully without the knowledge of this Treaty.

Article I. *Imprimis*, THE King of *England*, besides what he holdeth in *Guyenne* and *Gascoigne*, shall have for himself and his Heirs for ever, and shall hold in like manner as the King of *France*, or his Son, or their Ancestors, Kings of *France*, did hold them, the Provinces of *Poictou*, *la Saintoigne*, *l'Agenois*, *le Perigord*, *le Limousin*, *le Quercy*; the Country of *Bigorre*, that of *Gaure*, *Angoulesme*, and the Land of *Rovergne*. And,

II, III, IV, V, VI. *MONSTREVIL*, the Earldom of *Ponthieu*, Town and Territory of *Calais*, the Earldom of *Guisnes*, and all the Islands adjacent to the Countries above-nam'd.

VII. *Item.* 'TIS agreed that the King of *France* and his eldest Son shall, within a Year after *Michaelmass* next ensuing, transfer to the King of *England* all the *Honours*, *Obediences*, *Homages*, *Allegiances*, *Vassalages*, *Fiefs*, *Services*, *Recognisances*, *Rights*, *mere and mixt Empire*, *high and low Jurisdictions*, *Resorts*, *Safeguards*, *Patronages of Churches*, and all manner of *Lordships* and *Sovereignties*, with all the Rights which they have, or may have had under any Title or Colour of Right vested in them, or the Crown

Edw. III. Crown of *France*, to the Places before-nam'd, and their Dependencies, without reserving any thing for them or their Successors. Also the said King and his eldest Son shall command by their Letters Patent all Prelates, Counts, Viscounts, Barons, Nobles, and Citizens, to obey the King of *England* and his Heirs, and shall discharge them of all Homages, Fealties, Oaths, Obligations, Subjections and Promises made by any of them to the Kings and Crown of *France*.

VIII. THAT all Alienations made within 70 Years past that the Kings of *England* were dispossess'd of those Provinces, shall be repeal'd and abolish'd.

IX. THAT the King of *England* shall have and hold all the Places above-mention'd, which did not belong to his Predecessors, in the same manner as the Kings of *France* have held them hitherto.

X. THAT all Places in the said Countries, which belong'd to the King of *France* on the Day of the Battel of *Poictiers*, shall remain to the King of *England*.

XI. THAT the King of *France* and his eldest Son shall transfer to the King of *England* all manner of Lordship and Sovereignty over the aforesaid Places; and that the Subjects thereof shall be Liegemen to the Kings of *England*, who shall hold the said Countries as Liege-Sovereigns, and as Neighbours to the Realm of *France*, without recognizing any Sovereign, and without being subject to any Recognizance or Service to the Crown of *France*.

XII. THAT the King of *France* and his eldest Son shall expresly renounce the Sovereignty of the said Countries, and that the King of *England* and his eldest Son shall renounce

nounce all things to which the present Treaty doth not give them a Right, especially the Title and Crown of *France*, the Homage and Sovereignty of the Duchies of *Normandy* and *Touraine*, and the Counties of *Anjou* and *Maine*, the Homage of *Bretagne*, and the Earldom of *Flanders*, and in general all other Demands, *&c.* *A.* 1360.

XIII. THAT the King of *England* shall cause the King of *France* to be conducted to *Calais* within three Weeks after *Midsummer-day* next, at the Expence of the said King of *England*, except only the Charges of the King of *France*'s Houshold.

XIV. THAT the King of *France* shall pay the King of *England* three Millions of Crowns of Gold (two of which make a Noble) *viz.* 600000 Crowns, four Months after his Arrival at *Calais*, and afterwards 400000 every Year, till the whole Sum is paid.

XV. THAT as soon as the King of *France* has paid the first 600000 Crowns, and given the Hostages here under-nam'd to the King of *England*, with the Town of *Rochel*, and the Earldom of *Guisnes*, he shall be set at Liberty, on condition that he shall not make War against the King of *England* till the Treaty is fully executed.

The Hostages that are to be deliver'd to the King of England, *as well Prisoners taken at the Battel of* Poictiers, *as others, are,*

Names of the Hostages for K. John.

Lewis Earl of *Anjou* (afterwards Duke.) } *Both Sons to King* John.
John Earl of *Poictiers*, afterwards Duke of *Berry*. }

Philip Duke of *Orleans*, King *John*'s Brother.

 The

Edw. III.

The Duke of *Bourbon*.
The Earl of *Blois*, or his Brother.
The Earl of *Alenſon*, or his Brother.
The Earl of *St. Pol*.
The Earl of *Harcourt*.
The Earl of *Porcien*.
The Earl of *Valentinois*.
The Earl of *Breme*.
The Earl of *Vaudemont*.
The Earl of *Forreſt*.
The Viſcount of *Beaumont*.
The Lord of *Coucy*.
The Lord of *Fienles*.
The Lord of *Preaux*.
The Lord of *St. Venant*.
The Lord of *Garentieres*.
The Dauphin of *Auvergne*.
The Lord of *Hangeſt*.
The Lord of *Montmorency*.
Lord *William* of *Craon*.
Lord *Lewis* of *Harcourt*.
Lord *John de Ligny*.

The Priſoners who are to be Hoſtages, are;

Philip of *France* (who was afterwards Duke of *Burgundy*) King *John*'s Son.
The Earl of *Eu*.
The Earl of *Longueville*.
The Earl of *Ponthieu*.
The Earl of *Tankerville*.
The Earl of *Joigny*.
The Earl of *Sancerre*.
The Earl of *Dammartin*.
The Earl of *Ventadour*.
The Earl of *Salbruck*.
The Earl of *Anceurs*.
The Earl of *Vendoſme*.

The

The Earl of *Craon*. A. 1360.
The Lord of *Derval*.
The Marshal of *Denham*.
The Lord of *Aubigny*.

XVI. THAT the sixteen Prisoners, who are to remain Hostages, shall no longer be deem'd Prisoners, but discharg'd without paying any Ransom, *&c.*

XVII. IF any of the Hostages goes out of *England* without Leave, the King of *France* shall be oblig'd to send another as good, within four Months after the Bailiff of *Amiens*, or the Mayor of *St. Omer*, shall be certify'd thereof by the King of *England:* And when the King of *France* departs from *Calais*, he may carry with him ten of the Hostages, such as the two Kings shall agree upon. And it shall suffice that of the foresaid Number of forty * there remain the full Number of thirty.

XVIII. THAT the King of *France* within three Months after his Departure from *Calais*, shall deliver up as Hostages four of the most considerable Burghers of *Paris*, and two Per-

* THE Reader may observe that the Names of the Hostages, transcrib'd as above from the *Fœdera*, amount to 41. Mr. *Barnes* makes them exactly to answer the Number of 40, by leaving out the Lords of *Prienles*, *Preaux* and *St. Venant*, and by altering *or* after the Names of the Earls of *Blois* and *Alencon* into *and*; in which he corrects all the Copies, whether *French* or *Latin*. Mr. *Barnes* also makes this a distinct Article N° XVIII. contrary to the *Latin* and *French*. Originals in the *Fœdera*, and to *Du Chesne*; his Authorities for it are an *English* Manuscript of Dr. *Spencer*, and a *Latin* one of Dr. *Stillingfleet*.

Edw. III. sons out of each of the Towns following, *viz.*

Paris.	*Troyes.*
St. Omers.	*Chartres.*
Arras.	*Toulouse.*
Amiens.	*Lyons.*
Beauvais.	*Orleans.*
Lisle.	*Champagne.*
Doway.	*Roan.*
Tournay.	*Caen.*
Rheims.	*Tours.*
Chaalons.	*Burges.*

XIX. THAT the King of *France* shall stay four Months at *Calais*, but pay nothing the first Month for his Keeping.

XX. THAT he shall restore the County of *Montfort* to *John* Earl of *Montfort*, upon his performing Liege-homage to him for the same.

XXI. AS to the Dispute arisen about the Succession to the Dutchy of *Bretagne*, the two Kings shall appoint Commissioners to accommodate the Parties, without going to war with one another upon that Account, in case an Accommodation should not take Place.

XXII, XXIII, XXIV, XXV, XXVI. THESE Articles relate to private Persons, or Facts of little Importance.

XXVII. THAT the King of *France*, within a Year after his Departure from *Calais*, shall put the King of *England* in Possession of the Lands yielded to him by the present Treaty.

XXVIII. THAT as soon as the King of *France* has deliver'd up the Lands above-mention'd with the necessary Renunciations, *viz.* *Ponthieu*, *Montfort*, *Saintoigne*, and the Territory of *Angoulesme*, the King of *England* shall put

put him in Possession of all that is possess'd by himself, or his Allies, in *Touraine*, *Anjou*, *Berry*, *Auvergne*, *Burgundy*, *Champagne*, *Normandy*, *Picardy*, and in all other Parts of *France*, *Bretagne* excepted. *A.* 1360.

XXIX. That if any of the Subjects of the Kings of *France* and *England*, on either part, refuse Obedience, they shall compel them respectively at their own Expence.

XXX. That the Clergy shall be subject to that King of the two, under whom they hold their Temporalities: And if they have Temporalities under both Kings, they shall be subject to both.

XXXI. That there shall be a good Alliance and Friendship between the two Kings, notwithstanding any other Alliances they may have, and particularly those with *Scotland* and *Flanders*.

XXXII. That the King of *France* shall give no Assistance to the *Scots* against the King of *England*, nor the King of *England* to the *Flemings* against the King of *France*.

XXXIII. That the Collations to Benefices made on either part during the late War, shall stand good.

XXXIV. That the two Kings shall cause the said Treaty to be confirm'd by the Pope in the strongest manner.

XXXV. That the Subjects of both Kingdoms shall enjoy the Privileges of the Universities of the two Kingdoms.

XXXVI. That the present Treaty shall be confirm'd by the Letters Patent of the two Kings, by their reciprocal Oaths, and also by the Oaths of the Princes of each Royal Family, and by the most considerable Noblemen of each Nation. That they shall reduce the Re-

Edw. III. fractory to Obedience.——That the two Kings ſhall ſubmit to the Cenſures of the *Roman* Church for the Execution of the ſaid Treaty.— That they ſhall renounce all Hoſtilities, and all Acts of Violence in caſe of its non-performance. And that if thro' the Diſobedience of any Perſons diſaffected, any of the Articles of the preſent Treaty cannot be executed, the two Kings ſhall not therefore go to War with one another, but ſhall endeavour to reduce the Rebels to their Duty.

XXXVII. That by the preſent Treaty all others preceding are made null and void..

XXXVIII. That the preſent Treaty ſhall be ſworn to at *Calais* by the two Kings perſonally; and that within one Month after the King ſhall depart from *Calais*, they ſhall reciprocally ſend their Letters Patent confirming the ſaid Treaty.

XXXIX. That neither of the two Kings ſhall procure any Oppoſition or Obſtacle to the Execution of the Treaty from the Court of *Rome*; and that if the Pope goes about it, the two Kings ſhall do their utmoſt to hinder him.

XL. That the two Kings ſhall agree together at *Calais* about the Hoſtages who are to be deliver'd to the King of *England*.

Thus we have given the Subſtance of the famous Treaty of *Bretigny*, which is the principal Act of this ſixth Volume of the *Fœdera*. We proceed now to the other Acts, which are for moſt part depending upon the ſaid Treaty.

Edward's *Return to* England.

1. A Memorandum of *Edward*'s Return to *England. viz. May* the 18th 1360.

King John *conducted to* Calais. *P.* 198.

2. An Order to conduct King *John* to *Calais*; dated *June* the 17th 1360, at *Weſtminſter*. But he did not arrive there till the 8th of *July* following, as appears by his Letter he wrote to the

the Inhabitants of *Rochel*, dated at *Calais* the 18th *ditto*. *A.* 1360.

3. PRIVILEGES granted by *Edward* to *Rochel*; dated *October* the 22d 1360, at *Calais*. *P.* 217.

ALL the time betwixt *John*'s Arrival at *Calais*, and the 24th of *October*, was ſpent in preparing all the neceſſary Acts for confirming the Treaty of *Bretigny*. King *John* not only ratify'd the Treaty in general, but likewiſe made particular Acts for the Ratification of each Article of the Treaty, as well in his own Name, as in that of the Dauphin who was gone to *Boulogne*. All theſe Acts, which were Confirmations, Ratifications, Renunciations, Mandates, &c. being ready, *Edward* repair'd to *Calais*, where the two Kings ſign'd thoſe particular Acts, and ſolemnly ſwore to the Obſervation of the Treaty, on the 24th of *October* 1360. *Treaty of* Bretigny *ratified. P.* 219, &c.

TO all theſe Acts was added one, being an Obligation enter'd into by King *John* and the Dauphin, that on the failure of reſtoring one or two Caſtles on the part of *Edward*, they would nevertheleſs execute the Treaty. *Particular Obligation of K.* John *and the Dauphin. P.* 276.

EDWARD was willing to comply with the King of *France*'s Requeſt, that his Son *Philip*, who was taken at the Battel of *Poictiers*, might be one of the ten Hoſtages that he was to carry along with him from *Calais*. Edward *releaſes King* John*'s Son. P.* 285.

HERE is a particular Obligation which *Edward* enter'd into, with reſpect to his Treatment of the Hoſtages. *His Obligation as to Hoſtages. P.* 283.

AND the Renunciation of all Acts of Violence on the part of both Kings, their Sons, and the greateſt Noblemen of both Kingdoms, in caſe of Non-performance of the Treaty. *All Hoſtilities renounc'd. P.* 269, &c.

ALL theſe Acts, which are moſt of them dated the 24th of *October* 1360, are to be found

Edw. III. from *P.* 217, to *P.* 294, together with the Dauphin's Confirmations; dated from *Boulogne*. The others that follow are,

K. John's *Obligation as to* Burgundy. *P.* 351. 1. KING *John*'s Obligation, whereby he engages to pay the King of *England* what remain'd due to him for *Burgundy*, which was reunited to the Crown by the Death of the Duke of that Name; 'tis dated *February* the 21st 1362, at *Paris*.

Treaty about the Princes of the Flower de Lis. *P.* 396. *P.* 405. 2. A TREATY for the Liberty of the Princes of the *Flower de Lis*, who were Hostages, concluded at *London* in *November* 1362.

3. KING *John*'s Ratification with some Alteration; dated at *Avignon*, *January* the 26th 1363.

4. HIS pure and simple Ratification without Alteration; dated as above, the 13th of *March* following.

Letter to the Prince of Wales. *P.* 430. 5. *EDWARD*'s Letter to the Prince of *Wales*, dated *December* the 6th 1363, at *Windsor-Castle*, wherein he acquaints him that the said Treaty was broke: This was by reason of the Duke of *Anjou*'s Escape.

Passport for John. Ib. 6. A PASSPORT for King *John*, who was coming over to *England*; dated *December* the 10th 1363, at *Westminster*.

Summons of the Hostages. *P.* 452, &c. 7. A SUMMONS to *Charles* King of *France* to give up the Duke of *Anjou*, his Brother, and the other Hostages who had made their Escape; dated *November* the 20th 1364, at *Westminster*.

8. A SUMMONS to the said Hostages, and a Letter from *Edward* upon that Subject to the King and Peers of *France*; both of the same Date with the former.

Notice of their Escape. *P.* 455. 9. INFORMATION given to the Mayor of *St. Omers* of the Escape of the Hostages, pursuant

ſuant to the 17th Article of the Treaty of *Bretigny*; dated as above. *A.* 1364.

WE don't find any Anſwer in the *Fœdera* either to the Summons or Letter.

10. THE Duke of *Orleans*'s Grant of the Lordſhips of *Chiſec*, *Melle*, *Chivray*, *Villeneuve*, and of all that he poſſeſs'd in *Saintoigne* and *Poictou*, to *Thomas* of *Woodſtock*, one of the Sons of King *Edward*; dated at *London*, *December* the 27th 1364. *Grant to* Thomas *of* Woodſtock. *P.* 458.

11. THE full Liberty granted to the Duke of *Orleans*, in Conſideration of the Grant which he had made of his own Accord to Prince *Thomas*; dated *May* the 30th 1365, at *Windſor-Caſtle*. Orleans's *Diſcharge.* *P.* 467.

12. THE Obligation of the Earl of *Harcourt*, to whom *Edward* had given Leave to go to *France* on Condition of returning again by ſuch a time to *England*; dated *July* the 28th 1365, at *Windſor-Caſtle*. Harcourt's *Obligation to return to* England. *P.* 473, &c.

13. SEVERAL Acquittances for the Payment of King *John*'s Ranſom; dated at *Weſtminſter*, *January* the 26th 1366. It muſt be obſerv'd that part of the firſt Million was yet unpaid upon the 10th of *December* 1365, tho' according to the Terms of the Treaty, the three Millions ought to have all been paid before then, except 400000 Crowns. *Acquittances for* K. John's *Ranſom.* *P.* 490, 491.

14. CONVENTIONS for referring the Affair of *Belville* to Arbitration; dated *January* the 20th 1366, at *Paris*. *Affair of* Belville *referr'd.* *P.* 484.

15. AN Obligation by the Duke of *Bourbon* and the Earl of *Alenſon*, to remain Hoſtages till the Diſpute relating to *Belville* is determin'd; dated at *Weſtminſter*, *January* the 22d 1366. *Security upon it.* *P.* 486, 488.

16. A PERMISSION to the Duke of *Bourbon* and the Dauphin of *Auvergne*, to go to *France*, *Duke of* Bourbon, *&c. to go to* France. *P.* 489.

Edw. III. *France*, upon the Security given by the Duke of *Berry* for their Return; dated at *London* as above.

To the Earl of St. Pol. *P.* 494. 17. A FURLOUGH granted to the Earl of *St. Pol*, upon having two of his Sons as Hostages; dated *February* the 21st 1366, at *Westminster*.

Crown Lands in Guyenne. *P.* 494. 18. THE Revocation of the Grant of certain Lands in *Guyenne*, annex'd to the Crown of *England*; dated *May* the 8th 1366, at *Westminster*.

Convention betwixt the Kings of Castile, *&c.* *P.* 514. 19. CONVENTIONS between *Peter* King of *Castile*, *Charles* King of *Navarre*, and *Edward* Prince of *Wales*, whereby *Charles* obliges himself to give this Prince Passage into his Dominions; dated *September* the 23d 1366, at *Libourne*.

Castile's *Grant to the Prince of* Wales. *P.* 521. 20. *PETER*'s Grant to the Prince of *Wales* of certain Lands in *Castile*; dated as above.

Privileges to the English. *P.* 531. 21. A PRIVILEGE granted to the *English* that they shall always have the Vanguard, when they are in the Armies of *Castile*; dated also as above.

Prince of Wales's *Letter.* *P.* 554. 22. A LETTER in *Spanish* from the Prince of *Wales* to the Count *de Trastemare*, two Days before the Battel of *Najara*; dated at *Navaretta* in *Castile*, *April* the 1st 1367.

Answer. *P.* 556. 23. *HENRY*'s Answer, dated next Day from his Palace near *Najara*.

Battel of Najara. *P.* 557. 24. A MEMORANDUM of the Day of the Battel of *Najara*, viz. *April* the 3d 1367.

K. of Castile *to bear the Expence of the War.* *P.* 559. 25. AN Obligation, whereby *Peter* King of *Castile* engages himself to bear all the Expence of the War; dated *May* the 2d 1367, at *Burgos*.

More time granted for Belville, *&c.* *P.* 562. 26. A PROLONGATION of the Term for adjusting the Affair of *Belville*, and of the Furloughs of the Duke of *Berry*, and the Count of

Alenson

Alenſon; dated *May* the 15th 1367, at *Weſtminſter*. *A.* 1367

27. *EDWARD*'s Proclamation againſt his Subjects who ravage *France*; dated *November* the 16th 1367, at *Weſtminſter*. Edward's *Proclamation.* *P.* 577.

28. AN Acquittance for 100000 Crowns, part of the ſecond Million payable for the King's Ranſom; dated *May* the 13th 1367, at *Weſtminſter*. *Acquittances for the King's Ranſom.* *P.* 562.

29. ANOTHER Acquittance for 92000 Crowns, part of the ſecond Million; dated *November* the 18th 1367, at *Weſtminſter*. *P.* 579.

THIS was the laſt Payment made towards the Ranſom; ſo that inſtead of three Millions, *Edward* receiv'd but one Million 192000 Crowns.

30. A SUMMONS to the Earl of *Harcourt* to return to *England*, the Term of his Furlough being a long time expir'd; dated *December* the 1ſt 1367, and *January* the 5th 1368, at *Weſtminſter*. *Summons to the E. of* Harcourt. *P.* 580, 582.

31. A LEAGUE offenſive and defenſive between the King of *France* and *Henry* King of *Caſtile*, whereby the latter engages to aſſiſt the King of *France* againſt the King of *England*; ſign'd *November* the 20th 1368, at the Siege of *Toledo*. *League betwixt* France *and* Caſt. *P.* 598.

THO' *Charles* made Preparations for War, he endeavour'd to make *Edward* believe that he had a Deſign to maintain the Peace. But it appears that *Edward* was jealous of him, becauſe he ſent him back a Preſent, which he had made him of 50 Pipes of Wine, as we find by an Act dated *April* the 26th 1369, at *Weſtminſter*. Edw. *jealous of the* Fr. *King.* *P.* 617.

32. A PROCLAMATION by *Edward* of the ſame Date, to protect the *French* Hoſtages from being inſulted by the *Engliſh*. French *Hoſtages.* Ib.

33. ED-

Edw. III.

Edw. *resumes his Title to* France. P. 621. P. 626.

33. *EDWARD* by the Advice of his Parliament resumes the Title of King of *France*, as appears by a Memorandum of *June* the 3d 1369.

34. His Grant of the Lands in *France* to such as conquer them; dated *June* the 19th 1369, at *Westminster*.

Letter to the Lords of Guyen. P. 643.

35. *EDWARD*'s Letter to the Lords of *Guyenne* upon the Rupture with *France*; dated *December* the 30th 1369, at the Tower of *London*.

Treaty with the D. of Bretagne. P. 699.

36. Treaty of Alliance betwixt *Edward* and the Duke of *Bretagne*; sign'd at *Westminster*, *November* the 4th 1371.

Alliance between France *and* Scotl. P. 696. P. 747.

37. The Alliance betwixt *Charles* V. King of *France*, and *Robert Steuart* King of *Scotland*; sign'd *October* the 28th 1371, at the Castle of *Edinburgh*.

38. A Passport for the Ambassadors of *France*, nominated to treat of a Peace; dated at *London*, *February* the 20th 1372.

39. A Memorandum of the Day of *Edward*'s embarking for *France* to go to the Relief of *Thouars*, viz. *August* the 30th 1372.

Full Power to the Ambassadors. P. 760.

40. A Full Power to the Ambassadors of *England* to treat of a Peace with *France*; dated *January* the 8th 1373, at *Westminster*.

II. *Some Reflections upon the Treaty of* Bretigny, *and the Violation of it by* France, *for the fuller understanding of the Acts contain'd in this Sixth Volume of the* Fœdera.

Remarks on the Treaty of Bretigny, *and the Breach of it.*

Every body that is not well vers'd in the History of *England* would be apt to think, after having run over this Treaty, that *Edward* improv'd his Advantages beyond all Reason, and without any Mercy; for to consider the Treaty

Treaty alone, it appears that he was not content with raviſhing a great number of Provinces from *France*, but that he likewiſe depriv'd her of the Sovereignty of thoſe ſame Countries, without giving her any other Equivalent than a few rambling Places, which he had lately conquer'd in ſeveral Provinces. Yet 'tis certain that this Treaty, far from being unreaſonable, was on the contrary exceeding moderate, whether we conſider the State in which the Fortune of War had plac'd *Edward*, or whether we have regard only to his Rights, and to Juſtice it ſelf. *A.* 1360.

WE have already ſeen what Pretenſions *Edward* had to the Crown of *France*; Pretenſions, which far from being ſo frivolous as the *French* Authors would have it thought, had a very good Foundation, if they are conſider'd on the Foot of Equity, independent on State Policy, and on his Advantages in *France*. Be this as it will, at the time that *Edward* demanded the Conditions ſtipulated by the Treaty, he ſaw himſelf juſt in reach of the Mark which he had all along in view from the very beginning of the War, I mean the Crown of *France*, which he intended to wreſt from that Prince, whom he look'd upon as an Uſurper of his Eſtate; for he had King *John* Priſoner in *England*. The *Scots*, whoſe King was alſo in his hands, were in no manner of Condition to give him the leaſt Uneaſineſs. *France* was in ſuch Confuſion by the Diſcords which prevail'd in the Kingdom, and by the Cabals of the King of *Navarre*, a ſworn Enemy to the Royal Family, that it was not poſſible for the Dauphin to raiſe an Army fit to defend the Kingdom. Moreover, *Edward* was got into the very Heart of *France* with an Army of 100000 Men, which nothing could ſtand before.

Edward's *Circumſtances at the Conclusion of the Treaty.*

Edw. III. before. He had alſo made himſelf Maſter of a great number of Places in *Normandy*, *Touraine*, *Anjou*, *Maine*, *Poictou*, *Auvergne*, *Berry*, *Burgundy*, *Champaigne*, *Picardy*, &c. and had carry'd his Conqueſts into the Iſle of *France* as far as the Gates of *Paris*. What was it then that cou'd incline him to put up with ſo ſmall a part of the Kingdom of *France*, at a time too when he had ſo much reaſon to expect the whole? Certainly it can be aſcrib'd to nothing but his Moderation, and to the Vow which he had enter'd into to make Peace upon equitable Terms. This Moderation of his was the more remarkable, becauſe we ſeldom ſee Conquerors ſtop ſhort on a ſudden, and confine themſelves without Force, or ſome apparent Cauſe, to a ſmall part of their Pretenſions, when they are juſt on the point of ſeeing the Accompliſhment of their Deſigns. Thus much for the Condition that *Edward* was in at the time of the Concluſion of this famous Treaty. We proceed now to his Rights.

Edward's *Rights.* WHEN *Henry* II. one of his Predeceſſors, came to the Crown of *England*, he was in quiet poſſeſſion, by Hereditary Right, of *Normandy*, *Anjou*, *Touraine* and *Maine*; and by his Marriage with *Eleanor* of *Aquitain*, he was in poſſeſſion of *Guyenne* and *Poictou*, and all their Dependencies. This is a Fact which cannot be diſputed. *France*, contenting it ſelf with the Reſervation of the direct Sovereignty of thoſe Provinces, never troubled her ſelf to diſpute the Poſſeſſion of them, either by that Prince, or by his Son *Richard* who ſucceeded him. *John Lackland*, *Richard*'s Brother and Succeſſor, took poſſeſſion of the ſame Provinces, without the leaſt Obſtruction from *Philip Auguſtus*, who then reign'd in *France*, and was ſenſible that he had

no

no other Right to it but that of Sovereignty. *A.*1360. But afterwards *John* being accus'd of having put his Nephew *Arthur* Duke of *Bretagne* to death, upon this bare Accusation, *Philip*, without causing the Witnesses to be heard, and without the necessary Forms of proceeding in an Affair of such Importance, caus'd *John* to be condemn'd, and all the Lands which he held in *France* to be confiscated. It was in pursuance of this Arret pass'd by default of Appearance, that *Philip August* put himself in possession of *Normandy*, *Maine*, and part of *Anjou*, while it was impossible for King *John* to recover what was so taken from him.

HENRY III. *John*'s Son and Successor, a Prince of a very mean Genius, and not qualify'd for War, made an Effort to recover those Provinces; but by so doing he only drew *St. Lewis*'s Arms upon those Parts which yet remain'd in his Possession, so that he robb'd him of the rest of *Anjou*, *Poictou*, and part of *Guyenne*.

WE observ'd in our Account of the second Volume of the *Fœdera*, how *Edward* I. lost *Guyenne* by the Treachery of *Philip the Fair*. 'Tis true, that this Province was at last restor'd to him, but not without leaving a part of it in the Hands of the King of *France*.

EDWARD II. lost the *Agenois* by means of the Affair of *Sardos*, of which mention was made in that Reign. *France* not only took this part of *Guyenne* from him, but also made him pay the Charges of that preposterous War. And afterwards, when she granted him leave to transfer *Guyenne* to his Son *Edward*, she did not consent to the Bargain till she had exacted a Sum of 60000 Livres from him; so ready was *France* to

 take

Edw. III. take all Advantages against *England* that Opportunity presented.

We may see by this short Dissertation, in which there's nothing aggravated, with what Injustice those Provinces, which lawfully belong'd to the Kings of *England*, were seiz'd by *France*, which had no other Right to them than what Power had given them. The Countries we have been speaking of did not come to the Crown of *England* by Conquest, or by Treaties made at the Point of the Sword, but by a lawful Succession from Father to Son time out of mind. As to the Earldom of *Ponthieu*, it devolv'd to *Edward* by the Right of his Mother *Eleanor*; and the King of *France* himself gave him the first Investiture of it, tho' there was some Injustice too in the case, because he demanded of *Edward* that he should in the first place relinquish all his Claim to *Normandy*.

Now let the Treaty of *Bretigny* be examin'd upon that Footing, and it will appear that *Edward* III. by this Treaty only reclaim'd those Provinces which *France* had unjustly torn from his Ancestors, by mere Force of Arms. For all those Countries which *France* yielded to the King of *England*, if we except *Guisnes* and *Calais*, were Dependencies on *Guyenne* and *Poictou*, and had been quietly possess'd by *Edward*'s Ancestors. 'Tis true, that this Prince demanded *Calais*, and the Earldom of *Guisnes*, with the Sovereignty of all the Provinces which *France* deliver'd up to him, into the Bargain; but in requital thereof he left him *Normandy*, *Anjou*, *Touraine*, and *Maine*, with the Homage of *Bretagne*, to which he had as good a Right as to the former, and which, as well as all the rest, was part of the Inheritance of his Ancestors. He likewise yielded him

him all the Conquests which he had made in several Provinces of *France*; and what was more than all, he dropp'd his Pretensions to the Crown. *A.* 1360.

As to King *John*'s Ransom, I know not whether it can be properly call'd an excessive Sum for so great a Prince whom the Fortune of War had cast into the Hands of his Enemy: such Examples are so rare to be met with, that 'tis a difficult matter to ascertain the Ransom of a Captive King, in proportion to the extent of his Dominions, by the Rules of Justice and Equity.

As to the Hostages that *Edward* demanded for his Security, can any one think it strange that he took such Precautions at that Juncture, to oblige the *French* to the Execution of a Treaty which was so much to their Disadvantage? It was plain that those Securities were no more than necessary, because they were not strong enough to guard against the Treachery of *Charles* V. nor against the Baseness of some of the most considerable Hostages, who made no scruple to violate the publick Faith, and even to serve against that very Prince to whom they had engag'd themselves both by Parole of Honour, and by solemn Oaths.

Inquiry into the Breach of the Treaty of Bretigny.

THESE are the Reflections which I thought necessary, in order to give the Reader a just Idea of the Treaty of *Bretigny*; in which one cannot but perceive a Moderation which is not common to Princes flush'd with Victory. We proceed now to take notice of the Breach of this Treaty, and at whose Door it lay. But that we may not be too precipitant in passing judgment upon this matter, 'tis necessary to know first of all what was the State of Affairs between

Edw. III. between *France* and *England* at the time of the said Rupture.

King *John*, whose strict Adherence to his Engagements can be never enough commended, had put *Edward* in possession of all the Countries which he had engag'd to deliver up to him, except the County of *Gavre*, situate in *Armagnac*, and the Territory of *Belville* in *Poictou*, about which there arose some Dispute. As to the first, I know nothing of it; but as to *Belville*, I find in one of the Acts of this Volume of the *Fœdera*, that *Edward* claim'd that some other Lands which depended on the said Fief, should be deliver'd to him, which King *John* did not agree to. As to the Hostages, they had all been deliver'd up except two Burghers of *Tholouse*, Persons not considerable enough to be the subject of any great Contention. Tho' *John* nicely kept his Word in those Articles of the Treaty which related to the Provinces yielded to *England*, he found it impossible for him to be as punctual in the Payments of his Ransom. After the Payment of the first 600000 Crowns before his departure from *Calais*, the rest came in but very slowly; for of the three Millions which, according to Agreement, ought to have been paid at the end of the Year 1366, there was but a Million and about two hundred thousand Crowns paid in 1369, when the War was declar'd. 'Tis very probable that *Edward* was so generous as to admit of the Excuses made to him from time to time, on default of Payment, the rather because he had always Hostages in his hands who were answerable to him for what was due.

Among these Hostages, were five Princes of the Blood of *France*, *viz.* the Dukes of *Orleans*, *Anjou*, *Berry* and *Bourbon*, and the Count of of *Alenson*. There being nothing wanting towards the entire Execution of the Treaty, but the two Lordships of *Gavre* and *Belville*, and the Payment of the rest of the three Millions, *Edward* probably was scrupulous of keeping so many Princes as Hostages for such a Trifle. Therefore, of his own Accord, he propos'd the absolute Release of the four first, and of the Lords of *Brenne*, *Grandpre*, *Montmorency*, *Clare*, *Hengeest* and *Andresel*, the last of whom was of the Number of the Prisoners; with a Proviso that the County of *Gavre* and the Territory of *Belville* shou'd be deliver'd up to him, in the Condition that he demanded them; that *Mesle*, *Chisay*, *Chivray*, *Villeneufve*, and some other Territories in *Poictou* and *Saintonge*, should be pledg'd to him for Security of the Execution; and that if before the Feast of *All-Saints*, he was not put in Possession of *Gavre* and *Belville*, the Lordships so pledg'd to him should be confiscated to his Profit; and the four Princes and the other six Lords, be oblig'd to surrender themselves again as Hostages. The *French* Princes having accepted these Terms, King *John* confirm'd the Treaty on condition that for the Lords of *Grandpre*, *Clare* and *Andresel*, *Edward* would release the Earl of *Alenson*, the Dauphin of *Auvergne*, and the Lord of *Coucy*; but *Edward* refusing to consent to this Exchange, *John* ratified the Agreement as it stood at first. A. 1360.

WHEN the Ratification of the King of *France* was arriv'd, these ten Lords were conducted to *Calais*, and left at full Liberty not only to walk about the Town, but also to go where they pleas'd for three Days, provided they return'd to lie at *Calais* the fourth Night. Probably there arose some Difficulty with respect

Edw. III. to the Territories that were to be given in Pledge, and that this was what detain'd the *French* Lords at *Calais* longer than they expected. However it was, the Duke of *Anjou*, who no doubt was afraid of being oblig'd to return again to *England*, abus'd the Liberty which had been granted him of going out of *Calais*, and never return'd more: And the Counts *de Brenne* and *Grandpre*, and the Lords of *Clare* and *Derval* following his ill Example, escap'd as well as he; after which there was no more talk of the Execution of the Treaty for the Liberty of the others. Soon after King *John* returning to *England*, either to excuse the Duke of *Anjou*, or for some other Reason, dy'd there in the Month of *April* 1364.*

* Mr. *Barnes* says he arriv'd at *Dover* the 4th of *January* 1364, and dy'd the 8th of *April* following at the *Savoy*, then one of the fairest Mansions in *England*, where he was lodg'd with those Hostages, that were of the Royal Blood, and often made and receiv'd Visits to and from the Kings of *England*, *Scotland*, *Denmark* and *Cyprus*. *Stow* tells us in his Survey of *London*, that these five Kings were all feasted at one time, together with the chief Hostages of *France*, K. *Edward*'s Sons, and many of the chief Nobility of *England*, by Sir *Henry Picard* Wine Merchant, who some Years before had been Lord Mayor of *London*. Mr. *Barnes* quotes *Knighton* and *Walsingham* to prove, that King *John* on his Death-bed sent for King *Edward*, and confess'd to him, that from his first coming into *England* he had Confederates in *London*, &c. who secretly collected the finest Gold of the Kingdom, made it into Plates, and put it into Barrels hoop'd with Iron to send to *France*, with Bows and Arrows, and a great quantity of other Arms; and that he had unjustly withheld the Crown of *France* from him, until the Peace of *Bretigny*; for all which he heartily begg'd the King's Pardon, and for which *Edward* entirely forgave him, and caus'd all the Gold and Arms to be seiz'd, and severely punish'd those *Englishmen* who had offended, among whom were many *Lombard* Merchants, who were clapp'd up in the *Tower* till they had compounded as the King pleas'd.

His

HIS Son *Charles* V. ascending the Throne of *France*, the Face of Affairs was changed; and if *Edward* had not blindly believ'd that this Prince was as honest as his Father, he might have easily perceiv'd that he had some ill Design. *Charles* gave him no Satisfaction as to the Escape of the Hostages, tho' he earnestly demanded it, nor as to the two Burghers of *Tholouse*, nor the two other Hostages which he requir'd in the place of the Lords of *Estampes* and *Hengeest*, who had dy'd in *England*. He never troubled himself to pay the rest of King *John*'s Ransom; and if he remitted him any Part, it was but a small matter, and only to amuse him. Four Years run on after this manner in fruitless Negotiations upon the Affair of *Belville*, which was never decided, tho' referr'd to Arbitration; because, in all appearance, *Charles* did not care whether it was or no. *A.* 1360.

ONE cannot help suspecting, that the Hostages who were in *England*, were appriz'd of the Design of the King of *France* to break the Peace, when one finds by the Collection in this Volume that it was chiefly about that time they made the greatest struggle to obtain Furloughs, on various Pretences, or to compound with *Edward* for their entire Liberty.

THE Duke of *Orleans* obtain'd Liberty for himself and the Lord of *Andresel*, by granting some Lands in *Poictou* to *Thomas* of *Woodstock*, *Edward*'s Son.

THE Duke of *Bourbon*, and the Dauphin of *Auvergne*, had leave to go to *France*, upon the Security of the Duke of *Berry*; and their Furlough being prolong'd, the Duke of *Bourbon* made an Agreement with *Edward* for 12000 Crowns, which *Edward* paid to him who took the Duke Prisoner at the Battel of *Poictiers*.

Edw. III. THE Duke of *Berry* having obtain'd a Furlough to go to *Paris*, never return'd.

THE Earl of *St. Pol* obtain'd the same Permission, on leaving his two Sons as Security for his Return.

THE Earl of *Harcourt*, who had a limited Furlough, upon his Parole of Honour, excus'd himself from keeping to his Engagement, tho' *Edward* recall'd him several times.

MONTMORENCY, *Boucherche*, and *Maulevrier* did the same; but 'tis probable they gave the King some Satisfaction afterwards.

CHARLES of *Artois* retir'd without taking Leave.

ENGUERRAND de Coucy, by what means I know not, procured his entire Liberty.

GUY of *Blois*, who had obtained a limited Furlough, never return'd more to *England*, having made his Accommodation while he was abroad.

THE Dauphin of *Auvergne* obtained a Furlough, on Condition of paying 10000 Crowns, in case he did not return by such a time.

THE Earl of *Luxemburg*, the Lords of *Estampes* and *Hengeest*, died in *England*; and *Charles* never sent any other Hostages to supply their Place. Add to these the ten Hostages that *John* carry'd with him from *Calais*, who probably were the chief; and we shall find that at the time of the Breach of the Peace, there were none left of any Consequence in *Edward*'s Hands.

ALL this appears from divers Acts in this Volume: From whence it may easily be conjectur'd, that the King of *France* could not be much disturb'd about those Hostages that still remain'd in *England*; consequently he was no longer concern'd for the Execution of the Treaty, after he had withdrawn his Brothers, and the chief of the Nobility. On the other hand, the Distemper of the Prince of *Wales* growing every day more dangerous, *Charles*, who saw that this Prince was not in a Capacity to do any thing, thought he ought to make his advantage of this Opportunity, while *Edward*, who was in a State of perfect Security, could not imagine that *France* was in a Condition to renew the War. *Charles* being resolved upon it, made several Alliances with the Princes of *Germany*, and particularly with the King of *Castille*, before he discover'd his Design. He obtained great Sums of the Estates of the Realm, who, to be sure, were not ignorant of his Intentions, tho' those Sums were granted upon other Pretences. When his Affairs were almost arrived to the Maturity he wish'd for, he complain'd bitterly of the Ravages committed by the *English* Troops in *France*. We have seen that *Edward* gave him all the Satisfaction possible in the like Case. But as *Charles* was bent upon picking a Quarrel with him, he shew'd that he was not satisfy'd, and pretended that *Edward* actually made War against him. In order to give the more Colour for the Rupture which he intended, he complain'd that the *English* had not evacuated all the Castles that were to be restored to him: But as no Historian has specify'd what those Castles were, there is Reason to believe that his Complaint was trifling. In the mean while happened the Clamour against the Tax the Prince of *Wales* had establish'd in *Guienne*; which Clamour was probably fomented and supported by the King of *France*. Be this as it will, tho *Charles* had no Right to meddle in the Affairs of that Principality, the Sovereignty

A. 1360.

Edw. III. ty of which the King his Father and himſelf too had expreſly renounc'd, he took occaſion from thence to ſummon the Prince of *Wales* before the Court of Peers; and upon his Refuſal to appear, ordered all the Lands which the *Engliſh* held in *France* to be confiſcated.

HAVING thus examin'd the State of Affairs betwixt the two Crowns, nothing now remains but to judge whether *France* had good Reaſon to break the Peace. *Edward* had Subjects of Complaint, which were very real and ſubſtantial. *Gavre* and *Belville* were yet in the hands of the King of *France*. Near two thirds of King *John*'s Ranſom were ſtill unpaid, and the chief Hoſtages were either eſcap'd, or were not return'd according to the Terms of their Furloughs, or had compounded for very ſmall Sums in proportion to the two Millions of Crowns of Gold which remain'd due to him. Mean time *Charles* pretended that the Treaty of *Bretigny* was void, becauſe ſome Caſtles, of which no Hiſtorian has given us the Names, were not reſtor'd; becauſe *Edward* had not hindered his Subjects from ravaging *France*, tho' he had diſowned them; and finally, becauſe the Prince of *Wales* had refus'd to appear as a Vaſſal, tho' it was certain that *France* had renounc'd the Sovereignty of *Guienne*.

FROISSARD ſays, that *Charles* having cauſed the Treaty of *Bretigny* to be examin'd in Council, they dwelt chiefly upon that Article whereby the two Kings renounc'd all Hoſtilities in caſe of Non-performance of the Treaty. He adds, that 'twas upon this Conſideration that *Charles* was adviſed to found his Declaration of War, becauſe it was pretended that *Edward* had not ceaſed to make War againſt *France* ever ſince the Peace of *Bretigny*. It were to be wish'd that this Historian had been a little more explicit, and had shewn upon what Particular the Complaint was founded. If it was upon the Ravages committed by the Prince of *Wales*'s disbanded Troops, it seems that since *France* her self could not get rid of them, it was yet more difficult for the Prince of *Wales*, or the King his Father, to reduce those vagabond Troops to their Obedience, because they were in a foreign Country. *A.* 1360.

MEZERAY, who was very sensible of the Iniquity of this Rupture on the part of *Charles*, passes very slightly over it, and speaks of it in such a manner as demonstrates that Policy had a greater share in it than Equity. This is what he says of it in his Extract of the Year 1369. '*Edward* believed himself absolute Sovereign of '*Guienne* after the Peace of *Bretigny*; but as on 'his part he had not drawn off the Garisons, 'and had moreover committed divers Hostilities, the King pretended the Treaty was null 'and void, and that therefore the said Prince 'still remain'd a Vassal of the Crown. It was 'upon that Foot that he sent a Declaration of 'War to him; and that afterwards in an Assembly of his Parliament on the Eve of Ascension, he then sitting on his Bed of Justice, 'pass'd an Arret, which for those Rebellions, 'Outrages, and Disobediences, confiscated all 'the Lands the *English* held in *France*.' Let the Reader compare the Terms of *Rebellion* and *Disobedience* with the Article of the Treaty of *Bretigny*, wherein both King *John* and his Son *Charles* renounc'd all manner of Sovereignty to the Provinces which they yielded up to *Edward*, and then let him judge whether the Parliament had the least Colour to make use of such Expressions against a Prince, who since the

Edw. III. the last Peace did not possess so much as a single Village in the Kingdom of *France*, for which he was a Vassal to that Crown.

THIS Rupture, which was made so expressly for the Purpose, and which restor'd *France* to her former State, was one of the principal Reasons for assigning the Surname of *Wise* to *Charles* V. But I would fain know what Name would have been given him if the War had miscarry'd, as might have been the Case. Could he be sure of the Consequences? And may it not be said, that if *France* had happened to have been plung'd again in the Abyss from whence she was but just extricated, she would have had none to blame but her King? Fot the rest, though this Prince had very fortunate Success, yet to him, as the first Cause, ought to be ascribed all those Miseries that *France* suffer'd in the Reign of *Charles* VI. his Son and Successor, during which the *English* took a sweet Revenge.

III. *The Affairs of* Scotland.

UNDER this Article there are few remarkable Circumstances. It was observ'd in our Account of the fifth Volume, that by the Treaty which was concluded for the Liberty of King *David*, he had engag'd to pay 90000 Marks *Sterling* for his Ransom. This Treaty, which remain'd without Execution, was renew'd in the Year 1357, but with this Difference, that the King of *Scotland* should be obliged to pay 10000 Marks more. This last Treaty is dated *Oct*. 3. 1357, at *Berwick upon Tweed*.

Ingagements for the King of Scots *Ransom.* P. 46, 56, 59, 61.

A GREAT many Acts follow it, by which the Prelates, the Temporal Lords, and all the good Towns of *Scotland*, engag'd to pay the Ransom of their King.

HERE

A. 1358.

Pope won't consent for the Scots *Clergy to be bound for* David, *P.* 59.

HERE is a remarkable Brief from Pope *Innocent* VI. to the King of *Scotland*, in which he declares that he cannot consent that the Clergy of *Scotland* should be bound for him; 'tis dated at *Villeneufve*, in the Diocese of *Avignon*, the 11th of the Calends of *July* 1358. The other principal Acts relating to *Scotland*, are,

David's *Passport. P.* 363.

1. A PASSPORT for King *David* going into *England*; dated at *Westminster*, *April* the 18th 1362.

Treaty with him, *P.* 375.

2. *EDWARD*'s full Powers to treat of a final Peace with *Scotland*; dated at *London*, *June* the 25th 1362.

Edward's *View to the Crown of* Scotland. *P.* 426.

IT appears by a Memorial dated at *Westminster*, *November* the 27th 1363, that *Edward* try'd to persuade the *Scots* to declare him King *David*'s Successor, in case that Prince dy'd without Children; and that he made them large Promises to bring them into it: but this Project did not succeed.

Truces with Scotland. *P.* 464, 468. *P.* 632.

3. A PROLONGATION of the Truce for four Years; dated at *London*, *May* the 20th, and at *Edinburgh-Castle*, *June* the 12th 1365.

4. ANOTHER Prolongation of the Truce for fourteen Years; dated at *Edinburgh Castle*, *July* the 20th 1369.

David's *Death, and his Successor's Treaty with* Fra. *P.* 696.

DAVID dying in 1371 *, *Robert Stuart* his Successor, who was his Nephew, being Son of his eldest Sister, no sooner got into the Throne but he made an Alliance with *France*, dated *October* the 28th 1371, at *Edinburgh-Castle*.

* THIS discovers a Mistake of Mr. *Barnes* and other Historians, who place his Death in the Year 1370. *Robert*, his Successor, was the first King of the Race of the *Steuarts*; of the Original of which Family Mr. *Barnes* gives the Genealogy, and explodes an old Error of the *Scots* Historians concerning *Robert*'s Children.

Edw. III. THIS is all that is of any great Consequence in this sixth Volume of the *Fœdera*, with respect to *Scotland*.

IV. *Domestic Affairs*.

THIS Article consists only of some loose Acts relating to *England* in particular, or to the Royal Family, of which these are the chief.

Death of Isabel *the Q. Mother. P.* 140.

1. AN Order of King *Edward*, dated at *Sandwich*, *October* the 16th 1359, to pay the Charges of the Anniversary Service for his Mother Queen *Isabel*. It appears that this Princess dy'd in 1358, at the Castle of *Rising*, where she had been confin'd twenty Years before*.

* MR. *Barnes* who says she dy'd the 22d of *August*, was certainly mistaken in the time of her Interment, which he says was on the 27th of *September* following, in the midst of the Choir of the Gray Fryars, now call'd *Christ-Church*; whereas there is an Order in this Volume of the *Fœdera P.* 110. and dated at *Westminster*, *November* the 20th, for cleaning the Streets without *Bishopsgate* and *Aldgate*, against the Arrival of her Corps in *London*. As to her Imprisonment, tho' tedious, Mr. *Barnes* tells us it was easy and respectful; that she had Freedom enough under the Eye of her Keeper, and an Allowance of 4000 *l. per Ann.* that the King paid her a Visit at least once a Year, and gave her many Princely Recreations. As to her Guilt in the Murder of her Husband, our Author is of opinion, that upon her first coming with an armed Force into *England*, she had no Design against the King her Husband, but only against the *Spensers*; but that *Mortimer* and others, who were already obnoxious to the Law on account of their Treason, artfully drove her on so far for their own Security, that she was not able to retire; and that when the King was depos'd, they so terrify'd her with making her believe, that if ever he came to the Crown he would burn her, that she comply'd with the Design for his Destruction.

2. AN

2. An Act for erecting the Dutchy of *Guyenne* into a Principality, in favour of the Prince of *Wales*; dated *July* the 19th 1362, at *Westminster.* *A.* 1362. Guyenne *a Principality.* *P.* 384.

3. An Act of the same Date, by which the new Prince of *Aquitain* engages to pay an Ounce of Gold every Year, as an Acknowledgment to the Crown of *England.* *Acknowledgment for it.* *P.* 388.

4. An Order against idle Sports and Pastimes in use among the common People, and an Injunction to the Sheriffs to make them exercise the Bow; dated *June* the 1st 1363, at *Westminster.* *Order for the exercise of the Bow.* *P.* 417.

5. A Passport for *Waldemar* King of *Denmark* coming to *England*; dated *February* the 1st 1364, at *Westminster.* *K. of* Denmark's *Passport* *P.* 432.

6. Articles of Marriage betwixt the Earl of *Cambridge*, *Edward's* Son, and the Dutchess Dowager of *Burgundy*, Daughter to *Lewis* Earl of *Flanders*; dated *October* the 19th 1364, at *Dover-Castle.* *Marriage of* Edw's *Sons with the Ds. of* Burgundy. *P.* 445.

7. The Marriage Articles betwixt *Lionel* Duke of *Clarence*, *Edward's* second Son, and *Violante* Daughter of *Galeaz* Duke of *Milan*; dated *May* the 15th 1367, at *Westminster.* *And the Duke of* Milan's *Daughter.* *P.* 564.

8. An Order for the Departure of the Duke of *Clarence* for *Milan*, with a Retinue of 457 Men and 1280 Horses; dated at *Westminster*, *May* the 10th 1368. This Prince dy'd in *Italy*, in the Year 1370*. *D. of* Clarence *goes to* Milan. *P.* 590.

9. A Protection for three Clock-makers, coming from *Delft* to exercise their Profession in *England*; dated *May* the 4th 1368, at *Westminster.* *Protection for Clock-makers.* Ibid.

* Mr. *Barnes* says he dy'd not without Suspicion of Poison, upon the 17th of *October*, the same Year that he was marry'd.

V. *Af-*

V. *Affairs relating to Religion or the Popes.*

THE old Differences still subsisted betwixt *England* and the Court of *Rome* about the Collation to Benefices, the foreign and non-resident Clergy, the Benefices of Royal Collation which the Pope usurp'd from time to time, the Temporality of the Bishopricks which the Pope pretended to confer by his Bulls, and the Provisions which he gave to Benefices before they were vacant, whereby he depriv'd Patrons of their Rights. These were the Subjects of the greatest part of the Acts in this Volume, relating to Religion; but as they are the same with those mention'd in the former Months, 'tis needless to insist long upon them here. I shall therefore only take notice of some Acts, which shew that neither the King nor the Pope receding from their Pretensions, those Differences remain'd undetermin'd, each Party taking hold of every fair Opportunity that offer'd to maintain their Rights.

Order against the Bulls. P. 65.

1. AN Order from the King to the Lord Mayor of *London* to imprison all Persons in the City carrying the Pope's Bulls; dated *October* the 10th 1357, at *Westminster*.

Payment of the Procurations. P. 68.

2. AN Order to pay to those Cardinals, who were sent to treat of Peace, the Procurations which were due to them upon the Bishoprick of *Ely*, which was then in the King's Hands; dated *November* the 7th 1357, at *Westminster*.

WHEN the King wanted any Favour from the Court of *Rome*, he caus'd those Procurations to be paid; but at other times he stopp'd Payment.

3. A BULL of *Innocent* VI. whereby he consents to the Execution of the Treaty of Peace concluded at *Bretigny*, tho' it contains Articles prejudicial to the Holy See. The Bull is dated at *Villeneufve*, in the Diocese of *Avignon*, the 2d of the Calends of *July* 1360. This had a special View to the 39th Article of the said Treaty.

A. 1360. *Pope's Bull about the Treaty of* Bretigny. P. 201.

4. A PROHIBITION to carry Money out of the Realm, that is to say, to *Avignon*; and an Order to take up those that carry'd Bulls about the Kingdom; dated *July* the 28th 1365, at *Westminster*.

Prohibition to carry Money out of the Realm. P. 475.

5. AN Attestation by the King, that a Woman committed to Prison for the Murder of her Husband, subsisted in the said Prison 40 Days without eating or drinking; and his Pardon granted to her in acknowledgment of the Miracle; dated at *Westminster*, *April* the 25th 1357.

A Woman lives forty Days in Prison without eating or drinking. P. 13.

6. *EDWARD*'s Present to the Abbey-Church of *Westminster* of the Head of St. *Benedict*, Abbot and Confessor; dated *July* the 5th 1358, at *Westminster*.

Edward's *Present of St.* Benedict's *Head.* P. 93.

7. *EDWARD*'s Attestation that a certain *Hungarian* Gentleman had pass'd a whole Day and Night in St. *Patrick*'s *Purgatory* in *Ireland*; 'tis dated at *Westminster*, *October* the 24th 1358.

St. Patrick's *Purgatory.* P. 107.

8. THE Restitution made to the foreign Priors of their Revenues which were seiz'd at the beginning of the War; dated *February* the 16th 1361, at *Westminster*.

Restitution to the foreign Priors. P. 311.

9. AN Order to the Archbishops of *Armagh* and *Dublin* to agree about carrying of the Cross, and to permit each other to bear it reciprocally in their several Provinces, after the Example of the Archbishops of *Canterbury* and *York*; otherwise

Order to the ABps of Armagh *and* Dubl. P. 467.

Edw.III. wiſe he orders them to come to Court to decide the Difference there: 'tis dated *June* the 9th 1365, at *Weſtminſter*.

Order for impriſoning a Heretic. P. 561.

10. A PERMISSION to the Biſhop of *London* to impriſon a Heretick; dated *March* the 20th 1370, at *Weſtminſter*.

THE

A. 1373.

THE most important Acts of the four last Years of King Edward, *viz. from* 1373, *to his Death, which happen'd in* June 1377, *are inserted in the beginning of the Seventh Volume of the* Fœdera; *the chief which relate to the Affairs of* France, *are,*

1. AN Order for the Embarkment of *John* Duke of *Lancaster*, King of *Castile*, with design to go and make War in *France*; 'tis dated at *Westminster*, *April* the 28th 1373. *D. of* Lancaster *goes to* France. P. 7.

2. THE like Order for the Earl of *Cambridge*, who went over for the same Purpose; 'tis dated at *Westminster*, *November* the 18th 1373. *And the E. of* Cambridge. P. 48.

3. A TRUCE with *France* till *Easter*; dated *February* the 11th 1375. *Truces with* Fran. P. 53.

4. THE Prolongation of the Truce to the 30th of *June* 1376; dated at *Bruges*, *June* the 27th 1375. P. 68.

5. ANOTHER Prolongation of it to the 1st of *April* 1377. 'tis dated at *Bruges*, *March* the 12th 1376. P. 100.

6. A FULL Power to make a Peace with *France*; dated at *Westminster*, *June* the 12th 1376. *Treaty with her.* P. 110.

7. THE like full Power, dated at *Westminster*, *April* the 26th 1377. P. 143.

As to the Articles of Religion, or his Affairs with the Pope, we have only these three Acts.

I. POPE *Gregory*'s Letter to *Edward*, acquainting him of his Intention to go and hold his Court at *Rome*; 'tis dated at *Villeneufve*, in the Diocese of *Avignon*, the 5th of the Nones of *July* 1376. *Pope's Letter to the King.* P. 115.

II. A

Edw.III. II. A Composition of the Differences betwixt the King and the Pope, by which *Edward* engag'd himself to confer no Benefice that was vacant and unprovided, before the 15th of *February*, in the 50th Year of his Reign, but without drawing the same into Consequence for the future; the Instrument is dated at *Westminster*, *February* the 15th 1377, in the 51st Year of his Reign.

Accommodation of their Disputes. *P.* 136.

The Pope enter'd into several Engagements on his part; but he did it in a manner so general, and with so many Restrictions, that it was plain he did not intend to cramp himself by any Engagements of this Nature.

1. He promis'd for the future to be more moderate in his collating to Benefices in *England*.

2. That he would grant a convenient time for Elections, and that he would not fail to admit the Person elected, provided he was fit to serve the Church.

3. That he would give Benefices to those that were in a Capacity to reside on them.

4. As to the Complaint which had been made to him, that a great number of foreign Ecclesiasticks possess'd Benefices in *England*; he answer'd, that he had conferr'd but one to any such Person, except to Cardinals.

5. As to the Representation made to him, that the Cardinals had more Revenues in *England* than in *France*, tho' *France* was three times bigger than *England*; he made answer, that for the future it should be more moderate.

6. That he could not recede from the first Fruits; but that he hop'd to find a way to moderate them.

7. That as to Reversions and Provisions, he would not for the future be so ready to grant them,

them, but without any Restriction of his Power. A. 1374.

III. A FULL Power to treat with the Pope's Nuncios; dated at *London*, *July* 26th 1374, by which it appears that *John Wickliff*, who made such a Noise afterwards, was one of the Ambassadors whom the King sent this Year to the Pope.

J. Wickliff *sent Ambassador to the Pope.* *P.* 41.

The chief Acts in the beginning of this Seventh Volume, relating to Domestic Affairs, in the Remainder of Edward's *Reign, are*,

1. A COMMISSION appointing his Son, *John of Gaunt* Duke of *Lancaster*, and King of *Castile*, to be the King's Lieutenant beyond Sea; 'tis dated at *Westminster*, *June* the 12th 1373.

Commission to John *of* Gaunt. *P.* 13.

2. *EDWARD*'s Grant to *Alice Perreres* of some Jewels, which had belong'd to his deceas'd Queen *Philippa*. This is the only Act we find here that gives any Indication of the Affection which *Edward* conceiv'd for this Lady in his old Age. She is by some Authors call'd *Alice Piercy*, by others *Piers* or *Pierce*; but in this Grant, which is dated at *Woodstock*, *August* the 8th 1373, she is call'd *Perreres*, which probably was her true Name.*

Edward's *Grant to* Alice Perreres. *P.* 28.

3. A

* MR. *Barnes*, who calls her *Alice Perrers*, quotes *Stow*'s Survey of *London*, to prove that she was a Person of such extraordinary Beauty, that about the Year 1374 she was made Lady of the *Sun*, and rode from the *Tower* of *London*, through *Cheapside*, accompanied with many Lords, Knights, and Ladies; every Lady leading a Lord or a Knight by his Horse's Bridle, till they came to *Smithfield*, where presently began a solemn Just or Tournament, which held for seven Days together. But

Edw. III. Edward's Death. P. 151.

3. A MEMORANDUM of the Day of *Edward* the Third's Death, *viz.* *June* the 21st, *A.* D. 1377, and of his Reign the 51st, at his Manor of *Shene* in *Surry**.

But tho' it appears from a Record mention'd by Sir *Robert Cotton*, that this Lady was in such Credit with King *Edward* III. that she sat at his Bed's Head, when others were fain to stand at the Chamber-Door; and that she mov'd those things to him which they of the Privy-Chamber durst not; yet Mr. *Barnes* will by no means allow what is asserted by very many Writers, that she was King *Edward*'s Concubine, because of the Improbability that he who was so chaste in the Flower of his Years, should burn with Lust in the very Impotence of Age; and that so noble a Baron as the Lord *William Windsor* should afterwards take her in Marriage, if she had been thought so lewd at that time as she has been represented since.

* EDWARD *the Third's Character.*

WE cannot well dismiss this great and glorious Reign, without giving a Summary of *Edward*'s Character and Successes, from his Historian Mr. *Barnes*.

HE was a Prince, says Mr. *Barnes*, the soonest a Man, and the longest that held so of any we meet with; his Stature not exceeding the usual Bigness of Men, but of the middle sort, that is, just six Foot high; his Limbs neat and well-made, his Body strong, his Shape exact, his Visage something long, but exceeding comely, graceful, and angelical; his Nose long, strait and manly; his Eyes sparkling and Majestick, but with so much Sweetness, that it was reckon'd a good Omen to behold his Face, tho' only in a Dream. Fortunate he was beyond measure, especially till the six latter Years of his Reign; Wise and provident in Council; well-learned in the Laws, in History, Humanity, in Divinity. He understood *Latin*, *French*, *Spanish*, *Italian*, and high and low *Dutch*, besides his Native Language. He was of quick Apprehension, judicious and skilful in Nature, elegant in Speech; sweet, familiar, and affable in Behaviour; stern to the Obstinate, but calm and meek to the Humble; magnanimous and courageous above all the

Princes

Princes of his Days; apt for War, but a Lover of Peace; never puffed up with Prosperity, nor dismayed at Adversity. He was of an exalted, glorious, and truly royal Spirit, which never entertain'd any thing vulgar or trivial, as may appear by the most excellent Laws which he made, by those two famous Jubilees he kept, and by the most noble Order of the Garter, which he first devised and founded. His Recreations were Hawking, Hunting and Fishing; but chiefly he lov'd the Martial Exercise of Justs and Tournaments. In his Buildings he was curious, splendid and magnificent; in bestowing of Graces and Donations free and frequent; and to the Ingenious and Deserving always kind and liberal; devout to God, bountiful to the Clergy, gracious to his People, merciful to the Poor, true to his Word, loving to his Friends, terrible to his Enemies. And because he was so strictly observant of his Faith and Honour, and withal so valiant, politick and fortunate, his Subjects imagin'd that to live under him was to reign in Triumphs; and his Renown ran abroad even to barbarous and foreign Nations; and all thought themselves happy and secure, if they were either under his Protection, or any way Confederate with him. The *Turks* and *Saracens* fear'd him; the oppress'd Christian Princes humbly implor'd his Assistance; the *Germans* he had at his Command during the time of his Lieutenancy under *Lewis* of *Bavaria*, and might have had them entirely, had he accepted their Proffer of the Empire: The *Flemings* were his Confederates; the *Italians* he oblig'd to him by the Bond of Affinity; the *French*, *Spaniards*, and *Scots* he subdued by force of Arms; he won *Calais*, recover'd *Aquitaine*, *Normandy*, and *Ponthieu*; and took *John* King of *France*, and *David* King of *Scots*, his Prisoners; being the first of *English* Kings that bore the Arms and Title of *France*. In short, he had the most Virtues, and the fewest Vices of any Prince that ever I read of; he was valiant, just, merciful, temperate, and wise; the best King, the best Captain, the best Lawgiver, the best Friend, the best Father, and the best Husband in his Days. And after all this, adds Mr. *Barnes*, his very Enemies will be found to say much more of him.

To this we shall join the Testimony of a Person of Honour, *viz.* Sir *Robert Howard*, in his Comparison of the Reigns of the three first *Edwards* and *Richard* II.

EDWARD III. says Sir *Robert*, by the Virtues and Methods of his Grandfather, restor'd what his Father had lost. He observes, that he came to the Crown, after it had been *shaken* by the *Errors* of his Father: That like *Edward* I. he was a Man *ealier* than others, and *victorious* before others us'd to *attempt* Victory; so that before he *was King*, he shew'd *how fit he was to be so*. That tho' he was able to *judge*, yet he was never unwilling to hear the *Judgment of others*: That he was *deliberate* in *resolving*, and *firm* in his *Resolutions*; unshaken in *Dangers*, and steddy and equal in *Safety*: That his *Promises* were *Mankind's Security*, and *Truth* his *Wisdom*: That his great *Virtues* and *Courage* made the Nation expect *Success* from all his *Actions*: That he grew *fierce* by *Opposition*, and *gentle* by *Submission*: That he seldom deny'd *Pardon* to those who implor'd it, nor suffered any *abused Mercy* to pass unrevenged: That he was mighty enough to conquer Enemies, and powerful enough to forgive those he conquer'd: That he was equally *victorious* both to *himself* and *others*; and that those who *submitted* to him prov'd always more fortunate than those who *resisted*: That in his greatest *Hazards* he requir'd none to attempt more than he did in his *own Person*; and in the greatest *Prosperity* and *Safety* prescrib'd no more *Virtue* and *Temperance* than he gave *Examples* for: That he knew how to *gain Power*, and how to *use it*: That he who might have the *easiest* attempted to *break* Laws, made the *best*: That he knew how to *gain*, and how to *preserve* the Love and Confidence he rais'd in his Subjects Hearts, by requiting the *first*, and never abusing the *last*: That his great *Taxes* and *Supplies*, however large they might appear in *themselves*, would not seem so vast when compar'd with his *Victories*, the Conquest of *Wales*, *Scotland* and *France* being not such *light Victories* to be obtain'd with *small Assistance*; and that what the Nation gave him was *justly bestow'd* for what it was given, and *faithfully laid out* for their Honour and Interest: That he not only return'd *Security* and *Benefit* for his Subjects *Gifts*, by *Conquests* abroad, but by *excellent Laws* at home: That what *Edward* I. began well, *Edward* III. gave Perfection to: That this brave Prince was not more *just* in making *good Laws*, than *severe* in the *due Execution* of them; and never shew'd so much Severity as against those that abused the *Trust of Justice*; as if he had been more offended at the *Enemies of Mankind*, than at *his own*: That he mingled his *own Interests* with his *Subjects*, and never refus'd to *bear the Wrongs* of those that assisted him

him to *revenge his Injuries on others*: That both *Edward* I. and *Edward* III. were *equally valiant*, and *equally successful*; and both died uncheck'd by Fortune, only *Edward* I. *died himself*, and *Edward* III. *outliv'd himself*. But the Death of his *Glorious Son*, the *Black Prince*, join'd with the weight of *Old Age*, might justly make that *Sun* set *clouded*.

FROISSARD says that when *Charles* of *France* heard of the Death of his Enemy King *Edward*, he gave this Testimony of him, *viz*. *That he had reign'd most nobly and valiantly, and well deserv'd to be added to the Number of the ancient Worthies*. And soon after he assembled all the Nobles and Prelates of his Realm, and with them solemnly perform'd his Obsequies. We shall shut up his Character with the *Latin* Epitaph on his Tomb in *Westminster-Abbey*, according to the Rhyme of those Days.

Hic Decus Anglorum, Flos Regum Preteritorum,
Forma Futurorum, Rex Clemens, Pax Populorum
Tertius Edvardus, Regni complens Jubilæum,
Invictus Pardus, Bellis pollens Machabeum.
Prospere dum vixit, Regnum Pietate revixit:
Armipotens Rexit: Jam Cælo (Cælice Rex) sit!

Tertius Edwardus *Fama super æthera Notus.*
PUGNA PRO PATRIA.
M.CCC.LXXVII.

THE Institution of the most noble Order of the Garter, being universally allow'd to be one of the Glories of this Reign, deserves to be mention'd before we pass to the next. However uncertain the Original or Foundation of it may appear, from the various Accounts given of it by Mr. *Ashmole* and other learned Antiquaries, which we shall not undertake to reconcile in this Place, 'tis certain that it was instituted by King *Edward* III. in the Year 1349, and as Mr. *Ashmole* says, on the 23d of *April*, the Anniversary of St. *George*, call'd the Patron of *England*, and of this Order in particular. As to the common Opinion that it was inſtituted by this King in Memory of his taking up the Counteſs of *Salisbury*'s Garter, which dropp'd off her Leg at a Ball; and that the Motto *Honi ſoit qui mal y penſe*, was taken from the Anſwer he made to that Lady, when ſhe was ſurpriz'd to ſee him ſtoop down to her Feet: Mr. *Rapin* and the beſt Hiſtorians decry it, and reckon it a Diſhonour to an Order which has ſhone throughout ſo many Ages with ſuch Splendor, to aſcribe its Original to an Act of ſo much Levity. To omit the mention of other Opinions, which ſtand unſupported by any ſufficient Proofs, this is indiſputably true, that King *Edward*'s main Deſign was to engage all that had then or were hereafter to have the honour of being admitted into that Society, to diſtinguiſh themſelves by their Courage and Virtue: That no Order of the like Nature has ſo nicely obſerv'd the Rules of its Inſtitution: That it is more ancient than even thoſe of the *Golden Fleece* or the *Holy Ghoſt*: That it has always kept up its old number of Companions, which is twenty ſix, including the Sovereign of the Order, who is always the King or Queen of *England*. And the foreign Kings and Emperors to the Number of near forty, as well as many other Sovereign Princes, who have been admitted into this illuſtrious Order, ſhew the Eſteem that all *Europe* has had for it.

BISHOP *Nicholſon*, who makes the Improvement of the Regulation of the Coin another of the Glories of this Reign, takes Notice of King *Edward*'s Groats, coin'd after he took the Title of *France*, bearing his Head crown'd and inſcrib'd *Edward. D. Gra. Rex: Angl. & Franc. D. Hyb* and on the reverſe *Poſui Deum Adjutorem meum*, (a Motto continued by all his Succeſſors down to the Union of the two King-

Kingdoms) and the Biſhop infers by the numbers of them daily diſcover'd, eſpecially on the Frontiers of both Kingdoms, that they were miſtaken who obſerv'd, that his Victories and Expeditions in *France*, *&c.* drain'd almoſt all the Money out of the Kingdom. The Biſhop gives the Form of one of his Grants to the Abbot and Monks of *Reading* for the Coining of Halfpence and Farthings, and ſmall Pieces of *Sterling* Money; from whence he conjectures, that the Abbots, or other great Men in thoſe Days, were only permitted to coin ſmall Pieces, uſeful in Exchange, as our Kings this Day grant Patents for Copper Halfpence and Farthings; and that the Sovereign reſerv'd the ſole Power of coining the larger Money to himſelf by his own immediate Officers.

Rich. III.

WE now enter the Reign of Richard II.

'WHICH, says Mr. *Rymer* in his Dedi-
'cation of the Seventh Volume of the
'*Fœdera* to Queen *Anne*, affords but little Mat-
'ter that may shine in History, and cannot
'boast of any one great and distinguish'd Cap-
'tain, any one memorable Battel, nor one im-
'portant Siege; no Proceeding to St. *Paul's*,
'no *Te Deum* for Victory.

'BEYOND the *Pyreneans*, *John* Duke of
'*Lancaster*, without fighting, made a Compo-
'sition with his Adversary, and took an Equi-
'valent for the Crown of *Spain*.

'BEYOND the *Alps*, Sir *John Hawkwood*
'gave Law to the *Italian* Princes, and taught
'them the Mystery of commanding Armies.

'BUT on this side the Mountains continued
'a wavering, hazy, undetermin'd Face of
'Things, neither Peace nor War.

'PROROGATIONS of Truces, Abstinen-
'ces, Sufferances, Patiences, Tolerances were
'the Language and the Amusement of the
'Times; and all the while were kept on Foot
'Treaties for a *Perpetual Peace:*

'TREATIES hitherto fruitless, illusory and
'unpracticable.

RICHARD II. (says Mr. *Rapin*) Son to the famous Prince of *Wales*, succeeded his Grandfather King *Edward* III. *June* the 21st 1377, when he was but eleven Years of Age, and reign'd to the end of *September* 1399.

THIS Seventh Volume of the *Fædera*, and a small part of the Eighth, contain the Acts which relate to the Events that happen'd in the Reign of this Prince. Of all the Volumes I have

have run thro', this ſeems to me to have the fewest Pieces in it, which are capable of illuſtrating any part of the Hiſtory of that Time. There's but a ſmall Number of thoſe which regard the principal Events; whereas on the contrary, there's a Multitude relating to Matters of an independent Nature, of which I could not poſſibly make an Abridgment without running into too great a Length. I ſhall confine my ſelf therefore to the ſix chief Articles, which concern *France*, *Great Britain*, *Scotland*, *Caſtile*, Domeſtic Affairs, and the Church; there being few remarkable Events in the whole courſe of this Reign, but what are contain'd under one or other of thoſe Articles. *A.* 1377.

I. *The Affairs of* France.

THE Truce which *Edward* III. had made with *France* expir'd in *April* 1377, near three Months before his Death, at a time when the *Engliſh* had not made the leaſt Preparation to renew the War; whereas on the contrary, *France* was eager to improve the Opportunity of the Weakneſs of a dying Enemy, and of a Minority, which in all Probability would be attended with Conſequences fatal to *England*. However, *Charles* V. did not renew the Hoſtilities till towards the end of *June*, five or ſix Days after *Edward*'s Death. Then it was that the *French* made a Deſcent upon *England* and the Iſle of *Wight*, and committed great Ravages, becauſe of the little Oppoſition they met with from the *Engliſh*.

French *invade* England.

NEXT Year (1378) the King of *Navarre*, who had great Domains in *Normandy*, deliver'd up *Cherbourg* to the *Engliſh*; but tho' this Acquiſition gave them as fair an Inlet into *Normandy*, as

Cherbourg *deliver'd to the* Engliſh.

Rich. II. as they had before in *Picardy*, by the means of *Calais*, yet they made no Advantage of it.

In 1380, they made an Effort to support the Duke of *Bretagne*, but they fail'd of the Success which they expected.

Death of Charles V. *and Accession of* Charles VI.

CHARLES V. dying in that Year, and *Charles* VI. his Successor, being a Minor when he ascended the Throne, the War was carry'd on but faintly on the part of *France*, and more weakly still on the side of *England*, which was but in an indifferent Plight.

Another Descent, and a Truce.

In 1383, the *French* made another Descent upon *England*; but not long after, the two Crowns concluded a Truce of ten Months, which was next Year prolong'd for a short Space.

Design of France *against* England.

The said Truce expiring in 1385, the King of *France* sent a powerful Reinforcement to the King of *Scotland*, to make a Diversion in the Northern Counties of *England*, while he was preparing a Fleet to ravage the Southern Coasts. The Court of *England* was so alarm'd at the Preparations of *France*, that they assembled all the Militia of the Kingdom, and muster'd an Army of 300000 Men; which Precaution so terrify'd the *French*, that they dropp'd their Projects, and left the *Scots* alone to bear the whole Expence of the War.

In 1386 the Duke of *Lancaster*, *Richard*'s Uncle, having carry'd an Army of 20000 Men into *Castile*, *France* resolv'd to lay hold of that Opportunity to conquer *England*, and for that end prepar'd an Army of 60000 Men, and a Fleet of 900 Ships. But 'tis pretended that the Duke of *Berry*, who was Uncle to *Charles* VI. baulk'd the Expedition by an affected Delay. However that was, those Troops were not embark'd, the Transports design'd to carry them were

were ſcatter'd by a Tempeſt, and ſome of them actually taken by the *Engliſh*. *A.* 1391.

THE great Expence laid out upon this Armament was ſuch, that the King of *France* was not able to do much afterwards. *Richard* on his part was, equally unable to proſecute the War. Conſequently in 1389 the two Kings concluded a Truce for three Years, which in 1391 was prolong'd for another Year. *Truce.*

RICHARD's Diſinclination to Arms, and the exceſſive Charge he was at in other Reſpects, to no purpoſe, hinder'd him from thinking ſeriouſly on a War. On the other hand, *Charles* VI. being ſeiz'd in 1392. with a Diſtemper which very often depriv'd him of the Uſe of Reaſon, the Court of *France* fell into ſo many Diviſions, that inſtead of putting themſelves in a Poſture, to make an advantage of the Enemy's Supineneſs, they only aim'd at each other's Ruin; which was the reaſon that nothing conſiderable happen'd from the time the Hoſtilities were renew'd, till the Year 1395. that the two Crowns agreed upon a Truce for 28 Years, which was ſeal'd by the Marriage of *Richard* with *Iſabel*, *Charles* VI's Daughter. *Another* Richard's *Marriage.*

IT may eaſily be ſuppos'd that there are not very many important Pieces upon this Article, in the Volume before us: all that we find in it being only Orders to guard the Coaſts, Paſſports for Ambaſſadors, and Treaties of Truce, which were often renew'd.

THE following is a Letter which the Lord of *Coucy*, Son-in-law to *Edward* III. wrote to *Richard*, when he ſent him back the Order of the *Garter*; whereby we may gueſs at their manner of Writing in thoſe Days. *L. of* Coucy *ſends back the Order of the Garter.* *P.* 172.

TRES-

Rich. II.

TRESHONNOURE ET TRESPOISSANT SEIGNEUR,

VOSTRE Noble & Grant Seignourie scet & congnoit assez l'Alliance, que de la Grace & Bonte de Trespoissant & bon Roy, mon Treshonnour & Tresredoubte Seigneur & Pere, le Roy, derrainement Trespasse (que Dieux face Merci) a pleu que j'ai en aly & au encore avec vous: dont Treshonnoure Seigneur je vous Mercie tant comme je puis & scai.

OR est il avenu que la Guerre est entre le Roy de France, mon naturel & Souverain Seigneur, d'une part, & vous d'autre.

DONT il me desplait plus que de chose qui puist estre en ce Monde, se Admender le peusse.

ET m'a Commande & Requis que je le serve & acquitte mon devoir, comme je y sui tenus, au quel comme vous savez bien, je ne doy desobeir, si le servirai a mon poir, comme je le doy faire.

ET pour ce, Treshonnoure & Trespoissant Seigneur, que on ne puist, en aucune maniere, Parler ne Dire chose qui fust contre moy ne mon Honneur, vous fais assavoir les Choses dessusdites, & vous Renvoie tout ce que je pourie tenir de vous en Foy & Hommage.

ET aussi, Treshonnoure Seigneur, mon Tresredoubte Seigneur & Pere dessusdit vuolt moy ordonner & mettre en la tresnoble Compaignier & Ordre du Jartier; si plaise vestre tresnoble & poissant Seigneurie de pourveoir, en lieu de moy, tel ou ainsi que il vous plaira, & moy tenir pour excuse en ce.

CAR, Treshonnoure Seigneur, se en autre maniere vous ne voliez aucune chose commander, je le feroie de tout mon pooir.

TRES-

TRESHONNOURE ET TRESPOISSANT SEIGNEUR, je prie a Messire qu'il vous dont bonne Vie & longue. *A.* 1377.

Escript le 26 Jour d'Aoust, 1377.

i. e. Most Honoured and most Potent Lord,

YOUR Majesty very well knows the Alliance which by the Grace and Goodness of the most potent and good King, my most honoured and most dread Lord and Father, the King lately deceas'd (on whose Soul may God have Mercy) was pleas'd that I should make with him, and also with you; for which, most honoured Lord, I thank you with all my Heart.

IT happens now that there is a War betwixt the King of *France*, my natural and sovereign Lord, on the one part, and you on the other; which gives me more Uneasiness than any one thing in the World.

FOR I am both commanded and requir'd to serve him, and to discharge my Duty as I am bound to him, whom you well know I ought not to disobey, but to serve to the utmost of my Power.

AND most honoured and most potent Lord, that nothing whatsoever may be said by way of Reflection against me or my Honour, I advertise you hereof, and renounce whatsoever Fidelity and Homage I owe to you.

AND, most honoured Lord, whereas my most dread Lord and Father, above-mention'd, was pleas'd to associate me with the most noble Companions of the Order of the Garter, may your most noble and potent Lordship be pleas'd to provide one that you shall think fit in my place, and to excuse me.

FOR,

Rich. II. FOR, most honoured Lord, you may command me in any thing else whatsoever, and I will do it with all my Might.

MOST honoured and most potent Lord, I pray God grant you a long and happy Life.

Written the 26th Day of *August* 1377.

Richard's *Letter to the D. of* Lancaster. *P.* 407.

THERE is a Letter from *Richard* II. to his Uncle the Duke of *Lancaster*, impowering him, if he thinks fit, to propose to the King of *France*, in his Name, to put an end to their Dispute, by single Combat betwixt them two alone, or each seconded by his three Uncles, or else by a general Battel. The Letter is dated at *Westminster*, *September* the 8th 1383.

RICHARD was then 17 Years of Age, and *Charles* but 15; consequently there was no likelihood that the Challenge would be accepted, or that the Duke of *Lancaster*, whom the King left to his Liberty to propose it or not, would engage him in such a Duel.

Truces with Fran. *P.* 622.

THERE follow'd a Treaty of Truce, concluded at *Lenlingham*, between *Ardres* and *Calais*, from *June* the 18th 1389, to *October* 1392. And,

P. 820.

ANOTHER for 28 Years, from *September* the 29th 1398, to the same Day in 1426.

II. *Affairs of* Bretagne.

D. of Bretagne *banish'd, but recall'd.*

THE Duke of *Bretagne* had always espous'd the Interests of his Father-in-law, King *Edward* III. which was enough to incense the King of *France* against him, who, by the Connivance of the Lords of *Bretagne*, turn'd him out of his Dominions, and compell'd him to take refuge in *Flanders*. The Duke of *Lancaster* willing

willing to try if he could restore him, went and laid siege to *St. Malo*, but was oblig'd to raise it. *Charles* V. being yet more enrag'd against him after this Enterprise, caus'd him to be summon'd before the Court of Peers; and for his non-appearance got an Arret pass'd for re-uniting *Bretagne* to the Crown of *France*. Then the *Bretons* perceiving that he was for making that Duchy his own, recall'd their Duke, who to support himself made a Treaty with the *English*, by which he gave them *Brest*. In pursuance of this Treaty, the Earl of *Buckingham*, *Richard*'s Uncle, was sent into *Bretagne* with an Army of 8000 Men, whom he put ashore at *Calais*, in order to march by Land. While he was upon the Road, King *Charles* V. dy'd, leaving his Successor at no more than 12 Years of Age. This seeming a favourable Conjuncture for the Duke of *Bretagne*, he made a separate Peace with *France*, and sent home his Forces. The *English* nevertheless kept *Brest* till 1397. that *Richard* restor'd it to the Duke for a small Sum of Money.

A. 1378. *Siege of* St. Malo. Brest *given to the* Eng. *E. of* Buckingham *lands in* France. *Death of* Charles V. *Peace with* France. Brest *restor'd.*

Of the numerous Acts which relate to *Bretagne*, the two of most importance are,

1. A Treaty by which the Duke of *Bretagne* engages to give *Brest* to the *English*, on condition that the said Place be restor'd to him, when the War is made an end of, either by a Peace or by a long Truce: 'tis dated at *Westminster*, *April* the 5th 1378.

Treaty about it. *P.* 190.

2. A Treaty of Alliance, offensive and defensive, betwixt the King of *England* and the Duke of *Bretagne*, by which the two Princes engage to make neither Peace nor Truce without each other's consent; dated at *Westminster*, *March* the 1st 1380.

Betwixt Richard *and the D. of* Bretag. *P.* 236.

Rich. II. THIS Treaty was broke in a few Months after by the Duke.

HERE are many other Acts in this Seventh Volume of the *Fœdera*, relating to the Earl of *Buckingham*'s Expedition, and to the Town of *Brest*.

III. *Affairs of* Scotland.

K. of Scotland *takes* Roxburgh

THE Truce which *Edward* III. had made with *Scotland* was to continue till the Year 1384. but it was ill observ'd by both Nations, who reproach'd each other for breaking it. This was a fair Pretext for *Robert Steuart*, King of *Scotland*, who as soon as *Edward* III. was dead, surpriz'd and took *Roxburgh*.

And Berwick.

IN 1378, he also seiz'd the Castle of *Berwick*, which was presently retaken by the Earl of *Northumberland*.

Negotiations for a Truce with Scotland.

IN 1380, the Duke of *Lancaster*, who had got the *English* Council to pass a Resolution for sending Succours to the King of *Portugal* against *Castile*, thought it necessary, before those Troops were sent away, to confirm the Truce with *Scotland*. For this end he went himself to the Frontiers, but he met with vast Difficulties in the Negotiation of that Affair. The *Scots* asserted that the *English* were the first that broke the Truce; and that if they had a mind to renew it, they must come to new Terms: but to this the *English* would not consent, and only demanded a Confirmation of the Truce. Till this Difference could be made up, the Duke of *Lancaster* obtain'd an Engagement, that instead of confirming the Truce, reciprocal Securities should be given on both sides, that no Hostilities should be committed for three Years. It was very happy for *England* that this Affair was determin'd determin'd before they had the News in *Scotland* of the Insurrection in *Kent*, of which by and by. *A.* 1383.

IN 1383, *Robert* made an Incursion into the North parts of *England*, while the *French* ravag'd the Southern Coasts. But not long after *France* and *England* agreed upon a Truce, in which room was left for the King of *Scotland*, in case he had a mind to come into it. Mean time he delay'd so long to return an Answer, that the Duke of *Lancaster* enter'd *Scotland*; and *Robert* finding himself no longer supported by the *French*, he desir'd to be included in the Truce, which was granted.

Truce concluded with France.

And with Scotland.

IN 1385, while the King of *France* was preparing to conquer *England*, the King of *Scotland* made a second Incursion into the Northern Frontiers; and *France* miscarrying in her Design, as has been already observ'd, *Richard* march'd himself into *Scotland*, and ravag'd the Neighbourhood of *Edinburgh*. If he had been wise enough to have improv'd his Advantages, he might have conquer'd that Kingdom; but being soon weary of the War, he retir'd, leaving his Work imperfect.

Scots *and* English *invade each other.*

AFTER that time the *Scots* were included in all the Truces which were made betwixt *France* and *England*.

THERE's a great number of Acts in this Volume relating to *Scotland*, some of which may be of use to such as write the History of that part of *Great Britain*, especially on account of the Dates; but I have not met with any remarkable enough to be particularly insisted on in this Abridgment.

AMONG those Acts there are some in *English*, as they then wrote and pronounc'd it in *Scotland*.

Rich. II. [THO' Mr. *Rapin*, who wrote his Abridgment abroad, and design'd it chiefly for the use of Foreigners, did not think it necessary to insert any Example of this kind, the Translator has thought fit to exhibit one of these Acts in this Place, as supposing there are some modern Readers on both sides the *Tweed*, to whom an Act that contains so many obsolete *English* Terms, and such strange Spelling, will be at least entertaining, if not useful.

'TIS call'd *Indentura super Prorogatione Treugarum Scotiæ*, and runs thus.]

YIS ENDENTURE,

'MADE at the Water of *Eske*, beside *Salom* 'the xv Day of *March*, the Zher of our Lord 'M.CCC.XX. and IV. betwix noble Lards 'and meghty Seignuris, *Henry Percy* Earl of '*Northumbre* of the Ta part, and *Archibald* 'of *Douglas*, Lord of *Galway*, on the Toyir 'parte,

CONTEYNS AND BERREZ UITNES.

'THAT Day of Radress sal be halden be- 'twix yam in proper Persons, at the place be- 'for saide, the xix Day of *Auerill* next, for to 'do and take full Radresse, and Execution of 'all thinges done betwix yair Boundes apart 'the *Westmarchie*, begynande the xiv Day of '*Octobre* to *Candlemasse* Day last passyt.

'AND yan it fell in Speech betwix the for- 'said Lordes, that, in entent of common Pro- 'fit of bathe Reaumes, gif hit meght happen 'of langer Trewe, or els of Pees, gif God 'vald vouche sauf, and als for the Tyme is to 'schort to mak full Redrass beforsaid, the for- 'said Lordes *ARE ACCORDIT*, in spe- 'cialte, as after followes; that is for to say,

'THE Earl of *Northumbre* for him, and for 'the Lord *Nevill*, and the Lord of the *Galleway* for the Earl of *Douglas* and for hymself, yat speciall Trewe and Assurance sall betwix thaim and yair Boundes, betwix this and 'the first Day of *July* next, for to com, Contenant and Havenand the force and effecte, in all Poynts, as the nixt Trewe gangand 'before. A. 1360.

'*ALSO IT IS ACCORDIT*, that durant the tyme beforsayde, nane of the Lords 'beforsayde, ne nane of yair Boundes, sal do 'skate to ya of the Boundes of the tothir Partie; 'but ya sall ger it be redresset, als Lawe of '*Marchevill*, entrechaungeably.

'AND gif it happens that any gretter, auir 'of the ta Reame, or of the toyir, schapes 'for to ride white oste ilkham of the Lordes 'beforsayd, enterchangeably, sall set let yaie 'in, at yair Powair: and in cas yay may noght 'let it, yai sall ger warne ye toyer part of xv 'Dayes, and yai sall nought be at that Rydying, bot yay sall lely let yaim of yair 'Boundes at yair Powair, for owten fraude or 'gile.

'*AND ALSO IT IS ACCORDIT*, 'that this Condicion of special Treuwe and 'Assurance, sall stande and be kep hit fullely 'by sealls vell as for yair Bondes by Lande, as 'the Trewes beforsaid askys.

'*AND ALSO HIT IS ACCORDIT*, 'that gif yie specialx Trewes likes to the Erle 'of the *Marche*, to be comprysset whitein yaime 'that yai sall stand furght for hym and his 'Boundes, and he sall stand for hym and his 'Boundes, under the samen Condicion, anentys yaim and yair Boundes.

Rich. II. 'AND gif yir Covenantz beforsayd likis or 'misslikes to the forsayd Erle of *Northumbre*, or 'to the Lord *Nevill*, yay sal certify be yair Lettres, or be on of yairs, opon *Blakmonday*, 'that next comis, before none, at the Chapell 'of *Salon* be ye Water of *Eske*.

'AND in the samen manere, gif hit likis 'or misslikis to the Erle of *Douglas*, or to the 'Lord of *Galleway*, yay, or ane of yaim, sall 'certifie, be Lettre at the Place, Day, and 'Oure beforsayd. And in cace gyf yai certifie, that this specialtie stand, yat Day, yat 'chuld be halden ye xix of *Averill*, chald be 'chort to the xv Day of *May* next to come, to 'be halden in all force and effecte as the xix 'Day of *Averil*: and the Day on the *Este marche* 'sall be delayied, in the samen maner, as it is 'endendit to be halden the xxix Day of *May*.

'*AND ALSO IT IS ACCORDIT*, 'that all Prisoners, taken on boye the sidis, 'sall be frely deliverid, and all yair Borons 'freth it.

'*ALSO IT IS ACCORDIT*, gif ony 'stellis aceyr on the ta part, or on the toyer, 'yat he chall be henget or hefdhit.

'AND gif any Compane stellis any Gudes 'within the Trieux beforsayd, ane of that 'Company sall be hengit or hensdit; and the 'remenant sall restore the Gudys stollen in the 'Double.

'*IN THE WITNES* of wische thinges, 'leley to be halden and fulfyllyt, the forsayd 'Erle of *Northumbre*, and the Lord of *Galleway*, has set yair Signetz, enterchangeably, in 'absens of yair Selles, Day and the Yer beforsayd.

IV. *Af-*

IV. *Affairs of* Castile.

IT was obſerv'd in our Account of the Sixth Volume of the *Fœdera*, that *Peter*, ſurnam'd the *Cruel*, King of *Caſtile*, had been reſtor'd to his Kingdom by the Prince of *Wales*, who afterwards left him in Diſguſt. When he was gone, *Peter* was again attack'd by his Baſtard Brother *Henry*, who routed him, and kill'd him with his own Hands, in the Tent of *Du Gueſclin* the *French* General, where they happen'd to meet. After the Defeat and Death of *Peter*, *Henry* was recogniz'd King of *Caſtile*.

King of Caſtile *kill'd in Battel.*

PETER had left two Daughters, *Conſtantia* and *Catherine*, who retir'd to *Bayonne*, where, notwithſtanding their Father's Ingratitude, the Prince of *Wales* was pleas'd to give them ſhelter. And when that Prince quitted *Guyenne* upon account of his Illneſs, he left his Brothers there, *viz.* the Duke of *Lancaſter* and the Earl of *Cambridge*, who ſoon after married both thoſe *Caſtilian* Princeſſes. The Duke of *Lancaſter*, who had the eldeſt to his ſhare, immediately aſſuming the Title of King of *Caſtile*, it occaſion'd the Baſtard *Henry*'s cloſe Union with *France*; and from that time there was always open War betwixt *England* and *Caſtile*.

Marriage of his Daughters.

DURING the Reign of *Richard* a Rupture, which happen'd betwixt *Ferdinand* King of *Portugal*, and the King of *Caſtile*, oblig'd *Ferdinand* to apply to *England* for Aſſiſtance; and on that condition he offer'd his only Daughter *Beatrix* in Marriage with the eldeſt Son of the Earl of *Cambridge*, and to have him declar'd his Preſumptive Heir. This Offer being accepted, the Earl of *Cambridge* was ſent with an Army into *Portugal*: But *Ferdinand* having obtain'd all that he

Quarrel between the Kings of Portugal *and* Caſtile.

King of Portugal *puts a Trick upon the* Engliſh.

Rich. II. he aim'd at by it, which was to make a more advantageous Peace with the King of *Castile*, he gave his Daughter to his Son the *Castilian* Prince, and sent the *English* back again.

Another Quarrel. In 1363, or thereabouts, a new Quarrel broke out betwixt *Castile* and *Portugal*: for *Ferdinand* dying without any Child besides *Beatrix*, the Wife of *John* King of *Castile*, who had now succeeded his Father *Henry*, *John* pretended that the Crown of *Portugal* was devolved to his Wife *Beatrix*; but the *Portuguese* plac'd *John* upon the Throne, who was Bastard Brother to their last King. This occasion'd a War, which did not prove so fortunate for the King of *Castile* as he hop'd; yet being resolv'd not to recede from his Pretensions, he sued to *France* for Succours, while the new King of *Portugal* on the other hand made an Alliance with the King of *England*, and with the Duke of *Lancaster*, whom he own'd for King of *Castile*. *Richard*, who had no great Affection for the Duke his Uncle, was very glad of an Opportunity to be rid of him on so fair a Pretence, by giving him the Command of 20000 Men, to go and assert his Rights to *Castile*. The Duke landed at *Corunna*, and in the very first Campaign took *Compostella*, and many other places. During the Winter he made a Match betwixt *Catherine* his eldest Daughter by his first Wife *Blanche* of *Lancaster*, and the King of *Portugal*. Without dwelling upon the Particulars of this War, it shall suffice to say that it was concluded by a Treaty. The Duke marry'd *Constantia*, his Daughter by his second Wife *Constantia* of *Castile*, to *Henry* Son to the King of *Castile*, and resign'd his Pretensions to that Crown. The King on his part promis'd to pay the Duke the Sum of 600000 Livres, and a yearly Pension of 40000 Livres,

King of Portugal *marries the Duke of* Lancaster's *Daughter.*

The Duke's Resignation of his Pretensions to Castile.

Livres, during the Life of the Duke and his Dutchess. *A.* 1380.

THERE's a great Number of Acts in this Volume relating to *Castile*; but I pass over the Majority, and shall only take notice of some which are of most Importance.

1. THE Engagement enter'd into by *Ferdinand* King of *Portugal*, and his Queen *Eleanor*, for procuring the Supply which they desir'd of *England*. It appears by this Act that they positively engag'd to give their Daughter *Beatrix* to the eldest Son of the Earl of *Cambridge*, and to secure the Crown of *Portugal* to that young Prince after their Decease; 'tis dated *July* the 5th 1380, at *Estremos*.

King of Portugal's *Engagement to the Earl of* Cambridge's *Son.* *P.* 262.

2. THE renewing of the Alliance betwixt *France* and *John* King of *Castile*, wherein it is stipulated that in case the Duke of *Lancaster* be taken Prisoner by the *French*, he shall be deliver'd up to the King of *Castile*; dated *December* the 18th 1381.

Agreement betwixt the Kings of France *and* Castile. *P.* 285.

3. A FULL Power granted by *Richard* to his Ambassadors to treat with *John* King of *Castile*; dated *April* the 1st 1383, at *Westminster*. From thence it appears, that the King of *Castile* was afraid of the Succours which *Portugal* was like to have from the *English*. And the very next Act shews, that he had made some Advances towards an Accommodation with the *English*.

Negotiations with the King of Castile. *P.* 386.

4. CONVENTIONS between *Richard* II. and the Duke of *Lancaster* as King of *Castile*, by which the Duke engages to make no Peace with the King of *Castile*, till the latter obliges himself to pay *Richard* 200000 Doublons of Gold, for the Damages done to the *English*, as he had already offer'd once before; dated *February* the 7th 1386, at *Westminster*.

Betwixt King Rich. *and the Duke of* Lancaster. *P.* 495.

Rich. II.

Bull against the Anti-Pope and the pretended King of Castile.

5. AN Order for publiſhing a Bull of Pope *Urban* VI. in *England*, which granted Indulgences to thoſe who ſhould aſſiſt the Duke of *Lancaſter* in his Expedition againſt *John* the pretended King of *Caſtile*, and the Adherent of the Anti-Pope *Robert* of *Geneva* (*Clement* III.) dated at *Weſtminſter*, *April* the 11th 1386*.

P. 507.

Alliance perpetual with Portugal.

6. TREATY of perpetual Alliance betwixt *England* and *Portugal*; dated at *Windſor*, *May* the 9th 1386.

7. CONVENTIONS agreed upon as to the Succours which *England* was to ſend to the King of *Portugal*; dated as above.

P. 515.

P. 524.

Negotiations with Spain.

P. 587.

8. *RICHARD*'s full Power and Inſtructions to the Duke of *Lancaſter*, to treat in his Name with the King of *Spain*; dated *June* the 1ſt 1388, at *Weſtminſter*.——The Duke of *Lancaſter* had then made his Treaty with the King of *Caſtile*.

Protection to the King of Caſtile'*s Hoſtages.*

P. 603.

9. PROTECTION granted to the Hoſtages whom the King of *Caſtile* was to deliver up to the Duke of *Lancaſter*, and who were to remain in *England* as Security for the Performance of their Treaty; dated at *Weſtminſter*, *Auguſt* the 26th 1388.

* *Walſingham*, a *Benedictin* Monk belonging in theſe Days to the Abbey of *St. Albans*, ſays the Duke had got as large Indulgences as were granted to the Biſhop of *Norwich* in 1382, for his Croiſado againſt the ſaid Anti-Pope; but he obſerves that the frequency of granting ſuch Pardons and Relaxations had now render'd them vile and contemptible, ſo that ſcarce any body regarded them, or would give 2 *d.* towards this laſt Croiſado, tho' they were ſo extravagantly fond of the former: which is a Leſſon, that a *Cheat, tho' ever ſo religious, is not to be play'd over twice in one Age.*

The End of the Firſt Volume.

THE
INDEX.

A.

Anda-

Bre-

Coucy,

D.

E.

then

His

F.

G.

H.

Ire-

Holy

I.

His

K.

L.

M.

N.

O.

P.

R.

W.

Y.

End of the Table.

CPSIA information can be obtained at www.ICGtesting.com
Printed in the USA
LVOW09s1738130915

453988LV00015B/460/P